Children of Horizons

Children of

HORIZONS

How Gay and Lesbian Teens
Are Leading a New Way
Out of the Closet

With a new Epilogue

GILBERT HERDT
ANDREW BOXER

Beacon Press
Boston

Beacon Press
25 Beacon Street
Boston, Massachusetts 02108-2892

Beacon Press books
are published under the auspices of
the Unitarian Universalist Association of Congregations

02 01 00 99 98 97 96   8 7 6 5 4 3 2

Text design by Diane Levy

Library of Congress Cataloging-in-Publication Data

Herdt, Gilbert H., 1949–
    Children of Horizons: how gay and lesbian teens are leading a new
way out of the closet / Gilbert Herdt and Andrew Boxer.
    p.   cm.
    Includes bibliographical references and index.
    ISBN 0-8070-7929-4
    1. Gay teenagers—United States. 2. Coming out (Sexual
orientation)—United States. I. Boxer, Andrew. II. Title.
HQ76.2.U5H47 1993
305.9′0664—dc20   92-417933
                            CIP

*We dedicate this book
to the courageous youth of Horizons,
vanguard of a new generation*

CONTENTS

◆ ◆ ◆

Acknowledgments   ix

Preface   xiii

CHAPTER 1
Birth of a Culture: An Introduction   1

CHAPTER 2
From Homosexual to Gay in Chicago:
Transformations of a Culture   25

CHAPTER 3
"Horizons" and the Youth   70

CHAPTER 4
The Rituals of Coming Out   100

CHAPTER 5
Milestones of Sexual Identity Development   173

CHAPTER 6
Being Out   203

CHAPTER 7
Conclusion: Gay Culture and the Moral Career of Youth   243

Epilogue: Growing Up Gay and Lesbian in the Age of AIDS   254

Notes   265

Index   297

ACKNOWLEDGMENTS

❖ ❖ ❖

The project that led to this book would not have been possible without the generous support of the Spencer Foundation of Chicago, for which we are very grateful. The grant was made to Gilbert Herdt (principal investigator) for the project "Cultural Competence and Sexual Orientation: A Study of Adolescence in Chicago." We wish to offer special thanks to Linda May Fitzgerald and Nancy Foster for their encouragement and support of our project at the foundation. Additional support for data analysis came from grants of the Biomedical Research Fund of the Social Sciences Division at the University of Chicago, and we thank Dean Edward O. Laumann, in particular, for his support.

To the Horizons agency we are especially indebted for their good will, cooperation, and warm assistance. We thank especially Bruce Koff, L.C.S.W. (then executive director of the agency), and Scott McCausland (then chair of the board) for their kindness and help. We also wish to thank Bill Weeks, Starla Sholl, Liz Huesemann, and Melanie Sovine for their assistance during the course of the study. We owe an immense debt of gratitude to Bruce Koff, whose support, insights, and friendship were invaluable to the successful completion of the study.

This study would not have been possible without the tireless efforts and coordination of our field director, Rachelle Ballmer, and we pay special tribute to her for serving far beyond the call of duty. Her intelligence and good cheer, and endless commitment to the youth, provided an inspiration to all who worked with her.

Two colleagues who have worked with us for years deserve special praise. Psychologist Floyd Irvin, who helped to facilitate the training and shape the interview process, also served as clinical supervisor and referral psychologist for two years. We are very grateful for his active participation. Anthropologist Richard Herrell, who conducted an ethnographic study of Newtown and an archival study of the history of the community, was of immense help in the anthropological component of the study and coauthored chapter 2. We thank both Floyd Irvin and Richard Herrell for their collegiality and friendship.

We are very grateful to John Gagnon, colleague and friend, for his help in obtaining access to, and utilizing the interview data from, a 1967 study of Chicago homosexuals, reported in chapter 2.

Many persons have interviewed Horizons' youth for us, and we wish to acknowledge and thank them all here: Yvette Baptiste, Amy Blumenthal, Alan Dishman, Keenan Ferrel, Drew Feraios, Camile Gerstel, Monte Hetland, Adam Katz, Dorothy Knudson, Matt Koziel, Lisa Pickens, Martha Pintzuk, Leslie Pratch, Carole Warshaw, and Jeffrey Weiss. We also wish to thank Lisa Pickens, Leslie Pratch, Camile Gerstel, Andrew Mondt, and Jeffrey Weiss for their assistance in the ethnography of the youth group. We are also grateful for the assistance of Mike and Vivian Chanon, Gerda Muri, Nancy Johnson, and the Chicago Chapter of Parents and Friends of Lesbians and Gays (P-FLAG).

For theoretical and methodological insights we are grateful to several friends and colleagues, including Judith Cook, Bertram Cohler, Anita Greene, and Martin P. Levine. We are especially grateful to John Gagnon for his theoretical insights and support of the project.

We would like to pay tribute to our editor, Deborah Chasman, for her patience and kindness, and her astute eye.

The true name of the agency "Horizons" is used throughout this book. It refers to the existing agency in Chicago, "Horizons Social Services Inc.," and we wish to thank the agency for permission to use the real name. We also use the real name of the director of the agency during the time of our study, Bruce Koff; and we thank him for this too. All other names of individuals in this book are pseudonyms unless otherwise indicated, a step we have taken to protect their true identities, consistent with standard social science practice. We regret that we cannot use the true names of the teenagers we came to know and who so generously opened their lives to us.

Lastly, we dedicate this book to the courageous youth of Horizons, without whom we would not only lack a study, but whose bravery and openness, as revealed in the story of coming out they have shared

with us, have enriched and changed our own lives forever. We hope
that they enjoy this token of our respect and friendship.

Gilbert Herdt and Andrew Boxer
Chicago, Illinois

PREFACE

◆ ◆ ◆

A small storefront community center on North Sheffield Street in the city of Chicago bears a modest wooden sign in the window that reads "Horizons Social Services." The center serves as the major community-based social service agency for the gay men and lesbians of Chicago. It dates from the early 1970s and the "gay sexual revolution," when it emerged as the mainstream hub and heart of the gay and lesbian community. Originally founded as a nonprofit organization, it was staffed entirely by volunteers and funded by public and private grants. Its purpose was to provide legal, educational, and mental health services to adults who were struggling to come out.

Thus, the adult gays and lesbians of Horizons pioneered in the Midwest what was to become a new social phenomenon in the United States: the adolescent coming-out group. In New York, Minneapolis, Seattle, and San Francisco, gay- and lesbian-identified youth would participate in similar groups. And in the coming decade, new gay youth institutions would be founded, such as the Harvey Milk School in New York for gay youth, "Project 10" in Los Angeles schools, and the Institute for the Protection of Lesbian and Gay Youth in New York.

By 1978, more and more youth were finding their way to Horizons, which in turn created a support system in the form of a Saturday afternoon "rap group" for Chicago teens (aged fourteen to twenty) in the process of coming out as self-identified lesbian and gay youth. This book is a study of these youth and the agency that facilitates their coming out. But it is also the story of how these youth are the offspring of a historical process that has given birth to a new gay and lesbian culture in the United States.

We conducted a two-year study of Horizons' youth between 1987 and 1988. The support group for youth was the immediate setting of the study. The project was uniquely interdisciplinary, combining anthropological and psychological theory and methods with the holistic study of the emerging gay and lesbian youth culture. In addition to an ethnographic and historical study of Chicago's gay community and institutions, we conducted interviews with 202 (147 boys and 55 girls) self-identified gay and lesbian youth (aged fourteen to twenty) who are approximately representative of Chicago's population (though they are not a random sample). All of their names and identifying characteristics have been changed. We have discovered, through psychological testing and interviews, that the youth of Horizons are psychologically normative, in almost all regards, compared to their heterosexual peers. These youth are neither mental patients nor runaways; many are in school and most of them live at home, usually with their parents. Almost all of them aspire to have what they call a "normal" life.[1] It is a utopian goal, in the face of bigotry and harassment, because they not only want to be gay but expect to be accepted by society as gay and lesbian. They do not know if they can achieve such a cultural lifeway, but they are trying very hard to find out.

We wrote this book to explain the situation of gay and lesbian youth in Chicago as we have found it. Our research shows that there is no stereotyped "gay" youth nor one prototype of a young "lesbian." Desire for the same sex does not obey the strictures of age, class, ethnicity, religion, or political persuasion. Gay and lesbian youth come in all sizes, shapes, and colors, from all manner of social backgrounds. What we have found cannot be described purely as a matter of individual desires or of collective social structures. What brings youth together at Horizons is the very process that forges culture. Our work shows that gay and lesbian culture is the result of a process by which historical forces and social events and practices lead the youth out of the alienation of secrecy into the public solidarity of gay and lesbian culture.

This book is not meant to represent all youth who experience same-sex desires during adolescence. It is about a special group of these teens, a historical cohort who are in the process of self-identifying as gay or lesbian. They have been resourceful enough to find the Horizons youth group, though not without many trials and struggles, as we shall see. Their resilience makes them distinctive. We are aware that many youth who feel attracted to the same sex may not find their way to Horizons until later, or not at all; and we are equally aware of the need that exists in many other cities and towns to create groups where none exist. The stories of those youth who continue to be hidden are likely to be different than the experience of youth documented in this book.

As we have presented the preliminary findings of our research—to national scientific meetings in anthropology, psychology, psychiatry, education, and public health; to colleagues in seminars across diverse academic fields; to university task forces on issues of gay and lesbian education; to public high school counselors; and lay groups—we have found, time and again, a common concern raised by diverse Americans: "Aren't these youth at Horizons just confused? Aren't they like other teenagers who are going through a "stage" of sexual development, who are not homosexual, but who don't know who or what they are?" And then we have heard two stronger complaints. "Shouldn't these youth be protected from homosexuals—who might victimize them? Isn't this agency socializing these confused teens, brainwashing them into making sexual choices from which they should be protected?" These questions represent a misunderstanding of the development of lesbian and gay youth. They rest, in part, upon antiquated and misleading stereotypes from the popular and scientific folklore on the origins of "homosexuality."[2]

As we will show in the following chapters, the youth of Horizons are not confused about their sexual identities, but they are confused about what to do with them. Usually they have nowhere to turn in exploring and expressing the dimensions of their identity because they feel hindered from approaching parents, friends, and teachers whom they fear will disapprove of or dismiss their feelings, or worse. They turn, sometimes in desperation, to the Horizons agency for a refuge of social support and peace of mind; and for some of them the agency becomes a symbolic second home, a way station preceding the larger stage of adult life. They are not "brainwashed" or absorbed into a cult; they are not socialized into a sexual identity, nor do they have sexual "choices" made for them, any more than these choices are made for heterosexual teenagers. Rather, for the first time in their lives, they begin to talk openly about sexual feelings with peers and friends of their own age who show them respect, finding others like themselves, and adult role models, whom they can admire. Their worst fears are that they are "out of their minds," full of sin or disease, that they are doomed to dress as transvestites, molest children, hate the opposite sex, or contract AIDS, which may lead them, if they remain alone and isolated, into desperate acts of risk, including drugs or suicide. At the Horizons agency, these fears can eventually be laid to rest. Another country has opened up its arms to them: the gay and lesbian community.

But why study the cultural and developmental problems of gay youth? Of what general import are these youth—who are usually thought of as "deviant"—to an understanding of the problems of human life in other times and places? The answers, it seems to us, speak to basic processes of becoming and being a person, and of constructing social rituals to this end, all of which further the struggles of youth to feel good about their own society and to take their place as worthy members of the emerging lesbian and gay culture. The stories of the youth of Horizons tell of their search to find themselves and to locate the new culture of lesbians and gay men, which is to become so much a part of their lives. These narratives reveal the very opposite of the stereotypes we Americans harbor regarding the mythology of the secret homosexual. These are the brave pioneers of a new generation whose special nature affords an insight into the timeless struggle to be human in the larger sense.

In spite of the prejudice and stigma, these are resilient youth. They struggle to overcome hatred to others and guilt in themselves. They work harder than their heterosexual peers to gain understanding and acceptance from those around them, especially the people they love. They struggle harder to achieve excellence and success in school and competence in their jobs because of their hiding, isolation, and fear of discovery. And always—just beneath the surface of these everyday struggles—lies another noble task: to feel worthy and valuable, to find respect for themselves as objects of self-love. That most youth succeed and excel in social development, in their competencies at home, school, work, and with friends and lovers in social relations, is a testimony to the remarkable resilience of the human spirit.

Perspectives and Methods

Our study of sexual identity development is novel in certain respects; we are probably the first team of social scientists to tackle these issues in an interdisciplinary voice. We are a psychological anthropologist (Herdt) and a developmental psychologist (Boxer). We address both the levels of culture and of individual development, and this "bifocal vision," as the American anthropologist Edward Sapir once referred to a similar perspective, requires us to be somewhat more self-conscious about the narrative voice that we choose throughout the text. We thus feel compelled to identify ourselves more fully than has been the case in the past for reasons we shall explain; namely, the need to describe our theory, methods, and research procedures for those who would like to undertake similar studies in future; and we must identify our audiences in order to make clear our communications to the reader.

First, by sexual orientation we are both gay men, and we believe that this information is important to the reader as we shall make clear. Herdt is a forty-three-year-old man who is in a committed relationship to another man who is also a scholar. Boxer is a forty-year-old man in a committed relationship to another man who is a pediatrician. Our separate careers, relationships with our respective lovers and families, and our friendship and mutual research collaboration have brought us to this point of fitting our professional identities with our personal lives. Our book constitutes another level in the process of our own coming out, integrating the professional with the personal, though we are publicly "out" and are already recognized for work as individual scholars and also as a collaborative team in the area of sex and gender research.[3] Nonetheless, neither of us has placed our sexual identity in the forefront of our books or papers; like many other gay and lesbian scholars in the field it has remained implicit that we are gay.

We have utilized a collaborative team approach that combines the talents of several gay men and lesbians in studying culture (anthropology) and the individual life course (developmental psychology). Each of the components of our project were headed by a study director: an ethnographic and historical study of Chicago's gay and lesbian community (by anthropologist Richard Herrell); an ethnographic study of gay and lesbian youth and of the Horizons' agency (by Gilbert Herdt); a developmental study of the youth through interviews and psychological assessments (by Andrew Boxer, assisted by Herdt and Floyd Irvine, a clinical psychologist); and a study of the parents of gay men and lesbians (conducted mainly by Andrew Boxer). In this book we present the findings of the first two studies, together with information from the third study.[4]

Being a team of gay researchers suggested advantages and problems in the conduct of our study. Being gay made it possible for us, both by social identity and by sensitivity to the issues, to gain entry into the gay and lesbian community, including the Horizons agency. Taking the cue of anthropology we have sought to understand Horizons and the youth in terms of the language and culture of real actors in natural contexts. In fact, it was mainly because of our gay identities that we were allowed to work at Horizons. A special characteristic of the community is the small town, face-to-face quality of social relations. Although Chicago is a large city, its gay community is small, with a social network of intense and overlapping fields. This poses special problems for research in a different way than it does for psychotherapy with gay and lesbian clients, a point made by John Gonsiorek some years ago.[5] We were able to gain a level of trust from the Horizons agency that ensured the validity of our information.

In the past, it was assumed in science that the investigator was heterosexual, and this assumption, even in "cultural studies" today, is unchallenged unless the author indicates otherwise. In thinking about the new culturally conscious perspective, we have puzzled over why scholars have generally ignored the moral voice of gays and lesbians whose development is heavily influenced by cultural processes of coming out. One's identity, including the sexual aspect of identity, is no different than other factors in research that inhibit the discovery process. Thus it is important to communicate to readers in publications how the investigators presented themselves and their identities to informants or respondents in research, as this element entered the conduct of research.

It remains one of the remarkable social facts of sex and gender research that virtually all studies fail to identify the sexual identity of the investigators. Some writers today, particularly in humanistic studies, declare their identities as gay or lesbian, but this critical piece of information is still usually hidden in the social and natural sciences, although there are signs of change.[6] Yet, as Herdt and Robert J. Stoller have suggested in another context, all research—whether in anthropology, sociology, psychoanalysis, or any other field—must grapple with the fundamental problem of how the researchers' identities and experience enter into the observations and findings of a study.[7] Studies of "homosexuality" are no different; it is often assumed that the research scientist is gay or lesbian, but this is neither explicitly stated nor questioned; so researchers have, in general, remained as hidden as their homosexual or gay subjects (see chapter 1 on the distinction between homosexual and gay subjects). This is not just because of the proscriptions of the canon of normative science. Another powerful reason is the stigma attached to sex research in general and to homosexual research in particular.[8] There has long been a tendency to mute the researchers' identity, and some misuses of homosexuality research have resulted from this hiding. In fact, many works on homosexuality that have appeared during the past century can be historically attributed to writers who were explicitly homosexual or gay, though they did not reveal their identities in the text. We believe that the discovery narrative is important to findings in the history of homosexuality research. Today, when our identities remain hidden to the reader, it is difficult both to understand the conduct and validity of the research and to compare the results (positive or negative) to other studies.

While we have tried to minimize the potential bias of sexual identity in this work, this factor must be taken into account through training and interpretation processes. Otherwise the results are skewed. What kind of identities and behavior did we communicate to the adults and youth in our research? The interview and observational material you will read did not come out of thin air, nor was it derived from just any interviewer. The structure of the present study is based upon the advantages and difficulties of its being conducted by a team of gay investigators with the assistance of a group of heterosexual (male and female) and gay- and lesbian-identified interviewers. In retrospect, we recognize a slant toward the study of gay males. In part this bias results from the numerically large number of boys than girls in the 1987–1988 youth group (see chapter 3); it is also partly a result of the fact that the historical material from Chicago available to us was predominantly concerned with homosexual and gay men (see chapter 2). Furthermore, we self-consciously recruited white, black, and hispanic interviewers to give the youth a choice from a full range of people, regarding the sexual identity, gender, and the color of our interviewers. We believe this heightened the research "alliance" of rapport in the interview.

To locate and train interviewers for this study took more than a year. Many applicants were turned down. The training procedures related to interviewing were complex and laborious because we required empathic but rigorous people who could create an effective research alliance for three or four hours in interviewing youth. We experimented with various forms of training graduate students and lay persons to interview gay and lesbian youth. Time and again in our study we saw the difference that knowing the sexual identity of the interviewer makes in the response of the informant. Our sensitivity to the issues enabled the entire research team to bear witness to the coming out process of these youth: implicitly and explicitly to give youth "permission" to share candidly their life stories with us. Ultimately, our procedures suggest that with proper training in cultural and clinical interviewing, other projects of a similar kind can be undertaken around the country.

We have struggled to find the clearest and least offensive way of representing the voices of different kinds of persons. The impersonal language of "male" and "female" so often used in works on sexuality and gender does not correspond to ordinary language. "Boy," "girl," "man," and "woman" are preferable terms. But when in a culture does someone qualify as, say, a "boy" and not a "man"? At what age is it better to speak of a "young woman" rather than a "girl"? To avoid both clinicalism and sexism we have adopted the following conventions. We usually refer to people under the age of twenty-one as boy or girl, and collectively as youth. For those over this age we use man or woman, and collectively adults. Adolescent, youth, and teenager are used variably to refer to persons between the ages of thirteen and twenty.

Who are our audiences? First there are the Horizons' youth, who opened their lives to us and shared their life stories, but only on the condition that we would in turn share our knowledge with others. The reason for this was clear: the youth felt a sense of being trapped in out-moded stereotypes not of their own making. They expected us to help break down these myths, to ease the burden and fears of coming out for the next generation of youth. No less a challenge is their utopian desire to *change their society*—to eliminate the bastard forms of homophobia that stalked them in growing up, waiting for them in their parents' homes, school classrooms, friendships, and the neighborhoods of their own city. Our ʳesearch project provided these teens with another confirmation of their existence. As you will see in chapters 5 and 6, our narrative study gave the youth a new context in which to come out—and not just to anyone, but to older, adult gay and lesbian positive role models—who cared enough to understand and listen to them.

We have studied parents, too, and we are very aware of the problems they face in accepting and understanding their children. We hope that our study will speak to these adults in a new way that provides basic insights into their dilemma of accepting their children as gay men and lesbians. We also hope that adult gay and lesbian readers, looking back on their own development, will see both similarities and differences in the stories of the youth. Of course, times have changed; there is a new generation of youth, whose standards and ideals are possibilities unknown to those of us who grew up in the past. We have tried to show from our study, however, the lifelong nature of coming out, anticipating new futures for youth.

We also speak later to social service providers who find themselves confronted with the policies and problems of gay and lesbian development. Mental health and social service providers, public health officials concerned with AIDS education and prevention, and teachers and counselors will find new information here for the creation of effective strategies and policies of social action.

Finally, we hope that this book will make a contribution both to developmental theory and to culture theory. We would like to think that in asking how sexual identity emerges in context we have returned to a central problem of human life that our intellectual ancestors, such as Freud and Margaret Mead and Alfred Kinsey, have pondered.

We entered into our project at Horizons with a promise to the youth that we would tell people about the lives of gay and lesbian youth. Our book speaks to their experiences, and we write in the hope that young people in other places and times will benefit from the story of the challenges and struggles of Chicago youth. It is powerful to watch these youth find themselves throughout the youth group, wherein they explore and forge identities that "feel right" to them. Such a journey in the search for identity is heroic in the sense of searching deeply within the human spirit, and in society, to create loving social relations. The youth thus aspire to a utopian vision of the world and their place in it; and the adults aim to provide for this utopia in their culture building. From such a utopian idea once sprang "The Children of the Dream," psychologist Bruno Bettelheim's classic study of people born and reared on collective farms (*kibbutzim*) created by the visionaries of the modern state of Israel.[9] *Children of Horizons* represents a similar kind of historical outgrowth of a new culture, and our work on these "children" belongs to the study of all such utopian visions—a freedom movement born from the moral cry of "coming out."

♦ ♦ ♦

CHAPTER ONE

Birth of a Culture:
An Introduction

A new culture has sprung up. And although it has no patrimony or promised land, its swift and steady development in the late twentieth century springs from the oldest tradition of social reform and expressive individualism that is at the very heart of what we cherish in the American cultural tradition. It has already changed much in our society, and yet there is good reason to believe that far more change lies on the horizon.

This book is about the birth of this culture and its new offspring: a pioneering group of teenagers who identify themselves as gay or lesbian. They challenge a hundred years of social oppression, secrecy, and silence on the rights of those who desire the same sex, when they "come out of the closet" and courageously reveal themselves to their families, friends, teachers and employers. They tell how their "true nature" as gay and lesbian was hidden for years.[1] These youth are a new cultural phenomenon: a generation who self-identify as lesbian and gay, the first ever in human history. But they could not have come so far without the prior political and social changes that created a new and more powerful community of adults who were willing to brave discrimination and violence, harassment and isolation by committing themselves to the construction of a new culture.

We believe a fundamental break with history has occurred over the past two decades, and we propose a new theory of gay and lesbian development to understand it. Our theory hinges upon a conception of "desire" that expresses heartfelt feelings to obtain satisfaction be-

1

yond the self and the will to perform action that seeks appreciation of these feelings in all human affairs.[2] Like Freud and Kinsey, we assume that sexual desires emerge early in life and come to awareness before puberty.[3] Unlike them, however, we argue with such scholars as Foucault[4] and Gagnon[5] that the adaptation of individual desires occurs in specific social and historical contexts. The developing child has social desires, as well, and these restrict the expression of sexuality through cultural taboos and traditions of social roles and goals negotiated by adults. "Heterosexual," "homosexual," and "gay/lesbian" are the moral categories of identity and social relations through which the socialization of the child's desires is directed.[6] The result is a succession of interactions between erotic desire and the social desire to take pleasure from, and conform to, tradition across the course of life.

In the history of our society and many non-Western societies today, erotic desires and their place in social and sexual development are molded by the ideological imperative for reproduction. Many scholars of late have written critically of this ideology of reproduction, and they have suggested instead a new emphasis upon the concepts of "desire" and "pleasure" in social networks and roles of sexual conduct.[7] We join them in the critique—expanding the concept of desire—while offering a dual perspective on the cultural and individual aspects of the development of sexual identities and desires.[8] In a society that assumes an explicit heterosexuality as the "natural" process of individual expression, persons who desire the opposite sex do not experience *social* conflicts in conforming to the customary social "mainstream" conventions of being married and having children.[9] But for those who desire the same sex as their erotic and cultural object, many developmental and social problems occur in the struggle to be what they are not; and hence, adjustment to mainstream norms is a constant hurdle and source of *moral* and *physic* conflict.

When youth grow up being defined as heterosexual but experience a desire for the same sex, the result is the "push" to "come out." Yet coming out implies neither a cause and effect relationship nor a guaranteed "happy outcome." The reasons are that the process requires a strong base of social support, which it usually lacks; strong reactions by parents and others to the breaking of the taboo on same-sex desire inevitably occur; the youth may then question or deny his or her own desires; he or she may then exacerbate the denial through other actions, such as inventing fictitious girlfriends or boyfriends, pretending to "pass" again: conforming to "social heterosexuality." Many youth experience harassment and even violence, as we shall see, so it is no wonder that they try to come out but slip back. If they fail to make a successful transition into a new identity and role during adolescence, it may take them years to return to the fundamental compromise of integrity suffered in their youth. Passing, then, is a pull back into the developmental subjectivity of the past—one that will remain, for most gay and lesbian persons—a devilish Janus of daily compromise between their erotic and social desires for the remainder of their lives. Our study shows how important it is to understand individual development in cultural context as a system of interpretation. Adolescent lesbian girls and gay boys are developing a whole *way of life:* ways of being in a hostile society and lifestyles through which they can express that being in a world that little knows or understands them.

Why is "coming out" such a controversial event in American society? The sociological and historical evidence suggests that in western European countries, such as Holland or Sweden,[10] expressing same-sex desire is not so dramatic and marked with a ritual of coming out.[11] A few European countries, such as England or Ireland, may oppose same-sex desire in ways not unlike those of American society. Other societies, such as France and Spain, Greece and Italy, may enfold same-sex desire in traditional patterns of family and neighborhood life, with marriage and parenting expected—but illicit same-sex relations tolerated on the side, so long as no public scandals occur. Canada has also recently become more tolerant.[12] These European countries do not have "gay ghettos" at any rate; "coming out" is not a marked social process; and same-sex desires, in some cases more and in others less, are integrated into the fold of mainstream society. In American society, however, "coming out" is a polarizing process that leads to social roles being more clearly defined as "gay" and "lesbian" than in any of these other countries. Why is this the case in the United States? The reason, we shall argue, is that heterosexual and homosexual is a fundamental structural dichotomy of our American worldview, a dualism we project into culture and nature, more strongly and at a more intensely ideological and moralistic level than in many other modern nations. Coming out is a social and psychological "mediator" of this dualism.

At our presentations of our study around the country many Americans have asked us why these teenagers feel it so necessary to declare their sexual orientation in public? We have heard even supportive heterosexual parents and friends of gay youth say such things as, "Of course I understand their feelings, but why do they keep harping on them? Why do they have to make such a big deal of them? Why do they have to keep coming out—over and over—seemingly obsessed by it? None of their straight friends or family members make such a big deal of their sexual attractions and feelings. Why can't they let it rest?"

It is all too easy for the gay or lesbian person, including the scholar and scientist or the professional health care provider, to dismiss these questions merely as "ignorance" or "homophobia." Indeed, we take them seriously because we are ultimately concerned with understanding the assumptions that underlie them. To answer these questions is to demonstrate that unlearning heterosexuality and learning to come out require unusual social and psychological conditions. Youth who are coming out today keep harping on their newfound identities because, if they do not, common assumptions of heterosexuality return to gain sway: "We are not who you think we are; in fact, we are gay and lesbian and proud of it," they retort. Our perspective on their experience takes its starting point from the insight that this unlearning and learning require a ritual process—in the usual anthropological sense of the term. But such a ritual did not exist prior to the late 1960s. Thus we must examine historically the reasons why coming out has emerged to take a ritual form. As we see it, the rites of coming out derived from the historical circumstances of the gay and lesbian movement since the turbulent 1960s, the second sexual revolution of this century.[13]

The Stonewall Tea Party

The United States in 1969 could hardly have been less prepared to greet the birth of a new social movement. After years of an unpopular war in Southeast Asia, almost a decade of racial and civil strife, and long smoldering public discontent over the new "sexual revolution" of the 1960s, homosexual rights were the last priority on an already overburdened national agenda.[14] Such was the attitude that many persons brought to a hot and humid evening in late June of 1969, when police harassment led to a riot at an ordinary homosexual tavern in New York. This marked a watershed in the budding gay liberation movement.

The famous riot at the Stonewall tavern in Greenwich village, the heart of the emerging homosexual "territory" of the city, was not the beginning of this social process but rather its symbolic beachhead, when—as so often happens in the historical uplift of a reform movement—a singular dramatic event ignites an outcry and burns into the imagination of people near and far. Police raids in bars and homosexual gathering places in New York and other cities such as Chicago were old hat, an accepted fact of life for decades in the United States.[15] This was the era of the "closet homosexual," when those in hiding simply assumed that violence and harassment, even blackmail and complete ostracism, were a way of life: the ugly price that one had to pay for the sin and crime of having a desire for the same sex or for socializing with others of like nature. The 1969 police raids on "closeted" homosexual bars in New York were, however, particularly unnecessary and therefore troublesome—the bored overkill of an establishment whose other social problems, such as picketing students or the racial riots of the ghettos, would not go away and were too visible to crush. The homosexuals were an easy target and rather powerless prey. One of these raids, directed at the Stonewall, caused the patrons to fight back. They took to the streets, these closet "queens," and were soon joined by others of a more muscular sort, brandishing their anger, flinging beer bottles and stones. Their violent response to the police raid formally marked the beginning of a new cultural wave of radicalism that has continued to this day.[16] Chicago suffered police raids and harassment for several years more, but by the early 1970s, as we show in chapter 2, the city was to undergo the same freedom strike and ritual rebellion spearheaded by New York.

That famous battle from late June 1969 marks the Independence Day of gay and lesbian culture, celebrated each year by Gay and Lesbian Pride Day parades. The Stonewall "tea party" is now a living symbol of the "minority status" of gays and lesbians, commemorated in small towns and large cities across America. This new culture of gay men and lesbians is also represented by other increasingly visible national icons and symbols—the rainbow flag and banner, pink triangles and gay churches, the Quilt of the "Names Project," a burgeoning number of local lesbian and gay community organizations, and in Chicago by the gay and lesbian youth group who march as the colorguard at the head of the Gay and Lesbian Pride Day parade. What Stonewall ushered in could not have been predicted back in those days: there was no notion of a gay culture twenty-five years ago, and no one foresaw the great tragedy of AIDS that would darken the lives of tens of thousands of lesbians and gay men. The transition from secret homosexual to public gay has been a bumpy ride. Certainly it was not anticipated that a new and younger generation, all of them not yet born in the late 1960s, would want to claim a share of this new social life, creating what would become a new cultural nation for the lesbian and gay children of tomorrow.

One dramatic effect of this political movement in the structure of American society has been the steady lowering of the age of coming out. A review of the research literature from 1968 to 1990 suggests that the mean age of coming out has dropped by at least five years.[17] No longer is the declaration of same-sex desire postponed until adulthood. Coming out in the early 1970s was an event that typically occurred in a twenty-two-year-old male and a twenty-five-year-old female, while today, the scattered but accumulating studies suggest that these ages have fallen to the middle and late teens in the major cities. What this trend suggests is not only that Americans are coming out at an earlier age, but that they do so now as teenagers. They have an opportunity, unique in the history of our species, to self-identify as a gay or lesbian person while still in the time of the transition between childhood and adulthood, when love and sex, friendship and social idealism, are strongly marked.

The Four Historical Age Cohorts of Chicago

Central to our study of culture and sexual identity development is a distinction between "homosexual" and "gay."[18] We have learned from our previous research[19] that the adults and youth of contemporary Chicago implicitly define the meanings of "homosexual" and "gay/ lesbian" identities as fundamentally different and sometimes even in opposition. In subsequent chapters we show that these cultural identities have a historical basis with real-life psychological effects upon development.

Homosexual and gay, we believe, are different creatures of social life. They are different psychological and cultural entities, that is, different constructions from social facts, based in alternate values and beliefs, norms and social roles. As an ideal form, the homosexual does not ever reveal himself or herself; whereas the gay and lesbian always does. As social categories they have differing historical origins: the "homosexual" is a nineteenth-century invention; the "gay" is a product of the later twentieth century.[20] To historical society the closet homosexual was primarily a bearer of a secret sin or crime; later he or she was believed to have a flawed biological nature which had represented the sign of a disease as well (that belief was not contested until the 1970s). The gay or lesbian person has had to face and attempt to cope with these conceptions of his or her "nature"—sin, crime, and disease—and whatever success was wrought from these attempts can be attributed primarily to the reform and rebellion movements that have politicized the gay body and identity.[21]

To study the contemporary forms of the expression of same-sex desire thus requires that we know the historical forms that have proceeded them in cultural places such as Chicago. Many experts in the field, especially clinical psychologists, have taken a different view, we believe, because they have studied only the current generation of adults, and not lesbian and gay youth.[22] The adults remember their youth from a different historical and cultural epoch; perhaps some of their informants have so dispelled the past that they have reconstructed their memories.[23] They stress traits of same-sex desire as an eternal reality; they are not disposed to see how social conditions may actually alter the ontology or cultural reality of the person. Whatever the case, these surveys and clinical studies represent the prior generations who grew up with cultural conceptions of secrecy and stigma and hiding that matched those of the closet homosexual, not the gay man or lesbian.[24] Some scholars who write of coming out therefore ignore lesbian and gay culture; others who are especially concerned with development have failed to appreciate the extraordinary cultural break with history that distinguishes gay youth from adults.[25]

To chart the cultural world of Horizons in the gay and lesbian culture of Chicago is to confront the changing configuration of historical age cohorts living within the area who are involved, in greater or lesser ways, with the youth who are coming out. A twenty-year-old coming out in rural Nebraska shares more in common with a twenty-year-old coming out in Chicago than would be expected. They are exposed to similar media and Hollywood movies, and the social and historical categories of the identity "gay and lesbian" link them across space. A fifty-five-year-old man who has lived his whole life as a "closet homosexual" resembles his heterosexual peers more than he resembles these youth. He is also alienated from the openly lesbian and gay men of his city. By contrast, a forty-year-old who has been married with children but is getting divorced and coming out for the first time shares more problems in common with gay teenagers than with other men and women of his or her own generation whose sexual and romantic development occurred at an earlier age.

The sociologist Glen Elder has used the concept of historical age cohort to define a group of persons whose development—especially their coming of age—occurred within particular social/historical conditions.[26] For instance, those who passed through the Great Depression, or World War II, share many common events and experiences which have left an indelible stamp upon their identities. Although these Americans differ in many ways, being male or female, black or white, northern or southern, they nonetheless participated in these great global trials and tribulations, with similar form and content, that strongly influenced their developmental subjectivities. As Elder argues, "Depressions, wars, and periods of extreme social ferment often produce major reorientations of society. That the life course of individuals may also be reshaped by such periods of crisis is apparent from personal experience and from biographical studies."[27]

The Stonewall revolution, and its reflections in individual lives, we now understand, shaped the form of coming out, its secrecy or publicity, the kinds of social relations that it denied or opened up, and its probable effects upon future events in the life course of the person. The individual does not invent these grand historical events or create the relevant cultural categories, but through social development the individual participates in collectively shared experiences, linking himself or herself to other persons of similar status, according to where they were at the time and what they did in relation to the historical events. In the memory culture and historical records of Chicago, we find distinctive cultural age cohorts that bound the "coming of age" of diverse persons. Coming of age boundaries are denoted by virtue of the stories people tell, the events of their sexual histories that they remember, the common events and roadblocks they experienced, such as harassment and discrimination, and their present-day social relations that reflect upon contemporary cultural norms and institutions. In Chicago we can locate a cohort system comprised of four historical age-groupings as follows.[28]

1910	**Cohort One**	Came of age after WW I
1940	**Cohort Two**	Came of age during/after WW II
1969	**Cohort Three**	Came of age after Stonewall/Gay Activism
1983	**Cohort Four**	Came of age in the era of AIDS

Cohort One marks the earliest coming of age cohort, principally defining the same-sex desires of people by the folk category of feeling and acting "queer." The older category of "queer" (not to be confused with the new identity of "Queer" as in "Queer Nation") encompassed the notion of "pervert" that preceded it in the bio-medical language of "inverted" gender from the nineteenth century. It referred to persons who desired the same sex, usually identified as men, who expected to act and possibly dress as "women." They could be jailed or killed for their sexual acts, and some of them were. They did not call themselves "homosexual" or "gay" because these category terms were either nonexistent or not in circulation. But in accord with the concepts of queer and pervert, they thought and acted in cultural ways that expressed these identities, including hiding and pretending to be heterosexual. They would not think of "coming out" in the sense of today: this rite did not exist. They would not openly express their erotic desires to their families, friends, and employers. Radical or reform activities, such as attempting to change the laws, did not exist. They would not usually think of finding a same sex partner for life, but would rather think of being heterosexually married ("for convenience or survival"). If they engaged a same-sex partner, they did so discreetly, and the relationship was kept hidden from everyone else, perhaps including other self-identified queers. Today, most of these persons are deceased, though some of them live on in the memory culture of the older members of the following cohort. A few of them did, in the late 1960s, begin to emerge from their hiding by going to more openly gay bars. However, most of them were opposed to the gay liberation movement, and they were afraid of its effects upon their remaining years. Those of this cohort still living have nothing to do with Horizons today, and in the minds of youth coming out, they have never existed.

Cohort Two is defined primarily by the events of World War II. Some political and social change occurred around the large-scale mobilization of men and women in the armed services of the "Good War." GIs who served abroad and Wac's who served at home experienced new possibilities of meeting others from diverse backgrounds. They were brought together in the dramatic and intimate circumstances of wartime, creating unique possibilities to be sexually or romantically involved with each other; some permanent partnerships emerged. These men and women might sometimes self-identify as "homosexual" or something else.[29] However, for the purposes of cultural description, they remain largely closeted today; they did not reveal their desires to their families and friends; many were harassed and suffered indignities, including court-martial and "dishonorable discharge" from the service; the majority of them never became involved in reform activities, such as the Mattachine Society of the 1950s; and they should, therefore, be represented as "closet homosexuals." They came of age during the war; they met friends or lovers in that context. Women learned that others who desired female bodies worked alongside of them in the factories or in the service. Police raids and harassment actually accelerated after the war, reaching their peak during the Cold War period, when the torment of secrecy and suspicion was so generally high in American society.[30] Thus, one seldom "came out of the closet" in the present sense, but rather lived in ways that permitted socializing in private circles, or in the dark, mafia-owned bars, that thwarted intimacy and enhanced alienation. Some gender-reversal of behavior occurred, with dressing or acting like the opposite sex, and "drag shows" were common. Alcohol and drinking were major venues of socializing and courting, with the resultant problems of drug-abuse and disease in this generation.[31]

Many of these men and women acculturated completely to middle-class or lower-class heterosexual norms, including "marriages of compromise," making them invisible in their blending. Their same-sex desire routinely resulted in arrest or loss of employment if discovered. They were blackmailed. But by the late 1960s and early 1970s, a rare few began to "come out" later in their life course, in their forties and fifties. The closet homosexuals of this cohort have been perceived as a greater threat to the gay community than its heterosexual critics, as suggested by Randy Shilts.[32] Their existence provides a negative role model of "what not to be" for the youth now in the process of coming out.

Cohort Three is identified with the radicalism of the late 1960s which led to the Stonewall riot and the formation, in the early 1970s, of gay and lesbian communities around the country, including Chicago. Political challenges to the police and raids began; the old secret bars either gradually went out of business or became publically acknowledged gay taverns. Other radical challenges resulted in the decriminalization of some laws and the declassification of homosexuality as a disease by the American Psychiatric and Psychological Associations.[33] Drinking and sexual courting became prominent features of gay life in the bars and bathhouses of the period. Many individuals coming of age and entering into adulthood during the time announced their same-sex desires to friends and college roommates. They did not all come out to all significant others, however; indeed, many did not explicitly come out to their families, particularly their parents. The idea of the gay and lesbian "ghetto" evolved. New alliances were initiated with the police, politicians, and between gay men and lesbians, in part thanks to the women's movement and the gay movement. The founding of institutions such as Horizons was the order of the day. It was possible to expect to find a gay or lesbian partner and possibly live openly as a couple for the rest of one's life. Newly self-identified gay men and lesbians generally derided those who failed to come out of the closet. They disliked closet homosexuals; and in many respects they especially disdained the old queers from the first cohort. These new lesbians and gay men, now in their late thirties or forties (the oldest members, into their late fifties, were those who "converted" their identities, leaving behind the closet homosexual identity of the earlier cohort and becoming self-identified gay or lesbian) formed the bulwark of the gay/lesbian community and of Horizons. This cohort, incidentally, has suffered the greatest losses from AIDS.

Here again the old dualism of heterosexual/homosexual continued to press upon the everyday consciousness of Americans. For instance, one difference between cohorts two and three concerns the kind of social relationships they form in intimate partnerships. Many closet homosexuals of cohort two attempted to mimic the heterosexual husband/wife relationships of the heterosexual mainstream of the time, an understandable consequence of the social order. In fact, the point actually mirrors a psychosexual attitude among gays and lesbians themselves. Many heterosexuals say that they enjoy the feeling of "difference" between themselves and their partners; that is, the sex difference in anatomy and psychology is pleasing and exciting. Many current studies show that the emphasis of men upon sexual drive and pleasure and of women upon emotional expression form a complex, tension filled, image of heterosexualism.[34] Difference may translate into complementation or into hierarchy, mingled with power and subordination, as traditionally represented by the category distinction "husband/wife," the notion being that the "husband" is masculine and "active," and the "wife," feminine and "passive." An offshoot of this hierarchicalism is the sadomasochism of the husband/wife, supported by standard Freudian theory of gender differentiation. When carried over into same-sex relationships, sadomasochism reached a stronger contrast than ever, characterized by such distinctions as "master"/"slave" and "butch dyke"/"fem" lesbian.[35] By contrast, the ideology of the gay movement extolled the love of "sameness" between self and sexual partner as "equals."[36] The key is the resistance by gays and lesbians to notions of conventional heterosexual conformity; to the husband/wife bonds, changes which began in Cohort Three and took on greater momentum in Cohort Four.

Cohort Four identifies those who have come of age since the early 1980s and the onset of AIDS. These people can be in their teens or twenties of course, either male or female, of any class or race. It may seem curious to mark a cohort with the awareness of a disease; however, the life stories of younger men and women reveal that this epidemic equals the power of World War II and other sweeping historical events in impressing common experiences on a new generation. Their coming out and awareness of their same-sex desires are forever stamped with the sign of AIDS, the fear of sexual risk of HIV, the programmed campaigns to change sexual behavior, and the politicalization of "homosexuality" that has ensued over the past decade. Their sexuality is infused with changing norms of desire and sexual expression, including the "punk" style that "gender blends" everyone, to erase what is left of the old male/female, masculine/feminine cultural distinctions of heterosexualism. Some of these and a few of the older gay cohort now begin to identify with alternative categories, such as the new "Queer," or "Radical Fairy," and so forth. They are a minority. The great majority of youth come of age self-identifying as gay or lesbian, and thus expecting not only to live their lives openly, but to tell all of their family and friends, and their employers of their desires and lifestyles. The struggles of the historical past come back to them in part by their reading and listening to accounts of those who have gone before, the adult gay men and lesbians who support their coming out. Take note that for the first time, in this cohort, two different generations are brought together, creating the sense of a past and a future. A collective story of the gay and lesbian culture is thus woven, for instance, at Horizons, from the shreds and tatters of meanings surrounding their coming out and coming of age in the presence of the older adults.

Ironically, the older cohorts of closest homosexuals and adult gay men and lesbians have had little or no contact with gay and lesbian youth. This is a historical product of the oppression of the past. Margaret Mead once used the notion of a "generation gap" to describe a strong political and social disjunction between the past and present, such as is reflected in this generational discontinuity.[37] We find that there continues to be an intense reluctance on the part of gay and lesbian adults from the older cohorts to socialize with or engage youth. As many adults have said, they fear the old stereotypes—the notion that (especially closet) homosexuals prey upon youth (see chapter 3). This "cultural survival" of an antique pattern directs adults to fear and even shun younger members of their own culture, for fear of arrest, harassment, or exploitation. The cultural stereotype, confuses having sex with the socialization of youth, suggesting the incomplete formation of gay and lesbian culture.

Every culture, to be a viable and continuing entity, must reproduce itself, not only recreating its social practices and relationships, but transmitting its cultural knowledge, folklore, and values to the next generation. In spite of much progress, as outlined in the historical unfolding of these cohorts in Chicago, old structural barriers to becoming a gay and lesbian person—oppression and homophobia—are still in place. The new task of entry into gay and lesbian culture requires a social practice of sufficient power and sacred durability that it can override all the various obstacles, both social and psychological, while providing a powerful means of support to ensure its success. The Stonewall Tea Party unleashed a vast storm of change in our society—with families and friends altered by the radical cultural act of individuals declaring that they were lesbian or gay—a fury that required a human practice of great power to quell it.

The Rituals of Coming Out

Teenagers who desire the same sex are often isolated and mired in the social problems of internalized homophobia, alienation from family and friends, and sometimes exploitation and violence. They come to Horizons in search of a place to discuss and express their desires, a new way of learning how to be a person, both inside and outside; a way of doing things differently from anything they have known or seen in their previous life. The mind of the anthropologist links these youthful experiences of coming out in Chicago to those tribal rites of initiation we know so well from places such as New Guinea.[38] But, the rituals of coming out are so distinctive of American culture that they deserve a special status in the archives of anthropology. The rituals of coming out differ from the rites of certain cultures of Melanesia and of particular Archaic civilizations that had age-structured homoerotic relations for the purpose of passing from childhood to adulthood.[39] The rituals of gay youth in America are not aimed merely at changing their social role in male/female relationships or their status in society.[40] They are instead explicitly directed at changing the *whole conception of the nature and being of the desires of the youth.*

Of all of the social processes that enable the transformation of the individual body and mind, none is more powerful or important than that of ritual. Its ineffable and sacred practices adjust the individual to a stable social system in the face of a constantly changing biological and social nature. Its qualities suggest the power and authority of tradition, the sanctity of transcendent powers, and the faith in the group to satisfy the needs of the individuals. Only in ritual do we find the symbolic roles and mechanisms necessary to do the job of binding the energy of individuals into new and complex cultural forms. By binded energy we mean the desires of the person to belong, participate in, and make commitments to, a gay and lesbian worldview and culture.

The rites of coming out bear a family resemblance to what anthropologists would call a "life crisis ritual" as this social practice has been studied over decades across cultures around the world.[41] In fact, the kind of identity change that "coming out" creates should, most properly, be called a *ritual process of passage.*[42] Like the rites of birth and death, puberty and marriage, coming out necessitates transitions from one social role and cultural field to another throughout life; and through these ritual transformations "society" recognizes that the change is immutable and irreversible.

Coming out is the acknowledged social process of entering gay and lesbian culture. While it is not sanctioned by the mainstream society, today coming out is prescribed for socialization into gay and lesbian culture. Emerging cultural institutions in the gay community recognize the struggle by providing group support for individuals, allowing them to express their desires rather than conform to society's heterosexual assumptions. Suspended in the chasm between feeling tabooed desires for the same sex and feeling the pressure to conform to the mainstream, coming-out rites provide a solution to an intolerable dilemma. Though coming out is optative for the individual actor, like many initiation rites around the world, it acknowledges a compelling match between the personal and the social: the promise and impetus of a new being and status powerful enough that gay and lesbian teenagers risk complete ostracism to enter an approving culture of gay men and lesbians. It is through this culture, and the promise it offers youth of an alternative and more satisfying life plan, that ritual becomes a necessary social practice to accomplish the dramatic change.

The challenge to the individual comes in the way that expressing same-sex desires undermines the received theory of "human nature" in American society which is learned in growing up. To be a male is to desire a female, and to be a female is to desire a male, and "What falls between is a darkness, an offense against reason."[43] This folk theory revolves around three basic cultural principles of mainstream beliefs and practices. In each of these, youth must undergo radical change inside and outside of themselves, as the sufficient and necessary conditions for being out. First, he or she must unlearn the principle of "natural" heterosexuality, especially the "essentialist" assumptions that to marry and parent with the opposite sex is the only right and normal mode of development. Second, they must unlearn the stereotypes of "homosexuality" as these apply to their own development. This requires them to separate the concepts and images of "homosexuality" from "gay/lesbian," identifying with the latter in the intense struggle against social taboos, contaminated identity, and status loss which leads them to pass as heterosexual. Third, they must learn how to be gay and lesbian, which requires them to reconstruct their social relationships in American society, based upon new and emerging social status and cultural being in the gay and lesbian culture. This latter process is the end product of coming out, except that, in fact, the process is lifelong and never really ends.

Let us explain: all Americans, regardless of their ethnic or class background, have grown up with heterosexual roles, assuming that all people everywhere are "heterosexual." We are taught that it is normal and natural to desire and love only the opposite sex, never the same sex. Such a "natural state" conception—which psychologist Evelyn Hooker called "heterosexual ethnocentrism" and the poet Adrienne Rich has referred to as "compulsive heterosexuality"—is as much a part of the American folk theory of human nature as it is a mark of social homophobia in our time.[44] All Americans, the white middle-class in particular, are still socialized via the quiet but powerful nineteenth-century ideology of the "melting pot," which plays down the differences between individuals and groups. In social groupings, such as the educational classroom, our society works very hard to consistently suppress differences between groups, on the grounds that social treatment in common ensures equal recognition and access to opportunities for advancement. Such attempts at liberal democracy and affirmative action are always politically controversial and incomplete. As de Toqueville foresaw long ago, suppressing differences between groups has the ironic effect, not of enhancing personal liberties or freedom, but of creating sameness.[45] Proof of the point resides in the continuance of taboo: neither the popular culture nor the government recognize desire for the same sex as a means of differentiating individuals for the purpose of securing "life, liberty, or the pursuit of happiness." Indeed, most social rights continue to be denied to those who claim same-sex desires, on the grounds that the Declaration of Independence was not intended to cover the rights of same-sex love. The burden of proof thus continues to fall upon the individual to ensure that he or she is granted the liberty and freedom to express his or her desires.

Wherever intense and "naturalized" cultural ideas of heterosexuality oppress a people, these will be rebelled against, ultimately paving the way for a "counterculture" of ideas that validate personal freedom. This cultural process creates new myths and rites to uphold the countervailing cultural formation against the old. The old dualism, heterosexual and homosexual, is so basic to the American tradition, that it was impossible to eliminate "homosexuality." This is because same-sex desire is too dangerous a threat to the dualism.[46] Today, "natural" taboos continue to suppress same-sex desires in children, such as exploratory sex "play," with powerful social pressures in adolescence, especially from parents and peers, reserved to inhibit the discovery of these desires in oneself.[47] This is the main reason why coming out as a rite of passage in teenagers is still surrounded at every step by secrecy.[48] Today, the sharpest form of cultural competition between the older homosexual category and the newer gay and lesbian category is vested in the events of coming out. Ultimately this competition has led "Queer Nation" at least to the more radical practice of "outing" closet homosexuals.[49]

The coming-out rites have evolved because of the breakdown in the secrecy of homosexuality which has occurred since prior generations. Where before same-sex desires were kept hidden, the result of a duplicit contract of social control on the part of society and "the passing" individual, today gays and lesbian shun secrecy in every way. They thus challenge the old social boundaries and moral rules that segregated the sexual spheres of social life. The post-Stonewall generation, the people who came out in the late sixties and during the seventies, have endeavored to desegregate the public and private barriers, revealing their same-sex desires to the world, but not always uniformly or completely. Can one be identified as straight and then later self-identify as gay too? The coming-out ritual was to provide an answer, however provisional. Once the person has come out, social perceptions change, but there remains a collective memory that is difficult if not impossible to alter, thus suggesting the great loss of status and fortune that follows from rumors of "homosexuality" about public figures and celebrities.[50] Such challenges to moral rules, as the anthropologist Max Gluckman once predicted, result in new rituals that spontaneously appear in complex societies.[51]

But if coming out is the key ritual of gay and lesbian culture, then it is, simultaneously, a healing process, indeed, a *healing rite* of considerable power for the self and society alike. Anthropologists, from Van Gennep to Victor Turner,[52] have long known that the rites of passage effect not only change in social status and identity, but also bring about transformation in the inner world of the persons undergoing the existential life crisis, through a soothing and holding support of the surrounding ritual group. We see gay and lesbian youth who are happy and confident, who move on to successful life adaptation, and others who are troubled and guilt ridden by the effects of homophobia and harassment, broken family bonds, and discrimination at school and work. Coming out begins a long and sometimes arduous process of healing these wounds in their lives. It does so by all the processes of unlearning and relearning described before, aided by the creation of new bonds of friendship and support that will sustain them, often for the rest of their lives.

To return to the question asked by parents and friends: the reason why gay and lesbian youth must continue coming out is that, for the ritual to "work," they must present the new gay or lesbian self again and again, to each significant other, and in the full range of each social situation in which the actor has rights and duties. Otherwise, its intentional, desired inner and outer transformation cannot be completed. Basic boundaries of group and self relationships are thus stretched and refigured in new, uncharted ways by the ritual presentations of the gay self-conception. The stable formation of social roles in the broader society is likewise tested in unprecedented fashion. Might one, for instance, be gay and also be a teacher? Could a lesbian serve honorably in the military? Might a gay man be a loyal and worthy member of the United States Senate? Could a lesbian also be a parent? These are the kinds of fundamental questions raised by gay and lesbian youth every day.

Culture is a fabric of moral norms and sensibilities; its rituals weave together this fabric, but not altogether seamlessly. A key to understanding the power of ritual to effect change has to do with the neglected fact that ritual can deconstruct and construct "natural" rights and "social" privileges in societies. Claims for new natural and social rights in society require new endorsements—by rituals. As Robert Bellah and his colleagues have written more generally of American society: "We cannot know who we are without some practical ritual and moral 'structure' that orders our freedom and binds our choices into something like habits of the heart."[53] The coming-out ritual, it turns out, is one of the few truly new habits of the heart in our so complex and changing American cities. But how does coming out actually heal? Knowing how the rituals facilitate healing and adaptation for those who desire in their social and sexual being the same sex requires an understanding of the gay and lesbian moral voice in society.

Homosexual versus Gay:
Critique of Moral Development

A moral question is foremost in the minds of many gay and lesbian youth. They still come out in a society that places them at risk of many forms of bigotry, and they know it. Thus teenagers must revise their moral thinking on what is good and just in society in order to take the risk of coming out. They venture to redefine for themselves, like budding anthropologists, what is authentic or spurious in that greatest and most cherished of all of human beings' adaptive resources: culture.[54]

Scholars in the past have not generally addressed the issue of "homosexuality" and coming out in the context of moral development and social injustice. Why is this? Perhaps the main reason has to do with the historical climate of prejudice that has colored scholarship for so long. The psychoanalyst Erik Erikson, for example, tended to treat developmental stages as timeless.[55] He pathologized homoerotic relations in youth as matters of juvenile delinquency, identity confusion, and the peer group pressures of street gangs.[56] Another powerful reason has to do with the psychological image of sexuality as a drive or a trait that was biological and purely internal to the individual. Freud, for example, did not, at least at first, see any connection between the psychological well-being of the homosexual and the presence of social injustice in the society. Later in a famous letter to an American mother, he changed his views.[57] Long after Freud, however, a tendency remains to see the homosexual or gay identities as defined purely by sexual need or desire, sexual behavior or sexual orientation, as did even Kinsey in his enlightened conception.[58] Certain psychoanalysts and psychologists, moreover, continue to believe that homosexuality is based in "psychopathology," that the "problem" can be cured by inhibiting the "impulse" and treating it. They maintain this belief in spite of the clinical evidence and in disregard of the opinions of clinical scholars, from Freud to Robert Stoller, who have argued that developmental same-sex desire over many years is not a choice but a permanent identity.[59] Treating same-sex desire as a "sexual compulsion" is perhaps the latest form of this medical and moral attack.[60] Ignoring or denying the real-life consequences of social injustice for gay men and lesbians was a mistake in the social science of the past, as much of an error as the male-biased models of moral reasoning that slanted the understanding of women.[61]

Our emphasis upon the moral dimension of coming out may surprise the reader, especially the gay and lesbian reader who finds the "morality" debates about the legitimacy of homosexuality repugnant. After all, there are many aspects of coming out; why single out its morality?[62] We take a cue from anthropology that all of culture and its conventions are, after all, morally laden phenomena, beliefs and values which define a socially constructed reality. In coming out into gay and lesbian culture, virtually no aspect of the developing person's existence is left unchanged. We are thus inclined to see many of the changes that occur in gay and lesbian adolescent development as moral in the sense of being indicative of major value orientations that emerge to challenge the hegemony of the mainstream heterosexual society. Is it just and right to assume that that all persons who desire the same sex are "bad," for instance? It is right to assume that everyone is "naturally" heterosexual? Is homosexuality a "choice" or a "natural right" of individual development? Over the course of our project it was through questions such as these, posed by the teenagers themselves, that we began to see that the change in their lives marked a new moral thinking regarding their future social relations and productive work.

We want to suggest that gays and lesbian culture is, more than anything else at this moment in our history, a powerful critique of moral ideals and justice in our society. It is from gay and lesbian teenagers that we have learned this; they have forced us to recognize that their desire and struggle to come out is a new form of moral career. They are exercising a moral "choice," the liberty to come out and live as self-identified gays and lesbians, whose pursuit of happiness means that they no longer agree to live under the moral corruption and compromises of prior generations. These young people's lives suggest that they desire a new culture that will enable them to be the most creative and productive people; and for this purpose, it is not merely the choice of a "lifestyle" that matters, although that it is very important; it is also the question of a new cultural consciousness. Let us explain.

American culture continues, in spite of much progress in social equality, to define the nature of sexual and gender development by virtue of the old heterosexual v. homosexual duality. For all too many Americans this dualism is equated naively with a moral dualism of "good" and "bad," the homosexual, of course, being all "bad," even "evil."[63] The shift in the social and psychological landscape of the past twenty years has changed categories of personhood, from the secret closet homosexual to the publicly self-declared lesbian and gay, but it has not eliminated the moral dualism. As we shall see in subsequent chapters, teenagers learn negative sterotypes about the "evil" of homosexuals: child molesters, compulsive masturbators, men who wear women's clothes and others in leather masks, women who hate men and others who are lonely or alcoholic, serial killers. To identify with such dark or monstrous figures, as portrayed, for instance, in the mythology of a hundred Hollywood movies, and to be denied the images of positive role models hidden in the Rock Hudsons, is a very oppressive way to grow up.[64]

Growing up harboring a secret nature, as we discuss in chapters 4 and 5, burdens the development of same-sex desire in the child with alienation from self, family, and society. Eventually, the result of hiding one's desires is to split up morality, less in terms of the "good" and "bad" ideology discussed before, and more in terms of what is "true" and "false" in society. If one must suppress one's "true" desires to be accepted (acculturate to heterosexual life) many teenagers reason, then all of society becomes a "lie" or a "joke" to be ridiculed at every point. Hiding and passing as heterosexual becomes a lifelong moral hatred of the self; a maze of corruptions, petty lies, and half truths that spoil social relations in family and friendship. Recall for a moment Oscar Wilde's still powerful image from the late nineteenth century of the secret portrait of "Dorian Grey." The portrait became increasingly sinister and hideous with each selfish harm Dorian committed upon society, crimes that reflected back upon the secret mirror of the soul; and all the while, the public face of Dorian remained beautiful and ageless, the result of a life of exploited love and hollow intimacy.[65] Perhaps this moral duality helps to explain the humor of homosexual "camp," that clever but jaded genre of the closet homosexual that caricatured the opposite sex and betrayed the hidden social hostility between men and women.[66] If kitsch is art with its hatred left out, camp is heterosexuality with its hatred left in.[67] Those on the margins of society, who have to hide their desires, have a ringside seat at its ongoing social drama and develop a special sensitivity to its foibles and self-deceptions, it is true; but in prior generations, before it was possible to come out, the moral hatred of having to conform to "reprosexuality"[68] conventions usually meant that life was humorous only if it was a bitter and lonely humor.

Coming out is the most radical form of *unlearning* anti-gay prejudice and bigotry ever invented. Hiding one's desires and passing as something other than one is—heterosexual—is no less injurious to the normal heart and the healthy mind of gay youth than was, say, passing as a Christian if you were Jewish in Nazi Germany, or passing as white in the old South or in South Africa today.[69] In many parts of the country, as in Chicago too, people report that they have no choice but to hide, for fear of exposure and worse, just as once occurred in these fascist regimes. Today, "sodomy statutes" continue to criminalize same-sex relations in twenty-four states and the District of Columbia.[70] The person who does not come out, who refused to acknowledge deeper desires and being, is someone who has not unlearned the warnings of oppression and bigotry from the past, the moral voice of gay and lesbian rhetoric suggests.[71] Closet homosexuals today may recreate the bigotry in a frantic effort to hide from others, or to prove to themselves that one should not come out because of the terrible destruction wrought upon the self by an oppressive society. Here we see that to the closet homosexual and to the heterosexual in opposition, coming out threatens destruction to society and the danger of death of the heterosexual self, both of which belong to the same world of hide and seek.

Much has been written by conservative and religious critics of the gay and lesbian movement, and by their defenders, about what constitutes a "choice" in sexual identity development and moral action.[72] Chicago gay and lesbian youth do not see the matter in such black and white terms; they reject the idea that they have "chosen" their sexual desires, but they do not want to reject personal choice in the matter of expression: Some of us have a choice, we would agree, but not in the creating of our sexual desires; we have some room to maneuver in how we express our desires socially.[73]

The moral rhetoric of reductionism that equates being gay to having sex remains one of the most powerful constraints on sexual identity development in young people. To be homosexual or gay is to want sex with the same sex—so goes the folk psychology of our heterosexual tradition. Particularly for youth who come from a strong religious background and multicultural youth who view sexual relations as part of a broader social pattern of cultural and family traditions, the equation of having "sex" to being gay or lesbian is wrenching, the turpitude of the unclean. The reductionism of the human spirit to the sex act never seemed so perniciously antisocial and anti–culture-building than in this bit of folk wisdom.

By highlighting "sexual contact"—that precious technoterm the public health establishment exploits to measure frequencies and population trends for sexual disease surveys—the whole person of the gay man or lesbian is reduced to a cold statistic that hides the underlying social relations of a cultural world. (The AIDS literature is replete with this language.[74]) The effect of this is that we do not understand what part, if any, sexual pleasure or romance play in the kinds of relationships that typify "heterosexuals," "homosexuals," or "gays and lesbians." As teenagers come out, they come to challenge the rhetoric that equates being gay with having sex, and they oppose the prudishness of the underlying ideology that signals its acceptance. Might we not appreciate love more, given that it comes without necessary legal support, a gay asks? Might the children of a lesbian relationship be more appreciative, a young lesbian asks? Thus, the youth reject the moral assumption that to be gay or lesbian is, simply, to have a sexual orientation or preference for the same sex, or to want only sex with the same sex. They claim instead aspirations and ideals of the whole person: that is, the personality or self, the body, their social spaces and roles, their spirituality and concept of the soul.

Coming out of the closet is the key to establishment of new social justice, as the reformers and activists in the "homosexual rights" movement have known since the time of the early scientific reformer, Dr. Magnus Hirschfield in Germany, at the turn of the century,[75] to the rebels of Stonewall in 1969 in New York, and on to the youthful lesbians and gay men who march in Chicago's Pride Day Parade today. For the adolescents, the rituals of coming out mean confronting what they consider the hateful, unjust, and false social values of prejudice in our society that have forced generations into the lie of "passing" as straight. The youth, that is, yearn to change their very conception of human nature, of what it is to be a good and valued member of society. Their effort to reform is no less vaulting and utopian than the many efforts of the civil rights movement that have fought bigotry based upon someone's skin color, gender, religion, or national creed.

Gay and lesbian culture seeks to define a vision of the good and just society that would include gay and lesbian persons as normal and natural. Such a utopian value may seem impossible to reach, yet it is closer at hand than was the case a century ago, when the homosexual could be hanged or jailed; or even twenty years ago, when the mayor could make a "queer joke" in public, when the police would not fear raiding without cause gay taverns, and when the right to hold a parade in commemoration of the gay community's "liberation" day was treated as a nuisance that was dismissed with a disparaging epithet. The political response to such behaviors today would be swift and largely negative from most segments of our society. Those anticipated responses are progress. They signal many ways in which development can be more positive and less disjunctive than in the past. Where once, hiding in the closet protected the old homosexual, today it is visibility, political power of numbers and voting, and social solidarity in the gay community that assures protection and freedom. What this amounts to is a recognition that the gay community's utopian vision of the good and just society can become a personal value for the self in development and in acculturation into the new gay and lesbian culture.

Breaking down the moral structure of the past is implicit in every part of the coming-out process. It conjoins a past and future, hitherto unknown to gay and lesbian youth. In growing up they could see no positive future. The past looked ugly and monstrous to them, populated as it was by the hideous stereotypes of the closet homosexual. Without a supporting tradition, it was impossible for them to undo the moral stigma of same-sex desire and locate a different voice within themselves, the mirror of an alternative culture.

Today, however, the change is taking hold, and gay and lesbian teenage development has no meaning without the concept of striving for a future "gay life." By the creation of communities, gay men and lesbians have provided the *traditions* for teenagers to change and strive toward in their coming out. It is the rituals which make these traditions a lived reality; they codify and socialize gay and lesbian ideals, knowledge, and social roles, binding past and future in a timeless present that could be created only through social tradition.

It is not easy for those of us in the American tradition to write of gay and lesbian development as a moral critique of society without sounding moralistic. Recent events in American politics make this even more difficult to do, given the rhetoric of pundits who attack "homosexual lifestyles" on the grounds that they oppose "family values." In their grandstanding, they continue to confuse "homosexual" and "gay and lesbian," though such a rarefied distinction is, of course, of no importance in their political strategy to continue picturing same-sex desire as "all bad." We are well aware that issues of gay and lesbian coming out have been cloaked in moralistic rhetoric by the critics and the defenders of the gay and lesbian movement. It is not our intention to fan the flames or to put the fire out. We have tried to focus on the place of the individual's experience and development through the coming-out rites; to see that it is individual liberty and freedom that matters; we do not take the rites as ends in themselves that might uphold yet another moralistic movement or counter-movement. It is for the reader to decide if we have succeeded.

Gay men and lesbians can celebrate the achievements of their traditions by realizing that the purest confirmation of the existence of their culture today is the rituals themselves—the symbolic capital they have bequeathed, like "good parents" do everywhere, to their "children" for their future. But they must also allow these "children" their own freedom in deciding how they shall construct that future for themselves.

CHAPTER TWO

◆ ◆ ◆

From Homosexual to Gay in Chicago: Transformations of a Culture

by Richard K. Herrell and Gilbert Herdt

A central concern underlying [the] options and the management of a homosexual career is the presence and complexity of a homosexual community, which serves most simply for some persons as a sexual market place, but for others as the locus of friendships, opportunities, recreation, and expansion of the base of social life. Such a community is filled with both formal and informal institutions for meeting others and for following, to the degree the individual wants, a homosexual life style. Minimally, the community provides a source of social support, for it is one of the few places where the homosexual may get positive validation of his own self-image.

—William Simon and John H. Gagnon,
"Homosexuality: The Formulation of a Sociological Perspective"

In terms of homophobia in the larger society, I don't think much has changed [since Stonewall]. But the gay liberation movement has meant that I can have integrity, that I'm not hiding anything. I can live in a rational world. Before Stonewall, we were mostly isolated individuals. Since then, a community has developed—gay churches, gay choruses, gay athletic events. All that had started before AIDS, but dealing with AIDS—having to educate ourselves about it, raise money for treatment, set up buddy programs, and care for the sick and dying— that has solidified it. We did a very fast job of growing up. That has been the miracle of the past twenty years

—Al Wardell, Illinois Gay and Lesbian Task Force

In the summer of 1987, as in the summer for many years preceding, a contingent from the Horizons Community Services Youth Group for gay and lesbian teenagers led Chicago's 18th annual Gay and Lesbian Pride Day Parade, carrying its banner and heading its color guard. Farther back in the parade, others from the youth group sat on a car and chanted, "Two, four, six, eight! What makes you think your kids are straight?" The parade, the single most public and socially encompassing event in Chicago's gay and lesbian annual calendar, offers the one time when the entire community comes together, and, thus, one of the few points of social interaction with teenagers.

As early as 1967, two years before the Stonewall Riots in New York that galvanized gay liberation, sociologists William Simon and John Gagnon identified the functions of what they then termed the "homosexual community." While there was, no doubt, a marginal homosexual world in the face of overwhelming political and social oppression, it would have been impossible at that time to imagine the achievements of gay liberation during the late 1960s and 1970s in beginning a new culture. In much of traditional Chicago it was (and remains) typical for children to move away from their parents only when they marry, leaving many closet homosexual men and women at home indefinitely into adulthood with their parents. The emergent gay lifestyle grew as attitudes toward "homosexuality" changed and a new gay and lesbian territory made it possible for men and women to move away from their natal families and childhood neighborhoods. But what kind of a cultural change has resulted?

Gay and lesbian cultural values, institutions, and roles in Chicago have created a community context for the coming-out process of today's gay and lesbian youth. As the first historical cohort of adolescent gays to come of age in an established gay community, Horizons teenagers are drawn from a wide arc of cultural and social groupings. Yet ironically, the teenagers interviewed for this project knew little of the gay and lesbian community's social history, either locally or nationally. The Gay and Lesbian Pride Day Parade draws them into its commemorative drama and political controversies. While adults speak of Chicago's gay neighborhood and institutions as recent and fragile, today's teens take them as a given for their adult lives.

Coming out in Chicago means membership in these institutions and belief in the worldview of the emerging gay and lesbian culture, with its own cultural history and geography. In exploring this current social history, we will draw upon archival historical material collected from Chicago in the earlier part of this century and demographic data collected from city records in the recent period. We will also look at an ethnographic study conducted in 1987 and 1988, involving participant observation in many cultural scenes, events, and institutions of Chicago's gay and lesbian community; ethnographic interviews with dozens of individual adults and youths during this period; and a cultural analysis of key events, especially of the Chicago Pride Day Parade.[1]

Perverts, Queers, and Homosexuals

To chart the cultural world of Chicago's contemporary gay territory and the Horizons institution that belongs within its orbit is to confront the changing configuration of historical age cohorts living within the area.

By the turn of the twentieth century, Chicago had established itself as the crossroads of America. The railroads had opened up the heartland frontier at the expense of Native Americans and a hasty rush to civilization. A great band of capitalist barons and respectable industrialists, developers, and retailers drove the unbridled boomtown. The teeming metropolis failed, however, to conform to the proper Victorian morality of its official leaders and challenged their exhortations to cling to the strait and narrow. In the winter of 1910 Mayor Busse of Chicago drew heavy fire over accusations of rampant vice from a group of influential clergymen. By spring he had appointed a special commission to "clean up" the sin and vice in Chicago. The aim of this elite of respectable citizens was to determine a policy of social purity, a plan of sexual hygiene to "consider the moral and physical harm which results from vice."[2]

The very idea of a Vice Commission seemed at first scandalous. The heartland of the United States, this city of God-fearing German and Scandinavian Lutherans and devout Catholic immigrants from Eastern Europe, of carpenters and factory workers so bound to tradition, was surely different from, say, decadent Berlin, effete London, or even cultivated Boston.

An outside investigator brought in from the "social hygiene" movement of New York scoured the city. Soon he was to confront the signs of queers in the city. One of the local Chicago investigators recommended that he put on a red necktie and walk down the east side of State Street between four and five in the afternoon to "see what happens." When he followed the advice, he reported that he was accosted by fifteen to twenty men who wanted to go with him, usually to one of the prominent hotel lobbies to make "assignments." Later investigators pursued such perverts into rooming houses, whose residents were found to be mostly young homosexual men, often counter-jumper store clerks, such as from the showcase Marshall Field's department store.[3] Interracial cafes known to be frequented by homosexuals are also reported.[4]

The Vice Commission investigators reported on "notorious saloons" and the "literature" of the "cult" [of homosexuals], which is "incomprehensible to one who cannot read between the lines." They told how "in one of the large music halls recently:"

> A much applauded act was that of a man who by facial expression and bodily contortion represented sex perversion, a most disgusting performance. Evidently it was not understood at all by many in the audience, but others wildly applauded. Then, one of the songs recently ruled off the stage by the police department was inoffensive to innocent ears, but was really written by a member of the cult, and replete with suggestiveness to those who understood the language of this group. It appears that in this community there is a large number of men who are gregarious in habit; who mostly affect the carriage, mannerisms and speech of women; who are fond of many articles ordinarily dear to the feminine heart. . . . Many of them speak of themselves or each other with the adaptation of feminine terms, and go by girls' names or fantastic application of women's titles.[5]

But by the Roaring Twenties, as Wall Street boomed, so did the first sexual revolution of the twentieth century. Fueled by massive industrial growth and large immigrations from Europe and rural America, Chicago emerged as the dominant city between the coasts. Here was the connection between the industrial east and agricultural west. Gangland Chicago, with both shady and legitimate establishments, provided entertainment, diversion, and liquor to the burgeoning population. In 1928, two researchers from the Department of Sociology at the University of Chicago documented a dance hall, "Diamond Lil's."[6]

> [Diamond Lil's] is owned and managed by Roy Spencer Bartlett, known as "Diamond Lil," after Mae West's play of that name now running in New York. This place is going into its third month of existence, and seems to be making a huge success. On Saturday nights by two o'clock they are filled up and people are turned away.
> Lil says that his plan is to lease the entire building . . . and to have dancing upstairs. He is, he asserts confidently, keeping strictly within

the law. He serves no gingerale, in fact nothing but coffee and sand-wiches.

The place is frequented by homosexuals. Not many women go there. Until very recently, there was a room at the back where men danced together, but because Lil had no license for running a dance place, the police stopped this. When the place is enlarged, there will be dancing, Lil says; what kind he does not specify.

The crowd is extremely Bohemian, although there are a lot of college men there. . . . Everyone stares quite boldly at everyone else, and if you want to talk to the person across the room or at the next table you simply walk over and begin talking.

Lil wears a red tie with a huge imitation diamond stick pin. He makes no attempt to conceal what sort of a place it is, in fact, by the use of such a name, he advertises it.[7]

While the social life available to Chicago's "queers" lingered into the 1930s, World War II and the mobilization needed to respond to Nazi Germany wrought unprecedented social change in Chicago. The massive dislocation of individuals and families throughout American society, the entry of women into factories, and the exodus of GIs to foreign shores created an indelible historical cohort marker between the generations. As men and women joined and were conscripted into the armed forces to fight the "Good War" (as Chicago's Studs Terkel termed it), the cities that were home to transportation centers and military bases became magnets for men and women from all walks of life—from both the small towns and sophisticated cities of American society. The war affected the lives of closeted homosexuals, too, and in spite of repression and discrimination, the war proved a critical turning point in their lives as well.[8]

The largest military port between the coasts by 1942, Chicago saw some "50,000 soldiers and sailors pouring into [the] downtown 'Loop' each weekend looking for a good time."[9] Persons who were attracted to the same sex but had hidden such desires their whole lives were thrown together for the first time.[10] They were, within limits, more free to pursue their interests. As in the other major port cities of the nation, many Americans found themselves for the first time in an en-vironment free of the kind of traditional constraints with which they had grown up. Some of the oldest closet homosexual establishments sprang up in Chicago during this time.

The war created not only a new mobility but an entrepreneurial market for the homosexual bar. Indeed, this institution was for the next generation to serve as the hiding place, haunt, and initiation ground for a new cohort of men and women pursuing same-sex desire. With only a few hours' furlough, the pent-up needs of GIs for a refuge from military and social pressures found an outlet in the bars and cafes of the inner city areas. "These establishments often were clustered in the parts of town that were flooded with GIs, introducing the [homosexual] life to a wider population of young men and women."[11] Among these hangouts was the expensive and fashionable "Town and Country" bar, located in the basement of the famous downtown Loop hotel, the Palmer House. New areas for solicitation and sexual cruising opened up; the "Wabash Baths," not far from the Palmer House, was one of these. New homosexual social events emerged, such as large interracial "costume balls" and "fashion shows" featuring a drag theme at "Finnie's Club" in Chicago beginning in 1939. Soon the "spillover" effect of bars in outlying areas began, with the "Circus Inn" in Rock Island, Illinois, coming into prominence, especially among black and white mixed crowds.[12]

Chicago—more similar to New York and San Francisco than to other midwestern cities—became a haven for homosexual men and women. With the end of the war and return from foreign duty, many homosexuals discharged from the military never went back to their small towns. Urban centers in the postwar period were thus to witness the development of a new cohort of urban-dwelling and secretive homosexuals.

But more than secrecy was soon demanded. Traditional gender roles and sexual conventions were taken out of mothballs and dusted off, and new kinds of heterosexual conformity were implemented following the war. "Rosie the Riveter," who had known such unprecedented freedom as a single or married woman working in the factories, was sent home to bear children and feed them. Her exit made way for the millions of GIs left unemployed by the war and hungering to begin traditional families. The moral mythology of the Cold War fell like a thick fog over the country, obscuring any alternative to conventionalized family life, the norm for the baby-boom generation.

Living in cities like Chicago was not easy for homosexual men and women as they entered the 1950s. The moral fabric of American family life centered on the suburban "split level family" of the suburbs, upholding the values and beliefs of heterosexualism, as pictured in the novels of Edmund White and other recent gay writers.[13] There were closet homosexual bars and secret meeting places, but the homosexual's personal life remained alienated from his or her public life. A

South Sider reported: "We used to go to Sam's [a bar on the Near North Side]. I never made out there. On the way home I'd ask to be let out at 63rd Street and State. I always knew I could find somebody wandering home at that hour who would be interested." It was during this period that a notion of entering the homosexual world through the secret networks and closet bars seems to have become a cultural practice. One did not "come out" in the contemporary sense. Homosexual persons entered ever so carefully and perhaps with reluctance into hidden spaces and places frequented by other persons who desired sex with the same sex. Yet this did not mean that all such others were "homosexual," as the South-Sider tells us. We find that the same kind of implicit tradition continues in South Side Chicago even today. It contributes to a cultural barrier against coming out which many youthful African-American boys and girls continue to experience in the city.

By the 1960s, Chicago began to lose the seemingly limitless prosperity of an earlier era. The city map was scarred with new expressways that destroyed old neighborhood boundaries to make way for commutes into the city from the suburbs. Racial strife was common. Panic-peddling radically and rapidly changed the demography of a city previously built from neighborhoods of relatively homogeneous class, race, and ethnic description. This was the city of Richard J. Daley, who had firmly consolidated the infamous Chicago Democratic machine, using political patronage jobs and close dealings with unions to weld the city together. The riots in Chicago in 1968 following the death of Martin Luther King, Jr., and at the Democratic Convention ripped the mask off the "family town" image Daley wished America to see and Chicagoans not to challenge. For homosexuals in the surrounding area, Chicago had become the only place to live if you were actively pursuing social and sexual relations in the closet scene. And while racism in the secret homosexual network was present, more contacts between blacks and whites were possible than in the mainstream.

Homosexual Life in 1967

The period just prior to liberation was the object of a significant study of homosexual life in Chicago funded by the National Institute of Mental Health and conducted by John Gagnon and William Simon while they were members of the Institute for Sex Research (1965–68).

The ethnographic materials we quote from the Simon and Gagnon study were gathered by David Sonnenschein, Alan Bell, and Albert Klassen, who were part of the research staff of the study. The quotes are taken from research files held by Gagnon, though the interviews conducted by Sonnenschein have been privately published by him (David Sonnenschein, *Some Homosexual Men: Interviews from 1967*, Austin, Texas: David Sonnenschein, 1983). Some of the quantitative results of the structured interviews were reported in Alan Bell and Martin Weinberg, *Homosexualities: A Study of Diversity among Women and Men* (New York: Simon and Schuster, 1978).[14] The Gagnon and Simon study creates a vivid portrait of this phase of closet homosexual life as a "bad scene," as recalled by informants from the mid-1960s. As one man remarked: "Raids were common. Same-sex couples were arrested for dancing. Names were published in the papers. People lost their jobs from that."[15]

The overwhelming sense of life it reveals until the period after the Stonewall riot is one of persistent danger and chronic secrecy. One informant summed up the secret world in this way:

> None of these homosexual situations is haphazard. The typical promiscuous situation takes place only in certain places. People know other homosexual males frequent these places and can meet people there. You don't have to worry if this person is homosexual or not, because the clientel is almost one hundred percent homosexual. So these things are very definite. They're planned and institutionalized. They include bars, shows, hotels for men (particularly the YMCA's), steam baths, parks, beaches, streets, hitchhiking, transportation stations, public toilets [These places] combine in a distinctive way as an opportunity for homosexual contact and danger of police action. A sudden, disastrous danger. This is where the profit comes in of catering to homosexuals. Running a homosexual bar, a steam bath—these are extremely profitable enterprises. The person who is not aware of taking risks and is promiscuous will inevitably end up in jail.[16]

The men in the study reported clandestine meeting places in which they made sexual contacts and sometimes friends, such as the bus station in the Loop and the American Airlines waiting area at O'Hare Airport.[17] A young newcomer to Chicago in the early 1960s tells how he found his way into the hidden scene:

> The first thing I did was go to Bug House Square [Washington Square, a public park frequented by hustlers and homosexual] and I just tried

to get information. Where are the bars? I finally stumbled onto a few places in the Clark and Division area by myself.[18]

I walked into my first gay bar, I think quite by accident, not knowing what it was at first. When I was in there I didn't know what to do. I stayed for a time and then came back to talk more and more frequently; and of course talking with people and bartenders you learn of other places to go and things to do.[19]

Yet, ironically, the dangers of the mid-1960s were accompanied by rebellious signs of an emerging homosexual neighborhood. Homosexual bars were well-known. These were in areas where "lots of gay people live, the areas around Dearborn and Division streets" as well, and "up north of Diversey."[20] Already we begin to see a push to the northern part of the city, the present area of gay life. The Old Town area of Chicago (Wells and North Avenue) was already becoming established as a place where homosexual men lived, and what is more important, as a neighborhood where two single men could take a lease on an apartment or get a mortgage to buy a house together. One informant complained: "Until recently it was very difficult for two males to get a mortgage. They will lease to two women, but they wouldn't lease to two men unless they were students or the building was on the rocks. I know two guys who are ready to put a third down on a house and the bank won't give them a mortgage."[21]

It was the fear of raids, entrapment, and arrest that most plagued the lives of these men. During the two years before the interviews were conducted (1965–67), a "big purge" forced many bars to close. "The bars were all closed for a time. Before, things were very free and open, and it was a swell place to live."[22] Chicago was the most open city around. "Some fifty bars catering to homosexual people have been harassed, to the extent that there are only a half a dozen left. Licenses were revoked and patrons of bars reported police brutality."[23]

The climate of fear was endemic. Another man told an interviewer in November 1967: "There is no such thing as a safe bar in the city of Chicago today. In the bars that do reopen there is a constant apprehension with the boss looking out the window waiting for the trucks to pull up in a line and carry everyone out. You simply can't go to a bar without feeling that you're not going to bar—you're going to jail. Even if the charges are thrown out of court it still costs each of the individuals several hundred dollars before they get through with it."[24]

Loss of employment was the greatest fear arising from arrest: "Since my job is connected with the Federal Government, I have a little bit of worry on the account . . . because I have clearance and all that. I generally will not give my name out except for my first name, and I won't tell anyone specifically where I live until I get to know them better. The number of people I have told where I live or my full name has been limited to half a dozen."[25] Such accounts reveal the threats of harassment and homophobia that maintained closet homosexuality: the secrecy of hiding; the fear of arrest and loss of income; the shunning of close contact in public places; the turning away from any public social life that would facilitate the emergence of a homosexual community. It is hard for Horizons youth, when they hear of such stories, to realize the prevailing stigma that ruined the lives of closeted people exposed in such ways.

And of course the private lives of these people were forever affected. The contamination of fear infected not only their sexual adventures but also their pursuit of friendship. Private parties and events were not immune from harassment: "I remember the few gay parties I went to. They had a light rigged up for a warning in case of a police raid. All these people were doing was enjoying good dance music and dancing with one another, talking and having a few drinks. Yet they had to act like they were some clandestine spy ring."[26]

Men had to choose between the dangers of raid and arrest or the loneliness of no social life at all. Many felt the need to find a permanent partner for this reason. "Why I'm so much for settling down with one person—so you don't have to go to these places with the dangers and grit. Aren't most people who are with the gay life looking for a companion? Most people don't find them, but isn't most promiscuity a matter of a search?"[27]

In fact, for many men—in spite of the secrecy and the dangers of arrest—the closet bars were their best chance for a social life. When men were asked how they got established in the homosexual world, most of them reported that the bars provided the best opportunity. "You have to make acquaintances, and this is the only place other than cruising streets and parks," one man said.[28]

One alternative to the bars was reported by some men—the Mattachine Society. This was the earliest public organization in the United States that struggled for reform of the laws and attitudes regarding homosexuality. Ironically, many of its members remained closeted throughout the period of its visibility, although the founder, Henry Hay, was a devoted public figure in the cause.[29] As one informant noted, "It's so important that a group like Mattachine put on social functions for precisely this reason to get established. This is the thing Mattachine has made possible for me. For the first time I'm being invited to some other guys' places for an evening where there will be half a dozen or a dozen people."[30] But here, too, secrecy and the closet loomed even large. A fieldworker from the Gagnon and Simon study who attended a function in May 1967 reported on the guests' apprehensions of strangers. Precautions were sometimes extensive. For example, a social function held at the apartment of two Mattachine society members provoked fears of arrest: There had been several anonymous tips (harassing calls) about the prospect of a police raid at the gathering. The seventy-five men and two women wore name tags with first names only. An announcement asked anyone in possession of alcohol or other drugs to leave immediately to avoid incriminating others if there were a raid.[31] No area of social life, including the private party, offered secure shelter from the torment of institutionalized homophobia in Chicago.

The social alienation and feeling of powerlessness wrought from this historical period were reflected in the attitudes of many who refused to join the Mattachine society. Some men did not view their lives as being sufficiently threatened to care; others were politically frightened. "I'm not a member of Mattachine," one man said, "I just don't feel persecuted, I guess, so I don't feel the need to join any movement."[32] Still others believed that it was useless to join an organization: "One reason I'm opposed to Mattachine is that I don't believe that marching in front of the White House will help. Would you go up to people and say, 'Look, I'm normal in every way, but I like to have sex with men?'"[33] Another man disagreed with political activism of any kind: "No, it wouldn't accomplish anything; it wouldn't get me anywhere. We don't fit the definition of minority groups. The homosexual world isn't an organized group. And all minority groups are organized. It's more like an underground. We only come out in a secret kind of way and express our own little way."[34] This last commentary captures the mood of many closet homosexuals of the time; activism was not only dangerous, it was just plain useless. Things would not change.

Liberation Comes to Chicago

The sentiments of the 1960s closet homosexuals who opposed activism were apocryphal. The radical vision of gay liberation had not yet been born. How could a culture possibly be created out of such alienation? Soon, however, and in a surprisingly swift way, a transformation began to occur. It started in isolates around the country, with Stonewall being the most publicized.

By 1970 the impact of increasing radicalism, from the Stonewall riot to other liberation events in American cities, began to surface in Chicago. The old Mattachine Society, long a forerunner of change through social and political pushes of accommodation, was giving way to the Gay Liberation Front as a nascent political nationalist movement. The old closet homosexual hangouts continued in operation for some time; in fact, the last survived well into the late 1980s. But the effects of gay liberation were growing.

Our informants in the late 1980s remembered this period in strong and—in spite of the continued harassment—sometimes nostalgic narratives.

> Before Newtown was at Clark and Division [on the Near North Side]. Just a handful of bars. Mafia-owned. Very dark. Very little light. Bars like Ruthie's. You couldn't touch, dance, eat, no tables. Only lean against the bar or wall and get drunk. Find someone attractive. Go home and fuck 'em. Then go back to the bar the next night. It only provided for alienation. That's it. If you did touch anybody you were bounced out the door. But the bouncer could walk up to you and put his hand down your pants. There wasn't anything you could do about it. You had to stand there and take it. Or be thrown out of the bar. There were no other social outlets. Nothing.

Another man described the extent of the early gay territory in these words:

> The [gay] ghetto extended from Diversey north to Belmont along Broadway. The concentration of gay people was enormous. It was like a barrio. I got here in 'sixty-nine and it was like that, residentially speaking. I don't know when it was established. Some gay people lived in Old Town. There was a bunch of gay folk around Orleans—down in that area, along the side streets, such as the "Eugenie." It was very oppressive. The social scene was oppressive. There were bars on Broadway. The original "Annex." Three other bars on Clark Street. There was a bar on Rush Street, called the "Normandy," near the Carnegie Theater.

The "Haig." And "Kitty Shean's." The lesbian bars were west on Irving Park.

Liberation was for some people unexpected:

It started being called Newtown in '69 and '70. It was the name of the gay neighborhood. It had clear boundaries. It started drifting north when the straight singles bars opened on Broadway. On summer nights in 1970 the stoops of buildings and curbs of sidewalks were filled with gay people. And all your friends would walk by. That's what you did on a summer night: just sat there and drank a coke and blew a joint. It was like the West Village [in New York] . . . then. People just being out and friendly. But the singles bars came in and gay people started fleeing . . . in droves. Not till much later did they start coming back in.

And what kind of place was the early gay bars? Another man comments:

The bars were shadowy places, but the street life in the early 1970s was out in the open, in the daylight or at night. We countered that bar scene the way we could. I remember when the gay liberation movement began in Chicago, the first places to get hit were the bars. I went one night after the bars had closed and I broke windows. It was terrifying. I was sure I would get busted. The bouncer at "Ruthie's" told me I had to buy a drink. You had to buy a drink or you would be thrown out. I had my arm around my friend Jerry. He took my arm down and he said, "You can't touch anybody in here, faggot." I put my arm back. He got abusive. He came back later and started to open my pants to grope me. He had just called me a faggot. But he wouldn't let me put my arm around Jerry. I came back with a bunch of bricks and broke the windows.

The quality of social life in the bars was bad enough that the patrons demanded changes on their own. The same informant tells the story.

It was difficult for gay-owned bars to get started because they were torched. I figured it was the syndicate. One of the first to make it was the "Bistro," and another was "Eddie Dugan's" place. It was great. It was fun. One night we were picketing the "Normandy." We were demanding that it be better lit, that there be tables, food, and that we be allowed to dance. They refused all these demands. We tried to stop people from going in. We wanted to destroy their business. We pretty much did.

Chicago's cultural geography reconstructed the moral geography of the marginal. The city's history, as we have seen, reveals an oscillation between radical crusades for sexual social control and libertine openness that extended to the liquor and vice interests of the criminal underworld. The geography represented the city, with rather hostile social oppression, and the relatively benign social environments outside the city limits. Calumet City, a suburb of Chicago, continues to offer an island of gay bars just outside the city. Over many years the crusading mayors in Chicago have often shut down establishments of vice, but through it all corrupt little Cal City, just over the border, always remained available, like Newport, Kentucky, across from blue-nosed Cincinnati. The wild city threatened the clean city, and life at the moral margins was always subject to vice investigations and shakedowns by organized crime. An informant who frequented the gay bars in Chicago in the 1950s and 1960s remembers men emerging from the back seat of limos, coming into the bar, and collecting large sums of cash taken directly from the cash drawer by the bartender.

These narratives suggest the existence of established groups and networks of homosexual people from the earliest years of the century. The history of the homosexual bar provides a key to understanding this change. Who owns the bars? If the owners are not homosexual, do they support homosexual people? Until alternative spaces became available (mostly at the universities and in churches who offered rental space), the beginnings of an organized gay political life took place in bars. The magazine *Gay Chicago* was first issued in the mid 1970s; its first issue published a list of gay bars, identifying which were gay-owned and which were "gay-supportive." The early gay-owned bars led in turn to many other cultural activities and community meeting places, to churches and a community center. Gay liberation gave birth to two decades of institution building. The growth has not subsided in present-day Chicago.

The culture and institutions of the Newtown neighborhood are what matters for this story. It is home to most gay organizations and entertainment spots. Nevertheless, what most Chicago people think of as "the gay neighborhood" is far from uniform: Where is it? What is it? What should it become? Persons of different ages, genders, races, and classes hold very different views of the matter. Many of the places in which lesbians and gay men meet outside of the ghetto are not seen as "gay" in any conventional sense. In fact, the shadowy and neighborhood bars that offer clandestine same-sex contact, frequented primarily by Hispanics, African-Americans, and blue-collar workers, are outside the orbit of gay and lesbian culture. Bars on the far south end of the metropolitan area in Calumet City, and in other suburbs, are each distinctive of a social niche. Organizations for suburban gays and lesbians have been formed throughout the towns that ring the city. But by the late 1970s Newtown was home to gay and lesbian-identified individuals, bars, businesses, and institutions—including, of course, Horizons. And by the late 1970s Horizons had formed a group for teenagers, recognizing them not as some kind of proto-adults, but as a new kind of adolescent in need of a safe space beyond the streets and sexualized bar life available at that time.

Newtown: The Gay Territory

With the emergence of a defined gay and lesbian geography, a sort of "ghetto" as distinctive of recent gay history in the United States as it is foreign to the cities of Europe, Chicago took on a new profile.[35] The North Side area of Chicago began to be residentially homosexual in the 1970s. The "Newtown" neighborhood emerged as a new social scene as we have seen, first for closet homosexuals, then for gays. It was not yet a "gay neighborhood"; that would require several years more. It would never be a "real gay ghetto" like Greenwich Village in New York or the Castro in San Francisco; rather, it would remain more diffusely and densely "gay"—in social and political flavor, cultural and economic interest—much as smaller American cities and larger European cities, such as Amsterdam, are today. The neighborhood dramatically changed from an all-white, Northern European enclave, commercially developed in the mid-nineteenth century, to an ethnically mixed neighborhood in the late 1960s lacking the local institutions that preserve neighborhood homogeneity throughout much of the rest of the city.

As a name for a fixed territory, "Newtown" refers to the eastern half of the Lake View neighborhood on Chicago's North Side lake front, bounded on the east by the great insulated apartment houses along Lake Shore Drive. The territory of the Lake View neighborhood, bounded by Diversey, Ravenswood, Montrose, Clark, Irving Park, and the lake, is part of an older (and much larger) Lake View township (1865) and, later, city (1887). The whole area was annexed by Chicago in 1889. Although industry did expand in the southwestern sector of the area during the 1880s and 1890s, manufacturing developed largely outside the residential district known today as Lake View. Two major shopping areas grew up around Belmont, Lincoln, and Ashland, and at Clark and Diversey. The Chicago Cubs baseball field was bought by the wealthy Wrigley family after World War I and remains a major feature of neighborhood life. Today the area is largely residential.

As a major destination for European emigrants, Chicago neighborhoods developed the distinctive character of émigré institutions. They reflected the local control of residence and voluntary affiliation. Between 1910 and 1920, the population of Lake View grew from 60,535 to 96,482. More than 70 percent of the community's population in 1920 was native white, many the descendants of the original German and Swedish settlers. These two immigrant groups predominated among the foreign-born residents as well. In the 1950 census, the population of Lake View was 99.2 percent white. During the 1950s, there was a significant increase in persons of Asian descent, by 1960, 3 percent of the population was nonwhite, and by 1980, 5 percent of the population was of Asian descent.[36]

Before the emergence of Newtown, the gay scene centered largely in the "Near North" area. The bohemian district around "Tower Town" (near the Water Tower today) and later Clark and Division Streets, was a political and social epicenter. In the 1960s, "Old Town," a residential and commercial area centered on Wells Street and North Avenue, was home to Chicago's hippie counter-culture. As Wells Street became rundown and shabby, developers christened as "Newtown" the area north of Diversey along Broadway. Chicago has been characterized by its homogeneous neighborhoods and ugly histories of abuse by sellers and buyers alike when panic-peddlers manipulated fear and prejudices as a neighborhood begins to change. Given this history of neighborhood strongholds, a sure index of neighborhood transition, indicating changing local control, is a change in racial composition of a neighborhood. The sharp decline in Lake View's population parallels a period of decline elsewhere, when many of the city's residents left ethnic neighborhoods (and also important for many, left their parishes) for the suburbs.

For the first time there was a significant increase in the black population of Lake View. While the black population of the western half of Lake View grew only to 3.7 percent, in the eastern half of Lake View that makes up Newton, it had grown to 10.2 percent by 1980. Eighty-four percent of the black population of Lake View in 1980 lived in the Newtown area.

These statistics reveal only part of the change—that of changing from an overwhelmingly European to a mixed neighborhood. During the same period, many Hispanics moved into the Lake View area. The central portion of Lake View has a large Hispanic population, includ-ing important business districts catering to the large Puerto Rican and Mexican populations in the district. While the percentages for 1970 and 1980 censuses are not comparable (1970 asked for "Spanish lan-guage," 1980 for "Spanish origin [surname?]"), they nevertheless dem-onstrate further changes. The homogeneous, tightly bounded ethnic neighborhoods—still found in the northwest and southwest of the city—were giving way to a new territory.

In the late 1960s, homosexual establishments were left alone in mar-ginal and nonresidential areas, such as the Near North along Clark Street, just north of the Chicago River. Here, for many years, a bar district flourished amid warehouses and marginal businesses. With the decline of the older local institutions in East Lake View as the older population moved away, such as churches and other ethnic orga-nizations, the neighborhood was, in a sense, wide open for the changes that a racially and ethnically mixed population without com-mon cultural authority and traditions could bring about without chal-lenge. Thus it was a residential formation that created in Chicago (as the Castro did in San Francisco) a gay and lesbian neighborhood cul-tural life in its fullest dimensions.

Among these changes were foundling institutions, gay-owned bars and organizations, that found a home in neighborhood churches. Without their space and support, the institutional growth of the gay and lesbian community in this neighborhood would have been nearly impossible: the Wellington Avenue Church (United Church of Christ, home of the Metropolitan Community Church and site of a jammed house for State of Illinois hearings on gay rights legislation), St. Sebas-tian's Catholic Church (home to Dignity, and site of former Mayor Jane Byrne's request for the Gay and Lesbian Democrats' endorsement—enthusiastically given), the Second Unitarian Church (meeting hall for many gay political events and the Lesbian and Gay Academic Union and LGAU History Project), and St. Peter's Episcopalian Church on Belmont (meeting place for Gay Alcoholics Anonymous).

Meanwhile, other establishments besides the bars became visibly "gay" in the area. Although two large dance bars were present for a period of time, and a small neighborhood bar for both women and men flourished on Broadway for many years, the bars were limited. A growing number of small gay and lesbian establishments began to flourish. Newtown was where many people spent time together out-side the gay bars—at the record stores, restaurants, a shopping mall carved out of an old movie palace, a theater that screens films popular with lesbian and gay audiences, not to mention a "very gay" hardware store mentioned by informants who like high-tech furniture and housewares. The Dominick's, one of the large supermarkets in the area, was regarded as a place to meet "hot gay men." Nearby there stands the Metropolitan Community Church, Second Unitarian Church, Gay Horizons, and later the Illinois Gay and Lesbian Task Force. In the early 1980s Horizons had a weekend coffee house at the Jane Addams Center (social welfare group) near Belmont and Broadway Streets. The Golden Nugget Pancake House, at the corner of Belmont and Broadway, was jokingly referred to as the "Golden Faggot." Among other special shops, a leather and "sex toys" store, and an adult bookstore that specialized in gay men's erotica and pornography.

Two popular bars for men were on nearby Halsted Street, although the area was considered outside of the Newtown gay neighborhood. A few businesses further north catered to the gay/emergent yuppie clientele. The Marigold Bowl has for years been home to gay and lesbian bowling leagues. On Addison near Wrigley Field was His 'n' Hers, a bar popular with both gay women and men that featured food and entertainment.

Newtown grew in the midst of a deteriorating neighborhood. As a residential destination it became a place to get away from the confines of family, to be free of the traditionalism of small town and suburban communities. For many, it was the place they chose to live; for others, it represented an involuntary exodus after their families discovered and rejected lesbian or gay members. For these reasons, distinct breaks appeared between the economic class of Newtown residents and that of their families of birth, as well as of the original inhabitants. Class differences remain a significant reminder of this history of Newtown.

Consider, for example, Paul and Jose. They are a white and Hispanic gay couple in their thirties. Paul's father is a wealthy dentist in Tennessee. He had planned for his son to pursue a similar, well-paying profession. But Paul's father cut him off entirely when Paul came out to him during his second year of college. He fled to Chicago, where he took one of the readily available but poorly paid jobs for gay men: retail sales. Many other men and women wait tables in similar situations. Paul would like to pursue a graduate degree program but sees it as impossible. On the other hand, Jose, who grew up in Puerto Rico and moved to Chicago, is on good terms with his family, in part because they live far away. He has a well-paid union job with a public utility. Unlike his brothers who are married and have several children, he maintains a style of life well above that of his family of origin.

As the neighborhood has changed from a seedy commercial strip in the 1960s to an affluent residential district in the 1990s, the cost of running a business or living there has also dramatically grown. Gay men, especially, live there and are notable as its symbol. As one old-timer complained: "First the gays moved in. Then the guppies moved in. Then the yuppies moved in and forced the guppies out. I skipped that stage. I just moved directly to Uptown."

The kernel of this statement offers a story familiar in many American cities since 1970. Gay men and some lesbians began to move into ethnically or marginally residential communities that did not have organized community forces to resist them. Not only was there no formal opposition to the migration, property owners were usually glad to sell or rent to these more steady and affluent customers. Properties were cheap to rent and buy. On Saturdays, the local hardware stores were full of gay men buying paint and new furnishings for their apartments who spoke with pride about their achievements in improving the buildings. During the late 1970s and through the 1980s, the frenzy of real estate development—of which this was a part—drove up rents and purchase prices, as older buildings were converted into condominiums and smart rentals. Older and poorer residents were thus forced to move out as the area became too expensive. More attractive and settled, then, nongays with money bought into the neighborhood. The area would subsequently lose much of its ethnic character as it simultaneously became a residential neighborhood of "ethnic" gays.

Contemporary Cultural Voices

Newtown is, thus, Chicago's "gay turf." It now has both a social structure—its institutions and their networks of social relationships—and a culture—the symbols, meanings, and values that reflect the lives of its gay and lesbian residents, and the new gay immigrants who come there. The neighborhood itself has become a complex symbol of the wider community—of its place in the city and of the social life of Chicago's gay men and lesbians. Its boundaries shift with perspective. To some it is an entertainment district, in which case the neighborhood centers on the bar strip of Halsted Street. For others it is a residential neighborhood, in which case it is located between the shops and surrounding residential streets. And it is a center of the gay community's social and political life, centering on the "Rodde" Center, home to many of Chicago's gay and lesbian social service organizations—notably Horizons.[37] Newtown has become a complex symbol which binds the tensions among residential, commercial, and entertainment interests in the service of an emerging gay collectivity.

Although Newtown was established as a gay residential and to a lesser extent entertainment area by the early 1970s, few of the organizations, bars, and businesses that anchor the community date back to that time. A map of the area produced by *Gay Chicago* magazine in 1976 shows a very different picture from what we see today. Businesses—all kinds of businesses, especially bars, but also restaurants, card shops, resale shops, clothing boutiques, etc.—come and go at a rapid rate on the North Side of Chicago, and the gay businesses of Newtown are no exception.

What makes Newtown the gay neighborhood? People gave many responses. One man who lives in the neighborhood asked first, "Isn't 'Newtown' a developer's word?" (It is, but so is "Lakeview.") He then continued, "What makes that neighborhood gay for me is that gay people live there. The Jewel [supermarket] is gay, and so are the nearby Dominick's and Treasure Island [supermarkets]." Why? Not only "because gay people shop there," but because they are now perceived to be part of the territory. Indeed, so powerful is the reach of the gay idea that today many organizations and businesses in the neighborhood name themselves after the popular if unofficial conception "Newtown."

All of the organizations and businesses listed in table 2.1 were located in the Newtown neighborhood, or at least were headquartered there, at the time of our 1987 survey.

The reactions of immigrants to the discovery of gay turf ranged from an amused to a deeply emotional recognition. A young man new to the city from years at a college in downstate Illinois said, "I still remember walking down Broadway the first time I was in Newtown. I bet it was when [my lover and I] were apartment hunting. It was summer and they had the tables out at the Melrose [restaurant]. It was real obvious that most of the people were gay, notwithstanding the fact that we tell straight people that you can't tell who's gay by looking at them. We know you can." A woman who had no social experience of being with lesbians other than her lover recalled how it

Table 2.1 Newtown Gay/Lesbian Establishments, 1987[a]

34 bars patronized by gay men and lesbians; of these
   15 are patronized by men and women
   17 are patronized primarily by men
    2 are patronized primarily by women
    4 are patronized both by gays and straights
   15 are dance bars[b]
    5 serve food
    8 show music videos
    2 are nonalcoholic and thereby accessible to minors
   22 have a 2:00 A.M. license
   10 have a 4:00 A.M. license

20 major businesses are on the "gay map" of Newtown; of these
   11 are gay owned
    2 bookstores offer gay and feminist literature
 5 businesses sell erotica (3 exclusively gay erotica); of these
    4 provide the opportunity for anonymous same-sex activity
 1 gym patronized primarily by gay men
 1 gym patronized primarily by lesbians
 1 bath house

24 community/social organizations; of these
    6 are exclusively male
    3 are exclusive female

14 social service organizations

11 political organizations; of these
    6 are activist organizations
    3 are the community offices of nongay politicians
    2 are nongay churches which provide space for meetings

 4 gay and lesbian professional associations

 3 weekly community publications

12 religious organizations; of which
    8 have regular or semi-regular services specifically for a gay/lesbian
       congregation or specifically welcome gays and lesbians into
       their congregations

 8 athletic and sports organizations, most of which organize regularly
    scheduled team and individual activities for lesbians and gay men

[a]Although we have tried to offer a comprehensive list, this table is only approproximate, and many of its categories overlap. It intentionally omits the many businesses outside of Newtown, such as the smaller cluster of shops in Old Town and Calumet City.
[b]There is no bar that now presents drag shows in the neighborhood.

felt to walk into a lesbian bar: "The first time I went to a women's bar [there] I was with my lover. We were still living in the suburbs. You want to know about the time my throat choked up? And being ready to cry? This room full of women was all lesbians. How can a place that smells like stale beer move you? A bar! I don't play pool! We don't drink! But we walked into the bar and until [then] I really believed we were the only two lesbians in the world."

Many of our informants expressed the need to feel safe and secure in a "community" of their own. Anne, the owner of a Newtown restaurant, laughed when we told her a man known to us reports eating at her restaurant because he can feel "gay" there. "You see a lot of affection between gay people here. Touching. Holding hands. The things people who like each other do. Nobody who comes here cares."

More than twenty years ago people were moving into Newtown to claim the social space to come out. Here is a white woman, a lesbian in her forties, who links then and now:

When I wanted to come out, I wanted to live somewhere where I could be as out as I comfortably could. When I first lived here I remember seeing the gay people mostly on Broadway. It seems to have moved. Now it's Halsted. Broadway has gotten more straight. I remember I used to take walks there at night, being real excited about things like being able to walk down the street holding hands with a woman. Living here facilitated that. It provided options that I wouldn't have had anyplace else. A friend of mind [who lives in another part of the city] is worried about getting gay mail because the mailman might notice. Here, who the fuck cares?

For many gays and lesbians who came to Newtown for the first time, it was an oasis of taverns, a kind of bar culture left over from the historical homosexual period. Many a gay man has commented how going to the bars was an initiation into the older gay male cohort of the time. As one of our black male informant's described the 1970s, "Going out to the bars for the first time was a very big deal." A difference between coming out in the 1970s and today impinges upon the role of the bars and alcohol in general (see chapter 4). But there has always been a great disparity between the number of gay male bars and lesbian bars (see table 2.1).

What of the women's experiences in bars? Many commentators have discussed the smaller presence of the bar in lesbians' lives. Chicago's paucity of women's bars is no different, but it still poses an ambiguity of "belonging" or being "out of" Newtown and gay/lesbian life to some women. One woman informant remarked: "What makes this neighborhood gay? Probably, Horizons. That's been around forever. MCC [the Metropolitan Church]. The bars. [Where do women go here?] The Closet, Augie's. [pause] Out to dinner [laughs]. I used to go with gay men to the men's bars. The Lady Bug. That was my bar. Where DO women go? There aren't really a lot of places now."

Few bars attract women and men equally. Most bars will have at least a few patrons of both sexes. The "leather bars" are virtually male exclusively. Men and women informants have described ambivalent feelings about these gendered spaces. A woman activist in Newtown complains of the predicament:

> Augie's and CK's is the only bar in the neighborhood. I only know three women's bars. When you get politically involved, you don't go to bars because you have something else to do. "Paris Dance" [a prominent lesbian bar] is outside of Newtown. I tend to go to bars for bar night fundraisers and stand around raising money. I can't live in Newtown because I need a three bedroom apartment, and my kids live with me five weeks a year ... I feel comfortable with gay men, but I get pressured not to forget I'm a lesbian.

But if gay commercial places register loyalty, and lesbian bars provide a place to socialize and be seen, even more does Newtown constitute a security circle that draws notice in the cultural voices of Chicago's gays. It is not only the place to be with other gays and lesbians, but a place wherein the feelings of fear located in other quarters of the city are significantly reduced.

Indeed, this creates an opposition to straights—a kind of ethnic humor of neighborhood exclusion. Occasional humorous and actual resentments are expressed toward straights who presume to violate the gay and lesbian ethic. For example, Linda, a thirty-five-year-old resident of Newtown, said: "I feel most comfortable walking down the street. Like I belong. Most of the people I see are just like I am. As a matter of fact, I get resentful of straight couples walking down the street. 'Hey! Don't you have your own neighborhood? Don't go hugging and kissing on the sidewalk!'"

Still other residents dismiss the presence of nongay people in the neighborhood. Another lesbian expresses clear "rules of behavior" for "breeders" (heterosexuals) who visit Newtown. "It's okay if they come here and spend money as long as they don't talk or touch each other," she said.

The youth who venture to Newtown to come out and be out express relief and joy at discovering their own territory. A founding member of the Horizons Youth Group said he discovered the neighborhood through a *Chicago Reader* advertisement for a Northeastern Illinois University gay group. He pointed to a building that now houses a retail business and said, "My friend Bob and I used to sit in the window at the restaurant that used to be there watching people go by. I thought I had gone to heaven."

Yet some informants expressed highly ambivalent feelings about belonging to the "ghetto." Some dislike the impetus gay turf represents for gays and lesbian adults to withdraw from the city at large. "I don't like the ghetto as culture—but ghettoization does wonderful things. It's important for me to live there. I breath easily when I get back to my neighborhood. I'm so aware of my 'difference' when I'm elsewhere. It's life-giving to go back to Roscoe Street and walk on Halsted Street, to be part of my people. I love my people. The ghetto is essential. It's how we grow but we have to be able to move out of it."

But Joann, a woman who rarely goes to bars—though she is involved in gay community organizations—was nonplussed when we asked her to name Newtown's boundaries: "What anchors the neighborhood? Good Shepherd Parish [church]. A lot goes on there. A lot of gay people's identity is church-related. That's where they put their effort. Or they divide their efforts between Horizons and Good Shepherd. For those who need that kind of outlet, there's a real outlet there. I'm not a Christian. Or 2U [Second Unitarian Church], and the 'Rodde' Center, where so much goes on."

Here we see the divergent voices of Newtown and their differing relationships to the neighborhood. Many locals agree with Joann in defining the neighborhood by the places wherein community meetings are held and by their understanding of what draws others to Newtown. Joanne, who has recently become involved in the "Gay Parents Group" at Horizons, views it as the heart of social networks that connect lesbian and gay institutions.

Is Newton a gendered space? The gay men who live in the neighborhood typically call it "Newtown." But a young lesbian, for instance, who resides here, laughs when she calls it "Boy's Town" and comments:

A lot of lesbians have moved north and west because this neighborhood has gotten expensive. Mainly, I think of it as Boy's Town because of the bars. If I'm talking to someone I don't know, I say 'Lakeview' or 'near

Cubs Park' or 'Wrigleyville.' I don't think of it as the name of the community. It doesn't have a neighborhood sense like, say, Hyde Park [on Chicago's South Side where she grew up]. Now it's full of Lincoln Parkers who can't afford Lincoln Park anymore, and they are taking over my neighborhood [laughs]!

Since the beginning of the women's movement in the 1970s, many lesbians and heterosexual feminists have insisted on the importance of separate places and resources for women, sometimes termed "womenspace." This has made Newtown difficult for those women who see it as a man's neighborhood. The woman director of a leading gay and lesbian rights advocacy organization cited the provision of "female" space as a key item on the lesbian political agenda. The possibility of a "gay community" that includes both men and women—frequently stated as the ideal goal by individuals and organizations—is more often realized only as a network of institutions since most of these are male-only. Some women say that the disparity between their incomes and those of men explains why there are fewer women's bars. Others say that Newtown has become too expensive as a place for lesbians to live. High rents have caused women's establishments to move out of the neighborhood. Four businesses with a significant or exclusive lesbian presence are now just beyond the usual boundaries of Newtown.[38] On the other hand, women spoke of areas where lesbians live, though they wouldn't define these as lesbian neighborhoods. For instance, a woman activist remarked: "There's no lesbian neighborhood. I had always heard that Rodgers Park was a place for lesbians, but all the gay people I know there are gay men!"

We met women who were nostalgic for a past when there was more available to women in Newtown. One woman told how the women's space had shrunk in the growth of the neighborhood.

> Especially right here along the bar strip—on Halsted. Christopher Street, Little Jim's, Ricky's (used to be Ladybug), closed down. In the immediate area, no women's bar except for CK's. The Swan Club is gone. I was basically under age during a lot of the really wild times. But [the bar owner] Marge knew me. Marge's lover had a beautiful eagle tattooed on her wrist. Whenever she saw me there, she would shoo me out. "You can't be here!" I'd say I was just eating. Then she'd say, "As soon as you finish your chili, you have to leave." I always felt as though I had been found out by my mother!

Many commentators on the gay and lesbian scene in the United States have noticed the difficulties in how men's and women's lives are linked. We found the same thing in Chicago. One woman's history must stand for many:

> I used to bounce back and forth between the men's community and the women's community. I really like the humor and wit that a lot of gay men I knew were displaying because bitchiness was really in. It was very politically incorrect. I never had an outrageous sex life like the men I knew did. At that time before AIDS, there was nothing to stop you from being a shameless hussy. You were supposed to be as much of one as you could. I really enjoyed that freewheeling sexuality. The women were really stuffy about people like that. Sex was not so very big.

Social service, political, athletic, and religious organizations more than anything seem to draw women and men together. Leslie, a divorced mother of three, first got involved in the community through the support group for lesbian and gay parents. This is but one of the many functions supported by Horizons: "Many people in our community have no children and no plans to have children. I'm out to all my kids. I took them to the Gay Pride Parade. I haven't had any problems in the community other than that people without children respond askance at people who do. People think of them as a problem. But you never get hugs like you get from your kids. But here [at the support group], I've had good support for being a noncustodial mother."

This expanding neighborhood is defined also by the lesbian and gay-owned businesses that provide a common ground for socializing and networking. Professionals are visible too; the gay and lesbian doctors, dentists, lawyers, accountants, and others whose services are critical to the emerging gay middle class. These businesses and persons inspire loyalty to them as part of the community, even to the point of defining the neighborhood as the gay business district. For instance, a gay lawyer who lives outside Newtown, nevertheless makes a point of shopping there: "I think of it as the business district of the gay community. The businesses are gay-owned, or if not gay-owned, they advertise in the gay papers. It's important to me if a business is gay-owned or if they advertise. Leona's [restaurant], Unabridged [bookstore], Molly's [restaurant], the card shop. If they advertise, that's important to me. Okay, then they can be there and be part of the community."

Solidarity with a community may sometimes conflict with profits. Activists in the community often call on gay and lesbian businesses to solicit contributions: money, advertising, raffle prizes, and so forth. A member of a political organization who finds herself constantly pleading with business owners to contribute revealed an underlying contradiction: Is this for culture or for profit? "I know that gay businesses like all businesses are out to make a profit. So gay business people have to reach out to others [nongays] to come to their neighborhood too. The merchants do so much for the community. If I were a gay merchant, I don't know if I could take it. Every organization in the community feels that because the merchants take money from the community and they are gay, too, they 'owe' us something."

A case in point comes from Anne, a restaurant owner, who sees herself as part of the community, but who also needs to separate her business interests from her political commitments. "This is not a gay restaurant, but there is a high percentage of gay clientele. I'm political, but I don't use the business as a temple of involvement. I'm personally political, but I don't push that on my staff." But I pointed to the reprints of reviews of her restaurant on the wall and said that with her success—good, imaginative food and reasonable prices—some people would be nervous about being seen as a gay business: "You have to be a person first. Some of the gay business people around here think they have to hide that. You have to be out. They're afraid. If you want to be a person first and gay second, you have to be out. Otherwise you're nothing, just in-between someplace. I've only had one anti-gay incident in the three and a half years I've had the business here. I didn't want it to be seen as a lesbian business either. I always have a balance in the staff between men and women."

The "helping" agencies are critical. Many women and men, especially women, see their relationship to Newtown primarily—even exclusively—in terms of their involvement in social service organizations. The community's institutions are drawn centrifugally to the "Rodde" Center, where Horizons is housed. The nearby gay churches, such as Metropolitan Community Church, and the Illinois Gay and Lesbian Task Force, are nearly all headquartered in the neighborhood nowadays, as are the arts, professional, and sports associations that see themselves as gay. Several people named Gay Alcoholics Anonymous as a crucial community organization.

Thus Horizons anchors the cultural community as much as it brings together the genders in new ways that attempt to bridge the gap between them in the broader hegemony of mainstream middle-class society. Through its extensive program of services and support groups, Horizons has become a key institution throughout gay and lesbian Newtown (see chapter 3).

Newtown is not immune to the harassment and violence of the old days. As a marked "gay" neighborhood it has become the target of a new homophobic assault. Gay-bashing and verbal abuse are common, sometimes reflecting conflicting claims over the turf. Most informants reported incidents, although none regarded it as a major problem in their living there. They tended to associate the problem, though, with characteristics other than its' being a gay neighborhood; for example, being home to Cubs Park, having drug sales on the street at night, or falling within gang turf. "I've witnessed a lot more fag-bashing during the last couple of years," reported one woman. "Last summer I interceded a couple of times. I heard a guy screaming who was being attacked by a couple of teenagers." The sense of living in a liberated neighborhood is always matched with caution. One man constructed his life this way: "I've never personally been the victim of it. I am out at work. They all know. I'm out to my landlord. Nobody cares. It's not the norm. I've been lucky. My lover and I will hold hands at the Lincoln Park Zoo, but we look around. We're careful. I don't worry about reading *Windy City Times* or *Outlines* [two gay and lesbian newspapers] on the bus or train."

Chicago's racism is routinely cited by locals as a problem plaguing the gay and lesbian community. Newtown replicates the troubled life of the city, both in racist behavior and in years of work by community organizations to address racism in the city and the neighborhood. The notion of a gay and lesbian community is frequently phased in terms of an internally diverse group of people defined by a common sexuality. Newtown is home to two bars that cater to primarily Hispanic and African-American clients. Racial difference is often eroticized, and the choice of a bar may reflect this aspect of sexual pursuit. However, one black lesbian expressed the view that being black and being a woman are far more serious causes of abuse than being homosexual. "Every once in a while, I have had homophobic abuse directed to me. A friend and I were walking down Southport Street—there are a lot of lesbians and gay men in that area now—and a guy starting yelling, 'Dykes! Dykes!' I think the problem I face more here is from being black. I get more 'nigger' slurs directed to me around here."

On the other hand, a new kind of racial equality is emerging in the area. Unlike the Castro District in San Francisco, where the Irish community was still intact when the early gay influx began, Newtown had already reached a period of transition, including a significant change in racial composition. For many African-Americans and Hispanic Americans, Newtown as a possible residence and as a destination to be with other gays and lesbians was an entirely new development. The organizer of Chicago's first group for black lesbians described its beginnings in 1980:

> That was when support groups were really big. All kinds of support groups. Black lesbians with ingrown toenails. There was probably a group for that. I laugh about it, but it was necessary. In terms of contributions that I made, the one thing I'm really proud of, is the black lesbian support group. Paula and I started it. It was the first group of its kind. We held it at the Lesbian Community Center. What was really exciting, at the first meeting we had twenty or twenty-five. We thought that was a spectacular turn out. The next week thirty or forty came. By the end of the first four meetings, we were all crowded into one little room. Eighty black lesbians! There was nothing like seeing them all together.

Some sociologists have suggested that communities in a city are defined by inter-community markers and counter-characterization, as well as by bounded residential areas and territorially self-limited populations.[39] Yet insofar as Newtown signifies gay turf, it remains contested. It has no formal status in the city (as other neighborhood names do) and as a name is thereby subject to highly variable use by different people and in different times. Populated by gay residents as well as by outsiders who come for the day or the night, it is defined by its mimesis of gays, and by gays' own caricature of gay life. The marketing name "Newtown" became a gay symbol through the actions of those who live, work, and commute there. And yet they agree only partially about what it is and what it should be as a gay culture.

Joining Groups: Gay Organizational Life

Observers of the United States from Alexis de Tocqueville in the 1830s to Robert Bellah in the 1980s have noted the American penchant for joining groups.[40] We Americans are distinctive because our ideology of individualism has always lived uneasily with the search for social communalism. The possibility of a genuine gay and lesbian social life has burgeoned from the early beginnings of the secret bar scene to a cultural enclave which now parallels that of other cultural minorities in American society. Gays and lesbians have increasingly come together with their fellows for collective purposes.

The social landscape of gay Chicago is filled with the interlocking, multifunctional voluntary institutions that help to structure daily lives. The secret social networks of prior epochs of homosexual life have been replaced by today's activist organizations. Before the emergence of a gay community, as we have seen, there were few opportunities for socializing, and many gatherings were fraught with fear of raids and arrest. The emerging gay and lesbian culture has contributed to the growth of new forms of sociality. What is new is the proliferation of clubs, businesses, churches, and political activist organizations, which are increasingly formalized or professionalized by state and city charters, bylaws, boards of directors, not-for-profit status, and a new generation of leaders. The urban "associational life"—a term created by anthropologist W. Lloyd Warner decades ago to describe a New England town[41]—of persons who define themselves as "gay" and "lesbian" is now creating untold possibilities, which were not only unavailable to earlier generations of closeted Americans, but remained unthinkable by the earlier cohorts of Chicagoans who desired the same sex.

Much of gay associational life is private, and it occurs beyond the territory of Newtown. Ed and Raul, a gay couple in their thirties, for example, live in a bungalow in a West Side neighborhood. Most of their social life involves the company of the other members of a previously all-lesbian bowling league that now is composed of lesbians and gay men. They rarely come to Newtown. Yet, it is still difficult to imagine that such a league could have emerged without the developments occurring in Newtown itself. The participants in gay community institutions are seldom limited to residents of Newtown, even in the case of organizations dedicated to ward politics.

But with this growth in cultural consciousness have come new collective conflicts: life in the gay community reproduces the lives of the men and women who come from the mainstream society. The gay community is not transmitted from parents and peers throughout the period from childhood to adulthood. The facts of homophobia still limit how "community" can be built. Social life in a gay community can be seen, for example, as either a place to hide or as a platform to be visible. At the meeting of a sports club, members argued bitterly about whether or not the club should participate in the Gay and Lesbian Pride Day Parade. Some members felt that it should remain "just social." Others retorted angrily that to do so would be like creating "another closet" to "hide in," rather than participating in the collective, public ceremony of the parade. As people see "gay turf" in terms of their differing social relations to it, they also come to see their involvements in the "gay scene" as having divergent purposes.

The "gayness" in this conception of "gay community" cannot be found in the sexual conduct of its "members," as some have argued, for sexual behavior with the same sex was not invented by gay culture. Rather, gay communal life can be indicated by three images that represent a new social "contract" between the individual and society (as de Toqueville reminds us) that creates the "gayness" of "gay communities" and "gay persons." One image of the gay community is the older construction of empowerment born in the struggle of the 1960s. Here, lesbians and gays find the strength to oppose a homophobic society through association with other gay people.[42] Another image is of an alternative, parallel society, a refuge from the heterosexual hegemony. A third image is the ethnicity and minority conception. Here, gay people are viewed as an ethnic type among themselves, in the way that Polish- and Irish- and Mexican-Americans are of a kind among themselves—a kind of Wilsonian League of Nations, each with a unique way of life.[43] All of these images represent and express the gay and lesbian community and its politics, and no single one of them is adequate to explain the rich cultural life now emerging.

It would be impossible to do justice to the institutions available to gay men and lesbians in Chicago. Political organizations, with ideological commitments ranging from conservative to radical reform, lobby for the passage of legislation, and others take radical direct action. Catholic, Protestant, Jewish, and many other religious congregations offer regular services as well as social and political activities. Throughout the year, bars organize parties, fundraisers, and sports events. Street fairs draw thousands to the Halsted business district. Two sports leagues and other athletic clubs organize team and individual events in basketball, volley ball, softball, football, racquetball, tennis, bowling, wrestling, running, and swimming. Teams are organized through gay bars and other businesses that bring together people on the field who would rarely interact otherwise. Many of the universities and colleges in northeastern Illinois have gay and lesbian organizations, and the Lesbian and Gay Academic Union organizes lectures and reading workshops. The Gerber-Hart Library, staffed by volunteer professional librarians, is home to the only major midwestern lesbian and gay archive. Business and professional associations provide common grist for entrepreneurs, physicians, psychologists, and lawyers. A community center formerly housed in Newtown (and recently relocated to another neighborhood further north) provided rental space for many gay and lesbian organizations, including the Horizons Youth Group. A popular neighborhood restaurant, Molly's, has become another, de facto community center, through the extensive use made of its banquet and meeting rooms by gay organizations and the generous contributions of its owner. Three choruses mount concerts each year, performing a wide spectrum of classical and popular music. The Lionheart Theater Company gave first performances to original plays by Chicagoans on gay and lesbian themes, contributing profits to community organizations. Two weekly newspapers and one monthly, circulated throughout the metropolitan area, provide national and local news coverage and opinion and publish extensive calendars of events and lists of community resources, such as those named here. Many additional special interests groups, such as Gray Pride, Girth and Mirth, Asians and Friends, and the Committee of Black Gay Men, crowd an ever expanding spectrum of social associations.

The Living and the Dead

Nothing in contemporary Chicago has drawn gays and lesbians together, and strengthened their organizations, as much as has AIDS. The politics of gay and lesbian rights always seemed distant to many in the community, who were rarely brought together, except for an occasional political demonstration or for the Gay Pride parade.[44] The loss of lovers, friends, children, parents, and siblings to AIDS has forced lesbians and gays as never before to create new symbols, such as the Quilt of the "Names Project," to speak to and for gay and lesbian culture and to the public unfamiliar with same-sex lifestyles. AIDS remains pivotal to the experience of gay men's community organizations burdened by the need to fill in for an unwilling and even hostile government. Lesbians, though actually at lowest risk in the epidemic's course, have shared the social onus of being seen as "plague-carriers" in Chicago. Gay and lesbian culture has thus been confronted with another stigma on top of the old stigmatized representations of "homosexuality" as it simultaneously struggles with the need to care for the terminally ill. Eventually new social practices have been created to memorialize the dead as well.

Every culture must deal with death and dying, and rites of passage are implemented to handle these; here again gay and lesbian culture is unusual. Anthropologists have often used the life course and rites of passage to construct accounts of a culture. They have studied the passage from one status to the next—from childhood to adulthood, from birth, to puberty, to marriage, and to death, sometimes followed by observances for souls that enter the timeless world of ancestral spirits.[45] Gay and lesbian culture is still only in its adolescence. Its immaturity is revealed in the fact that it has yet to define these status passages. The immense loss of life brought by AIDS has been all the more burdensome because these aspects of the formation of a culture were still in progress when the epidemic struck. The community of gay men and lesbians in Chicago, like others across the nation, has suffered the death of loved ones in a way unknown outside of war-time. Nothing has affected the living more than this loss. It increasingly has burdened older men and women with financial and emotional costs of all kinds, including their continuing grief. Some gay men and lesbians in Chicago tell of having lost dozens of friends to the disease already. Ironically, however, the epidemic has had the counter-effect of solidifying the gay culture in the minds of gays and lesbian people.

AIDS has altered the coming-out process too. By sparking a debate about the meaning of being gay and lesbian, and about what kind of a social group the "community" is, AIDS has created new prospects and problems of coming out (see chapters 3 and 4). It has most greatly affected men of the second and third historical cohorts, the "closet homosexuals" who came of age after World War II and the gay men who came out after the Stonewall "tea party." Being infected and then symptomatic has forced some men to come out reluctantly to family and friends. In this regard, AIDS has had a profound leveling effect because the virus respects no barrier of age, class, ethnicity, or residence.

For some men of color, being sick with AIDS and being homosexual or covertly gay has posed a double stigmata for their families and neighborhoods. The hostile reactions to these men reveals tenacity with which the old prejudice against same-sex desire prevails. For gay and lesbian youth, coming out today is virtually synonymous with learning about "safe" sex practices and the risk of HIV (see chapter 4). Furthermore, there sometimes is no authoritative voice beyond gay and lesbian culture to speak of the problem. For example, in Richard Fung's video on gay Asian HIV-positive men in Toronto ("Asian Positive," 1990), a young Chinese man explains that he cannot come out to his family in China because he learned not only about AIDS in English but he has learned to "be" gay only in the English language. He has no idea how to talk about being gay or having AIDS in the Chinese dialect of his parents. It is an analogous cultural task for a gay man, who immigrated to Chicago from Georgia, to tell his fundamentalist parents not only that he is gay, but that he has AIDS, in the language and culture they can understand. The issue, we have found in Chicago, is especially difficult for African-American men who have contracted AIDS because many grew up as closeted "homosexuals" or have called themselves "bisexuals," making it difficult to change their image in the eyes of others.[46] As AIDS has afflicted them, they had neither gay and lesbian friends nor families aware of their same sex desires at the time the disease began to disable them, leaving them ever more vulnerable.

Gay and lesbian culture was too young to have collectivized practices of mourning in place before the epidemic hit. When the mounting toll of deaths steadily increased through the late 1980s, more and more comparisons were made between the survivors in the gay and lesbian community and the survivors of the Holocaust. Their loss has surpassed individual grief to become a collective tragedy. A culture nourished in youthful energy and ambitions had lost its youthful innocence in the death knoll. Many of the men taken by AIDS had a same-sex orientation, but not all of them were out; some of the early deceased belonged to the second historical cohort of closet homosexuals, who, like Liberace, engaged in the secrecy of forbidden sex. But the largest loss has been to the third historical cohort; the obituaries daily report the deaths of men in their late twenties, thirties, and forties. These men were often gay-identified and out, with a network of lovers, friends, and family to support them. It is the latter cohort that has galvanized grief observances in such a way that the passage into death is becoming a new means of solidarity for the culture. Churches hold healing rites, and there are other community events as well. The "AIDS WALK," for example, draws thousands. Weekly services are held in the AIDS ward of a hospital near Newtown, and communion is offered in the rooms to those too sick to attend. Rites of Holy Union are held in the hospital to join same-sex couples, one of whom is sick.

And a candlelight vigil and march to memorialize those who have died from AIDS is now an annual event.

AIDS awareness pervades the community in nearly all of its social activities nowadays. By 1991, thirty organizations provided AIDS support services in Chicago, including many gay and lesbian providers of medical or alternative medical care, and educational, fundraising, support group, and meal services. New "coping" and "helping" groups reach into every corner of Chicago's gay network: PWAs (Persons with AIDS), support managers, and "Buddies," care givers, the "worried well," AIDS ACT UP, and many other activist organizations work together. Education for safer sex practices has become the key line of defense against the disease, at least insofar as people feel they can actively do something to stop the spread of AIDS. The bars, clubs, churches, and other community organizations provide and promote safer sex education for their patrons and members. Nearly every organization has sponsored some kind of fundraiser for the Howard Brown Clinic, Chicago House, and the other AIDS service organizations created during the past decade. AIDS has thus forced the community to educate itself about public health and politics, to organize for the care of the sick, and to lobby for government support of PWAs and positive legislation.

Yet the disease has transformed the gay worldview by forcing utterly new institutional arrangements upon the culture. The epidemic has come to dominate political discourse and agendas in the community. Fundraising efforts have reached a fever pitch. The female co-chair of the Illinois Gay and Lesbian Task Force (IGLTF) sees the current agenda as having been "taken over" by AIDS, displacing other critical concerns. She talks of the burden:

> The Task Force had to take on the task this past year of handling AIDS legislation. We started with a little campaign trying to handle [legislative bills] 884 and 885 in the [State of Illinois] House, gay civil rights and anti-violence, thinking we were going to get them out of Committee this time. All of the sudden we're slapped in the face with armloads of frightening legislation. If you figure the amount of time and effort that has gone into preventing those bills from going into law, which is a vital effort, and add the time and money and the efforts at Chicago House and Howard Brown, then you subtract from that the human resources lost because people are PWA's, they have no more energy or resources,— I'm surprised we have a political movement at all!

Many Chicagoans do not believe AIDS has increased homophobia but that it has given homophobic people "permission" to express it. One woman activist remarked on how the epidemic has affected the community: "The AIDS crisis isn't going to be the cause of more homophobia—it'll be the hook to hang things on." With the cultural representations of AIDS everywhere in the public mind, from the first homophobic depiction of AIDS as a "gay plague"—in all of the moral victimization implied by such a metaphor—the disease threatens to undo all that gay liberation has accomplished before.[47] There is also the division between the genders here, as elsewhere, in the response to homophobia. Speaking to an activist in both AIDS work and in the lesbian community, this same woman continued:

> I have a couple of friends—women—who have been tested. That was ridiculous. One way or another it affects us. It isn't killing us the same way, but women who see it as a "gay" issue and who have lost friends are deeply affected. I'm going to see a friend's brother who has AIDS next week. I'm pleased to see how [the response of women is] going. I hope that as issues come up for women, the men's community remembers our support. If this disease had primarily affected lesbians, we would not have been up to it, because—I think many women think this—no one would have responded, including gay men.

The "Names Project" Quilt

A contentious debate between gay and lesbian organizations and the mainstream has long existed over the fact that obituaries frequently omit that the cause of an HIV-related death is AIDS.[48] Because death is caused by a secondary infection rather than the HIV virus itself, those with money and power, especially closet homosexuals or the families of the deceased who are ashamed of a gay family member, have sometimes succeeded in covering up the cause of death, as shown in the media farce following Liberace's death.[49] Homophobia and the secrecy of closet homosexuals have combined to bolster the notion that AIDS was killing gay men and thus eliminating an unpopular and "deviant" element. Gay reactions to this bigotry have not removed the secrecy completely. In the obituaries and in the "Names Project" Quilt, even following their death from AIDS, some people continue to live in secrecy: their true names could not be used on the Quilt panels. Either through their own wishes or those of their families and friends, they preferred to remain anonymous. Some panels were thus inscribed with only a name, sometimes only a first name;

others were even more obscure. Hence it became important for gays and lesbians to "name the names" of those who had fallen to the disease.

The now famous Quilt has brought together in death such diverse celebrities as Rock Hudson, Leonard Cohn, Terry Dolan, Liberace—something that would have been incomprehensible in their lifetimes and after had it not been for AIDS. Some do condemn the 1970s "golden age" of gay liberation for what they call the "wild sexual abandon" that precipitated the holocaust in Cohort Three.[50] Yet few people are so judgmental about the "promiscuity" of the gay community that they now openly say (correctly or not) that casual sexual contact led to the current epidemic.[51] Others dismiss this moralism, seeing "sex" as the behavioral response of many gay men who had been denied a period of sexual exploration during their teenage years or later.[52] What is not debated is the immense size of the gay and lesbian community's loss, including some of its most beloved leaders, artists, and celebrities. One of our informants grieved: "The thing that is so devastating to me about the AIDS crisis is to see my people die, my culture disappear, to see the gifts that my people bring to the world being taken away without the world recognizing it. I see a people disappearing. The world doesn't realize that it's a people disappearing, not just individuals."

In Chicago plans for the March on Washington for Lesbian and Gay Rights in October of 1987 included the making of Quilt squares. The local committees for the march organized quilting bees to solicit contributions from around the country. By the time of the march there were two thousand panels from forty-eight states. The Quilt in Chicago connected local aspirations with the national event to be held in the capital. The "quilting bee" held in Chicago was sponsored by the "Chicago March on Washington Committee for the Names Project." Organized nationally in San Francisco, the "Names Project" asked people to remember those who had died by making cloth panels three feet by six feet. The squares were usually very personal, inscribed with tokens of the person memorialized, such as a reference to the sports team on which he had played, or the chorus with which he had sung, or a fondness for teddy bears. One panel had a huge pair of red lips in satin because the deceased had admired Marilyn Monroe. Each creator of a panel was asked to write the name of the person or a pseudonym memorialized on a piece of paper, along with a one-page reminiscence. The panels were to be collected and shipped to San

Francisco, where they would be finished and knitted together in larger panels, and hence, shipped on trucks to Washington

The first "Quilting Bee" was held in September at the Wellington Avenue Church in the Metropolitan Community Church Parish Hall. Some twenty-five panels were completed that night. The hall was full of people, some sixty in all, at work on a warm evening. Local merchants had donated food for the event, so there were cases of New York Seltzer, meatballs and chicken wings, and piles of cinnamon rolls from Molly's Restaurant. The committee had collected cloth, paint, brushes, yarn, Magic Markers, stencils, and other materials for making the panels. Chicago artist Jon Reich was there to help; he produced a panel to memorialize several artists who had died. At least a quarter of those preparing panels were women, many of them lesbians. A panel from a Memorial Service the year before, on which worshippers were invited to write the names of friends they had lost to AIDS, was put up on the wall so anyone not knowing someone who had died could draw a name from it. There was a lot of quiet conversation, and although it was not gloomy, there was little joking. A young Asian-American man quickly produced a panel with "new wave" lettering. Two other men worked on a panel together, one a PWA. Some organizations have hosted events to memorialize members who have died from HIV, and they have made panels to represent the deceased members of the "Windy City Gay Chorus" and "Black and White Men Together." Each organization used a distinctive design for all of their panels with one individual's name on each. The quilt had the same commemorative quality as the Gay Pride Parade, in this sense, a section of the quilt representing an organization.

One woman talked for a long time about what to put on a panel. "It's easier to memorialize with rules than without them," she said. Her panel was a testimony to the difficulties that many have experienced in the epidemic: she apologized to the man she memorialized for not having gotten closer to him because she had feared losing him to AIDS. After he died, she said she felt enormous guilt for having kept him at a distance.

What was formerly privatized and isolated became communal. Those who contributed panels that warm summer evening in Chicago felt that they had been able to share their personal grief with others who also suffered grief. While there has been genuine dissension in the community over how to memorialize the dead—especially between persons of widely differing religious backgrounds and affiliations—the Quilt has provided an utterly original and unprecedented way to transform the personal into the publicly shared. This transformation was another crucial step in the making of gay and lesbian culture, not only in Chicago or other cities, but when the Quilt was assembled for the March on Washington in 1987, a step was taken in the formation of a national gay and lesbian culture. In "naming the names" of those who have died, the Quilt created a new cultural symbol with which to fight the invisibility of gay people and to support others suffering from AIDS.

Today the quilt that has become a major cultural object of gay and lesbian culture, a memorialization of its lifeways through observances for its dead. Here we see a powerful link between the tradition of expressive individualism in American society and the forging of gay commemorative culture. As anthropologist Michael Gorman has reported: "At the . . . March in October 1987, over 100,000 people milled about and wept over the quilt as if over a battlefield. For many gay people . . . the quilt is a painful as well as hopeful symbol. On the one hand, it signifies loss, sorrow, disbelief and neglect, if not betrayal. Yet it also has come to symbolize permanence and a legitimation of the lives of those felled by the virus, people who would otherwise go unnamed and unremembered. By extension the Quilt also represents the gay community. In the words of one man, 'The Quilt is for us something holy.'"[53] The Quilt has, in this way, become a sacred symbol of a people, an element in the emerging social consciousness of a new cultural nation.

Gay and Lesbian Pride Day: Cultural Nationalism

Every year throughout the United States the annual Gay and Lesbian Pride Day Parade memorializes and celebrates the liberation of gays and the aftermath of the Stonewall riots in New York and elsewhere. It is fitting that we complete our account of Chicago life by setting a study of the parade at a juncture that led on to the March on Washington during the time of our study.

This historical account of Chicago gay and lesbian culture opened by reference to the Horizons Youth Group heading the Gay and Lesbian Pride Day Parade in Chicago. It is in such public rituals that the concrete transmission of gay culture to newcomers, including both teenagers and adults, can be demonstrated. The parade is one of several held annually in cities across the United States to commemorate the Stonewall riot in 1969. Estimates of the participants in Chicago's 1987 parade ranged up to 80,000. More recent parades have had estimated attendances of more than 100,000 people. In the 1987 parade there were 126 entries, including gay and lesbian churches, professional organizations, musical organizations, political groups, bars and other businesses, social service organizations, and sports leagues. The Horizons youth were entered into the parade around this time and have since served as its color guard—a sign of their importance and an appeal to the heart of the larger society. By 1987 the message of the parade had thus been transformed into, "We are just like you." Herein we see the basis for a communal strategy of power and integration into Chicago's life.

Conceptions of culture typically include its transmission from one generation to the next, epitomized in the education of the child by the parent. If this is the case, what can be said of a gay culture barely aware of lesbian and gay-identified teenagers who, it is usually assumed, will find their way into the gay world just as the current adult generations did? Contests for authority and legitimacy among gays and lesbians from all walks of life, and between gay organizations and American society, have yielded to no single voice. What it means to be a gay or lesbian person in America is changing; what it means for the upcoming generation of youth is even more uncertain.

As a critical symbolic and organizational ritual of Chicago's gay and lesbian community, the parade and teenagers' perceptions of it reveal the many ways that it contributes to their coming-out process. First, the parade provides normalization, one further step in their development. Second, the parade demonstrates the diversity of people who are gay- and lesbian-identified. Third, the parade brings the teenagers directly into the gay and lesbian community, engaging in social action and political fieldwork alongside of adults. And fourth, the parade is a transition of youth into the cultural life of the community. As we shall see in the following chapters, the parade becomes the penultimate rite of coming out for most gay and lesbian youth. Yet because the parade is a national event, linking the youth of Chicago with those of other American towns and cities, it also represents the funneling of adolescent lesbians and gays into an emerging national culture.

What further transformations will occur when the current generation of gay and lesbian youth inherit and reproduce this new culture can be anticipated by looking at the largest single gay and lesbian event ever, the protest march on our nation's capitol.

The March on Washington

Like the great gathering and dispersing rituals recorded by anthropologists in societies around the world, the 1987 March on Washington, D.C., filled the capital with gay men and lesbians from every state and many countries. This was a civil rights march of immensity, pointed like a political missile at the administrative bureaucracy in the Capitol. As a political demonstration, the March seems to have had mixed results, but that is only one of its dimensions. The March represented the culmination of years of gay and lesbian emergence as local communities and regional political activism across the country. At Chicago's first Gay Pride Day celebration in 1970, one hundred gathered and walked to City Hall. In 1987 in Washington, D.C., Chicagoans joined the estimated 650,000 who marched from the White House down Pennsylvania Avenue to the Mall. The March, in short, bridged for the first time the local manifestations of gay and lesbian community by a national confederation of a people in action. This change, from a local to a national consciousness, from what F. Tönnies[54] called *Gemeinschaft* to *Gessellschaft*, provides a key perspective from which to examine the general significance of the story of Chicago's gay culture for the United States as a whole.

While there were many contingents in the March, the state and city contigents stood out above all. The Elipse, where the marchers lined up in the shadows of the White House, was so crowded that walking across it was difficult. What was most dramatic about the American geography represented by the marchers was the way in which it spread beyond the major cities. Every state and many smaller cities also had delegations. The gathering was national, both in its composition and in the emblems of American nationality that surrounded it. Over a period of five hours, the March circled the president's residence and proceeded down Pennsylvania Avenue to the Mall. Behind the stage where speakers addressed the rally loomed the Capitol Building. Behind the crowd the Washington Monument pierced the sky.

Chartered planes and busses brought marchers to Washington for seven days of activism. This was not a parade like those held in cities across the country to celebrate Gay and Lesbian Pride Day. It was a march with a political agenda: the civil rights of lesbians and gay men. For two days, gay and lesbian representatives from every state lobbied their congressmen and senators, strong-arming and imploring. Despite the significance of the March, the event was ignored entirely by the nation's news weeklies and reported generally only as an "AIDS march" in the daily newspapers. With 650,000 strong, it is likely the largest civil rights march in American history.

For Chicagoans, the city's contingent represented months of organizing to raise money, coordinate travel and accommodations, and stimulate interest. The Chicago delegation took as its motto: "We, too, have a dream," referring both to Martin Luther King, Jr.'s, historic ties to Chicago and to the famous speech he gave in the Mall in 1963. The banner linked the Chicago skyline with Washington's, while helium-filled balloons held aloft a vertical sign spelling out the city's name. A woman informant told us that she wanted to go with the delegation in spite of the fact that she would have to borrow money to pay for her expenses. She was certain that whatever the financial cost, the memories of the March would sustain her for years to come.

The March was not without its glitter and ceremony too. A public gay wedding was staged the day before the March. Two thousand same-sex couples gathered at the Internal Revenue Service building to celebrate their commitment to each other in a polity that denies them the legal and financial benefits of heterosexual relationships. Among the Chicago couples was the director of the Horizons agency and his long-time lover. A memorial to Harvey Milk was also dedicated at the Congressional Cemetery. A wreath-laying ceremony at the Tomb of the Unknown Soldier in Arlington National Cemetery also honored gay men and lesbians who had died in military service to the country but were largely dishonored by the policies of the military.

On the Tuesday following the March, hundreds of activists were arrested at a demonstration outside the Supreme Court Building. There were dances, concerts, and art exhibits. Before and after the March on Sunday, Washington's subway trains and stations were as crowded as they are during rush hours, but crowded with gay people singing and chanting. The occasional family of tourists could not hide their stunned amazement. Gay and lesbian couples walked through the city arm-in-arm and hand-in-hand without fear of reprisal. Older radicals called it the Gay Liberated Zone—at least for a weekend.

No one had ever seen such a massive gathering of gays and lesbians. The rally following the March included a line-up of gay celebrities and national supporters, which once again reminded the crowd of the emerging national consciousness of gay culture. First-time participants in Pride week parades are often overwhelmed by the number of participants. But the number who gathered for the March over-whelmed even those who have participated in Gay Pride parades for years. Many of those who had come were young, too young to remember the early years of tiny demonstrations. A young man who marched with his parents carried a sign that read: "My mom and dad, Oscar and Peggy, made me come."

Walking away from the rally toward the Washington Monument, one could see the Quilt. The roar of chanting and clapping was suddenly left behind, and approaching the Quilt, one heard only occasional hushed voices, muffled crying, and the clattering of camera shutters, as though entering one of the great war cemeteries in Europe. Here the city of the living was exchanged for the city of the dead, another national gathering, but in remembrance. Unlike the identical crosses that precisely punctuate the green of those military cemeteries, each of the Quilt's panel was unique and demanded attention, even for just a moment, to the stories of loss and the remembering of the dead.

Among those who attended the AIDS memorials and Quilt exhibition was Joey, a nineteen-year-old member of the Horizons' Youth Group who was then very sick with AIDS. He had to be transported in a wheelchair, as did many of the PWAs. His frail body was itself a symbol, both of the effects of the disease on the community and of the potential link of the new nationalism across the generations. Soon after he returned to Chicago he succumbed to the disease. After his death, another member of the Horizons youth group memorialized Joey in a quilt panel, and the youth group journeyed in a new kind of pilgrimage, another rite of passage, to Navy Pier in Chicago to pay homage to him (see chapter 4).

The Quilt, a massive memorial whose two thousand panels represented only 10 percent of those who had already died by 1987, did not diminish the overwhelming feelings of unity and strength which the March engendered. Nationalist gay and lesbian consciousness was demonstrated time and again by participants, in acts and expressions similar to those experienced by demonstrators in the March on Washington led by Dr. King in 1963, whose participants still remember the personal impact of that watershed for the emergence of the civil rights movement. Activist and comedian Robin Tyler thundered to the crowd at the opening rally, announcing the march's theme: "For love and life, we're not going back!" The long journeys back to every state by participants in buses and trains were filled with exhilaration. These people carried with them from Washington to the provinces and towns the message of an unprecedented national gathering for gay and lesbian rights.

Richard Herrell reports:

The day following the March on Washington, I stopped in front of Grand Central Station in New York to talk with a middle-aged woman wearing a button from the March. She was returning to San Diego that day, having come to Washington to march with her gay son. Later that week in Chicago, I had walked off the plane at Midway Airport with two men I had never met, both of whom were also wearing the buttons from the March. A national sign of gay and lesbian civil rights activism was everywhere present for a time. Among the photographs I took at the March was a picture of a woman, standing by the side of the crowd, who was holding a small sign that read: "We Love Our Gay Children— Akron, Ohio, P-Flag" [Parents and Friends of Lesbians and Gays]. I sent a copy of this photograph to the Akron chapter. Soon, I received a warm note from this same woman in return: "P-Flag received the picture you sent to them. I have received so many pictures from parades. I hope I can get out to California next year for their Parade. Thank you so much."

Since the 1987 March on Washington, a new element has emerged in the rhetoric of gay leadership, one that conveys an understanding of gay and lesbian youth as the future of an emergent culture. At the rally following the Chicago Gay Pride parade in 1988, an activist working for the passage of the Human Rights Ordinance, a law that would add protection against discrimination on the basis of sexual orientation to Chicago law, remarked that it was needed to protect "our children," that is, lesbian and gay youth. Steve Schulte, the former mayor of West Hollywood, wrote in a fundraiser mailing for the Gay and Lesbian Adolescent Social Services of West Hollywood: "I believe that all gay and lesbian adults should think of them as our children." And immediately following the 1987 March, at the dedication of Harvey Milk's grave in the Congressional Cemetery, Leonard Matlovich said: "We need to never forget. We need to know our heros, our heroines. We need to know the ones who went before us. Everyone of you, you are a parent. And who are your children? Your children are tomorrow's lesbians and gays coming along. And being caring, loving parents—we are going to leave a history today."

· · · · · · · · ·

Such is the stuff of which gay and lesbian culture is built in the United States as a whole. Chicago's history is a microcosm of it. The emergence of a gay neighborhood, the founding of secret clubs, the harassment and raids, the change to an era of liberation with new gay and lesbian organizations—these are the signs of local gay culture. Horizons, with its youth marching in the Gay Pride Parade and commemorating the Quilt, and the political and social outcry in Washington for the protection of gay rights are the signs of a cultural nationalism. These are the fragments that meld a cultural tradition, reflected in the particular history of American life.

The power of culture derives from its sacred symbols—myths and rituals—which create, bind, and reproduce groups across historical periods and generations. In sacred symbols, Clifford Geertz has said in another context, "values are portrayed not as subjective human preferences but as imposed conditions for life implicit in a world with a particular structure."[55] And in this sense the culture of gay and lesbians poses a special problem. A people who depends upon the willful invention of new cultural forms rather than the inheritance of tradition, is especially concerned with the construction of sacred symbols. What gays and lesbians have achieved is nothing less than the creation of a new cultural consciousness.

Chicago provides the story of the historical construction of successive cultural forms of "homosexuality" and the lived experience of age cohorts of persons since the turn of the century: queers and perverts, hunted and hated; homosexuals, closeted but entrenched; lesbians and gays, symbolically reborn and politically active. Major events, practices, and social rituals, such as "coming out," reflect to each of these age cohorts the sacred symbols of a forbidden way of life, and, in turn, they express individual experiences in ways both oppressive and liberating. We have traced these major symbols up to 1990 to connect the world view of Chicagoans with their times. Their history is one of a rising moral critique of American society and, in particular, of the local circumstances of the gay and lesbian cultural movement in the quintessential midwestern American city. What these events, practices, and social rituals gave birth to was a new generation, the subject of our next chapter.

CHAPTER THREE

◆ ◆ ◆

"Horizons" and the Youth

I read a couple of letters to the editor a while ago from gay youth who were pushing for bars to have some social hours for teenagers. It sounds like the same thing you hear from any adolescent group—that they want more respect and consideration from the adult community. And we're the adults in their community. I don't notice them when I'm in Newtown. Not on the street. I've never noticed a young gay couple. Maybe when I see teenagers I assume they're straight because they're teenagers. Gay for me is something you don't do until you're an adult, because I didn't do it until I was an adult. So it's hard for me to conceptualize gay teens. Many in our community have no children and have no plans to have children. They see teenagers as "jailbait" and not as real people. You know, like a piece of a citizen. When they get to be adults they get to join—then you're a person.

—An older lesbian, a divorced mother of three

An eye-catching newspaper article from May 1979 features a drawing of a smiling, "All American" boy, books under arm, making his way home from school—the very face of normality. However, the newspaper is *Gay Life*, the first local gay rag of its kind in Chicago, and the title of the article is "Gay Youth Speaks Out." The article reports the first meeting of a new youth group—at Horizons. "What are the problems and aspirations of gay high school students," the writer asks, "who are living at home, going to school and trying to cope with the success-oriented, straight society their families represent?"[1] The writer both applauds the youth for coming out of the closet and expresses surprise to learn of the existence of the new generation. "We are gay, glad of it and proud of it," is the message of the youth, a message directed at the Chicago gay and lesbian community.[2] In the space just below the gay youth piece, appear advertisements for a bathhouse in Indiana and a bar in Chicago. The difference between the new and old generations could not have been more clearly stated than in this ironic juxtaposition of pieces on the newspaper page.

It was through media stories such as this one and the social contacts and personal networks that ensued that adult gays and lesbians came to know of the Horizons community services and center. Its distinctive atmosphere stems from its qualities as a voluntary organization and its location in the heart of Chicago's gay territory. Many American grass-roots groups, of course, have a similar volunteer base; volunteerism is as close to the American heritage of expressive individualism as the poetry of Walt Whitman is to the history of gay and lesbian culture.[3] Yet, while the youth group has since become a highly visible and much discussed part of Chicago gay and lesbian culture, many adults have no contact with youth; and it remains an enigma that the youth group is such a key symbol of the community.

The invisibility of gay youth and the "generation gap" that divides gay adults and adolescents is largely a holdover from the oppressive era of the closet homosexual. The older historical cohort of closet homosexuals, and to a lesser extent gay men and lesbians—those which we have called cohorts two and three—have virtually no contact with gay and lesbian youth. These generations regard the youth, as the quote which opens this chapter makes clear, as "jailbait." This is because of the severe laws that restrict sexual activity with minors and even between consenting adults, a taboo to which we shall return later. Virtually every adult that we interviewed in our ethnographic study admitted their ignorance about gay teenagers. Most seemed to be completely unaware of the youth. For instance, a forty-one-year-old white gay man who lives in Newtown remarked: "I don't see youth in the neighborhood. I know the group exists. Neon Street [a runaway shelter for homeless youth—not gay youth], the Youth Group: I know they're around. I see them at the church [Metropolitan Community Church] sometimes. They seem to stay by themselves. They seem not connected to the street life on Halsted." This lack of consciousness suggests the depth of the problems faced in the building of a gay and lesbian culture that would include youth. The Horizons organization grew under these historical conditions and eventually created a new place for the gay youth of Chicago.

A History of Horizons in Newtown

When "Gay Horizons" was founded in 1973 it did not have a program for youth; it was simply a homey center for adults in Chicago to meet others who desired the same sex and needed social and psychological support to come out and live openly gay and lesbian lives. It began as a small basement storefront shop in what was then the dreary heart of Newtown. Much later the neighborhood was to become trendy and upscale. Like many such gay and lesbian grass-roots agencies around the United States, its purpose was to create a special kind of community center that would support the efforts of local people to overcome harassment, to feel better about themselves, and to find others like themselves. From the beginning it was meant to be a nonprofit organization, so its staff was entirely volunteer. Bake sales and raffles were relied upon to make ends meet. For many years and during the time of our project, the agency was located directly west of Lake Michigan at the center of Newtown. But success has brought great changes to the agency, which changed its name in 1985 to "Horizons Community Services, Incorporated" to reflect a broader lesbian and gay community. By 1990 Horizon's success allowed it to enlarge into a more professional structure, with fifteen paid staff, an $800,000 budget, and a full-time director. Such an expansion has, of course, led to some problems and aimed the agency in new directions; however, Horizons remains a gay and lesbian symbol of enormous credibility in the Chicago area.

Horizons was an inspiration of the Stonewall revolution. It was created out of a need for a kind of "drop-in center" like the old hippie "crash pads" of the 1960s, where people could seek temporary shelter. Six or eight white, middle-class, progressive baby-boomers got together one evening to brainstorm and dreamed up the center. The organization began in a cold-water basement, with naked water pipes and light bulbs visible on the ceiling, and furnished with old sofas and hand-me-down donations. In the 1980s Horizons moved to a location near the corner of Belmont and Sheffield streets, in the hub of Newtown. But in the old location, a tiny room served as the only private space for personal interviews, and it was hardly private. A small table with two telephones constituted the "secretarial" desk. It was a homely beginning.

The founders believed, as one of them has said, that, "We could provide each other with better and more accurate information than the professionals." In fact, many of the founders didn't trust the establishment doctors and psychologists and lawyers. Their experience as members of the third historical cohort who came out after Stonewall had shown them time and again that many of the professionals they dealt with were blatantly homophobic. The first offshoot of Horizons was the founding of the Howard Brown Clinic in Chicago, which began as a neighborhood center for the treatment of sexually transmitted diseases, primarily for gay men. Later in the 1980s it would function as a large professionalized health center for gays and lesbians, specializing in AIDS services. A few gay (and some straight) doctors who volunteered to staff the clinic eventually wanted more professional arrangements, and so they split off from Horizons.[4] To provide an alternative to the bars as a social environment, Horizons opened its doors as a coffee house for a short time as well. There was even briefly a program for blind gays at Horizons. The creative front runner of the agency was a Chicago man from a wealthy family whose insight led to many of the original plans of Horizons. Paradoxically, he could not be out to his family, and so he remained an early leader of a pioneering gay organization who never managed to break free from the closet.

Today the Horizons center serves every social need of the gay and lesbian community. The agency offers training and education services to all manner of organizations, including successful "outreach" programs to the public schools and professional groups. It sends speakers to classrooms and Kiwanis clubs to spread the word that "gay is okay." Counseling for mental health needs is a prominent service and is supported by an extensive network of gay and lesbian psychologists and social workers in Chicago. Lesbian and women's support groups and legal counseling services for men and women are available, as well as a newer project combating violence against gay men and lesbians. Horizons sponsors numerous social and political events, including citywide annual conferences, and mini-workshops and cultural happenings as frequently as once a month. These events are related to gay community development, women and health, and AIDS awareness and benefits. Public meetings and workshops of special interest are constantly advertised in the local press and gay newspapers, keeping Horizons ever visible in the public eye. AIDS information is circulated by Horizons through many means, including outreach programs in Chicago.

Information about AIDS as a disease and about safe-sex prevention is included in all of Horizons educational programs. Most recently, the State of Illinois AIDS hotline was brought to Horizons as well. A general services telephone number staffed by volunteers for Horizons constitutes the gay "directory" of Chicago, where answers are provided to people with questions about AIDS, response is offered to the cries for help of youth coming out, and information is available to out-of-town gay tourists looking for a good time. But the telephone number is best known for its emergency "crisis line" counseling service to assist those in distress, as, for instance, gays and lesbians being harassed by their families, friends, or employers. Professionally trained and supervised peer counseling is provided both in person and over the telephone, both to individuals and to couples. New support groups, such as "gays as parents," are being added. A special program is provided for men at risk of AIDS, including those who worry about being HIV tested. A local arm of P-Flag (Parents and Friends of Lesbians and Gays) also co-sponsors events with Horizons. The agency is the hub of gay culture.

During the time of our study the Horizons agency had two broad aims and five distinct programs. The agency's current handbook lists its aims as follows: (1) "To identify social service needs of the gay and lesbian community of metropolitan Chicago, and to establish and conduct programs responsive to those needs"; and (2) "to provide the opportunity for gays and lesbians (and persons sympathetic to this community) to volunteer their time in an environment that enhances friendship and self-esteem."[5] The six programs of Horizons include: information and referral; counseling; self-help/mutual support; community education; training; and administrative volunteer services. The youth group falls under the auspices of several programs, in particular those of professional and peer counseling.[6]

The diversity of the gay and lesbian life in Chicago is reflected in who staffs and runs the agency. The diversity of the staff testifies to the agency's effort to achieve equal representation from diverse quarters of the city and the gay and lesbian community.[7] As stated earlier, Horizons was historically derived from the middle class, as we have seen, and was constituted almost entirely by whites. It has proven difficult, in the racially structured climate of Chicago, to find persons of color who would participate in Horizons activities with equal visibility as whites. Women were less prominent at Horizons in the beginning than they are now. But changes over the past few years have brought many new voices into the agency, especially persons of color and women participants at all levels, including management positions.

During the time of our study Horizons was headed by Executive Director Bruce Koff, M. S. W., a widely respected man in the gay and lesbian community. The director of youth services, a volunteer at that time, was a male social worker in his late twenties who had been active in the agency for some years. The board of directors numbered fourteen, including twelve men and two women: the chair was a prominent management consultant, a very enthusiastic man in his mid-forties; the vice-chair was a man in his mid-thirties, the planning director of a large human services organization, and once referred to as the self-appointed "queen" of fund-raising in Chicago; the treasurer, a male assistant professor of business at a local college; the secretary, a woman executive director of a psychiatric care facility. The common members included a female graduate student at a local university, a professor of law at another local college, an insurance company executive, a local merchant who is active in Chicago Democratic machine politics, a marketing vice president for a manufacturer, a survey researcher with a local college, a suburban dentist, an insurance company clerk, a middle-level mental health agency official, and a retired businessman. All of these persons, save one, used their real and complete names in the official publications of Horizons.[8]

Demographic Profile of the Youth Sample

We studied gay and lesbian culture and the coming-out process during a time of tremendous expansion and controversy over the place of gays and lesbians in Chicago. For the first time the gay community began to recognize the youth group in its regular calendar of activities, including the annual Gay Pride Parade. The Horizons agency records suggest that the average number of clients in the youth program (limited to the ages from fourteen to twenty) was twenty-five youth per week during the period of our study. A guesstimate would also place the average annual number of youth who attended Horizons on at least three occasions at about seven hundred people. The former director of Horizons believes that the number of adolescents who might be called "gay youth" in metropolitan Chicago numbers about forty thousand.

In our study we assembled a sample of 202 youth who volunteered to participate, to be interviewed and tell their coming-out stories. We attempted to collect stories from youth who are roughly representative of the distribution of social, ethnic, class, and other population characteristics of Chicago. We were hindered in getting a proportion-

Table 3.1 Background Characteristics of the Horizons Youth

Gender		
Male	70%	
Female	30%	
Ethnicity		
Black	30%	
White	40%	
Hispanic	13%	
Asian-American	3%	
Mixed	14%	
Religious Orientation		
Protestant	29%	
Catholic	27%	
Jewish	2%	
Atheist/Agnostic	18%	
None	24%	

ate number of girls in the study due to the smaller number of females who attended the youth group during the time of our study. The characteristics of the youth are provided in tables 3.1, 3.2, and 3.3.

The Early Youth Group

Much of what is important about the emergence of a lesbian and gay community in Chicago can be summed up in the changes that have occurred within Horizons itself. The change that occurred during the past two decades has represented the cultural transformation of a larger order in the United States; but its manifestations in Chicago were striking. It was not only a change in the political power and maturity of the community, as we have discussed in chapter 2, but it also represented the maturation of the founding adults of the original "Gay Liberation Movement" in Chicago. Older and wiser, they sought an institution for the transmission of their knowledge and lifeways, that is, the reproduction of their culture.

The youth group at Horizons began as the stepchild of gay hippies and leftover reformists within the community who felt an obligation to assist the small number of teenagers who were willy-nilly stumbling through the agency doors.

Table 3.2 Social Geography of Horizons Youth

Place of Residence	
Downtown Loop	1%
North Side	33%
South Side	24%
West Side	9%
West suburbs	11%
South suburbs	6%
North suburbs	11%
Other	5%
Cohabitants	
Both parents	39%
Mother only	25%
Other family	16%
Roommates/Lover	11%
Alone	5%
Shelters/Group living	4%

At first the group was small. It began with less than ten youth. There was a lone advisor, the youth group coordinator, who was a mental health professional volunteering his services. The youth group was endeared to him, and former members of the original group speak of him as the first and most important gay role model in their lives, back in the late 1970s. The group on its first meeting in January 1978 consisted of middle-class and working-class white teenagers, joined by two black youth. It was not until later that women joined and Hispanics and other minorities entered the group. During the first year of the group, a young lesbian would on occasion drop in, but she would feel too alone to continue, due to the absence of women advisors and other young lesbian group members. Within a year or so, a few kids from the suburbs found their way in. Then more blacks joined the group, and by the mid 1980s blacks comprised more than a third of the teenagers served. By the same time, women comprised a third of the Horizons coming-out group. By the early 1990s, they were to emerge as the majority of participating youth.

The youth members were older at the time the group started; they were just out of high school, eighteen, twenty, or twenty-two years old. Only later was a rule for youth under twenty-one implemented. The original youth advisor did a good job. Later a few more adult

Table 3.3 Current Grade in School of Horizons Youth

Grade	Males	Females
First year college	21%	17%
Second year college	11%	10%
Third year college	7%	2%
Fourth year college	2%	0
Grade 9	1%	2%
Grade 10	0	0
Grade 11	13%	10%
Grade 12	17%	25%
Not in school	29%	33%

advisors were added, though none were professionally trained, and eventually this lack of credentials caused problems. The boundaries were too "loose" between youth and counselors, one old-time advisor suggested. The same informant continued: "Most of the adult advisors were barely out of adolescence themselves! Years ago rumors of a sexual affair between an adult and a youth eventually led to reforms." How much of this is true matters less than its effect as a moral charter, a myth that upholds the way in which things must be ordered as they are today. As a former youth group director once told us, "Before I came along, the youth group was in a state of nature."

Two of the most important reforms stand out. One is that only youth between the ages of fourteen and twenty are allowed to join the group. After twenty-one, members must leave, no matter what stage of coming out they have attained. The other reform involved the creation of a rigorous training program for advisors, which prohibits social contact with youth outside of the group meetings. Both policies are strictly enforced.

But what was this legendary state of nature of the youth group really like? To discover some of the qualities of the early founding group, we assembled a circle of five of the original youth and held a rap group meeting to jog their memories. Now in their late twenties and early thirties, these men (white and black) discussed some of the feelings and activities that came from the group. They included Tom, a white suburban man (now aged thirty-two), who was the first "president" of the youth group. These men remembered, for instance, the first "car wash" sponsored by the group to raise money. "It was a very big deal because it was our first time to appear in public," said Rick, a thirty-year-old black man who also helped organize the group. Coming out from the beginning was "the real issue of discussion," he said. Dale, another man, said, "I enjoyed the informality and humor; it helped me to cope with the bad times; you could also see on many levels what being gay is."

In 1979 harassment was bad, worse than today. "Even the cops roughed you then," Tom said. Rick and Dale remain angry about harassment in high school. "They picked on me," Tom says, "I was fat and very shy."

Rick: "I was so angry that people called me a fag."

Dale: "We still are gawked at—like recently we had lunch in Oak Park. 'You should be ashamed [of being gay] and you aren't!' one woman said to us."

Tom: "We were terrified of being naked in the showers with other guys. Fearful of having an erection. . . . What do we do then!"

Ron says, "I was completely closed. About feelings and other things . . . there were some gays who came out and were accepted. . . . Not me. Some came out from harassment."

Lanny: "I went [to Horizons]—my first day was March 21 [1979]. And uh, I met Tom that day. We found out we lived only a mile from each other. And, um, I called him the next day and we started dating each other for, like three weeks [laughs].

Tom: "Well, it was really funny, though, because we had no car. I would just be forever on the bus to get there. And that's how it started. It was like he would pick me up and we would be together."

GH: "So you two have been friends ever since?"

Tom: "Yeah."

Lanny: "We went to our first gay bar together, I mean everything, the whole coming-out process—we went through together."

Tom: "We came out to our parents together, and through all kind of things . . . What it evolved into for our gang, was we would, you know, get there real early in the (Saturday) morning, and, meet together before the group. And then—just turn ourselves loose on Newtown afterwards . . . And just have the best time running around. And we'd all get together and go dancing that night. It was like—Saturday was just—nonstop playing. What was unique, about it, I guess was that—I didn't see these people through the week. We really didn't call each other that much. Sometimes. But, um, we were people from all over the city. Just all different types of people. And we just spent that whole day together. IT WAS GREAT."

Tom's narrative from more than a decade ago still conveys the magic and ritual flavor of Horizons today. It is a place where such diverse people can become chums, a place where the same people can meet after not having seen each other during the course of the week. These people can become each other's most trusted and intimate cronies—the people one is coming out with, people with whom—some of them, at least—one can remain connected, into the indefinite future, as the closest of friends (as Tom and Lanny are today). The story told by the original Horizons youth conveys the sense in which a special process unlike anything else in the secular urban environment is going on.

By the time several years later that twenty to thirty youth were attending weekly meetings, the group was dynamic and diverse. But it continued to suffer from a lack of direction and structure. The youth group director, one informant said, "spent too much time on individual kids and forgot the group function. Training was poor. Some of the kids did not get their needs met." Eventually, this director left to enter graduate school.

Two years after the first youth group began to meet, in 1980, Horizons opened a coffee house, largely as an alternative to the sexualized atmosphere of the bars and the alcoholic penchant of their clients. One reason for this move had to do with the needs of the youth group. Not only were gay teenagers legally shut out of the bars because of their age, but there was also concern that the bars were not the "proper atmosphere" in which to socialize young people. Thus, within two years, the youth group was having an effect upon the cultural organization of Horizons, shifting the focus away from the bars as a central meeting place. About this time too, Horizons came under the direction of a charismatic leader, and through leadership many changes came about, including the upward move to the prime location in which we conducted our field project.

For many years, and long before our project began, the youth group has had the same organizational structure: it meets for two hours beginning at noon on Saturdays, in the building of the agency. The advisors meet prior to the youth in a staff gathering and then open the building. At 12:15, the assembly of adults and youth, which varies in numbers enormously from week to week, splits into two groups: a "new people's group" and a "main group" of regulars. They meet separately for about one and a quarter hours. Then at 1:30 they take a coffee break. Some youth will smoke, or grab a coke or sandwich.

They begin again at 1:45 and meet until 2:30. During this period the "new" and "main" groups are usually lumped together in one large group. When the meeting is adjourned, there are often informal activities of many kinds. During the time of our study, the size of the total group varied, from some fifteen youth to approximately thirty-five teenagers at the largest meeting.

The Horizons youth group has grown in stature as a result of the social and political importance which adult gays and lesbians attribute to the agency for helping to socialize youth into their culture, and by virtue of the contact point which Horizons provides across age groups and social, ethnic, and class segments of the lesbian and gay population in Chicago.

The emphasis from the start has been on the normalcy, the "everydayness" quality, of youth who attend the Horizons group.[9] The same attitude is directed toward the normalcies of the adults. Advisors see their role as a way of continuing their own social development, that is, their own coming-out process.

Another emphasis of the group is on "self-help." The youth are encouraged to confirm their own identities, to explore what they feel is true to their own desires, and if this search suggests that they are lesbian or gay, to support them in their effort to come out. Often, youth come with a desire to come out immediately, sometimes as the result of movies or media presentations that have triggered some existential panic about their "secret." In the mid 1980s, for instance, two movies spurred youth to come out, with good and bad effects. One of these was *Consenting Adult*, the story of a freshman in college who comes out to his family and friends under difficult circumstances. The other film was *Early Frost*, a television movie that depicted the life of a young professional man in his twenties, living as a closet homosexual but with a lover, who contracts HIV illness and decides to come out to his family and social world. In our interviews we found that many of the Horizons youth mentioned these movies, or television and magazine stories, as influences which had motivated them to seek Horizons. The movies and related events became the focus of youth group discussion on occasions.

In general, the teenagers are encouraged by the adults to take responsibility not only for their own social plans, but to participate in building up the youth group program itself. In fact, a good deal of the actual "agenda setting" for youth group discussion every week, and the extracurricular activities presented by the group spring from the ideas of the youth. The youth elect their own leaders, who share the responsibility for making the group a success. They conduct fund-raisers and bake sales and hold raffles to make money for youth group activities. Regular parties and the annual prom are the primary goals of fund-raising. However, in recent years, the youth have taken to fund-raising for AIDS campaigns and hospices in Chicago. A newly elected Youth Council with a president fulfills many of these functions. The names of these teenager leaders were published in the local *Windy City Times* gay newspaper, showing the visibility of the gay youth group in the wider community, and also evidencing that such youth are the most visible and publicly "out." The council meets and plans agendas separately from the group as a whole. In practice, a small cadre of individual youth do much of the work for the group. They get to know each other intimately and are often social friends outside of the group.

As the youth group has grown in visibility, it has become popular to invite youth group members to be on public forums, transforming them from pariahs to celebrities. From 1986 to 1988, some youth were participants on more than one occasion on the "Sex Talk" show, a prominent radio talk program hosted by Phyllis Levy in Chicago. Such shows and news spots brought word of the group's existence to a wider spectrum of metropolitan Chicago.

The best known publicity event in the history of the Horizons youth group occurred in 1985, when a handful of the youth appeared on television for the first time on the popular "Oprah Winfrey Show." This appearance brought widespread attention to the group and perhaps drew the first national recognition to the needs and problems of gay youth.[10] The general aim of the show was to have youth talk about their feelings of being gay or lesbian identified and the effects this created in their lives. They told their coming-out stories in that telegraphic style of television that makes the complex sound ridiculous. And yet, they appeared as sensible and sincere, and more than anything they seemed "normal" and not monstrous, at least in the minds of many of the television audience who spoke during the show. Others objected and condemned the entire enterprise, of course. Some of the youth really wanted to be on the show; later it was discovered that two of them wanted it so badly that they lied about their ages. Oprah Winfrey indicated that only youth who were nineteen or under should participate, to underline the youthful nature of the issue. In fact (and unknown to the Horizons agency), two of the participants were actually twenty and twenty-one years old. The twenty-year-old girl unwittingly came out on national television to her estranged father, who lived in another state but happened to be watching the program, in what was a dramatic and long-remembered event in the group. The show made a hit in the gay and lesbian community. But not everyone in the Horizons group liked the content and tone of the show; several women felt that it was in "very bad taste." [11]

Over a period of years, then, Horizon's reputation as a "magnet" for gay youth—as the only steady and functioning place in which youth who felt themselves attracted to the same sex could go—grew throughout Chicagoland and spread throughout the midwestern region. A few kids from Milwaukee, Wisconsin, for example, periodically attended the Horizons youth group. Having sampled and liked its organization, and having none to return to at home, they created in 1990 a new coming-out group for youth in Milwaukee. Over the years a small number of youth groups in surrounding regions were thus to emerge, including groups in Indianapolis, Detroit, Michigan, and the suburbs of Chicago. Individual youth from Indiana, Michigan, and Wisconsin still attend the group on occasion. The national visibility of the group has also grown such that it has a small media presence, difficult to measure, but nonetheless visible. Similar youth groups exist in New York, San Francisco, Los Angeles, and Minneapolis, which through national conferences are now loosely linked in a network of gay organizations. During the time of our study, for instance, youth visited the Horizons group from as far away as California and New York, as they happened to be vacationing in Chicago or hitch-hiking through the area. An advisor once quipped that these gay adolescents from other states drop by, especially in the summer, as if they were doing "Gay Studies 101, on tour!"

An especially moving sign of the national visibility of Horizons came in the form of a letter from a Native American youth from South Dakota. It arrived one summer day in 1987 and was passed around the group by an advisor. The teenage Native American appealed to this unknown group for friends and "pen pals." He felt so "very alone on the reservation," he said, and he yearned to meet other gay teenagers. He enclosed a photograph of himself from his high school album. Scribbled across the back of it were the words: "I'm better looking than this now."

But it is not the visibility of the program as much as the feeling of belonging it creates in the youth that has made Horizons so popular.

One often hears kids refer to Horizons in the idiom of its being their "family" and their "second home." One characteristic expression we heard during our study was how gay youth regarded Horizons as their "family of choice," which meant to them a secure and confident feeling of belonging to a vital and affirming group that cared for itself and took care of its own.

As the youth group grew in size, and outreach into the city bolstered the number of youth coming into the program, it was inevitable that it would burst its seams. Some youth could not make the Saturday afternoon meetings, usually because of jobs or extracurricular activities at school, such as sports or music practice. There was no place for these youth to go. Furthermore, there was no group for youth who wanted to meet with other gay/lesbian youth after they turned twenty-one, which was especially problematic if their coming-out process was incomplete, as often happened. This situation led to many controversies, as we discuss in chapter 4. But during the time of our project a second meeting was established—Wednesday evening—which became instantly popular for a different crowd of youth, one somewhat older, tougher, and more sophisticated.[12] Most of the ethnographic observations and individual interviews on which this study is based pertain to the Saturday morning group, which typically tends to be a bit younger than the weekday crowd. In fact, the two groups overlap, with some individuals attending both groups at different times, and some, who need the most support or who are looking for the greatest social interaction, attending both the Saturday and Wednesday youth group meetings.

Violence and the Context of Coming Out

The history of homosexuality in Chicago, as shown in chapter 2, reveals a deep oppression, violence, bigotry, and racial prejudice that necessarily bends and distorts the process of coming out in the city. The cultural context of Horizons continues to reveal these same processes of oppression. We want to draw attention to this fact at the beginning of our ethnography because we are aware that anyone who deals with bigotry—with the problems of the oppressed—must grapple with how to describe the conditions that create and reproduce fear and secrecy and hatred. In the historical account given in chapter 2, we tackled the issue by representing multiple voices—young and old, male and female, black and white, loud and soft—that have suffered from harassment and discrimination, infusing the study with divergent perspectives on what it means to hide and seek. These voices are the inheritors of power struggles; they stem, in part, from history and the folklore of the cultural minorities in the United States, of which we consider openly gay and lesbian persons to be a part. Wherever oppression occurs, it resides within a power structure of social relations, ultimately kept in stasis by the fear of standing against it and chancing the violence of one's own destruction. In the United States—the world's most powerful, living liberal democracy— oppressive processes are ever at work, and the number of incidents of "hate" crimes (motivated at least in part by the sexual orientation of the victim) registered against lesbians and gay men has risen steadily.[13] As it is now understood, hate violence directed toward gays and lesbians shows that "perpetrators are predominantly average young men whose behavior is socially sanctioned rather than intrapsychically determined."[14] Thus it is this socially sanctioned homophobia (hatred toward homosexuals) that conditions the context of coming out for youthful Americans.[15]

Chicago is, if anything, subject to a higher level of violence than many other places in the United States, and the social consciousness of this potential ramifies into many domains and settings of social behavior. In our study we many times witnessed how the actions of youth derived from fear of violence and harassment; and in our struggle to describe this continuing process of oppression we are aware of the difficulties of making the struggles of gay adolescents "real" enough to have the reader know and "suffer" their experience of fear. By showing the setting of our project, including the context of violence in which all American youths must come out, we reveal a necessary part of understanding the culture of oppression that lies behind the coming-out process. These elements are never far from the situation of youth who are in the process of coming out, as is dramatically illustrated in the following account of events we witnessed in early 1987, which were reported in the Chicago newspapers and the *New York Times*.[16]

It was a lazy March afternoon, warmish, with a bright sun outdoors beaming through the opaque windows around the cheap, well-used door to Horizons. Our research team (Herdt, Boxer, and graduate students) had conducted four interviews by three o'clock and were now sitting and chatting among ourselves while two interviews were being completed. Floyd Ervin still had to finish a long and difficult interview with a woman who had just turned twenty-one. She was distraught and angry because the Horizons policy required that she leave the group. Outside a few of the teenagers milled around waiting for another kid who was being interviewed by one of our staff. Occasionally they checked in to see when their friend would be done so that they could leave.

Suddenly the door burst open and a very large man rushed in, bleeding profusely. He was naked from the waist up, bleeding from his arm, shoulder, and head. "Where is Bruce Koff?" he shouted. Without pausing for an answer, he shouted again, more frantically, "They got to us. Two men, with baseball bats. They climbed in from the back [of the building next door]. They bashed us!"

We were stunned but realized that the man needed medical attention. We wondered if others had been hurt. "Have you called the police?" we asked. We did so. Within minutes we heard the siren of a police car.

Meanwhile, one of our student interviewers (from the University of Chicago) went into action, playing nurse, finding towels, and treating the man's bleeding until the ambulance arrived. Blood was on the floor and the counter, everywhere. He turned around to glance outside, anxiously expecting another attack at any moment, and we saw terrible ugly black and blue bruises where a weapon had bludgeoned his back. The victim was Jeffrey McCourt, the editor of the *Windy City Times*, the local gay and lesbian newspaper housed in the adjacent building. (This building, incidentally, served as the meeting place of the Wednesday evening Horizons youth group, thus presenting a direct threat to the youth.) The bashers, it turned out, had calmly asked for "the manager" and singled him out for attack. He was nervous and angry with anxiety and fear: the unprovoked attack was for no other apparent reason than that the newspaper had spoken out that week on AIDS.[17]

Then the police arrived, in what seemed a routine matter to them. (This sense of routine was itself a shock to the youth. How often does such violence occur, they wondered?) Two uniformed cops quickly searched the grounds. Another unmarked car pulled up fast, and two plain-clothed men jumped out, one Hispanic and the other white. They peered inside quickly and then ran down the street. A third police car screamed to a halt with its sirens blaring. A crowd of curiosity-seekers assembled. The teenagers were pushed off to one side. The assailants, we learned, had entered the back door of the building in which the *Windy City Times* was housed. They had clubbed several people.

One member of our research team, a graduate student, naively (heterosexual and nonurban) asked the cop: "What do you suppose they did to provoke this attack?" The cop glared at her in disbelief, but then retorted, jaded but civil: "Did? They were probably just there! You don't have to do anything to be a victim. They're victims."

The crowd dispersed as McCourt was ushered away to the ambulance. We were all disappointed, to put it mildly, that the gay-bashers had gotten away. Again. All that remained of the attack were the new black spots of blood on the floors.

The youth had almost been forgotten in the melee. In fear, they had huddled together against the building, off to one side of the crowd, in that unselfconscious way of children who know when to get out of the way of the adults. This was because they were reduced to a helpless state: from being in charge of their lives—inside the youth group where they aspire to be grown up—to the outside where they were pushed aside and became again as children. And this helplessness frightened them. A few moments before the attack they were happy; they had forgotten their vulnerability. This aspiring to be gay—free from the shackles of their parents and the high school, acted out in a group that is protected by lesbian and gay adults—was reduced to a harsh reminder of the dirty reality beyond the doors of Horizons. Queer-bashing is too common a reminder of the homophobia that lies outside; its victims' bodies yield too easily to blows. Recognition of this reality is a process the youth refer to as their "vulnerability syndrome"—the sense that outside of the security circle of the group they can be hurt.

Such violence raises a dilemma for gay and lesbian adults. How much should they protect the youth from the "real world"? Are they being overly protective when they try to shield them? Real-life violence inflicted on the youth is difficult to locate because neither adults nor youth are sure where they can feel safe in society. Little wonder that the youth are fond of saying that Horizons is their only "real safe space" and their home away from home.

The Youth Group Advisors

No account of the rituals of coming out would be complete without a study of the ritual leaders. In the contemporary setting of Horizons these are the youth group advisors, adults of both sexes who range in age from their mid-twenties to their fifties. Pick any one of these good and worthy citizens, middle-class clerks, psychology interns, and teachers, who make up the pool of advisors, and you will find their dual goals are helping the youth and furthering their own coming out. They are also the role models and organizers of the process of changing from secret to public, and from homosexual to gay/lesbian, which the teenagers experience under the umbrella of Horizons.

Why do they volunteer their services to spend time with the youth, for instance? They all share, to one degree or another, a belief in the social value of "commitment" to building gay and lesbian culture. This social value suggests that the advisors feel a personal responsibility for what we might call the "sacred" trust of the community, put into practice through their guidance of acculturating gay and lesbian youth in the Horizons group. The concept of "culture" is represented by and created in the small events and great ceremonies of the calendar year, from the youth group meetings and Gay/Lesbian Youth Prom, to the Gay Pride Parade and numerous other social practices in the community. The adult advisors might not think of themselves this way, but the anthropologist sees that the group cannot function without its proper rites and ceremonies and that it needs the youth to carry on these practices. Socialization of the youth into the reproduction of these cultural practices, then, requires the commitment of advisors who are close to the youth and protect them during the rituals of coming out.

What does this ritual responsibility mean? The advisors have certain tasks and responsibilities regarding the sacred trust. They set rules and provide limits and boundaries for youth who by definition are outside of the rules of society. The advisors act as new role models, moral figures of authority and affection. The youths' parents cannot serve in this role; many of them do not know that their children are gay. The advisors define the passage between the youth group and its secret discourse, and the outside, oppressive, sometimes violent world. In the inner sanctum of small rap groups, the kids can spill their guts, telling the stories of fear and loneliness and rejection and hate experienced because they are gay and lesbian, and they will know that they will be accepted here. At the end of the meeting they will get hugs and kisses from their peers in the group and a friendly pat on the back from the adults who supervise them.

The problem is, the advisors must work around the laws, which say that they should not teach the youth directly, or otherwise they are accountable legally for the things that could go wrong. These dangers are coded into two key rules: the prohibition against using drugs on the premises, and the general taboo against having contact with the youth outside of the group. In general, drugs have not been an issue at the agency, either for adults or youth. On the other hand, the question of intimate contact and the taboo against sex with youth is foremost on the minds of the advisors. It is related, however, to another matter that filters into it: what are the advisors searching for in their role? We shall see that many of the advisors use their role as an implicit means to continue to develop their own self-image as gay or lesbian; to continue, that is, to come out, in one way or another in their various social relationships and to strengthen their identities as gay men and lesbians.

To be a culturally assigned "role model" in the community of gays and lesbians is a privilege and an honor. Through these role models, the youth become aware of the key features that define their purpose in the group, as these are reflected in the advisors. To be an object of admiration and idealization and to allow themselves to be supportive in this way require an adult strength and the ability to derive satisfaction from the subjective experience of "parenting" the youth. This requires a sharing of one's self with the youth, as well as "permission" being extended to those youth who would like to model themselves after the advisors. The process works by internalizing the idealized features of the advisors (the ideal self) that provides internal self-support for the youth to rely upon in their own development. Such a process can promote inner growth and change in social relations. Some adults thus compare the advisors' role to that of parenting. The training of advisors, a process which has grown more sophisticated over the years, makes these functions more available to advisors. Although they are often aware of it, many advisors still seemed surprised when told that the youth in our interviews stated that the most important positive influence upon them was the youth group advisors.

The youth group advisor is, therefore, an especially important role model. An example will illustrate this process of implicit modeling. Shirley is a young woman and a lesbian leader who served as youth group leader for several months. She is attractive, white, middle-class, and twenty-four years old. She became involved in Horizons shortly after moving to Chicago from a small midwestern town. Recently, Shirley appeared alongside her lesbian lover in a handsome photograph that appeared in the local lesbian newspaper. The article described her role in the lesbian community and mentions what she is doing at Horizons. The photo shows her standing beside her lover, a smiling woman of similar background and identical age. Her lover is active in the community also, and she serves as an advisor in another program at Horizons. Indeed, the title of the story reads, "Women in Action." A short biography of both women shows their mutual and close engagement in lesbian and gay culture, with connections in many directions. They have positions at a local college and at a monthly magazine, in addition to their Horizon's activities. Shirley also works with emotionally disturbed children through another agency. The newspaper asked Shirley why other women weren't more active at Horizons. She replied that she had come from a small town where she had been activist, but there had been so few role models there. In Chicago there were more, and she doubly appreciated the spirit of lesbian and gay activism in Chicago. She said that she felt "honored to follow in the footsteps of older activists." An important part of her life in Chicago, she concluded, was the presence of "so many role models." The story appeared in the paper the day before the weekly youth group meeting on Saturdays. We were fascinated to see how the youth commented on the article and complimented Shirley. The young lesbians in particular were admiring. Later that year, Shirley and her lover appeared together in the Gay and Lesbian Pride Parade on their motorcycle.

The key to understanding the advisor's role is that they are all unpaid volunteers; in a word, folk practitioners, as the tradition requires. There is a simple but powerful symbolic reason for this, though understanding it requires a study of the wider pool of Horizons' volunteers. Like many other grass-roots, volunteer organizations, the success of Horizons depends upon the good will of its volunteers. They are its lifeblood, and their role in the mission of the institution is well appreciated. During the period of our study some two hundred adults served as part-time volunteers at Horizons in all of its programs. Agency records show that twenty advisors staffed the youth program, including eight white women, ten white men, and two black men. It remains among the most popular programs to volunteer for, suggesting a strong link into the formation of gay culture. Let us sketch a portrait of two other advisors.

Sharon is a woman in her mid-thirties, who came to Chicago from another city. She is a social worker in training. She has been a volunteer at Horizons for some time. Her original contact was through the director of the agency, who is a social friend. She has a good intellect and strong physical features, coupled with a rather soft but confident voice. She is a moderate in most matters dealing with the youth group, preferring to allow others to voice their opinions, but asserting her own if she feels that someone is out of line, or has crossed a boundary that suggests a personal problem is clouding professional judgment. She came to Horizons for professional reasons, to complete her clinical training through an internship at the youth group. Sometimes she served as a substitute group director. Yet she also came to further her own personal growth. She explains that for some years she had been out to her friends but not to her family. She continued to pretend that her lover was a "roommate," lying about this if necessary. After two years at Horizons she decided that the time had come. She told her parents and they were very accepting. Her next goal, she says, is to come out fully at her workplace.

Buck is young and good looking, a twenty-five-year-old graduate student in training to be a health care professional. He hales from Arizona and carries with him sad memories of his own coming-out process within the past three years. He is tall and somewhat shy, and tells that he came to Horizons both to have additional clinical experiences and also to make friends. His former supervisor, a closet homosexual in Arizona, had once made a pass at him in an hour of supervision; he remembers the experience bitterly and condemns "closet cases" for this kind of behavior. He has aspired to be out in all aspects of his life. He could not come out at college because there was too much homophobia. He came out to his parents; his mother was supportive but conflictual about his same-sex desires, while his father was generally negative and rejecting. He is contemplating coming out to his grandparents later. At Horizons he has a new opportunity to meet friends and prospective adult partners. He enjoys the setting and feels that by helping the youth he is learning new things about his own maturation every day.

In both cases we see that the coming-out process is not complete for these two people. They continue, that is, to "work through" their own individual concerns and questions of how to construct a lesbian and gay life through constant work with the youth group and other advisors. How conscious of the process is each of them?

How do these people come to volunteer at all for Horizons? There are two routes. First, strangers call on the phone and say they want to "help out," after which they are referred to the youth group director. Second, volunteers and advisors talk to their friends, spreading enthusiasm, and they are referred in kind. In both cases, the director screens each person, who may perhaps be interviewed again. Some applicants are rejected, for various reasons having to do with their "maturity" and psychological health, as judged by the instincts and intuitions of the director. Eventually the group of successful applicants go through training with the director and other advisors for a few weeks. During this time several other individuals may be excluded from the pool for the same reasons as before. However, even the persons with marginal skills or psychological problems can still contribute in all manner of ways, such as in staffing the secretarial pool. Others may answer the telephone hotline to offer low-cost or free psychological treatment or legal services, as well as inform callers about many community activities, such as Sunday picnics and socials that raise funds for PLWAs.

But the youth group advisors are selected quite carefully. They come in all sizes and colors and both genders. They are old and younger, urban and suburban, many men and a few women, and all but a handful of them over the years have been gay or lesbian. Persons who are heterosexual have volunteered; two mothers of gay sons come to mind. The average volunteer advisor is male or female, in his or her late twenties, white, college-educated, working in a service or white-collar job, and has been in the process of coming out for two years or more. Persons of color volunteer, albeit rarely; professionals volunteer, especially those in the helping professions such as clinical psychology and social work, but they are rare. The youth group is special in its selection, with more specialized training, and more careful monitoring. Being "comfortable" with one's own sexual orientation is a key to successful advising, informants have said, and here the influence of the parent/teacher/mentor role model quietly enters the moral arena of the selection of youth group advisors.[18] The youth group advisors are among the most active and enthusiastic; among other reasons why this is true is that their role at the center offers them a way to make friends among their fellow advisors and participate in social activities that are at the very center of gay and lesbian community life.

An Advisor's Meeting

Every Saturday morning, prior to the youth group, the advisors assemble informally at Molly's restaurant. The atmosphere in general is chatty and cozy—"a family affair"—as are most functions, formal and informal, at Horizons. The breakfast meeting serves, more than anything else, to socialize new advisors into the culture of the youth group. It orients the adults as to the goals and plans of the director for the week; it helps to set an agenda with the group advisors; it reveals significant problems that have cropped up in the youth group, for instance, with individual youth who are having emotional problems; and it forges a solidarity between the advisors as peers that is crucial for the success of the ritual process. The substantive content of the meetings usually revolves around the topic for youth group discussion for the week, such as coming out to one's parents, or awareness of "safe-sex" practices. These discussions, in a sense, are "rehearsals" and "role-playing" efforts to sort out views and disagreements prior to the youth group. Sometimes the meetings reveal conflicts and contradictions between adults over certain "hot" topics, such as the advisability of permitting leaders from outside groups, like "Biways" (a bisexual group in Chicago) to make presentations to the youth group.

On a typical Saturday morning in late spring, 1987, the advisors met over coffee and donuts. The business at hand was as follows: an agenda of "open meeting" topics was to be fixed for the coming eight weeks of the larger youth group discussions. Usually these subjects are suggested by advisors, but some are requested by youth, and sometimes they are agreed upon mutually. Regular open-ended discussion meetings are also scheduled, during which the youth can bring up any topic they want. Here are the topics that were selected in this typical time frame: Week 1, a talk by the director of Horizons, a former youth group leader himself, welcoming the new kids from the past three months and discussing the history of the agency; week 2, an "open rap group," led by two advisors; week 3, a youth discussion on "race and ethnic minorities," including discussion of racial prejudice in the gay community; week 4, a rap on "self-expression," left open-ended for the youth to bring in particular concerns; week 5, a rap on "parents and the problem of dating while living at home"; week 6, a "discussion of gender," with girls and boys being divided in separate meeting rooms for the day; week 7, a meeting on "gay history," led by a male advisor who pursues the subject as his hobby; and week 8, a "Parent Social Function," in conjunction with Gay Pride Parade weekend.[19]

The announcement of this list by the youth group director led to an open discussion of the issues related to advising. Here is a short account of the meeting.

An advisor asked, "Is this agenda [for the kids] too structured and planned? Maybe it is not necessary to have two advisors for the meeting." Some of these kids, a younger lesbian advisor jokes, "need a hygiene group!" Someone quips, "Slip them all into a vat!"

Someone says: "Attendance seems to go way down in the summer." Another advisor remarks: "We've got to have more "history." These kids don't know our history at all. But how can you integrate historical consequences at age sixteen!" Another person remarks, "We need a parents' perspective." Someone else says, "We have some kids who are extremely racist! Or nuts!" Sallie, an older heterosexual woman who has a gay son, comments: "I still don't think that these youth should come out too early. They should wait till they're a bit older (she implied after they were out of high school)." This arouses some disagreement within the group, and someone mutters that straights do not understand the pressures to come out that are felt by gays. The remark was directed toward the older straight woman, who looked offended. After a couple of innocuous remarks, the director quickly changed the subject. Clearly, the advisors did not agree on the optimal age of coming out.

The basic question of confidentiality arises, such as whether to report to state officials any abuse which is alluded to during the course of rap groups. Then there is secrecy: "We are mandated by the state to disclose these things,"someone says. Risk overrides confidentiality. "Dating" as a new social experience for the youth comes up again. "These kids don't know how to date," Sharon says. "Yeah, but do they know that we don't either!" the youngish advisor Buck pipes in. Jorge thinks that this is extremely funny, and Sharon grins too.

"We need an in-service training session on suicide. This should be addressed, and we need more training." Yet someone else is cautious: "But how much structured training will ever provide what you need to prevent suicide"?

Another person suggests the need for AIDS education. He also mentions having trained to assist PLWAs in the "Buddy system." But is there any real connection between training and recruitment at Horizons, the leader wonders? There is an uneven flow of people at all times. On the other hand, the Buddy system provides support for continued change with the friend.

Sandwiched between the agenda discussions are personal asides, news, and gossip thrown into the stream of talk. No one is self-conscious about a story someone mentions regarding the romantic troubles one of the absent advisors is having. Later in the meeting a new Hollywood movie is mentioned, and the discussion is diverted to the question, momentarily, whether the producer is homophobic or not. The meeting started with a discussion of the annual Valentine's Day party for Horizons. The youth were helping out in organizing the meeting, but there was some disagreement over the scheduled time. There was planning also for a social fund-raiser at Molly's restaurant for later in the month.

Someone questions the plans for the upcoming Lesbian and Gay Youth Prom, which is scheduled in two weeks. The kids are responsible for a lot of the organization and publicity. Is it going to flop, some of the advisors wonder? The youth aren't paying for their tickets yet. But "this always happens," an experienced advisor says; a panic shortly before the prom leads to ticket sales and a rush of last-minute preparations. It always works out beautifully in the end. The prom that we attended later proved her prediction correct.

Then the advisors approved an AIDS education survey for the youth which was proposed by a university student. Substance abuse training is also being planned. An "identity conference" for Horizons featuring out-of-town speakers and many people from Chicago is announced for October. The "Night of 100 Parties" is planned for October. This is always a big event. It occurs annually, with the money raised for worthy and charitable causes. The center usually raises a substantial amount of money and many promises of good will. (Horizons gets $10.00 per ticket for persons who participate.)

The advisors mention that some individuals on the youth council are fighting for a smaller discussion groups. The teenagers feel that shyer members would be encouraged to speak by having fewer people for intimate discussions. The advisors, Jorge and Buck, argue between themselves over this. One of them says that it is typical of "the adolescent experience" to be shy. The other says that the ideas show the kids are trying to take responsibility. But who in the teenage group is responsible, the other asks? Buck says, "We don't expect anything, and the kids don't do anything because of it! We need more expectations." This leads to the question of how the groups influence the identity formation of the kids. "Do youth really have an identity structure?" someone asks. She feels that there is a need to revise the youth group structure. "We need more of a system," Sharon says. People are saying "there are two types of people in the youth group—kids who are confident, and the others who are sensitive, shy, and are excluded." And the high school model of government kept gay kids out of power in the schools—so "we don't want that kind of system." We need a new way to interface youth and advisors that does not abuse power, one of the older advisors suggests. The meeting comes to an abrupt halt at noon, when it is is time to walk round the corner to the Horizons building.

The Sex Taboo

At Horizons, one of the strongest sentiments and social rules of training for the adult advisors is the prohibition on contact with the youth outside of the agency. Underlying the injunction is a very powerful taboo against sexual relations with the youth. We should see this as a cultural rule of the highest sort, what a sociologist has called in another context an "institutional incest taboo."[20] The incest taboo is designed to maintain the kind of role distance necessary to create a balance between the adolescent and idealist yearnings, and the ritual authority of the adults, which the youth group comes to represent.

The symbolic process of advisor participation in the coming-out rites must confront this delicate issue in American life. What kind of influence do adults have over the sexuality of youth? Historically, the stereotypes of older closet homosexuals, kinky gays, and smothering lesbians preying upon youth were so common in the public mind as to raise a general outcry leading to imprisonment or loss of employment at the hint of any "homosexual" influence over minors. Fantastic images come to mind: adult men who are "trolls" and women who are "bull dykes," with vampire eyes and a corpse-like touch; they prey upon youth, they recruit them as prostitutes for childhood sex rings and give them drugs in exchange for sex. These are among the most fantastic—but they occur. These stereotypes have sometimes motivated symbolic "mob lynchings." The teacher is still a figure of moral probity, a substitute parent, or a legal remnant of *loco parentis* in many states. Gays and lesbian are thus forbidden to be teachers in many places for fear that they will corrupt and seduce the young. Thus, from the very start of the entry of the adult advisors into the agency, and from the time before the youth find their way to Horizons to come out, the question of sex with advisors is a heady issue that cannot be separated from the rite of passage which the group process represents.

These stereotypes are very deep and old in the American social tradition. Their cultural representations are transmitted by virtue of jokes and folktales and old novels, a core mythology of the "homosexual ogre" that continues to imprison much of popular imagination. That this is so is reflected in the fact that many advisors and youth mentioned aspects of the stereotype during the course of our project. Underlying the prejudice is the notion that people can be "taught" sexual desires; that sexual orientation is a kind of "choice"; that youth are sexually naive and gullible; that homosexuals are driven by dangerous and uncontrollable sexual drives that they are unable to check; and that all homosexual men and women prefer children and adolescents, particularly budding youth, as their sexual partners. These myths have little basis in fact, but that is not what matters; it is their grip upon the social imagination of the actors who find themselves in the intimate quarters of the youth group that we must contend with.[21]

In fact, contrary to the mythology, the possibility of sexual contact with youth remains forever a social and psychological burden for the advisors. Far from being a desire, they experience the notion as an unwanted baggage of fears and prejudice which they must deal with, however implicitly, at every corner. They struggle with the problem not only in facing the anxieties of the youth as they first approach the new people's group (see chapter 4), but also in addressing the concerns of parents, teachers, and reactionary Christian fundamentalists who constantly preach about the sins of the "homosexual."[22]

Morey, a thirtyish advisor whom we got to know well, attacked another advisor for his "acting out." He said that he saw him kiss a boy and that the kiss was "not just a buzz." "It's inappropriate" he says; and he rang up the youth group director to complain. The taboo on sex with teens must be kept. All of us have to pay attention to this, he says.

He told us an apocryphal story. A few months earlier a youth had called him. Morey had not given his number out; the boy had looked him up in the telephone directory. This youth was a very needy and confused sixteen-year-old boy. He was still in high school, and he was suicidal. He called Morey every night for a week. Some eighteen months before, a Filipino boy, about eighteen, had killed himself. Both the advisors and youth had felt very badly about his death because no one had had any idea that the boy was suicidal. As a result, Morey felt reluctant to turn down this boy's plea for help. He agreed to meet the youth at a local restaurant, which was a "big mistake," he said. He forgot that other advisors went there. The next day he was really chewed out for this. "I felt bad. What did he need, that boy? He was tripped up," he said as his face grew worried. "I really wondered maybe if I had violated a taboo." There are reasons for the taboos. "It's rumored sometimes that youth show an interest that is reciprocated. The problems this causes are huge." Morey wondered, "Did kids sometimes use sex for favors in the past?"[23]

The adults provide a standard for moral probity and correctness; they teach about the new possibilities of being human and having a different code of ethics than people in the material world. For instance, their opinions regarding homophobia and sexual harassment are clear: they do not accept these norms of the mainstream society; they reject the idea that gays and lesbians should be discriminated against in the areas of partner benefits, housing, jobs, service in the armed forces, and social standing at large. While they do not bandstand on these issues, their likes and dislikes become clear to the youth over the course of time, thus providing a divergent moral sensibility and a code of ethics for the subsequent development of the teenagers. The adults are responsible for how things go during the meetings, including the rules to follow and the respect for individual privacy and dignity. They are responsible for helping the kids to feel loved and wanted for who they are, for having same-sex desires. Through this caring, the youth transmute experiences of strength and courage from the advisors.

In all of this long process of coming out, of ritual practices that form a rainbow of interactions and associations across the historical age cohorts, the adults have an assignment from the gay and lesbian community, however implicit it remains: to prepare the youth for entry into gay and lesbian culture; to fortify them for the problems they will face by coming out in mainstream society. It is true that the Horizons agency regards the youth group as a self-help organization, wherein teaching does not occur (with the exception of AIDS education). But this is an official cultural view, an ideology imposed upon them by a harsh and oppressive surrounding society. The advisors do, in fact, teach, as does every adult when interacting with youth in our society or any other. How could they not? Whether by direct classroom teaching, by observation or role modeling, a culture requires that its values and knowledge be carried into the next generation.

No culture could exist without socialization and the enculturation of its basic value orientations. As we will see in the following chapter, one beauty of ritual as a means of socialization is that no individual has to take responsibility for its teaching or effects. At the same time, the youth group has come to function as a means of the intergenerational transmission of culture, extending and thereby fortifying the life of the culture through the life course of its individual members. The gay and lesbian life course has thus begun to include, for some individuals and for the culture as a whole, the period of adolescence. It struggles with how to do this against the social oppression and legal confines of the mainstream society. That itself is a key to understanding the moral critique which Horizons helps to instill in the youth through the rites of coming out.

◆ ◆ ◆

CHAPTER FOUR

The Rituals of Coming Out

Coming out means a person who is very confused, doesn't know what he wants,
boys and girls. You're at a certain stage in your life, a confused moment. Then
you lie to yourself and say, "No, I'm not like that, I'm straight." But you're
lying to yourself, denying yourself. One of the most confusing moments in life
is coming out—that's the truth.

—*An eighteen-year-old boy of Mexican descent*

The youth who find their way to the Horizons group are at an extreme point in their lives. They are facing an existential crisis of personal identity (Who am I?) and a social crisis of belonging (Where do I fit in?). Their transition from the torment of secrecy and isolation to the celebration of the public activities of adult gay life, such as the Gay Pride Day Parade, years later is a life crisis profound and yet so commonly experienced that it has found its resolution in the oldest of human remedies—ritual.

A generation ago the closet homosexual furtively sought hidden circles that provided an induction of sorts, a secret socialization into underground homosexual life. Such an initiation into secret social relations not only lacked the active declaration of one's new status and identity, but it positively shunned openness for fear of ostracism by society at large and rejection by family and friends. Discrimination of all forms, including jailing or blackmail, that sanctioned such discrimination was endemic to the experience of the earlier historical cohorts of the twentieth century. Forms of bigotry continue, but in the large American cities it is increasingly possible for people openly to express their desire for the same sex. Individuals may come out; and the probability that they will do so increases with the passing of time. Their coming out rituals and the means by which these shape and reproduce the gay and lesbian culture at large are the subject of this chapter.

Coming out in contemporary America has had two key cultural meanings for some years.[1] In popular discussion "coming out" has meant the *personal* act or event of telling someone of one's same-sex desires. For the purposes of our work we will define this "someone" as either another person or one's self, though the two processes are obviously different. (In chapter 5 we focus on such experiences of the self.) The second sense of "coming out" is the meaning attributed to it by researchers who over the years have begun to see coming out as a longer *social* process of transforming one's social relations to accord with same sex desires.

History has transformed experience: As coming out has taken on more of a ritual flavor in recent years, individuals' experiences have tended to equalize the personal and social aspects, shifting what is personal into the public, and what is a public symbol into private experience.[2] The problem in interpretation is that the personal and the cultural elements are often conflated in the minds of those who have studied the meanings of the identity "gay and lesbian." In large measure this confusion results from the continued lumping of "homosexual" with "gay/lesbian." Historically, researchers—especially psychologists—have thought of coming out as something under the jurisdiction of the lone individual, acting without positive social role models or networks, without socialization or the cultural institutions which support their desires and struggle to come out.[3] Certainly this was true of the closet homosexual in times past. Yet the perspective continues to color the research literature, as we see for instance, in the widely cited work of Carol Warren: "In general, the gay world has two distinctions. It is almost universally stigmatized, and no one is socialized within or toward it as a child."[4]

As a social ritual, coming out is critical to the formation of a national cultural consciousness, as discussed in chapter 2. That collective consciousness is undergoing a revolution today. The stigma is lifting, and cultural institutions such as Horizons provide a new context for the socialization of gay youth. For gays and lesbians to succeed in constructing a culture in competition with other groups in the United States has required three fundamental steps: (1) the creation of institutions such as Horizons through which to socialize and affirm values and lifeways; (2) the integration of the older homosexual generation into the new gay and lesbian cohort, or, at the least, the provision of cultural means to deal with the alienation of the older generation from the young; and (3) the training of the young, who will transmit social values and cultural rules and beliefs—the utopian ideology—across time and space into the future. Thus we see why the focus upon the lone individual, rather than upon the relationship between culture and the individual, has been so misleading. It is these new rites of coming out that carry forward the aim of socializing the young.

Ritual may seem to be a slow, cumbersome, and old-fashioned device to change identity. How are the coming-out rites effective in transforming identity in a technologically sophisticated society such as ours? Coming-out practices create a context for binding individual energy and personal meaning with collective social action and imagination in the community. Birth, puberty, marriage, initiation into sexuality, and death are the most fundamental of human experiences; they cry out for sacred symbols—myth and ritual—to bind the individual to collective tradition in powerful yet graceful ways. As we shall see below, the "life crisis" practices and events of coming out are no less fundamental to life. Beginning for the youth in a secretive context, the events of coming out are supported by a growing tradition of gay and lesbian culture that requires being out as the "right and proper" means of achieving entry into the culture. Ritual has the force to bind the energy of individuals (psyche, body, and spirit) to communities and to legitimize the change from one status to another.

What makes coming out a social ritual of recognized form and content in our culture? Several recurring events and processes in the youth's experience at Horizons can be interpreted in the lens of classical anthropological writings on the *rites of passage*. First, though the rites are not dependent upon biological puberty, they are still "sexual [in] nature since they incorporate the boys and girls into adult society of the sexes."[5] Coming out is recognized as the necessary and right way to enter gay and lesbian culture. Though the youth may be shunned by the mainstream heterosexual society for participating in the rites of entry, these passages are effectively prescribed for adolescents to enter into social relations with adult lesbians and gay men. Second, going to the youth group is a "separation from normal society . . . initiates are outside of society and it has no power over them," due to the "suspension of the usual rules of living."[6] Third, ritual provides a process of "relearning" which "changes all the gestures of ordinary life."[7] It brings new learning and unlearning of basic perceptions, a form of "radical resocialization" of identities and roles.[8] Fourth, the youth forsakes secrecy in favor of coming out, which breaks down moral barriers—segregation of the hidden secret from the social body,

and the nonsexual from the sexual aspects of the youth's social relations with family and friends.[9] Fifth, coming out exposes youth and
their families to intense stigma, with an accompanying loss of face
and social status, due to the homophobia of society.[10] Finally, as the
coming out rites succeed in forging a gay and lesbian culture, they
will ameliorate the current social status of such youth. This suggests
that some day the parents and friends who might have or actually did
shun their children and friends earlier will reclaim them once they
have successfully adapted to new social roles.

A Secret Nature

For some youth the secrecy of childhood concerns hiding homoerotic
desires. It begins early, often with a feeling of being "different," as
early as age five, while others experience this sensibility after puberty,
according to their self-reports (see chapter 5). Central to how the child
learns to hide and fear is the fact of homophobia. Family, religion,
ethnicity, and social class all contribute to the push into hiding, into
conformity to heterosocial and heterosexual roles and norms at home,
in school, with peers in the neighborhood, at church or at work.

The first recognition of a desire for the same sex is the beginning of
the process of coming out that will, for some youth, lead them to Horizons. On the average, the youth of Horizons we studied report that
awareness of same-sex desire began at age nine, well before puberty.
Some teens discover their desires in the nascent arousal for a friend
or a school chum or teacher; for others it begins in fantasy, with sports
heroes or television stars. But whatever its origin, same sex desire is
a signal to the child that he or she has a "special" nature, which many
sense as "unnatural or bad," as one youth put it, and which must,
therefore, be hidden. For a few teenagers it is too strong to say that
they make a secret of it; it is more implicit and more gradual than
that—the whisper of a shout that will emerge, but only later. Yet for
most of the Horizons youth, secret is the right sense: the secret of
having a nature that is unusual or unique but should not be revealed.

If a household is presumptively defined as "heterosexual persons
only," eighteen-year-old Johnny says, then how can the youth who
desires the same sex exist, unless he or she is "crazy or weird?" "I
never knew homosexuals existed," he remarks. What can the child do
but "leave" the house—either in his head, or by virtue of television,
periodicals, or fantasies—to seek this strange Other, or later physi-

cally leave home to find other lesbians or gays. One function of the fantasy of the "gay ghetto" in youth development is to locate physically a place wherein one might actually escape from oppression and see these new gay men and lesbians out of the closet. Thus, some gay youth talk about getting on the train and going to Newtown. And some South Side Chicago black youth have a secret code: "Are you going to the North?" they ask, meaning to the freedom of Newtown. Later, they may move out of the house, to be gay in another neighborhood. Thus the heterosexual concepts of being, time, and space so inextricably bound up in the early definition of the self begin to be reshaped.

Basic to the social ritual of coming out is the ending of the secrecy of sexuality. By "sexuality" we mean the person's sexual desires and their expression in social relations. The counterpart to coming out in heterosexual peers is self-exploration in masturbation, sometimes accompanied by sexual fantasies; but soon this leads into dating the opposite sex, which is socially encouraged at increasingly younger ages by society.[11] For gay youth, this process is nearly always suppressed. Homoerotic desire and its development have often been ignored because they were dismissed as a "passing phase" or even worse, condemned as deviant psychopathology. Horizons youth are brought into a new gay-positive context, however, where they are permitted to express for the first time their feelings in the process of their cultural status change. The youth group serves to initiate them into a world of homosocial and then "progay and lesbian" relations, hitherto unknown.

In both respects then—new sexual avenues and new social relations—being at Horizons constitutes a fundamental category change in self, sexuality, and social being of their former and future lives. Their presumed heterosexuality up to that point is destined to lay behind them, but not without many trials and tribulations.

The Threshold: Danger and Safety

Many youth tell how they could not immediately enter the doors of Horizons even after they had located the agency. They fret and fear, circle round and round the block, walking past the doors of Horizons repeatedly. This ritual may continue for weeks; some say they ventured back over a period of months before they finally got up the nerve to enter. Other youths were bold and entered quickly, as if to get through a panic; and a few others sought the agency in such desperation that no last minute fear at the threshold could dissuade them from passing into the feared sanctum. Tom, a Caucasian suburban gay man (now aged 32), the first "president" of the Horizons youth group, comments on his 1979 entry: "I could remember circling the block [to find Horizons in an] old basement apartment . . . circling, like—five times before, and I went in. I was so scared. I was one of the very first people there. And I walked in . . . thinking, 'Oh, everyone's gonna be at their most swishy, with the dresses, I just know it!' [laughter] . . . And there was Robert [first youth group advisor], and I was thinking like, 'Whoa!!' . . . He was so professional, and so NORMAL . . . he had on cowboy boots!" The process of stealthful approach and avoidance is so legendary that Horizons' kids remain on the lookout for the signs of youthful "suspects" passing by the agency who seem to need a helping hand. As Tom put it: "We [were] to the point [of knowing] where—you would know when somebody was just circling and walking past the door—that they wanted to come in, but they were scared . . . So that you'd just go out [on to the street] and get 'em in."

If a single generalization about the ritual approach to Horizons holds true, it is this: all the youth, even the ones who have clandestine contact with other gay youth before they come to the group, are secretly terrified. The youth say that they have to fear harassment and violence. But their most profound fears are perhaps closer to home: the fear of exposure to their family and friends. "I'm scared to tell my parents," one girl confessed in an emotional interview with us. Parents sometimes react with anger to the knowledge of their children's sexual desires. In our study, seven youth reported that they were kicked out of their homes after their parents learned of their same-sex desires. While this was exceptional for the group, it conveys the strongest dread of the mythology of the homophobic reaction: fear the worst in what your parents will do if they discover that you are "homosexual." The many stories surrounding the issue serve as fearsome reminders of potential rejection. A youth at one group meeting warned another boy who spoke angrily of wanting to come out to his parents during group discussion. "Look at what happened to Lennie," he said, "His mother kicked him out of the house when she found out about him!"

The transition from feeling "different" from one's parents or peers to gradually "passing" as heterosexual conjures up monstrous myths in the minds of youth. These are clichés and stereotypes of ogres, usually bad and evil, who are dangerous to all that is "good" and who may pollute the self by contact with them. A nineteen-year-old Asian youth from an upper-middle-class background said, "When I learned of [the existence of gay], I knew that it applied to me. But I felt it shouldn't because they seemed weird, a mental disorder, not normal." Most youth fear that that once they enter the doors of Horizons, they will fall prey to horrible creatures, neither human nor normal, who will do terrible things, such as expose themselves. The boys fear that they will become the "prey" (the metaphor is "chicken") of aggressive gay men, especially older homosexuals, the "chickenhawks," who will attack them. The girls fear they will be caught in the clutches of "lesbian witches," vampire creatures of manly nature, who will attack them. (They later come to actually fear these "creepy" adults, whom they call "trolls," especially closet homosexuals in bars, who "lurch around" tying to make a pass at them.) No wonder dealing with the old stereotypes and myths of "homosexuality" provokes denial: what youth could identify with them?

Fears of entering Horizons are deeply connected to the process of denial of same-sex desires, whereby the youth tries to convince himself or herself that there is "really nothing wrong." Denial may be initiated from the child, from a significant other, such as a parent, a sibling, a counselor or a minister or priest. Indeed the denials of loved and admired adults may feed the fear and pain of the child, prolonging the agony and alienation from the same adults.

Entering the Horizons doorway, the liminal (from the French *limin*, or door) passage to the inner world, is what starts the ritual process. Beyond this threshold much of the timelessness and special character of liminal worlds, that is, spaces and places set apart from society, often secret, with special rules and norms, is evident in the organization of the experience of the youth.

Yet the entrance to the Horizons' building is muted: a sign, tattered and ordinary, reads, "Horizons Community Services." The actual enterprise is concealed. But why? It is not for fear of being politically "out"; the agency is aggressively open. Instead, Horizons continues a practice, much like the old closet homosexual bars of preliberation days, of having an unmarked entrance. The innocuous entrance helps to protect the youth from harassment and the building from vandalism. It also looks less alarming to the tenuous youth because the magical word "gay" is absent, so their fear of giving away "the secret" is eased. The advisors, we might say, are the symbolic guardians of the youth's secret, defenders who are stationed at the doors: not to keep people in as much as to prevent outsiders, adults who would upset the delicate balance of making the secret public, from gaining access to the youth group.

The way the kids come to know of Horizons makes a difference in their understanding of it. Their source of information not only colors their entrance into and expectations of the agency, it may compound prior stereotypes of "homosexuals." Some of the ways through which youth learn of the group are remarkable. Some youth call in to the Horizons telephone "hotline" to ask for help or to get a referral address for the youth group. A few youth—through queer jokes by straight friends—have the building pointed out: "Fags hang out there." Others have heard their friends slur Horizons as a place where "queers" and "fags" hang out, unwittingly tipping off the youth as to the location of the agency. Others may have heard of it on television or on the radio. Some of the youth come with peers from school or other "hang outs" who introduce them to Horizons. The youth who come with peers are usually more secure than the others. Some of the youth are so desperate that they go to the public library and look up the word "homosexual"—glancing furtively over their shoulders—to see if there are any leads on where to go for help. One boy once seriously suggested canvassing all libraries in Chicago and inserting literature on Horizons at the appropriate places in books, including the encyclopedia entry on "homosexuality," to access these frightened kids! Several young women told us that they discovered Newtown and Horizons through feminist support groups that included lesbians. Other youth came through referrals from gay and lesbian organizations of Chicago area colleges and universities.[12]

The extent to which the youth have to hide varies according to how much their family already knows about their sexuality. The range extends from the completely hidden and closeted individual, which is typical, to a family which has a positive understanding of the child's sexuality but precludes the child from being out beyond the family. Here is eighteen-year-old Bluey, of racially mixed origins, who considers himself gay and black: "I guess my folks know because when I was twelve we talked about it—my parents, both of them. We talked about it at dinner and the whole night. My father brought it up and said, "Are you gay?" I responded, "Yes, I am. I prefer guys to girls.""

They weren't mad, they didn't condemn it. My uncle [father's brother] is gay. So he understood. They stand behind me." This youth is generally out at college, where he is a freshman.

For youth who are more closeted it grows harder to invent excuses to friends and especially to parents about what they are doing in Chicago for such long hours every Saturday. "Lying is a major thing," one boy says. A day at the beach is easy to account for in the summer, and a day of shopping at the mall during colder weather provide plausible excuses. But if they do not come out, the youth must invent increasingly fantastic lies, such as a sudden interest in museums, fictitious field trips for geology class, and mythical boyfriends or girlfriends whom the family never quite gets to meet.

Coming to the youth group is a passage from tormented isolation to a different kind of hiding for a brief time—a shared group secrecy. As Carol Warren has described it: "The settings of gay life, in turn, are places where the secret is shared . . . But once inside . . . secrecy is removed by co-presence."[13] Today this process has a different meaning in the setting of Horizons because the shared liminal secrecy of the youth group will ideally lead to a public life as gay or lesbian. Indeed, the advisors, as we have seen in chapter 3, not only expect that they themselves will come out further, but they also have the explicit aim of helping youth to come out as a form of "graduation" from the "class" of the group. A new cultural consciousness which shuns secrecy begins to reign.

Letting go of the secrecy of the past can be intensely unsettling, as many youth have told us, because it may lead to new discoveries of the self. Here is nineteen-year-old Mark talking about his acceptance into Horizons:

> When I was growing up, in high school, I did feel as though I was obvious [gay]. I also felt that I still missed something: I didn't have a friend. Like . . . I still to this day don't even have a heterosexual male friend. But, um, you feel like there is no one else you can actually talk to. And, ugh, its such a strange experience—I mean to use the group, and actually feel accepted. And they're saying it to you: "There's nothing wrong—we actually all feel the same way!" So it's really weird, to make that transition—to be alone, even when you're in a crowded room, and then—you just walk to another crowded room [Horizons] and actually feel you're with the group.

This is the power of the territorial passage. Horizons is a "sacred zone," an area betwixt and between normal society and the invisible world of gays. The sense of the "sacred" is metaphorically marked by the emotions of revealing hidden desires, of ridding the self of shame, and is solid with new-found friends: the feeling of belongingness mortifies the old isolated self as it simultaneously energizes and protects the new self that is growing. Entrance and exit rites are marked, with observances of various kinds restricting who gets in and who goes out. Such boundaries are the means of containing not only the physical body of the youth but this new social identity associated with coming out of the dark secrecy of the past into the light of social day in the group.

Magical Thought

People who feel isolated become alienated from society; in turn they look toward secrecy for solace. Their secrecy, however, can create fear of the unknown, and inevitably they attempt to control the dangers on the outside by beliefs that have a tenuous foothold in social reality. The fear of what we might call the "loss of the self in any ritual transition," in this case loss of the "heterosexual self," is basic to the existential "life crisis" of youth who desire the same sex. Although they do not fully realize it, their fears are well grounded; their transformation from a negated and dogged "homosexual" or "bisexual" to a gay or lesbian being will give them a new kind of social and psychological identity. The coming-out rituals are one way of attempting to control these fears through magical presentations of the body and self.

All rituals that involve dramatic personal and social change are characterized by "magical thinking." Westerners may stereotype "magic" as a property of thought in primitive society and the peoples of those exotic cultures of simple technology who institutionalize beliefs about inanimate objects being alive. But as anthropologists have long known, magic is not a characteristic of a type of society as much as it is a type of thinking, or, if you like, a framework of hunches and hypotheses about the world in the absence of a scientific rationale that explains the working of this world. We all engage in magical thinking, some experts say, if only we care to look closely at how we reason in the world.[14]

Ritual makes special use of the propensity for what anthropologists call "sympathetic and contagious" magical principles; these have the power to alter basic perceptions of time and space. Sympathetic magic identifies a fantastical process that recognizes how an action performed on an entity or person in one place may effect a human elsewhere, such as the antique belief that a wax doll effigy will harm the person represented by the doll. With contagious magic, however, direct contact with an entirety or person infects someone by touching the other. For instance, the ordinary "germ" theory of American folk beliefs about sickness, such as the common cold, tuberculosis, or (wrongly of course) cancer or AIDS, are believed to be spread by physical proximity. And nowhere is this more apparent than in the coming-out rites—those experiences of extreme stress and doubt, of profound yearning and fear that transcend the material world, of the sort that gay and lesbian youth commonly face in approaching Horizons.

One magical thought concerns gender reversal: automatically wanting to dress and act like the opposite sex. The youth of both sexes fear this strange transformation. There is an underlying paradox in their fears of gender "inversion," one that is based on the oldest of the nineteenth-century representations of the "homosexual."[15] One nineteen-year-old boy remarked, "It cracked me up to see the drag queens and transvestites. They're ridiculous!" Many youth hold stereotypes that all lesbians are "man haters" and all gay men are "women haters." And yet, according to these myths, these same ogres desire to dress and act only as men if they are lesbian or effeminate male women if they are gay. One twenty-year-old girl talked about her first concerns in finding out about lesbians. She was eleven years old at the time. "They confused me. Whenever I heard about lesbians I wondered, if these women don't like men, then why are they masculine? They should be more feminine." Later, we will see, the youth turn this idea back upon themselves and society, via the notion of "gender blending," wherein the heterosexual role standards are made fun of and ritually reversed.

And yet another magical thought concerns the idea that if you interact with someone who is gay, "it" might rub off on you, like a contagious disease, and you will have it too. Youth group members report this attitude from some of their high school peers and family members too. The brothers of teenage boys in the group are reported to be among the most susceptible to the "germ theory" idea, fearing that if they interact with their brothers who are coming out they might "become gay" too.

Fear of "catching" AIDS is another of the most powerful magical fears that youth bring to the group. Many youth group members have commented soon after entering, "If I am gay does that mean that I've got AIDS?" or "I can't be gay, or else I'll get AIDS." Another version of this myth is that simply by entering the youth group they will "catch" AIDS, being around so many gays who must "obviously" have the disease. Overcoming the fear that AIDS will spread into their lives is no easy task. Conversely, many youths feel at some point that "safe sex" is obtainable—but only with younger people. As one boy expressed it, "If I only sleep with people my own age I am safe." This later idea is soon weakened but not eliminated by being educated about "safe" sex in the context of the youth group.

Of all such magical beliefs—the handmaidens of homophobia and closet homosexuality—none is more profound nor widely shared than the notion that if one pretends to be straight, and hides or ignores feelings of being gay or of desiring the same sex, eventually these painful and fearsome desires "will go away." Some clearly believe in this magic, at least at first. Here is a Filipino youth, a member of the group, who recently began college in Chicago: "I hate to admit it, I really hate to admit it—I would say I haven't come out, I am just confused. I'm not sure about ever coming out, because it is something to do with my family—which is my primary concern." At school, he says, "I am 100% hidden. I don't want to be labeled. I just feel that being homosexual is not accepted . . . if you are in a straight environment. And I don't want to be humiliated." This is an understandable reaction to same-sex desires in a society that is homophobic. Some youths have expressed the feeling that they are damned to hell by God if they express their desires for the same sex. They hope that by prayer or by avoiding sexual situations their desires will go away.

Just how great are these fears of sympathetic and contagious magical change? During the early process of coming out many youth have thoughts of destruction, and about a third of them have in the past attempted suicide (see chapter 5). They are clever at hiding these fears, especially at first, but eventually they "out" them as well. Of course they are skilled at deceiving themselves as much as others: for years they have lived with a secret nature. For instance, the youth group director once told an advisor to pay attention to a black youth at a meeting; the week before the boy had been very depressed and had alluded to suicidal thoughts. Yet the advisor was surprised to hear of this, even though he was talking to the youth and had gotten to know him. The advisor remarked that only the day before the kid had seemed "bright and lively." "Compartmentalization of feelings—

these youths are brilliant at it," the director responded. We must not forget that in the turmoil of the transition from the profane to the sacred inner world of Horizons the teenager must rattle the doors of heaven and hell to break free.

The Youth Group Meetings

The overriding feeling the anthropologist finds in the Saturday morning rap groups is one of exhilaration, the zest and bounce of youth eternal. They are full of life, these teenagers; one thinks first of a high school weekend event where the adults are gone. Being free of supervision, able to "be yourself" and "show off," are the privileges of American youth on Saturdays. The mood is characteristic of the meetings, though one sees quickly enough that it belongs more fully to the older members of the group who are well established in coming to the group. The newcomers are more reticent and anxious. As they engage in the group, their fears evaporate soon enough, especially once they become involved in its social activities. These youth are both hidden and partially out. Certainly there is a mixture of people in their degrees of being out, and sometimes within the same individual there are both "out" and "secret" sides of the self living together in a volatile truce.

The older members greet each other with hugs and kisses in the lobby, and sometimes the daring ones go into the street in front of the building and screech, kiss, and otherwise "carry on." They are showing off, or better put, showing "out." The safety of the doors are nearby, however. Once inside the kids mill around the lobby for a few minutes, a plain corridor with old lounge chairs, a coke machine, a hand-me-down secretary's desk, and a bulletin board with myriad announcements of gay and lesbian activities in the community. There is a strong physical dimension of belongingness always at first: touching and holding, embracing and clasping hands. It is a wild energy, friendly, not erotic, in any overt sense. There are boys on girls' laps and girls holding hands and kissing their male friends, not only to greet them but at also to thank them or express their joy in them. The advisors are subdued by comparison, friendly and smiling, but more sober and adult: after all they are not only guardians but the citizens of the nation. The advisors usher everyone into the main meeting room of the building. It is a space not unlike a high school "recreation" room. The floor is covered with tattered carpet; there are old metal folding chairs, and odd pieces of hand-me-down furniture scattered around the room. The lighting is not very good. Bright but worn posters from old concerts, benefits, and museum shows adorn the walls. In the larger inner room the advisors call the youth group to order.

The meetings vary in size, according to the season, the quality of the weather during the day, and whether there are holidays, such as Thanksgiving, approaching. The meetings during the time of our work had an average attendance of some twenty-five teenagers, with an average of five advisors in attendance. The youth group leader welcomes everyone. On a typical Saturday the advisor, Johnnie, a very kind and mild man in his early thirties, opens the group. He greets all of the members, asking if anyone is new to the group. The "newcomers" raise their hands and introduce themselves. Then the advisor leads the group in clapping for each of the new ones in turn and repeating their names, which may not be their real names. These new youth are usually uncomfortable to have attention drawn to them. They could barely enter the door, let alone take the spotlight. They are commended for their courage in coming to the group. He truly makes them feel special and appreciated. But this social reward, too, is part of the process: having journeyed this far, they are joined in a circle of youth who will become their most significant reference group during the entire ritualized transition, and perhaps for the rest of their lives.

Then the youth are split into two groups. The established members stay in the large room. All the new people are herded into a separate, smaller room, with a subset of the advisors, where they must stay and meet for the four weeks, according to custom. No exceptions are allowed. Some youth are exasperated and others enraged by this special treatment. But a ritual has begun.

The New People's Group

In the new people's group begins what we might call the "stripping" process that transforms these youth into ritual initiates. Between normative social states, they are treated as having special powers, as dangerous to society; they are considered morally irresponsible and bound to fail in advance unless they follow the moral rules that set them apart. They are, as the German sociologist Georg Simmel[16] might have said of their secrecy, entering a process of "de-individuation"—that is, the individual identity markers and bodies of themselves are wiped away, so that they can become members of the hidden group. Now they are members of a batch, an age-set, subject to common proscriptions and prescriptions of conduct, which their peers and adults will oversee.

And how do the advisors feel about them? From private interviews with advisors, and more importantly from observing their informal behavior "backstage" with each other, it is clear that handling the newcomers group is no fun. The advisors often regard the smaller group at best as a challenge, a "learning experience," and at worst as a burden. It is chore to struggle with the strong and fearful emotions of the newcomers. Some of the advisors dislike the job. They prefer the more experienced kids in the larger group. The advisors are there to "screen" the youth, referring the more troubled youth to the Horizons' Psychotherapy Service or other counseling services. They are also the people who will provide a general orientation to Horizons and the youth group, describing and explaining, intermixing folklore and practical knowledge. Advisors are charged with answering questions that the youth put to them. Doing so eases the anxieties of the kids' initial experience, but also burdens the advisors with unanswerable questions about the nature of life. ("Why is homosexuality so bad for society?") It may seem ironic, in the informal pecking order of who is asked and who "volunteers" for the job of staffing the new people's group, that the newest and least experienced advisors take on such an important and demanding responsibility. They may have "come out" themselves only within the past several years. The irony fades, however, when it is realized that these young adults—who never went through such a youth group themselves—have the opportunity to come out in a new way by identifying with and handling the brave younger initiates.[17]

The youth may feel the squeeze of being defined as "gay" simply by being in the group. After all, they arrive bringing as much denial as need. As if he knows what the youth are thinking, the next thing Johnnie does is to state pointedly: "Our objective is to assist young people" in exploring their identities. "We don't make assumptions about your sexual orientation ... Anyone can come here. We don't assume what your orientation is just by being here." He congratulated the kids again for their courage and strength in coming. In this way, the youth are freed to identify themselves as they will. A few refer to themselves as "homosexual" or "gay." But most chose not to label themselves, or they speak of being "unsure," or "bisexual." Clearly, not all of the youth who come to the group are gay or lesbian-identified; several individuals come in support of relatives or friends. One young woman attended for a few weeks because her younger gay brother was coming out and she wanted to understand the process he was going through. She identified herself as "straight" and she was well accepted by the group. Another boy, who came to be known as "Straight Sam," was self-identified as heterosexual. He said that he wanted to rid himself of prejudice against gays, and later he said (in private interviews) that he himself had been called "gay and queer" in high school—a stigma that stayed with him. (His case is complex and is discussed below.) He was not accepted at face value for what he claimed; many of the youth befriended him but did not believe that he was "straight." These two cases are exceptional. The great majority come to the group to express same-sex desires in the form of gay and lesbian identities.

Despite the exuberance of the larger group, the newcomer's fears sit heavily on them, and once they are removed from the experienced members of the larger group, the whole atmosphere changes. It is often tense and strained. One of the female members complained bitterly of the mood in the new peoples' group, about which she had a "very bad feeling." "It's more like a wake or funeral than a youth group!" she offered. The kids are emotionally pondering past and present, one might say; and the advisors, especially the younger adults, are often unsure how to proceed or what to say. One of the overriding emotions is the fear that they have brought into the group and the fear of what they will find in "it."

How does one prevent the youth from being further stigmatized by society during the secret transition? The issue is vital in the period before the youth decide to come out. There must be rules of collective secrecy to live by. These ritual rules—the process of "de-individuation"—are cemented in this first meeting. The youth lose their names, their regular, out-in-the-world social names, especially their surnames. In fact, many youth who enter the group use false names or nicknames when they are introduced, for fear of being discovered: they are not out yet. Later they might change this and reveal their true names. The newcomers are told that they must not use these names on the outside; doing so would violate the secrecy and privacy of the other kids. They are told not to approach the other youth in public places where their hidden identities might be revealed to their parents or friends. True to the spirit of ritual initiation, this dis-identification with their old selves not only paves the way for a new self to emerge; it lays the foundation for a kind of "heightened self-consciousness" characteristic of secret societies.[18] This ritual secrecy of the newcomers is a necessary precaution to protect them before they enter gay and lesbian culture.

The initiates lose other privileges too, being subject to a common lore of identity and experience. There are no class privileges, and no special notions are allowed. The hazing that they receive, such as it is, is common to them all. Soon enough, if they return to the group and begin to make friends, they will be joked with and gently kidded informally—about their hairstyles or clothes or their reluctance. Inside of the group meetings, however, their ideas and concepts will be the object of intense scrutiny and debate by the other youth, who will ridicule any sign of what they call "homophobia" or "internalized self-homophobia" in newcomers. To whom do the youth turn to in the coming weeks? To an extent they can rely on the advisors, to make a real difference. But they are told that they must not fraternize with the advisors outside of the group because it is "inappropriate."

The youth turn especially to their fellow initiates for solidarity. They befriend each other; they choose each other to first reveal their true names and exchange telephone numbers. Later they will some-times trade clothes, share money or food, and make loans to each other. They will invite their new friends for lunch after the meetings, and maybe later they will get invited to parties, to those special apart-ments of a few of the really lucky gay youth: the ones who live on their own. Meanwhile, they are exposed to the same crisis together. They cry together—they go through everything together. In fact, in the world of gay and lesbian culture, to say of a friend that "you came out together" is the greatest endearment.

A typical new people's group rap in 1987 was constructed around the theme, "What are gay people like?" There were five boys (two black, one Asian, two white), four girls (three blacks and one His-panic), and two advisors present. The advisor Johnnie opened the dis-cussion by asking the kids' opinions about the theme. The youth of-fered many words of praise for gays; they are "nice," "creative," "honest," "hard working," and "intelligent," in a discussion that was as glib as it was "polite and politically correct." Only when Johnnie changed the topic to elicit invidious comparisons did the group come alive. "What do people on the outside think about gays?" This initiated a wave of excited comments. People in "society" believe that "we are sissies, fags, dykes without any real personality," one boy said. Another remarked, "They think that all gays have AIDS." One girl mentioned that people who think gay men are "child molesters," and that all "gay women are masculine and weight lifters." Another volunteered that "gays are sex crazed, and lesbians hate men." "Gay men are florists or hairdressers, that's all they think we can be!" Guy, a black youth, said that gay men are supposed to "rape children" and he felt that this was based on the "John Wayne Gacey" case. The advisor responded, "In fact research has shown that the majority of child molestation is done by straight men." Then Guy added that he did not believe that "Gacey" was gay anyway; instead, he said, "Gacey was just a violent rapist who primarily chose young men as his victims." The advisor praised the point, adding that it was "helpful to show that sex, which should be pleasurable for both partners, was not rape, which was sheer violence and aggression, using sex as its instrument."

As the discussion proceeded a young black woman took offense to the word "lesbian." She said it sounded like a "disease," and "why can't we just be called gay females"? The other advisor then asked if anyone knew where the word "lesbian" came from. Tiffany, a young black woman, responded that she thought it came from "a legend about the poetess Sappho, who lived on an Island called Lesbos, with only women." The advisor suggested that women adopted the term "lesbian" to distinguish themselves from gay men. He did not say why. Tiffany then countered the first girl by saying that she liked the word lesbian because "it made her feel special and different from gay men."

Johnnie then returned to the original question: What are gays like? Could gays be parents, for instance? One black woman said she knew of two gay men and a lesbian who lived together and had decided to have a child. Both men slept with her "to avoid problems of determining who the father could be; they stayed together and reared the child." Someone raised the concern that this triad "might rear the child to be gay." Was it right to do that? Charlie, another youth, did not think it would happen. He was reared with brothers and sisters, and he always "enjoyed trading clothes with his sisters." He lived in the ghetto, where you might be killed for being a "fag." But he "had to be himself," Charlie said, and it "pissed him off that some of the same guys who harassed him in public used to come and visit him for sexual favors." He said that he often thought of telling everyone that these tough guys were "fags just like I am," but they would have "literally killed him" for that. Charlie concluded by saying that he feels his "upbringing hasn't affected his being gay" at all. Guy echoed the point. He said that he has two kinds of relatives; "those who are gay," with whom "he can be himself," and those who are "straight," whom he "avoids."

The advisor asked if being gay was only about having sex? The group resoundingly responded "No!" Most of the youth perceived being gay as a "way of life." To some of the kids, being gay or lesbian has made them "different" beyond their "sexual preference." Tiffany said that it influenced "all areas of her life"—how she dressed, what she read, where she went.

Most of the youth said that they had always known that they were "gay." They couldn't figure out how it was they knew. This idea intrigued the group and led to many stories being shared. Jack, the white boy in the group, said that he was from a small "redneck" community where he and one black lesbian were the only "gays" in his whole town. They both attended the same school. He was struck by her because she was "so tough." He could never understand how others knew that he was gay. "I tried to act tough, to talk about sleeping with girls, but it didn't work." Charlie said he also "talked about fucking girls, pimping, and being tough; he even wore his hat tilted to the side, like the tough boys." Yet they would still say, "There's the fag!" He both laughed and sighed when he said this. Advisor Johnnie emphasized that their effort to "hide their gay identity may have made them stand out even more in their schools."

"Do all gays have AIDS?" Johnnie asks. All the group agreed emphatically that this was not true. How did such an idea start, they wondered? One of the black youth told a story that some Americans "in the army had abnormal relations with men over there that spread it." The advisor then said that AIDS was first diagnosed in 1981, that the doctors called it GRID—Gay Related Immune Deficiency syndrome. The doctors said that many young previously healthy gay men began to die of strange diseases. The discussion soon turned to the sadness of the epidemic, and then they fell silent.

During the fifteen-minute break and away from the youth, Johnnie told a story about a friend he had in high school. They went through the coming-out process together. But his friend wound up "heterosexual." He said "everybody had always thought of my friend as gay, and my friend believed himself to be gay. At age fourteen this boy came out to be straight because he realized that he was not interested sexually in men." One could see from the expression on Johnnie's face that the story still perplexed him. Perhaps somehow, he seemed to insinuate, there is less certainty in our sexual desires than we might think. But why did he not share the story with the group? When such incidents have occurred in the past, the advisor usually responds that it would be "inappropriate" to place his own concerns or needs in the group. The view is consistent with the idea that the advisors continue their own process of integrating feelings from the past into their present coming out. But viewed as a ritual process, another possibility seems obvious: to intrude such a story—which suggests that someone might "come out" as gay but later "come out" again as heterosexual, a sort of contemporary Tiresias[19]—might undermine the tenuous confidence that the youth have in their own feelings. They look up to the advisor; they place faith in his or her role and sage advice. Such a story might shake them into the same panic they feel when the bisexuals make presentations in the group (see below). No one can be certain of how his friend's story relates to this group, Johnnie implies.

Silence is a familiar party to the newcomers. Sometimes there are long, uncomfortable silences. A youth will suddenly break through the gap and say, "Somebody say something!" Then the kids all laugh. Some advisors, such as Buck, are also new to this experience. Buck is very friendly but nervous; he smiles a lot but doesn't say much, and when things get tense he tends to look down at the floor. He doesn't seem to know what to do or how to express his feelings; and yet his naturalness draws some youth to him during the breaks, especially the shyer boys, who look up to him. Johnnie steps in and tries to draw the shyer youth into talking. The youth may respond with an "I don't know" or a smile, and then the group lapses back into the silence. Sharon, the older advisor, once said that the youth need to "learn to cope with the silences too," and learn how to be "like adults" in this way. "They have to learn how to take responsibility for themselves, and not lean too heavily on the adults," to make their own way, she concluded. Still, some observers complain about the severe and starchy atmosphere of the new people's group.[20]

During this time, the pressures may mount, and some of the youth never return to the group. Pablo, a twenty-year-old Hispanic boy from Chicago, told of his struggle to first find the agency, and then how he quit several times. He is back again. He defined "coming out" as a period of time "where you are becoming comfortable within yourself, and then later with the gay community." "Being in the closet equals being uncomfortable," he said. "When I didn't like myself . . . being open was like having an 'open door,' where I could feel okay about myself." But the pressure on him from his family was intense. He found it hard to come to the group and harder to open up: "I needed help as a gay. . . . I had seen the movie *Consenting Adult* on TV, and they flashed the telephone number [of Horizons Help Hotline] on the screen afterwards. I saw the number but I didn't call until nine months later. As I made progress, I would come to the group, but then leave immediately after. Eventually I felt comfortable and I could go out with the others to socialize at Molly's, and then I started to make friends."

The youth who do continue in the group are no less pressed to accept the consequences. One of the newer members is sixteen-year-old Kim, who hales from a small town near Chicago. She seems sad in the group, vulnerable but with a streak of toughness. She has been at Horizons for a month. She is popular at school but doesn't feel close to anyone. Gay males are her closest friends. She doesn't feel close to women yet. When Kim tried to come out to her mother, she said, her mother's response was "cold." Kim got depressed. She cried while telling her coming-out story. She tried to commit suicide at age thirteen and a year later as well. She is doing better in the group, but she is still struggling to come out.

About a third of the youth group, as we discovered after our interviews had been analyzed later, have tried to take their lives at least once. This is very surprising for many reasons, not the least of which is that suicide does not ever come up as a discussion topic. One might say that suicide, as much as incest, for instance, is considered a taboo in our society but is never discussed in families. To speak of taking one's life is a threat from the past strong enough to create a reign of silence, not only in individuals, but in the collective memory of the group. Old stories from the early history of the group, some years before, tell of the dangers of silence. The advisor Morey remembered this story: "In 1985–86, a kid killed himself." Morey said that the boy was Asian, about eighteen years old. He continued intently:

This was a big blow . . . the youth attended his funeral. The boy had had problems, but they were not that big. The group was shocked. We didn't know anything about this . . . We were taken by surprise. I was leading a group one Saturday, and another advisor came in; he said that some girls [friends of the deceased] had come by to see if the boy had any friends in the group. I was instantly concerned ... this had to be handled just right. Everyone knew something was wrong. They piled out to the funeral.

During the time of our study this story was little known to the youth and never discussed, at least in the rap groups. Like those fabled myths that tell of the dangers of destruction and death, the story points to the fears of loss, literally the fear of death of the body, but more symbolically, to the dangers of being silent and not sharing one's conflict during the time of coming out.

There are no short cuts into the larger youth group. The newcomer's enclave represents a transition, a healing mirror of rebirth critical to the transformation of homophobic assumptions about self and social relations that must be "unlearned" before new challenges can be introduced. To undergo the change and pass the hurdles is hard; but in spite of the hassles, burden, and tedium of the group discussions, it is recognized that there is no magic trick that will substitute for the slow and painful working through of the past. To do so would abort the radical resocialization necessary for coming out, and that is what this phase of the ritual process is all about. As one psychologist who has long worked with the group said of the problem: "These kids are exposed to a series of mazes, an obstacle course, that has a healing effect of its own. I know of one boy who didn't go through the newcomer's group; later he tried to seduce me; when that failed, he tried to seduce Johnnie (which also failed). He was anxious and he got overwhelmed. He is a failure in the process, because he didn't go through the newcomer's group."

The Main Rap Group

Between their first meeting in the new people's group and their passage into the larger group, the youth develop a greater feeling of coming into the open and of opening themselves to new friendships. They become regulars. The norms of society continue to be suspended. The most often mentioned idea at this juncture is what the youth call their "vulnerability syndrome." It is an enigmatic idea, referring to their feeling that they are "safe" but also "vulnerable" to threats from the outside. To the regular members it is an idealistic sense of belonging to the Horizons group, a happy confidence that nothing bad can occur inside Horizons. The youth have created for themselves a "security circle," around which they can leave the secretive space of the newcomer's group and enter the more public (but still protected) space of the regular rap group. By surviving the trials of the first month, and by returning again and again, they have proven themselves able to adapt and worthy of belonging in the larger batch of the experienced initiates.

The larger group is also a ritual space. Prescribed practices occur here, but they have a quality of timeless being and becoming—one meeting merging into the other, people coming and going—but always abiding is the feeling that something profound is happening here. It is a holding environment with its own alliances and commitments, a reserve of good feeling and much good cheer. The older members of the group are largely proud of themselves, and they show it, not only in how they talk but in their actions, including the responsibility they take in helping the newcomers to enter the more boisterous and much more independent, larger group. It is here in the larger group that the main themes of group life emerge—hassles at high school, the trials of dating the same sex or of developing a lesbian or gay self, and the tasks of coming out. In the larger rap group, as one youth put it, no matter what comes up the "real issue of discussion is coming out." Not only how to do it, but "how to cope with it."

The moral sentiments of coming out, of doing the right thing, are critical to the idealism of the youth and to the utopian mission of the agency. Much of their early group experience centers on the social and moral barriers to being lesbian and gay. The conflict turns upon not being able to come out, which constantly creates controversies that the youth accept—up to a point. One nineteen-year-old boy remarked: "No I can't come out," he says, "not yet. Maybe in my late twenties, after I'm settled down, in a job, out of school . . . When you don't have to worry about discrimination at school." "At school," he continued, "I just have to hide it totally." A couple of the kids argued with him, but the others sat quietly brooding.

The larger group expresses a constant stream of physical energy and affection between the teens that confirms a social value for "commitment." They are helping and holding each other, but their physical contact is striking. They touch, breaking down tactile barriers with the newer members. Kissing is common. A very large girl in the group, who was a frequent member during the time of our study, was the source of much hugging and kissing for many of the boys, especially the younger gays. She was "safe" to them, a "giant teddy bear to snuggle and not worry about sexual hassles," Bowie said. Tremendous energy fills the room in the manner of adolescents greeting a winning sports team at high school, wanting to touch them and make them more real in their own eyes. They exchange jokes and insults with each other: "A girl can be a queen too!" Bowie kids a girl friend in the group that he thinks is acting "too butch," but then he grabs her wrist and embraces her strongly. They tease and joke constantly about sex, and sexual innuendos often fill the discussions. Romance fills the air; they invite each other out; sometimes the invitations are ambiguously neither purely social nor erotic; they discreetly arrange dates with each other, and then return with exciting stories or shattered hearts.

"Equality" is a strong value in the group. The social attitude of treating all persons as equal and of like merit and worth has been one historical ideology in the United States, and Horizons as an institution certainly reflects this value. It strives to ensure that both genders and persons of color are part of the leadership and advising group. The egalitarian ethic is strongly reflected in the youth group rap in many ways, but most noticeably in discussions about gender and about relationships between lesbians and gay men. As we noted in chapter 2, the question of gender parity and equal treatment are enduring themes of the history of gay and lesbian social activism in Chicago as elsewhere. While gender often comes up in discussion, racism is seldom touched upon and never discussed in the new people's group. The tenuousness of the secrecy and hiding experienced by members of the smaller group make it difficult to engage the fearful youth in such discussions of "diversity." In the larger group, however, advisors regularly engage members in talk about "diversity" in the "community." Of course, racial diversity does not automatically assure racial sympathy. Nowhere is this more true than in Chicago, and racial boundaries inevitably crop up in the group. However, racial bigotry does not exist in overt form in the group. A person's gender, class, or color does not not preclude the person being actively involved—and affectionately accepted—in the group.

In short, for many of the youth, their social and affectional world comes to revolve around Horizons, making its core values of increasing importance over those of their natal families and neighborhoods. Social solidarity is the net effect. As Sydney says, "It was the thing to do. You lived—I lived—for that day. I was there, nonstop." And his friend Tom joined in: "We *lived* for those days, and you know, it was exciting."

The kids cling to the emerging world view in the face of the adversities that continue to occur in the "real world" of their families and friends. Thus they begin to confront the fear that they have held back their "true selves" by not coming out to their parents. This does not mean that they will come out to their parents, only that they will decide to handle the problem, which may mean postponing it. An initiate, a twenty-year-old white Polish Catholic male, told of his problems from the Northwest suburbs. He first "came out" to a couple of friends three years ago, but only for three months; then he stopped. He used this time to "catch up," he says. He is comfortable but shy. He started going to the group, but then he pulled back and covered up his gayness. He told his cousin, to whom he was close, and then his mother. He never came out to his father or sister either. He sought a counselor. He talked with a priest and was offered prayers of social disapproval. There is a remorse in this sliding back, and a strong moralism of self-criticism about hiding the "true self." Kim, the sixteen-year-old girl from the suburbs, reveals this kind of characteristic rebuke: "I should be able to let people know who I am. I would like to let people know. But it's hard."

The youth, the older members especially, say that when the "heat goes up," people stay away for a while. They go away for a week or longer to "figure things out." They are maneuvering between their former heterosexual lives and the new entry points into gay and lesbian culture. The pressure from outside comes from parents or friends. It can be intense if the significant others do not know what the youth is up to; and even more intense if the adolescent has come out to parents and is fighting with them about it. Secrecy still defies their effort at self-transformation. A twenty-one-year-old boy of mixed nationality (Asian and Hispanic) described his feelings of coming out for a brief period to the new people's group two years ago, and then exiting, only to return to the larger group after he entered college:

No [I still can't come out] . . . I have to be secretive . . . I hide it by lying. My sister always asks me, where do you go, what do you do? [But] I could never come out to my parents, it would hurt them too much. After I graduate, I want to live out from my family . . . I don't want to be closeted. I want to explore this life style. I envy these fifteen-year-old kids. [I have to hide with] other people, but not with myself. I just think that it's [homosexuality] bad. I went to a Catholic school. "God created man and women." [I was attracted to one boy, but it frightened me.] I just thought I had to go back to girls again, I was so confused (after masturbating and thinking about "that man"). I came out to a kid from Horizons two years ago. He's only sixteen years old and he knows more than me. He was advising me on all these situations. I felt so naive. He obviously knew that I was gay because I was here. He was the first person I talked to about my life . . . I would say he was my tutor. That was the first time I felt I needed to talk about myself. It was nothing difficult, he was sincere. I trusted him.

Listening In

We will listen in on a rap group meeting from May 1987. On this occasion the director of the agency, who for some years had also led the youth group, called the group to order. He began by asking for a show of hands of those who had attended for more than a year. Five raised their hands; five others indicated that they had attended for more than six months. The director then praised the remaining six relatively newer members and asked them to give their first names and say where they were from.

After the newer members had introduced themselves, the director described a conference on gay youth he had attended in Los Angeles. He told the group about the meeting and focussed on how information was being exchanged around the country. Youth groups are springing up nationwide, he said. He then passed around some printed material that other organizations are making available for gay youth. These included the following: a gay comic book, "Tales of the Closet" (Summer/Fall, 1987), put out by the Institute for the Protection of Gay and Lesbian Youth in New York; a pamphlet on a "name-calling workshop" in Massachusetts; a pamphlet on homeless youth in Los Angeles, with the emphasis on dealing with problems in sexual orientation; a pamphlet from "Project 10" on gay youth support, published by the Fairfax High School, Los Angeles.[21] A potpourri of the emerging national gay culture.

Next he turned to ask the youth what they thought about their experiences since being in the Horizons program. What did they regard as the most positive changes in their lives over the past year? Six youth made comments, including two black boys, one black girl, two Caucasian boys, and one Caucasian girl, all largely concerned with the greater support and respect they have found. The new people were more comfortable than before; they found others to be friendlier; they had accomplished more while being at Horizons; and they were more out about their feelings of being gay than ever before. Some youth commented that Horizons was positive because in the past gay youth were too "queeny"—they had exaggerated effeminate features in language, gestures, and dress. They now experienced less pressure in how to act and didn't feel compelled to act out stereotypes. People acted "more grown up" now. One boy noted that when he first came out he felt he had to wear make up, which he hated, and to dress in a flamboyant way. The youth all agreed that they now dressed and acted in a more "normal" gendered way.[22]

The discussion then centered upon problems related to coming out in the Chicago high schools. The youth complained about being physically assaulted. The advisor asked for a show of hands of those who had been assaulted at school; five raised their hands. One boy noted that he had "won" in a recent fight when someone harassed him. The group consensus was that high school in Chicago is now more liberal and there is more respect for gay youth. Now they are "more accepted," several of them said. But in a few high schools in the suburbs, the youth find it necessary to stay in the closet because it is too "dangerous mentally and physically to come out." A heavy-set girl with big glasses said that she would not dare to expose herself as lesbian in her suburban high school. Other teenagers talked about fears of being "too open" at school or in the neighborhood, of needing to take care not to reveal too much in too many different places.

A youth who has frequently been harassed at school said, "I'm switching to a gay high school." The school he mentioned in Chicago is for the arts and is, according to the boy, "about 80 percent gay, and the rest don't care." In fact, the number of lesbian and gay students need not be higher than in other high schools. The important thing is that the gay students are out and their straight peers have positive attitudes about them.

Many youth said that they want to have a program for gay youth in their own high schools. They want to see others educated about what it means to be gay. Someone suggested making a videotape about the Horizons groups.[23] Someone said that such a high school program would threaten the "straights." They talked of "passing" and "how to act straight." A lot of jokes about straights were told and even more were directed at gay youth who "act straight." One of the boys in his late teens told how he saw a gay friend hanging outside a bar recently, acting tough and "macho." "Oh you've got your leather coat on," he teased him. "You are so butch, man, so very tough! Yeah, I know Bobbie—you are such a MAN!" The discussion turned to the copycat nature of passing: "How to look, walk, talk, and smell straight," Jeffrey laughed.

Safe sex was another concern. One skinny white boy said that he handled it by not having sex at all. Many safe-sex campaigns target the youth. Awareness of AIDS and safe sex is generally at an exceptionally high level in the group, thanks to the constant efforts of the advisors. Indeed, many youth feel that the adults nag them and are obsessed with AIDS awareness. Being able to recite safe-sex guides is one thing; being able to follow the rules is another story. "The attitude exists among gay boys (and lesbian girls) at first that one need only sleep with young people to be 'safe.'" Jeffrey said. But that soon changes with the education campaigns. Nevertheless, "the norm," Jeffrey says, "is to be safe." He cites examples from the group to demonstrate how the practice is followed. Privately, he says that no one knows what anyone else does, but he thinks that not everyone "plays it safe."

The director then talked out about the history of Horizons—how it was founded, financed, and the role he plans in it as manager. He commented on its outreach to other groups. He also noted that grant proposals were beginning to raise money for Horizons. Finally, he spoke of his dream for the youth group that might be accomplished by the year's end: "to get a paid staff, to do more work with schools, to have a crisis counseling service for gay youth and their parents, and to get out the word better on the youth program."[24] He also said that he wanted to make Horizons more available to gay youth every day after school. And this was warmly approved by the group. One boy asked about how the youth could help at the center. Could they serve as advisors? He replied that there was a minimum age requirement of twenty-one. They should do more active things in the gay and lesbian community, the kids agreed.

During a break, a woman advisor told one of the older female members of the group about a women's feminist conference that was going to be held at a local university on the next weekday. She said that some important discussions would occur and encouraged the youth to go along on her own if she was interested. She implied that this was an important way of building the "community."

The following Saturday, Sharon and Johnnie led a discussion on "life goals." The advisors passed out pieces of paper on which the youth were asked to write their near and long-term goals. This exercise led to a lengthy but frustrating meeting for the kids and advisors alike. The girls dominated the discussion; the boys in general talked only briefly, and then only on what one of them called "physical" goals, such as "getting into shape" and "going to school." Karyn discussed her goals of moving to California after school, going to college, getting money for school fees, and becoming a musician. She could talk about feelings, and later expressed the thought that being a musician was her "father's dream for her." No boys volunteered their goals. Sharon then asked: "Are there any emotional goals or ways you want to work on personally?" Another boy added that he wanted to "lose weight." Karyn talked about quitting smoking, but felt that it was "unrealistic."

When Sharon asked the youth about their long-term goals, the group was silent. Sharon wondered aloud if this might not be because of what their parents had wanted. The youth were silent until Karyn broke the ice again, saying that her "life was in a rut." She only went to work, came home, went to work, and was out on the weekends. Mark, another boy in the group, said that being in a rut was frightening. He said that he didn't like what his parents' lives had become; sitting around, a television in every room, bored; it "scared him." "What do you do when you don't have goals?" Sharon asked. Karyn and several other female youth talked about relationships; but again the boys remained quiet. One boy then added, "You can't make someone into what he isn't or feel what he doesn't." During this time Bowie was making faces. He broke in impatiently, saying that he had no goals and lived life "totally with expectations or goals" because "I don't want to be disappointed." Roong said that he felt being gay "has not changed any of his goals." But a girl disagreed. Sharon ventured that coming out may make some goals hard to obtain—goals from the past such as having children. Johnnie concurred with her, but all the youth fell silent. The discussion ended.

Seldom had we seen the youths so reticent as in this meeting. The boys had been unwilling to talk about feelings, the girls only slightly more verbal. All of the youth seemed unable to freely form long-term goals. The liminal nature of their position in society makes this understandable. They are moving between states, with the only clear goal being to come out. Yet the barrier to envisioning future times suggests a major stumbling block in their development, a problem to which we shall return in chapter 6.

Liminal Bisexuality

Anthropologists have not always described the sexual aspects of the rites of passage, even in small-scale societies.[25] Sometimes the erotic content was not relevant, and sometimes their own prudishness steered them away from the issue.[26] Yet as it was described long ago, the "sexual nature" of initiation is basic to those "rites of separation from the asexual world" that are "followed by rites of incorporation into the world of sexuality."[27] For gay and lesbian youth, the romantic and sexual content of their selves and social identities are undergoing radical change, and thus learning new ways of how to handle all of their sexual desires, including those for the same sex, is the next phase of the ritual process.

As they enter the group more fully, they face one of the most profound fears and mythic beasts of the ritual process: the bisexual. The issue of fearing that they are "really bisexual" and not gay or lesbian is important for two fundamental reasons. Historically, the bisexual represents, in some ways, a mediating position between homosexual and heterosexual in the traditional American cultural system. The bisexual is a shined-up version of a twentieth-century species, the liberated hedonist, that mediates gay and straight, the newer cultural system of sexuality in the United States. Politically, it follows that if you can be "bi," the moralist rhetoric of the New Right suggests, perhaps you can really be "straight." That logic implies that there is more "choice" in the matter of sexual desires than gays argue. But there is another factor as well: the sense in which in order to come out the youth must come to grips with whether he or she may be bisexual, not gay or lesbian, in their desires.[28]

For a minority of Horizons youth—the exact number of which shifts depending upon what is "counted" and how one "measures" sexual identity development—"bisexuality" identity marks a transitional social time between what they were and what they will be.[29] Youth are pressured at home, at school, and even at Horizons; some are deeply conflicted about their sexual identity. In this circumstance it is no wonder that the rituals of coming out protect the youth from too much pressure; they provide a time "outside" of heterosexual development, and at Horizons a social space to breathe before having to say to adults, "I am a this" or "I am a that."

It is true that the "bisexual" is more accepted in gay culture—especially in the new rhetorical ideology of Queer Nation, and in local cultural scenes, such as the popular club, "The Berlin," just around the corner from Horizons. One cannot be certain from physical appearances or cultural style who is gay, straight, or "in-between," to use John Money's language.[30] In some circles, at least, "bisexual" is becoming a more stable cultural identity of some currency, though not as salient as straight or gay.

Not long after our project began in 1987 the youth group devoted its usual Saturday afternoon larger rap discussion to "bisexuality." To kick things off, a local bisexual organization sent representatives, one man and one woman, to speak to the youth, as they do once or twice a year. The group has lots of requests of this kind, "Some of them are quite crazy and bizarre," the advisors told me. "So we have to screen them out carefully." Afterward there was a group rap. A youth said spontaneously, "As we were coming out it was easier to say, 'I'm bisexual,' than one extreme or the other. It's less threatening."

Some youth expressed strong feelings of rejection when a partner went to someone of the opposite sex. "It was very degrading and hurtful—more than with the same sex," a boy said. Three youths reported in the discussion negative experiences with "bisexuals." But the self-identified bisexual adult woman who had spoken to the kids retorted, "Don't overgeneralize! We are not all like that!" Then the older bisexual man said ironically, "I've been faithful to my wife for seventeen years!" (But he did not talk about being "faithful" to his same-sex partners—a point that was not lost on the advisors, who joked about it later.)

The youth group leader said privately of the bisexual presenters:

> The bisexual group has a strong impact on the youth. The kids get anxious and crazy for three weeks after the bisexuals present. The bi man who came here said, "I can be butch and fuck a guy or be straight, and a breeder, and screw fish [pejorative term for women used by some youth]. And I can have it both." He was crude, yes. But the youth don't know what to do or to think after this. They are scared a lot. They think to themselves, "Maybe I could be straight too, or bi." It causes problems for their relationships for a few days.

Later, the group leader cautioned us about interpreting the results of the discussion among the youth prematurely. He suggested that we wait a few days to see what would happen with the kids.

He was right. The next two Saturday meetings had a different atmosphere. More than the usual number of the youth did not come back immediately; some seemed overly restless. A number of youth said during the following meeting that they can feel very "deep" with the opposite sex, but do not have sexual intercourse with them. "They get along better with the opposite sex" (especially males)," one advisor commented. Yet, the youth did not seem as confused about bisexuality as the advisors, such as Johnnie, had suggested they might feel.[31] "It made some of them feel like they do have options. They don't have to be one way or the other—and they don't have to reject bisexuals."

The advisor Sharon commented, "The youth feel inadequate with these bi partners. They can't satisfy sexually the partner who chooses to be bi." And another advisor added, "How can that guy come here and say," 'I can be butch and fuck a guy or be straight,' etc., etc. It's too much." The whole experience "really turned him off," he said. His colleague concluded, "We have to be more careful about allowing outsiders to talk."

A few of the older teenagers expressed negative feelings about "bisexuals." When a partner went to someone of the opposite sex, it was experienced as more painful and rejecting than if they had taken a same-sex lover. Janie, a sixteen-year-old lesbian, said that "her lover had up and gotten married on her a few months back." Janie thinks her former lover can't stay "monogamous." "She's such a slut," she said. "She overvalues sex." It is harder to accept their feelings about the opposite sex. Janie again: "It took me forever to get to the point of accepting that my sister really desired the opposite sex. I didn't think it could be as extreme as me. She desires the opposite sex and only wants the opposite sex!" Janie argued with another girl over the question of having children. Janie denied that she was much concerned with having children. But the other girl felt differently. She is in a lesbian relationship, but she is troubled. She implied that her desire for social acceptance is leading her eventually to want children—so must she get married or can she do this with her female lover?

Bisexuality implicates AIDS. In a group discussion, Bowie noted that some of his lesbian friends were not responding to AIDS in the way that males were. He said "some of his friends were angry with the lesbian community because they weren't taking AIDS seriously." They seemed "remote and distant." Marshie, his young friend, sitting beside him, said that she was "scared of AIDS." She knew there were bisexual people, and she was very concerned about having sex with them. Someone else remarked that the people "who were most dangerous to be with were bisexuals." Marshie wondered if she could "come down with AIDS as a result of being involved with women" particularly, when she didn't know if they had a "bisexual history."

There was some joking on the side about "Straight Sam" and how he would have reacted to the bisexuals if he had come to the group that day. Sam, the Caucasian teenager from the suburbs mentioned earlier, continued to maintain that he was "straight" for the weeks that he came to the group. Long after, he was the focus of endless jokes and puns and riddles.

But one of the youth defended being bisexual. Bluey, a heavy-set, good-natured African-American guy remarked: "At one time I was so horney I would screw anything with two legs. Now it feels different. I could have sexual feelings for a man or a woman; and if I had feelings for that person I could stay with them."

Given the old myths of our society, one might have thought that a large number of youth who come to Horizons would be "bisexual." After all, many youth at one time or other may have said to friends or social contacts, "I'm bi," and we have observed this on occasion. Youth who say they are bisexual tend to be more conflicted about themselves and their desires, as we have found from interviews (chapter 5). But they are few in number. In the main, the larger group of youth who refer to themselves as "bisexual" do so transiently and move on to self-identify as gay or lesbian by the end of adolescence. In general, youth advisors prefer the view that youth are not confused about their sexuality, they are only confused about how to express it.

It is in this sense that "bisexuality" represents a state of being that is transitional: the very essence of the rites of passage. Thus we see how the liminal effects of bisexuality, like all other liminal creations, must be contained at Horizons. As the advisors intuitively know, the anomalous is threatening to the sought identity—gay or lesbian. Bisexuals may even endanger the bodies of the wards they are entrusted to protect. The youth must be protected from too much exposure to the confusion of boundaries, the advisors feel, for clarity is sacred in this matter. The myths warn of the dire consequences of transgressing the taboo of being a bisexual or being with one. The myth is not reality, of course. It is another order. But in this way the mythic construction of bisexuality holds a powerful grasp on the construction of social reality for the youth.

New Places to Come Out

Social occasions of going out with other members of the group constitute a new and significantly deeper commitment to coming out. One
of the most important of these social practices is familiar to every
American: having lunch at a fast-food hamburger chain restaurant, a
youth "hang out" near Horizons. For the first time, the youth socialize
in public with others who may be identified as gay or lesbian, whose
association magically transmits the same image to himself or herself.
Many feel anxious and threatened at this juncture. One seventeen-
year-old boy was asked by the kids to go with them, but he invented
excuses to diplomatically "postpone" going. "I wasn't ready for that
yet." But most of the teens who have reached this point in the ritual
process are thrilled to be invited because the invitation confers the
status of friendship on them by the long-time members. Setting aside
temporarily the concept of whether they are "gay," other challenges
emerge once their participation has begun. They search for ways and
means, usually in the form of new places to wear the identity, to discreetly come out. In doing so they begin to confront a fundamental
aspect of ritual process: how to be a member of the youth group—
that is, a faithful citizen entering into gay and lesbian culture—and
how to be "true to the self" and their other cultural traditions, such
as their ethnic group or neighborhood.

Many of the regulars from the group go to a place they humorously
call the "Burger Queen" after Saturday afternoon meetings. One particular Saturday, a group of three, including Jeffrey, saw a youth group
member cross the street. Later they are joined by seven others. The
conversation turned to what people were doing, and what this boy,
about eighteen years old, Bobbie, was doing in particular. They hadn't
seen him in a while, they gossiped. One of the girls said that Bobbie
had taken a job with an "escort service" for gay men. The escort service, they assumed, was a transparent cover for a male prostitution
ring. Jeffrey tells the story.

> I was shocked. Bobbie introduced me to Horizons and was once a good
> friend. And he was the closest thing to a gay prude that I ever met! We
> passed into a shop, and I asked, "And Bobbie is a prostitute?" At that
> very moment, Bobbie, who was on the other side that we couldn't see,
> stormed out of the store, slapped my friend on the back of the head,
> and shouted that he had quit the group. He ran down the alley out of
> sight. I was totally flabbergasted. My friend's reaction was simply to

laugh, since he and Bobbie were no longer on speaking terms. The girl who was with us was deeply embarrassed. My friend told us to calm down. Later I found out that it was common knowledge in the group that Bobbie was a prostitute. The atmosphere returned to normal once we got to the restaurant. The others from the group were already eating. Nothing seemed out of the ordinary. We had fun commenting on the various eligible young men that walked by the windows. Someone brought a toy mouse as a prank. It was a riot to hear some queen squeal from a group member when he thought that he had a mouse in his French fries.

Sometimes the regular group is suspended in favor of another activity. During the Memorial Day weekend of 1987 the group met to put on a play. They had been practicing after hours. The cast was open to whoever volunteered. There were six people involved, four girls and two boys. The play was scheduled to compete at an upcoming AIDS fund-raiser in Newtown. In the summer these fund-raisers may be a picnic. One of these occurred soon after the Memorial Day performance. The picnic occurred in the grassy area behind the "Rocks," the gay part of the Lake Michigan beach where sexual "cruising" is prominent. Jeffrey reports:

> It was a sunny day. Included in this group were two new people. We went along the rocks comparing notes on the different men. One of the girls was complaining that all the women were in couples and that women would not just "trick" like the gay male population. The comments were about the looks of the men, including those made by the women. One that stuck out was how we lambasted a man who was very middle aged, and had an old body. We commented on how a man with that figure could have the nerve to wear a G-string. The group split and went different ways, agreeing to meet at the bar that had become the Saturday night hang out for the group.

Being at Horizons offers a new opportunity: a context in which to mingle with adult gays and lesbians who are over twenty-one and beyond the group. Many of the youth from the regular group also participate intermittently in the Wednesday evening rap group, which opened during the time of our study. As noted in chapter 3, the Wednesday meeting has a more social atmosphere, less regulated by adults. Youth who cannot come on Saturdays and young adults who work and are older, up to their mid-twenties, participate. They seem more diverse, older, and worldly. They meet in the large carriage house behind the agency, where the *Windy City Times* is located, on the fourth floor room reserved for Horizons activities. Thus the location as well as some of the participants are somewhat on the margins.

On a typical Wednesday evening one is struck by how dark the room is, with blaring music and a party atmosphere. There are small windows, dim lights, and chairs are scattered around the room. This night there were twenty-three youth, sixteen males and seven females. A minority were Caucasian. Many of them were smoking; drinking is not permitted. The regulars didn't mingle much with the larger group. The groups seemed independent from each other. So many youth are "gender blended," that in the dim light, one can hardly distinguish between the genders. Perhaps this is one of the desired effects of the androgynous clothes, streaked hair, nose rings and earrings, with an intimacy of hugging and dancing that blurs the boundaries of bodies. Though Queer Nation was not yet established in Chicago during this time and was unknown to most youth of Horizons, one can glimpse its aesthetic gestation in such youth settings. "Are you a girl or a fag?" a boy playfully asks another; and yet, one could not help but notice the sarcasm in his voice. By the window is a group of Hispanic boys dancing together. One of them is dancing flamboyantly, while the others generally ignore him, talking. One group includes a white girl, two black men, and a white boy who are playing "hangman" on the chalkboard.

In the regular Saturday afternoon groups, the long-time members seem to associate with each other, both sexes and all colors. They form a core. Black, Caucasian, and Hispanic are together. Yet the women advisors and the girls sometimes cluster separately for special events, the men and boys going into another room. At the Wednesday evening group, color becomes more prominent than before. There is voluntary segregation as the youth fall into subgroups. The feeling of the members is that people like to be with "their own kind" in more intimate settings such as this. "The only thing frowned upon is grandstanding. Comments such as , 'I wish she weren't so Hispanic' have been expressed, and then disapproved by the youth," Jerry says. "When you are being chased around and never accepted, you can't have people in this group doing the same," another boy offered. Other members have to be supported. "Commitment" and "equality" as social values take precedence.

A rowdy and showy group of slick and punk-dressed Caucasian men soon walk in, most of them looking older, in their mid-twenties. They are well dressed, smooth, and loud. They seem intent on appearing "cool." Their status-consciousness immediately sets them apart from the other youth. Indeed, the other youth stay clear of them. The room pales now, drab by comparison with these "GQ types."[32] They seem out of place.

Some of the kids talk about going to see the midnight movie showing on Saturday night, the *Rocky Horror Picture Show*. The movie is a cult favorite of many "new wavers," and it is emblematic of the crowd who see it, some of them hundreds of times, it is said. And what is the show to them? It is filled with the images of androgyny; of deviants and people living on the fringes; of the undead who inhabit neither the past nor the future; of night people who escape the rules of society and live apart in a world of make believe, whose fun and horror is at one in the same time frightening and freeing. It is also the source of many a metaphor and idiom in the group. For instance, the popular youth Bowie took his name, and some of his fashions, from the movie. Many of the youth of Horizons have seen the movie and they adore it. It allows them a freer opportunity to out themselves—in a never-never land where the world has turned upside down.

The Old Rite: Seeking the Bars

Before the late 1960s social homophobia limited closet homosexuals' options for building social relations beyond private homes to the atmosphere of drinking and anonymous contact that always threatened legal entrapment.[33] For previous generations, "coming out" was not an introduction to a public culture but rather the attempt to protect secrecy through the anonymity of the bars.[34] Kenneth Read's poignant *Other Voices*, an anthropolitical study from the 1970s, showed how the experience of the homosexual bar did not lead to a presentation of the social "gay or lesbian self" beyond the confines of the doors of the bar.[35] As this trend changed, sex came into the open; to have sex with the same sex meant that one was "doing gay."[36] The gay male sexual actor, in what John Gagnon once called the new "cult of manliness," did what he desired.[37] Given the history of homosexual bars, it is understandable that some experts link them to various adult developmental problems, such as the feeling of low self-esteem and the high rate of alcoholism suspected to occur among gay and lesbian adults of previous generations.[38] Visiting these places a generation ago one might observe individuals who "went out" to the bars, which led to many developments but not to "coming out" in its contemporary sense.

Nowadays the cultural meaning of the bars is different. As the historical account in chapter 2 showed, both the significance of the bars and the way they are perceived have changed in Chicago gay and lesbian culture. Today, in Chicago, many other social arenas and places to meet and entertain exist, including restaurants, shops, churches, and of course Horizons. Gays and lesbians entertain in their homes openly; they host barbecues and picnics in good weather, and arrange social occasions to shop, visit the museums, and attend the opera in the winter. It is not that the bars have disappeared. Their numbers have actually grown, and they are a major tourist attraction for visiting gays from other cities and smaller towns. Rather, the process of socialization for gay men and lesbians does not begin in the bars. Adults may begin or end the evening in a bar, but they do not feel that it is the only safe or promising place to go. In fact, many adult informants in our study decried the bars and found them distasteful even for short visits.

One of the themes of youth group discussion and informal interaction is the bars. Seeking the bars was more strongly marked in the early youth group. "Going out to a bar for the first time was a really big deal," our informant said of his coming out in 1979. Lanny and his friends from the original youth group found that outside of Horizons, the bars remained the most likely place to meet and socialize. It was the place to seek prospective lovers. By 1987—the time of our study—the cultural meanings of going to a bar had clearly changed for gay and lesbian youth. Although legally underage, the kids had other reasons for not going to bars. Some of the youth, especially the religious ones and those from more conservative families, or from families in which alcohol was not used as a social lubricant, did not find the bars "cool" or "awesome." In short, they are considered unattractive haunts. They said that they feel the bars are smoky and somewhat frightening. One of the reasons for this feeling is the presence of older adults in the bars. Some of the youth, especially the ones who are still not out, generally feel uncomfortable around gay and lesbian adults. They are especially nervous around the "trolls," whom the youth see as taking liberties that offend them in the bars.

There are many other places for the youth to "hang out" and meet people. "Medusa's" is a popular nonalcoholic "juice bar" catering to youth just down the street from Horizons. Before 11:00 P.M., no one over the age of twenty-one is allowed inside; after 11:00, when alcohol is served, only adults over age twenty-one are admitted. Other informal haunts and meeting places include, for instance, the "Alley," a small row of shops and tattoo parlors that line an alley off of Belmont Street, around the corner from Horizons. The "Mountain Moving Coffee" house was an exclusively lesbian cafe popular with young lesbians, featuring music and poetry readings advertised in the lesbian newspaper.[39] Nearby Horizons there are also a new gay and lesbian bookstore, Molly's Restaurant, the Yidro Coffee House (which has a gay and "new wave crowd"), and many fast-food restaurants frequented by the youth. It is notable that all of these establishments are within a short walk of the Horizons center.

But some of the youth enjoy the bars and still find them an appealing wonderland. Jeffrey, for instance, regularly went to the bars illegally with his friends during the time of our study. Like his friends, Jeffrey was fascinated by the bars' mystique and enjoyed being in an evening spot where gays could congregate, drink, and dance. Many youth do not feel accepted by straight peers or at least not free to "mix" with them as self-identified gays or lesbians. Others who are more closeted simply dread the thought of unexpectedly meeting their straight peers from high school or their neighborhood in a compromising situation at a "hang out" where mainstream teens congregate, such as the nonalcoholic "juice bars." For these youth, the bars remain a preferred option for socializing, meeting people, and picking up sexual partners.

On a typical Saturday the kids attend the youth group meeting in the afternoon and hang out around town or in the apartment of one youth, Bowie, who lives with his lover nearby. Now it is evening. Fifteen Horizons youth (there is one guest from outside the group) have agreed to meet at Johnnie Walker's, which the youth know as a "hot spot." They are boys and girls, but a majority are boys. Johnnie Walker's serves alcohol and according to state law the youth should not be permitted inside. Somebody, the kids say, "has paid off the cops" to get teens into the bar. Youth in certain bars (gay and straight) are a "big attraction" to adult clients. They are of course a potential source of casual sex, and in certain places as well, a target for prostitution or, in gay circles, hustling.[40] They are admitted but are scared of being "busted" or arrested by the police. Yet they get free drink coupons from the doorman, which helps to soothe their fear. At least they can go down to the basement bar, which is darker and less public, than the upper bars. And here several of the kids are known to the waitress "Dawn." She shows her pleasure in seeing her acquaintances from before. They seem more relaxed. She winks at them and they find a corner table.

They order drinks discreetly. Many of them are nervous, but the alcohol loosens them up, and soon they are joking. "The usual conversation at the bar isn't much different from the socials that Horizons hosts," one girl says. Bowie is in the bar with Jeffrey. They are best friends. "You are looking for a man, aren't you?" Bowie asks Jeffrey. "Just for fun, you flirt a little, hang out with friends. Everyone knows we are underage," Jeffrey says. "We're husband hunting," another kid giggles to the others. Jeff tells Bowie that a friend at Johnnie Walker's likes his looks. But Bowie simply grunts and complains, "Why should anybody want this bag of bones?" Jeff chastises him for his attitude, telling him to be more positive about himself. He accuses him of "internalized homophobia," the most popular admonition of the kids, especially in situations where they rebuke themselves. Bowie retorts with his favorite pet phrase about his own body: "They have discontinued this model." He thus justifies his decision to sit in the corner and remain uninvolved sexually.

Consuming alcohol or sexually "cruising" men is not the main purpose of going to Johnnie Walker's, Jeffrey says. Rather, the bar serves as a meeting place for some of the regulars of the group, who like to see night life. And moreover, it is a "center of action" in the gay community. It is a social place that provides good music, sometimes live music, with dancing. "The whole idea is strictly to dance," Jeff says. He continues: "Cruising occurs at the bar. But it isn't hot and heavy. I am not familiar with people going home with others they pick up in the bar. If the prospect occurred, I would be surprised if a one night stand arose. Even with the element of cruising, the main reason to go is still to socialize and dance. The main goal of the evening is to dance to your favorite song."

Yet Jeff worries about kids leaving the bar at five in the morning. He perceives Johnnie Walker's as being located in a traditionally "straight" neighborhood. Some youth have been verbally harassed on the street near the bar. (One of the adult members of our research team was verbally harassed on the street with his partner in this neighborhood.) Recently a youth of color was also harassed on the street, and the other kids came to his defense. The group members should not be so oblivious to the dangers of going to the bar nearly every weekend, Jeffrey feels.

The bars are of importance for two contrary goals. The first is to socialize, the second is to engage sexual partners. For youth such as Jeff and Bowie, the bars are for mixing and having fun. The teens on occasion meet prospective partners there, just as their straight peers might. The possibility of sexual interaction does pose a problem for them, however. With their awareness of AIDS, the teens realize that mixing alcohol with sex as prior generations have done, sometimes results in "taking risks" that would not otherwise occur.[41] But aside from the risk-taking, their social values are also different than the prior generation. Most youth of Horizons, in so far as they go to bars at all, would like to socialize and have the advantage of an expanded pool of potential life-mates. They do not generally have the goal of picking up someone to have sex. Of course there are many adults in the prior cohort who have held the same value; they, too, looked beyond the bars for much of what was important in their social life and love life. It is these adults, such as the advisors at Horizons, who are socializing the youth into gay and lesbian culture.

This distinction between going to the bars for socializing and going to find sex is not valid for all of the youth at Horizons, especially when they first emerge from hiding. These newcomers may continue to have a secretive sexual life for a while longer. They have not found a new context yet. Their sexual contacts are extremely varied, including sex with others of the same sex who either do not identify themselves as gay or are closeted and opposed to open gay life. They may feel themselves to be "bisexual," as we have seen. Sometimes these youth experience a furtive sexual life akin to that of the closet homosexual prior to 1970 or to those gay men in the 1970s, prior to AIDS awareness, and to gay men after the 1970s who, to a certain extent, continued to seek their primary sexual contacts in bars and baths.[42] We shall examine these questions further in chapters 5 and 6.

Going to a bar today is just another expression of coming out, but not the only one, and it need not carry the baggage from years past. It represents a subtle social transformation in how and what youth do about the romance and sex in their lives.

New Rituals of Love and Sex

Dating the same sex is an odd and perfectly unfamiliar idea to the youth of Horizons. Learning how to date and what to do erotically with the same sex are not only "unnatural" in the heterosexual socialization of these youth; they are completely foreign. How does a boy ask another boy to go to out for a date at a movie or to have a coke? How does a girl invite another girl she desires to listen to music or to go to the beach? If you have hidden your desires from your parents, how do you arrange such a romantic outing? Should you kiss and caress, and when is it the right and "natural" thing to initiate sexual advances or to make love? We should point out that, before coming to the youth group, most of the youth have had at least one sexual experience (see chapter 5). However, their prior experience is a *discovery* of their desires, whereas in the youth group, they learn the expression of their desires in romance and love. Here again the coming-out rites for the youth at Horizons facilitate the unlearning of heterosexual norms and the acquisition of new knowledge about how to be gay or lesbian in the absence of clear pathways.

In the "old days" of the group, Lanny said about his participation in 1979–1980, "[to be sophisticated] meant just to know about sex. I mean that coming out to me was—about sex. To know what it was like to be gay." Today, however, as one nineteen-year-old black male told us, "AIDS has made sex harder." He continued: "It's made it harder to have sex; it's harder to meet people because everyone's afraid of AIDS. As opposed to what I hear from older people it was open and you could meet people, but now you can't do that. It would be irresponsible." AIDS has thus presented a new kind of social responsibility as part of one's sexual being.

In the old days there was no concept of socializing youth either for dating or attending social events that did not automatically include at least the possibility of sexual encounter. As we have seen, only some of the youth go to bars today, but even they do not necessarily desire or expect to pick up sexual tricks there. Certainly their folklore tells them that one does not readily find a "partner for life" there. Now the youth are initiated into gay and lesbian culture through Horizons; following this, usually in concert with other lesbian and gay friends, they go to the bars for excitement and fun. Their sexual coming out involves much more.

In 1987, when some of the kids from the group appeared on one of the local radio shows, Chicago's Phyllis Levy program "Sex Talk," the director of Horizons asked to sit in and occasionally comment on gay and lesbian youth sexuality. Eventually the subject turned to the very sticky question of whether or not the agency "socializes" the kids. For obvious legal and political reasons, the agency avoids this language, especially in the area of sexuality. Ms. Levy surprised the director by asking if the agency taught the kids about "love and sex," and specifically about "dating." When he awkwardly suggested that Horizons did not do this, she surprised him even more by humorously chiding the agency. How did gay and lesbian adults ever expect the kids to develop socially, she suggested, if they weren't taught how to properly "date" the same sex? This exchange illuminates the complications faced by gay and lesbian adults in dealing with the taboo against sex with youth discussed in chapter 3 while attempting to decide what to do and not to do in preparing gay and lesbian youth for their sexual lives.

At Horizons, the youth group is an "open place" to discuss sex and romance at any time. The teens find it is more open than school and much more open than home. "You can just never discuss sex with straights," a black youth from the suburbs says. "Gays are more open than straights."

There was no teaching about AIDS or "sexual risk" in the prior generation, since there was no concept of "safe sex" as it is currently understood and taught at Horizons. This kind of education did not commence until the early to mid-1980s. In the group today, "AIDS= GAY" is a homophobic myth that many youth bring to the group. As we have seen, the idea that one can contract the disease merely by being gay or lesbian or associating with such persons is a magical idea shared by the youth upon first entry at Horizons. Unlearning this attitude is a primary task.

Ask anyone at Horizons about the question of sexual development in the youth group program, and they will quickly move the question into the area of AIDS education. The agency prides itself on being a leader in "safe-sex" education and AIDS awareness, not only within the youth group, but in the wider gay and lesbian community. We have found that the teens have a very high knowledge of what constitutes "safe sex." Even more important, we have found that they implement this concept in their sexual practice. Even when they practice sexual interaction that has a greater "objective risk" in it, such as anal intercourse, they do so by using condoms and other protective measures at a higher frequency than their heterosexual peers.[43] The Horizons' kids talk of "playing it safe," and "knowing who your partner is and what she or he has done." The standard joke, Jeffrey says, concerns "the catechism of safe sex," which says: do this and not that, less of this, little of that. "That's how we refer to it in new people's group: our 'catechism' of safe sex."

The task of socializing the youth for "safe sex" creates thorny problems—a double bind—for the advisors. Many of them are in coupled permanent relationships or seeking them. Some advisors do not approve of "casual sex" or "cruising," and they dislike the bars either as a place to socialize or as a context in which to seek sexual partners. They have either seen their friends die of AIDS or have known or read about the cases. They are not always shy about letting their views be known, and their direct influence in socializing the youth is seen in the latter's negative feelings regarding the bars discussed before. Consequently, some advisors at Horizons are hard pressed to handle variations among the youth in sexual risk-taking, especially among a small number of kids involved in what the adults consider "marginal" practices, such as sadomasochism. How does one instill a value of accepting "diversity" among gay and lesbian teens while teaching that sexual practices associated with such "marginal lifestyles" are dangerous? There was no consensus about the debate, nor how to handle adolescents whose sexual practices were "risky" or "unsafe." Could a boy like Joey, the nineteen-year-old youth group member who died of AIDS, be a member of the group and live outside its sexual norm of safe-sex practices? Some advisors thought not.

After a time at Horizons, the youth begin to complain that the adults harp too much on AIDS. They come to refer to it as the Big "A," and when the advisors announce another rap discussion on AIDS, an educational film on the subject, there are at times audible sighs and moans in the group. The older members feel that they have "heard it all" before, and some of the women feel that they are less vulnerable to the disease, or that it is of concern only because their male friends in the group may be exposed to the risk. Despite the protests of the youth, however, the Horizons advisors have good reasons to insist on continued AIDS awareness programs. One obvious reason is that uneducated newcomers are entering the group all the time—kids who express the same "magical thinking" about AIDS described previously. For example, an eighteen-year-old black girl who had newly entered the youth group said, "AIDS has not affected me. I will not involve myself with a bisexual female. I figure that way I'll be safe." Another reason is because the coming-out process is even more complicated than the older youth realize. Part of the learning process is to put the constant fear of vulnerability, derided as their "vulnerability syndrome" by the youth, in perspective so that the individual is free to be himself or herself, gay or lesbian, in the larger world beyond the Horizons agency's doors. However, this new courage can intersect dangerously with the tendency of teenagers not to worry about their future, their budding confidence that a long life lies ahead. We have discovered this idea is firmly rooted in the minds of the Horizons youth. Unlike other generations of youth, this one must overcome the fear that being gay or lesbian makes them diseased, while at the same time they must directly confront the possibility of contracting a fatal sexually transmitted disease. Here, youth must find the confidence to identify themselves as members of a new and legitimate culture, while looking directly into the eye of AIDS which threatens everyone, and must learn that only their own power to choose safe-sex practices, not some magically safe partner nor their youthful confidence in their own immortality, will protect them from the disease.

The attitudes expressed by the Horizons advisors sometimes place the youth in a quandary about the acceptance of sexual diversity in the group. They have come to Horizons to escape the homophobic and disapproving attitudes of their parents, siblings, and neighbors. Thus they do not like the subtle disapproval of some forms of sexual activity. However, many youth argue strongly for practicing safe sex. Robert, a twenty-year-old Caucasian male from the suburbs is blunt: "No, I've never been sexually intimate with anyone and I don't plan to until I develop a long-term relationship. I don't want to fuck just anyone. After a few years in a relationship we could throw away the condoms." But others feel that it is wrong for the group to impose taboos and standards. "Sex is the drug of the [youth] group," Jeffrey said, meaning that intimate sexuality is a powerful and enduring bond that they share in common. He continued: "Sex is very open here ... 'Do your own thing'; it is *you*. Acceptance and tolerance of others' preferences is important. There should be no judgements of others—nobody wants to jeopardize this group support. Keep your judgements to yourself!" As an illustration, Jeffrey points out how well people of color are accepted into the group and that sexual intercourse with anyone is okay. "Blacks have it tough. They have to act more macho. Or act bisexual. If they don't butch it up, they get eaten alive." In fact, it is now frowned upon to limit one's sexual partners by their race, Jeffrey says. Interracial dating is accepted. A Caucasian and Hispanic lesbian couple are members of the group. There is also a black and white male couple. Several males state their preferences for boys from other racial groups. "These [values] are tolerated and not discouraged. Prejudice is wrong. You can't have value judgments here like there is so much of in society," Jeffrey said.

But there is a lighter side to the acceptance of sexual diversity in the group. The jokes and humorous stories, common in every Saturday afternoon meeting, tell of it. For instance, Bowie laughs as he explains how one boy from the group, Matt, who is rather dramatic and flamboyant, recently triggered a security alarm at a hospital when he went there to visit a friend. He had stopped at home to change his clothes before going to the hospital for the evening visiting hours because he was ultimately on his way to a "leather" bar in the city. As he approached the hospital security gate, he forgot that he was wearing a "cock ring" around his penis, underneath his clothes. When he walked through the gate, the alarm went off and the cops rushed him, suspecting that he had a concealed weapon. He was moved to the "frisk" room. The police were as red with embarrassment as he was when they discovered the ring. Most of the kids thought the story was funny, but a couple of them, and an advisor too, didn't see much humor in the fact that he was wearing a sexual emblem of the leather world.

"Sex" symbolizes many of the youth's insecurities. Like many heterosexual teens they do not fully accept their own sexual feelings. Yet perhaps, unlike their straight peers, they feel freer with each other to discuss their concerns. Among themselves at a summer picnic at the "Rocks," along nearby Lake Michigan, a group of a dozen youth spontaneously talked about sex. To some extent they hold themselves back from expressing their insecurities in the group itself; "confession" makes for little comfort in a setting where there is a constant flow of new adolescents and changing adult advisors. They are embarrassed to talk of their bodies, faces, and their feeling of being undesirable to the same sex. For instance, Jeffrey tells Marvin that another boy in the group thinks Marvin is "attractive." Marvin responds by asking, "What would he see in me?" Jeffrey scolds him for saying this. But Marvin retorts that many people in the group that day have commented negatively on his new hairstyle. Marvin's hair had changed overnight from dark brown to peroxide blond. This was of course not true, Jeffrey insisted. People liked his new hair. Jealousy and intrigue also surfaced in the conversation on the Rocks that day. Several times a sixteen-year-old boy complained about his absent lover. "He should be here," he said. His boyfriend had "gone out" on him, with another guy, and they had argued very bitterly. He was steamed up: "I love him but I can't stand betrayal." His friend had not come to the meeting that day because of the fight. The boy at the picnic said to anyone at hand, "How could he do that to me?" In anger he threatened to "kill" his boyfriend when he saw him again, although it was clear no real threat was intended. In fact, by the following Saturday, they were together in the group again, side-by-side and seemingly happy.

Going on a date is "sexual healing," the youth say, because through dating they come to feel desired and better about their bodies and appearance than ever before. Many heterosexual adolescents enjoy dating and romance for similar reasons. Their self-esteem gets a boost and they experience the expressions of approval by the peers and families who recognize the inklings of romance and the eventual transition into independence, marriage, and family life. For gay and lesbian youth, however, the hurt of the past, their isolation, alienation, and secrecy, clings to their awareness of same-sex desires. Before they come out, they fear being unattractive to the same sex. They fear that they will never find someone to love them in a different course of life that will probably preclude heterosexual marriage and children, bring disappointment to their parents and families, and lead eventually to a fearful period of rejection and loneliness in old age.

The most powerful form of healing comes in the sexual and romantic experiences which Horizons opens up to the youth, the most critical step in the ritual process that follows. Here is twenty-year-old Paul, a Hispanic youth from Chicago's West Side, on his relationship:

> Fun—it makes us both feel more mature and older than we really are. We can enjoy being alone together or in a group. Whatever we're doing, we always have fun, always have a smile on our faces. Both always feel needed and wanted, we both feel secure—we need that desperately. If we have different views of straight people or different facts we'll argue, but there isn't jealousy. We have faith in each other. Overall its really a good relationship. We've been lovers for four months. He lives in the suburbs, but we still see each other every weekend.

Some sexual interactions emerge from meeting other kids in the group. An eighteen-year-old boy said this of his first same-sex relationship:

It was someone I met here, the first day I came here. It was the end of winter and it was cold. We didn't do too much later when we went out. We kissed and felt each other. I was really nervous. I couldn't come. I jerked him off. He lived in Indiana, but we talked on the phone a lot, but eventually I lost touch with him. It lasted four months. It was okay, I don't feel bad. I thought things went awfully quick; it was something I wanted.

Some youth describe how they found the comfort of their closest friend through an initial romantic contact as well. Simon, a twenty-year-old Hispanic/Asian male, who has not come out to his family, described his feelings about such a friend:

He's gay. We've been friends for one and half years. . . . We met at a party. . . and he started calling me and we started going out. But it never became sexual. . . . We can talk about anything. . . . I call him when my sister's not around. He took me out to a bar the first time. He is very understanding. I look at him like an older brother. We respect each other, we go to parties, to bars, and we share everything. We can stay in each other' apartments. . . . We care.

Zamil, whose family is South Asian, has never had a same sex relation but he imagines what it will be like for him:

There will be friendship, emotional and sexual ties, with sex coming through the first two feelings. The physical imperfection wouldn't matter so much because of the real pleasure, of the emotionality. Even the sex wouldn't matter. We could relate intellectually as well. We could go to plays, talk ideas, watch movies, discuss books, share friends and have separate friends, be in a monogamous relationship that we feel sexually fulfilled with each other so we don't need to get pleasure from other bodies.

By "healing" the feelings of hiding and shame for their past desires and present longings, the youth of Horizons find a special need fulfilled in their romantic and sexual relations. The culmination of these feelings in the public sphere comes when they attend the Prom, the next phase of the ritual process.

Annual Gay and Lesbian Prom

Every year in late May for about the past decade, an alternative to the high school proms is held in Newtown. Its purpose is to provide an all-gay setting for youth who have for years felt excluded from and denigrated by the mainstream heterosexual proms of the Chicago high schools. The Gay and Lesbian Prom is held in the large upstairs "ballroom" of Molly's restaurant, which firmly anchors it in the center of the gay and lesbian community and business district. The prom is thus another way of being acculturated into mainstream lesbian and gay spaces. No alcohol is served; only sodas, in respect of those under legal age. Most of the advisors come, usually with their partners, if they have them. The director of the Horizons agency comes, with partner in hand. The agency sponsors many events here, but the prom has the intergenerational character of a mainstream high school prom, complete with parents in the wings watching to make sure that things "stay in order." It is a happy occasion, with music, dancing, and all the accoutrements of collective "normalcy."

The 1987 Prom was our first.[44] There were sixty-five advance tickets sold, and a nice crowd of about eighty youth, advisors, and adult staff were there. Our second prom in 1988 had about the same number of people in attendance. It started early on Friday evening. Four members of the youth decorating committee and two new advisors had met earlier that day on the top floor of the restaurant to prepare the rooms for dinner and dancing.

The dancing room was decorated in gray and lavender streamers. Kyle, the young male advisor, was able to get a discount from a local gay florist, so flower arrangements adorned every table in both rooms. Carlie, another adult advisor, supplied what seemed like miles of strings of lights that ringed the dancing room; the dinner table was draped with hundreds of twinkling white lights. The excitement and enthusiasm of the two new adults was contagious. After the rooms had been decorated, the youth group committee had to get ready for the prom, so all four people, three boys and a girl, among them Jeffrey, went into the bathroom. The rules of modesty were abandoned. There was a blizzard of clothes, hairspray, and blow dryers. The atmosphere was fun and chaotic. "The unspoken law was that if you were in the restroom of the gender you were not, you had to have an escort of the opposite sex," one of the boys said.

By 7:30 P.M. people began to arrive. Their attire ran the gamut from casual dress to tuxedos, with lots of hats. All the tuxes without exception were worn by the women advisors and the girls from the group. A woman we know, the long-time partner of a youth group advisor, laughed with us: "All my life I have wanted to wear one of these!" Here was a hint of the old days of "camp" and its homosexual images amidst the crowd. But it was incomplete: there were no male cross-dressers. Several of the adults commented on this, and the director, who has attended the Gay Youth Proms for some ten years, noted how striking it was that some youth used to dress in clothes of the opposite sex, but now none of the boys had.[45] All of the advisors we had met during the course of the study attended. The dinner went well; the food was good and the staff of the restaurant seemed to enjoy the kids too. Dancing started right after dinner. There were no couples on the floor at first; people danced in groups; and the gender of the partners was secondary. The only time that couples were exclusively paired was during the slow dances. The teens were having a good time.

Who do the youth date? Some bring partners and dates from outside the group. They are introduced around for the first time, and greeted with the great expectations that youth foster from having talked about their steady date endlessly to their friends. The majority of the teenagers came with a date. "The amount of flirtation that night was higher than at other times; there was some gossip and bitchy comments," Jeffrey said. But it never ruined the festive atmosphere. The toast of the prom are, clearly, the youths who are in coupled relationships: several women couples and some of the men too, who have longer-term or "steady date" same-sex relationships. Several of them, such as Bowie and George, live together. Some youth may be a bit afraid to ask a date to the prom. They are still too new at dating, and so they ask another peer from the group. A couple of the youth also say they "don't want to have sex yet," they want to wait for the "right" boy or girl to come along; they are "saving" themselves. So when they come with dates it is felt either that it is purely platonic or they have finally found the "right" one.

At 11:00 P.M. the prom queen and king were announced. Ballots had been filled out at dinner. As in prior years the youth love to "gender blend" the conventions by electing someone whose sex is a reversal of the traditional roles of the royalty. The queen was the boy Bowie. The election of the king was more colorful. Before the youth group director could announce the results, the crowd broke into a chant of "Karyn, Karyn!" Karyn was elected king for the second year in a row. She was very popular and had brought her steady date with her; they kissed before the assembly of people and the crowd roared. She was obviously thrilled by their applause. After the coronation, the dancing continued until midnight.

Why do the youth "reverse" the gender of the kings and queens? "Ritual reversals" of this kind are common to many initiations. They are rebellions against the usual constraining norms, and they provide the festival release of energy necessary for regeneration of the group.[46] To gender blend, the youth feel, is to poke fun at the moral probity of heterosexual roles. Their "minstrelization" by the act of voting and then cheering for a gender-blended "royal order" attacks the highest structure of hierarchy in conventional society.[47] Rituals of reversal also included the chance to dance with the advisors, and many of the youth did so. At the end of the dancing the adult and teenager would politely kiss—the only time they may ever do so "officially." One new advisor, younger and less experienced, kissed a youth a bit too long, which raised eyebrows. As with all rites of reversal, the rites actually reinforce the normal rules of the group, telling members what not to do, if not on the outside in society, then inside of the group.

After the prom the youth broke into different circles of friends. Some went to bars. Others went for a late snack. At the end of the night some of them went to the "Rocks" at the beach to watch the sunrise. They brought their own champagne and toasted themselves. Thus a new way of finding love and sex has entered into the youth group, formalized in ways that reflect the wider society but speak to the needs of these teenagers who would be gay and lesbian adults.

For some youth the Gay and Lesbian Prom is not the confirmation of, but rather their very first entree into, the group—just as heterosexual proms may serve as the initiation of a date or friend into one's high school circle of friends. Here is the story of Jerome, a young black man who helped found the Horizons group.

> Well, I had heard about the group through Lanny. He and I were very good friends in high school . . . spent most of our time together, being called "fags." [He laughs.]—Trying to figure out which one of these people who were calling us fags we wanted [sexually]! [laughs] Listen, that was pretty good for me. But at the time I lived in a really straight, parental, thing. And, Uh! Lanny would talk about Horizons and,— but—I couldn't go. Because I played [piano] for church, and my momma

had a fit if I went anywhere that she didn't know where I was going. So I really didn't have an opportunity to go, until after high school, and I really hadn't too much planned to go then, but it was when they had their first prom . . . and Lanny invited me to come to the prom. I got there and I just really met these people. And it was the first time that I was around some teenagers, other than high school, and they found me and I was popular. Suddenly I had all these talents that I didn't know that I had. . . .' Cus at school, I was so busy arguing and fighting [chuckles]. You know, I didn't have a chance to, you know, let my real personality come through. So, um, I went there, and like, week or so later, Lanny would say, "Well, everybody's asking about you, how's your friend, and stuff like that." So then I started going out [to Horizons]. . . . And I remember that night at the prom, when they elected the first queen and everything, I thought, "Oh boy, that was just so marvellous!" So, you know, the next year at prom, I was the next queen! [laughs]

The turnout on the Saturday afternoon following the prom was lighter than usual. The teenagers showed the effects of having had a very late and rambunctious night. Bowie, the prom queen, was both frenetic and exhausted because he had not gone to bed yet. The topic for that day's discussion was "Sexuality and Spirituality," moderated by an ex-priest, himself gay, who is now involved in the Metropolitan Community Church. The discussion was odd in its juxtaposition to the frolic and toasting of the night before; and yet somehow, this too created an atmosphere of normalcy: whatever happens, the group goes on, taking care of its own kind. The quiet, low-key discussion was brought to an abrupt end when one of the members suddenly passed out and fell over on the carpet. The youth group was shocked. Someone dialed 911, and an ambulance came. The teen was revived. He had apparently collapsed from a combination of too little sleep and heat prostration caused by too many layers of clothing. His friends laughed at his embarrassment, and the group, with the blessings of the ex-priest, joined in the laughter. One of the older group members had brought along two new friends for the first time, a lesbian and a gay boy. They enjoyed themselves immensely and said that they would return.

We attended the 1991 Prom and noted some changes from the earlier ones. It was still held at Molly's Restaurant, but was larger now and had become more of a social event for the entire Horizons agency. There were more women than before, the women outnumbering the men. The clothes and dress had changed somewhat. There were still some tuxes, but more youth dressed in the androgynous and punk look of Queer Nation, with many earrings and new wave brightly colored haircuts. There were many unfamiliar younger advisors. The king and queen roles were still gender reversed, but the youth who occupied the roles seemed more confident than before, as though they were fulfilling an old custom from long before their time.

The Apartment

The night after the prom some of the youth assembled in the apartment belonging to Bowie, his lover, and their roommates, who live not far from Horizons. This apartment provides another setting for the intensification of their ritualized coming out.

No matter what happens to a youth, or how much he or she is assimilated into the Horizons group, the youth believe, as in so many other quarters of American teenage life, that they are not accepted as full persons until they come of legal age. As one boy says, "Until you are 21, you're not a full blown member of gay culture." Why is this? Many things of importance matter in this respect—having a job and an income, being independent from parents, having a lover. Jobs are symbols of maturity and status. "The counter-culture value of dropping out of society does exist," a boy in the group says, "but the vast majority of nonschool members are working or looking for work." Yet while work is only a means to an end, it is a critical means of attaining the key symbol of adulthood—having an apartment.

Being invited to visit or party at the apartment is a special privilege that suggests someone's deeper acceptance into the youth group. Bowie's apartment became a regular meeting ground, a "safe space" for meetings and parties, and a "crash pad" where youth group members could stay if they wanted a place to sleep the night, to take a date, or in case of trouble at home. It was a place for friends to turn in case of need. The apartment was officially leased by Bowie and his lover Ken. They had a roommate too, an older man named Herb. The apartment was accessible by public transportation, which was important because many youth do not own cars. It was a large ground floor apartment with two bedrooms that functioned as separate spaces, each with a bathroom. Bowie and Ken shared one of them, and Herb had the other. Other regular guests in the apartment included "little Sally", a fourteen-year-old lesbian, and her lover Lauren. Also Sid and his lover Rob, and Jeffrey, who is Herb's lover.

Herb is a gay man in his late thirties. He was never a member of Horizons. He moved into the apartment when Bowie's first roommate left and the others needed someone else to help pay the rent. Herb had known another group member. Soon, he was introduced by Bowie and the girls to Jeffrey, in their attempts to be "matchmakers." This succeeded, and Jeffrey and Herb have remained together, presently living together, since that time.[48]

The key actors often spend the weekend together in or around the apartment. Friendship is the first reason; the concept of the apartment being a "safe space" for the teenagers is also crucial. Sex is another reason. Most of the group live at home with the parents. The running joke of the apartment is that "more sex happens on a weekend night at the apartment than in most married couple's lives for a whole year," Jeffrey says.

The general rules of modesty are not strict in the apartment. Walking around naked is forbidden, but wearing a towel will suffice. Sleeping arrangements do not permit much modesty; as in historical times when large groups of people would share a single room, the youth must make do with what they have. Sally and Lauren take the day bed in the living room. The two mattresses in Bowie and Ken's room are used by them, and by Sid and Rob. If the latter aren't there, the girls move into their bedroom. People in the apartment can overhear each other, including their movements in bed, which is both amusing and embarrassing at times. The women and men in the apartment make for playful situations. The men will jokingly grab the women's breasts, and the women the men's crotches, in playful, not erotic, gestures. The sense here is of trust, a complete trust that permits body boundaries to be erased temporarily. It is a liminal atmosphere—betwixt and between home and the gay and lesbian culture.

Sally, it seems, prides herself on being what she calls an "oversexed" lesbian. She enjoys sex a great deal. She has "abandoned the heterosexual social rules for female sexual drive," she claims. Her actions "do not fit the typical lesbian either; she is sexually driven," Bowie feels. Sally fits the behavior some associate with gay men. She complains that gay men are so lucky: "They can just pick up someone for sex." This isn't to say that she has a frantic life. "She just wants more than she gets," her friends say. The other apartment dwellers think she is a "crazed sex maniac," in Herb's words. Much to Lauren's embarrassment, Sally is chided by the others for her nudity.

There are friendly alliances. Sid is more Rob's friend. And Sid is not well liked by Bowie. This leads to friction between Bowie and Rob. Rob complains that Sally and Lauren are in the apartment too much. Bowie responds that he never complains when Rob's friends drop in unannounced. Herb remains neutral. His only complaint is that Sally doesn't wear enough clothes.

The apartment, and others like it, thus become the one place the blissfully emancipated youth have complete control over. "He or she can make it as straight or gay as they want," Bowie remarks. These oasis spots of "gayness" let the youth feel that they are more "out." Coming out makes one "grow up faster and harder," Jeffrey has said.

"Joey Has AIDS"

During the time of our study, AIDS was a constant presence in the group; it took on a life of its own. The youth responded in many ways to this presence, and we have written of their "safe sex" concepts elsewhere.[49] However, early in our project the first youth group member became ill with the disease. The response of the youth and that of the advisors is a key aspect of the social ritual of coming out that deserves a careful look.

Joey joined the group in 1986 and attended irregularly until the summer of 1987. He was diagnosed with AIDS in May of 1987. We did not see him again until he appeared at a social function held by the youth group on the weekend of the Gay Pride Parade (late June). Although Joey revealed to us in a private interview in June that he was a PLWA, because he stopped attending the group he hid his condition from the group until August. His acquaintances and friends were perplexed about what had become of him.

When he thus reappeared in August it had been a long time since the kids had seen him and he looked terrible: anemic and pallid, with a chalky face. He entered the group on a Saturday, quietly socializing. The topic of the day happened to be "religion" and coming out. Joey, contrary to his usual demeanor, said nothing once the meeting started. He tended to look away to avoid the eyes of the other members of the group. At one point during the discussion there was a pause. When the group took a break, Joey looked ill and discreetly took out some medication, popping a pill in his mouth. But the water fountain in the lobby made it hard to hide what he was doing. Joey mentioned to Jeffrey, who was watching him from nearby, that he was taking AZT. Later, the youth group advisor told us that she had never seen someone so completely drained of color as Jeffrey looked at that moment. The youth group leader was able to take Joey off to one side and ask him what was going on. He said that the disease had been "a long time coming." His "testing 'positive' [for HIV] and then developing symptoms was inevitable," Joey felt. He seemed overwhelmed that day, but by coming back to the group, he had accepted that he was ill. He seemed to have reconciled himself to his end.

What was the immediate response of the other teenagers to all of this? Joey disclosed his secret when there were only two teenagers present. Two of the youth group leaders had also stayed behind. Joey had been more open with them. Why hadn't he been more open with the larger group? "Over and over," Jeffrey said, "we have heard about AIDS, lots and lots. We've heard about sex and the importance of safe sex. The youth group discussion has focused on it many times, but this was the first kid from the group who got it and it's scary."

Joey's illness was frightening not only because of its intrusion into the group; but also because there is a strong identification between members of the group, the kind of bond that comes from the feelings of sharing, equality, and commitment already discussed. The hopes, dreams, and common concerns of the group are projected into one member who then symbolizes, for a moment, all of the positive and negative feelings and associations of coming out for the group. It is not a matter of "scape goating," as much as a "compression" of aspirations into the subjectified image of one of their own: Joey.[50]

The illness progressed rapidly and Joey never returned to the youth group. He had to quit work, go on welfare, and was cared for by his lover and friends. He was hospitalized twice with pneumonia. However, when he learned of the opportunity to attend the National March on Washington, D.C., in late October, he decided to make the journey against his doctor's orders. In a wheelchair he attended the Quilt ceremony, but fell ill the same day in Washington. Several days after he returned to Chicago he passed away from AIDS. His funeral was noted in the papers but the Horizons youth did not attend.

Joey's "marginality" in the eyes of the advisors is a key to understanding the nature of the teens' reaction to this AIDS-related death. By "marginal" these adults referred mainly to his sexual practices. Joey was "into" older men, and his older lover distinguished him from the other youth. He made allusions on more than one occasion to his "master/slave" sexual practices, which were disconcerting to some teenagers.[51] He came to the group wearing leather togs from time to time. The advisors' discussion centered on whether Joey fit into the "norm" of the youth group. One male advisor argued passionately that his colleagues had too narrow a view of this norm and stated that the group was very "waspy" white and middle class. But a woman advisor debated the point. She said that the group was very "mixed," among the most "heterogeneous" she could imagine in Chicago. This issue of Joey's peripherality and normlessness, one advisor argued, "is different from his personality." He was surely disliked by some, but others chummed with him. He wasn't an outcast. His youth group friends, a group leader suggested, "liked and learned from him," even if he was outside the norm. "Joey wasn't crazy or bizarre," he said, defending the boy's memory.

The youth group discussed Joey's death for the first time in a regular rap meeting that we initiated with the agreement of the advisors some weeks later.[52] The group consisted of some fifteen teenagers and at least as many adults (the members of our research team plus the advisors). In the group were the teenagers, John, Bowie, and Jeffrey, who were seated between two young lesbians, Karyn and Kim. Also attending were Roong, Rob, Tiffany, and several other boys and girls.

The discussion began with the advisor asking if anyone was willing to share his or her reactions to a film about the life and death of a San Francisco youth who had died of AIDS. Many of the youth reported that they cried during the film. Bowie said that he was very, very scared, and felt strongly moved by the film. He also said that "the film had made me think of Joey" and that he was scared that he might contract AIDS. Later, it was clear that the advisors were completely taken by surprise about the depth of the feelings that lingered regarding Joey's death.

The teenager Karyn agreed with Bowie. She said that she felt badly about what had happened to Joey and wished that she "could have done more to help him out." Over in the corner, a black youth (about nineteen and wearing large glasses) said that he had "thought about this a lot" and was concerned about "how people said that if you practice homosexuality you would go to hell." He talked about his "bad" feelings on the topic and how conflicted he was when he went to church. Another black male standing next to him said that he was "very scared of AIDS." He didn't like to think about it or talk about it. Eventually, Roong, an Asian boy, was to say something similar, that he was very scared and didn't like to think about it. "There was nothing you could do about it and it was very frightening. Why do we have to deal with these issues? We have so many other problems."

Bowie talked a great deal. He was more coherent and seemed more willing than we had seen him before to take the role as a social leader. He said, "I feel guilty that I didn't go to the wake or funeral for Joey." He said his lover "Ken wouldn't let me go." It was "scary to Ken," and although Bowie wanted to go, Ken wouldn't hear of it. "Just thinking about going to the funeral disturbs Ken." Then Bowie raised the question of "why the group never discussed Joey's illness?" Bowie pointed out that it never came up and "it was really hard to do anything about it because you didn't know where he lived and you wondered where he was. Was somebody taking care of him?" Though his question seemed to be directed to the advisors, none of them responded at that point. Karyn said she too had wondered where he was living. She knew he had an older lover, and she wondered how the lover had reacted to Joey getting AIDS.

It came out later in the discussion that Bowie's lover Ken is someone who has much denied that he is gay. He has remained in the closet to his parents. Even though he and Bowie live together and his parents know that Bowie is gay, Ken continues to pretend to them that he, Ken, is straight. He has not indicated in any way that he and Bowie are lovers. Bowie said that Ken is so disturbed about AIDS that once, when Bowie told Ken that he had been tested for HIV, Ken refused to even let Bowie kiss him for a while. Ken rejected dealing with the loss of Joey to AIDS and would not permit Bowie to be supportive of Joey in life or in death, which Ken's absence from the group that day seemed to suggest.

Roong told a powerful and gripping story which kept many members of the group sitting on the edges of their seat. He said he had lost so many members of his family during the years of war in Southeast Asia. He said half of his family had been killed. His extended family clan originally numbered more than two hundred people, and now only a hundred were left. "Fifty in the United States, twenty-five over there, twenty-five scattered around the world." He grew more rigid as he spoke, the distress evident in his face.

One day Roong's brother, who is younger than him, came into his room and saw a copy of *Gay Chicago*. He looked at Roong and droned, "You must never tell this to mother and father. If you do that, everything will be ruined. If you are gay, you have to go away." Roong said with great sadness that his brother would now have the responsibility of being the "oldest" male in his family and, therefore, being the eldest son of the eldest male, he would be the leader of his clan. By being gay, Roong felt, he was losing his ancestry, his cultural heritage; indeed, his role in his family. We watched him as he told us that he had clearly contemplated "leaving his family, being on his own, and dying alone without family or heritage." We were aware of his grave concern with AIDS when he said that he feared not only "coming out" but dying. "I had to deal with so much loss and death when I was young. I thought when I came to America this was all over; I was safe and secure. And here I found that being homosexual, I have to deal with the same problem." For him the loss of family ties was inextricably related to his own attempt to "come out." For a moment, in the microcosm of Roong, we could see clearly the plight of a multicultural gay-identified teenager, courageously risking the profound loss of his traditional culture by coming out into the culture of lesbians and gays.

While Roong struggled with these large problems, the advisors and other youth did not offer him comfort in the way that he needed or deserved. Some sat watching him; others sat looking down, remote, glum, and sad, and occasionally exchanging nervous glances.

Because the presence of AIDS is such a powerful "magical" force that thwarts coming out, the reaction to Joey took on a flavor of avoidance and denial. The magical fear that to be gay is to have AIDS had become a threatening reality in the group. Somehow, in the stream of many other demands upon them, the advisors were unable to respond adequately to this dread. Joey's condition unexpectedly intruded into the progress of "coming out,"not only in for the youth, but for the advisors too. Suspended between life and death, Joey's illness was not just a warning of what could happen to their own bodies—he also conjured up the fears of what might become of someone who comes out. In this way he was not only "marginal" to the group, as some of the advisors believed. He was more than ever liminal—dangerously betwixt and between life and death, and between the teenagers and the gay and lesbian culture on the horizons that they seek. In death they would remember him more for the loss that he represented than for his personality. Their reactions support the idea that the acceptance of the grief and loss of being gay and lesbian is a critical rite of passage in the transition of coming out.

Pilgrimage to the Quilt

Going to see the Quilt when it came to Chicago was one of the most difficult tasks the youth group faced. Many would not do it. But for those who did, including the ones who went to commemorate and remember Joey's death, this was another key passage—one that contributed to the acceptance of the end of something from the past and the beginning of something new in their ritual transition.

The "Names Project" Quilt, as we saw in chapter 2, is a memorial to the people who have succumbed to AIDS and, more importantly, a celebration of these people and their contributions to society. The epitaph in large squares of fabric bear each person's name and personal emblems. Most of the squares of the Quilt were made for adults, but a few are for children and adolescents, as one can sometimes tell from their design. One youth group member said that "by just looking at a panel you knew that person, and what he or she was about; you mourn them because you know them."

The youth group became aware of the Quilt's impending arrival in Chicago in August 1988, several weeks prior to its presentation in Washington, D.C. There was a definite sense of discomfort about the Quilt. This uneasiness wasn't confined to longer-term members of the group, although the Quilt was more personal for them. A panel had been made for Joey, who had died the previous autumn. Except for one member, the group did not take an active part in its construction.

As the time for the Quilt drew near, the group didn't appear to be at all touched by it. These youngsters share so much of their lives with each other, and in general openly share their emotions about events in the gay and lesbian community so their silence about the Quilt was a notable exception. It was not brought up in conversations—not even in passing. The teens became very quiet and uncomfortable for a moment after the topic came up. "The Quilt allows them to realize their own mortality," Jeffrey said. "A nineteen-year-old youth, even being in a gay youth group exposed to AIDS campaigns, doesn't contemplate his own mortality," he concluded. Yet as we saw from the group reaction to Joey's death, there are many hidden fears of AIDS that touch the group.

When the time came, and the Quilt had arrived at Navy Pier in downtown Chicago, some of the group members organized an outing to see it on their own. It was the core group who attended, including Jeffrey, Bowie, Karyn, and some others. Navy Pier is an immense old warehouse, of such large proportions that the Quilt could be displayed almost in its entirety. The Pier was thronged with people the day the youth saw the Quilt. Their emotional responses varied, but it clearly left a "profound mark on their lives," as they later said. Jeffrey said that the responses of the youth "centered on the huge size of the Quilt. In a world that bombards us with statistics every day it was amazing to see what thousands of deceased really look like. The reactions were personal. It was silent mourning broken only by tears. For each individual the response differed depending upon the people represented by the panels. The members of the group came to each others' side as never before. People held each other as they cried."

We were in the crowd visiting the Quilt at the same time as the youth group, but independent of them. The image of those young people standing before Joey's panel, is forever frozen in our memory. They stood banded together, crying openly, burying their faces in each other's shoulders. They huddled so closely that they seemed as if one in the vast room, a small but brave island of protection to each other, sobbing in the sea of people. They stood out because there were so few adolescents in the throng of adults. They were not surprised to see us in the great room; but perhaps the fact that we had been crying too comforted them. So many people were crying that one felt the outpouring of a vast collective funeral.

The group themselves brought up the Quilt pilgrimage the following Saturday. As one of the youth summarized their mood: "Many friendships and love relations were reaffirmed and strengthened by the Quilt. In all, the experience of the Quilt was good for the group." The topic of Joey's death emerged again. Bowie said that it was "too bad that Joey had died the way he had. Couldn't there have been more support and help for him? He really died alone. He didn't have us to help him. Something needs to be done about that," but Bowie wasn't clear what that should be. And this made people feel sad.

Loss and vulnerability create strains in anyone, and in many youths this is handled through the denial of fear and loss. The question of loss in this case is compounded by politics and moralistic rhetoric in the United States on all sides. Gay and lesbian activists reacted to an earlier "sin and perversity" rhetoric. A whole generation up until the late 1960s could not be open without paying a great price. After Stonewall another generation of gay activists emerged who, in general, would claim only the positive effects of being gay and dismiss the complaints of their critics. Later, the AIDS epidemic produced a mass of death and loss that has altered the meanings of being openly gay or lesbian again. In the new generation, the Horizons teenagers can live more openly, but they struggle with the loss of AIDS as they grow up. Each of the three generations has experienced different kinds of loss and grief in "coming out." Until recently however it was unacceptable to talk about the negative effects of coming out except and only insofar as these touched upon homophobia and AIDS. But what of the lost normative aspirations of their former heterosexuality—the once admired goals of one's family and friends, such as their dream for a conflict-free life and grandchildren? The conscious acceptance of the loss of this older developmental subjectivity, of being "off course" in one's adaptation to American society through the life course, is vulnerable to alienating unconscious fantasies of past and present unless the new gay and lesbian culture provides clear customs and practices with which the youth of tomorrow can cope with the loss.

Joey's death and the Quilt introduced a new level of discord in the solidarity of the group. When they considered Joey's death, an advisor asked whether the kids would have "problems expressing their concerns about friends contracting AIDS." Some of the members said that they would be able to take it on. Their response was brave, but too quick and pressured. Their subsequent uneasiness and fear showed that they could cope only with a great effort of energy and intent—because they were confronting the denial of before. They had no tradition of grief to fall back upon, being so young, and being participants in a young culture that has not found its own way in preparing its symbolic children for how to greet death. The youth group advisors seemed uneasy as well; the ordinary role model failed. We begin to see that our understanding of "coming out" and AIDS risks can only be derived by viewing the full picture—of advisors and teenagers together—actors in a cultural process that must be seen as an emerging tradition. The ongoing struggle to deal with homophobia and coming out in the age of AIDS needs to address the dual problem of socializing both adults and teenagers, in gay and lesbian groups, about the sacrifices and rewards of "coming out."

Every rite of passage is simultaneously a process of the symbolic death of the earlier person and the rebirth of a new selfhood to take its place. In the youth group this occurred simultaneously on several levels: in the struggle of the individual youth to come out; in the continuing process that characterized the expressions of adult advisors; in the reactions of the parents to the loss of their formerly heterosexual children; and in the teenagers nascent participation in events, such as the Quilt, which represents their coping with the losses of AIDS as they become adult members of gay culture. The Quilt is a symbol of death par excellence. It was a brave act for the youth to visit the memorial and pay homage to the dead. By doing what they did in the face of their own uncertainty and even the queasiness of the adults, the teens showed that they had passed another hurdle in letting go of the past: the ability to face their mortality during the time of AIDS and the possibility of a future more secure in the knowledge of their newfound roles.

Annual Gay and Lesbian Pride Parade

Many youth have little or no understanding of the history of the gay liberation movement, or even of its primary symbol, the Annual Gay and Lesbian Pride Parade. A young woman, when asked about it, immediately connected it to the civil rights movement. "It's like the black community remembering Rosa Parks refusing to leave her seat [on the bus]." Despite their lack of knowledge, the parade in 1988 on the weekend June 25–26 marked the culmination of the youth group's enthusiastic preparations for the annual Parade Day, the highlight of the yearly calendar of events. The group has in recent years taken an increasingly active role in the festivities of the parade. In the youth group discussions beginning in June, members began to ask where they could purchase "pride week buttons" that advertise one's "outness." Newer members wanted information on past parades. Old timers were more than happy to give glowing reports of the previous years' activities. People mentioned with pride the news programs that had gotten them on television. The greatest social rite of all had begun.

Parents' reactions to having their children march in the Parade was a key topic of discussion during the month. As one boy said, "Some people were determined to march in the parade even if it meant coming out to or confronting their parents about their gay sexuality." Most of the regular youth group members did in fact march in the parade. Some did so with reservations—they were afraid to be discovered by family, friends, or co-workers. However, peer pressure from the youth and the support of other group members led most of them into marching, regardless of the consequences.

Sunday, June 26, 1988, was a perfect, cloudless day for a parade. The heat wave of the past few days had broken and temperatures had fallen into the low seventies. Horizons had sponsored a "pre-Parade" brunch at the center for people marching in the various contingents of the Horizons' delegation, which is typically among the largest throngs of marchers. The brunch was a "pot luck" dinner of various dishes volunteered by people at Horizons. The youth group represented a large number of folks at the brunch. Another group of people were members of P-FLAG, led by George and Selma Golden, a prominent older heterosexual couple and leaders of P-FLAG in Chicago, who have a gay son. More than anything else the youth were thrilled by these supportive parents of gays and lesbians.

Excitement in the group grew as the time for the line-up at the head of the parade neared. Some youth became nervous; but their "stage fright" was soothed by the older youth group members who had already been through this ritual themselves. Their appearance anxiety was understandable. Karyn remarked that the parade "is my absolutely favorite day of the year. . . . Like Christmas, Easter, and my Birthday all rolled into one fantastic day." Others commented that Pride Day was their favorite time because it encompassed all the joy, love, and warmth of the standard holidays, but without heterosexualist traditions.

One new youth group project for this parade was the selling of gay pride flags. The youth were enthusiastic; they sold many flags. Adults in the community enjoy meeting these youth group members, since many have never met a gay or lesbian youth in their lives! The slogan the youth group adopted for their work was "FLAGS FOR FAGS!"

To draw attention to the Horizons youth group at the colorguard, the women advisors all rode motorcycles in front of the Horizons' marchers. The advisors made a great hit with the youth and the public. The parade passed by two well-known Lesbian bars, "The Closet," and "AUGIE C.K.'s," and the women in front of the bars, along with the ones drinking outside, poured into the streets, swarming through police barricades. They went into a frenzy of clapping and hooting when they saw the motorcycles, with a beautiful lesbian couple on each, all decorated with Pride flags and signs that read YOUTH GROUP ADVISORS or YOUTH GROUP COORDINATOR. To show their appreciation for the warm response from the women spectators, the contingent known as DYKES ON BIKES revved their engines and raced their cycles, which drew an even larger cheer from the crowd.

The strong Lesbian presence was welcomed by the youth group. The director of Horizons was elated. He hoped that this would spur more women into getting involved in the agency. The youth group responded with cheers of: "Dykes on Bikes!" and spelling out "D-Y-K-E-S." The men by contrast spelled out "QUEENS!" Other words such as "HORIZONS" were spelled out. The two most favorite cheers were "2, 4, 6, 8—How do you know that your kids are straight?" and "Gay Pride! Let's Get Gay Pride!" A muffled cheer of "1, 2, 4, 6—Lets all get some dicks!" was shared among the male youth group members as a private joke, but they did not shout it. Whenever the police passed the youth, the kids would taunt, "2, 4, 6, 8—How do you know the police are straight?!"[53] The reactions from the police were polite and usually unsmiling; there was no contingent of gay and lesbian police in the parade yet.[54] When the youth group passed George and Selma Golden, the youth group shouted in union: "We love our parents!" The P-FLAG representatives responded with, "We love our kids and you too!" The youth and the parents' groups received the largest cheers and the most tearful responses from the crowd.

Reaction of the youth group members to parade viewers was equally positive. The exuberance of the youth group seemed to rub off on the crowd. The kids enjoyed flirting with the 100,000 people. When the parade passed a couple of gay men's bars, some older men laughed and shouted, "Chicken" and "Fresh meat." Jeffrey said, "The youth didn't mind that," because "the day that many had been looking forward to for months had finally arrived." After the parade the group broke into its well-established cliques to attend the rally. "The only group notably absent from the parade were the teenage black men— for them it is very hard to be openly out in this way," Jerry said. After the rally, some kids went to eat at the Melrose Cafe nearby, another "hang out," with the group walking arm in arm, openly displaying their affection. For some youth, this is the first time they have ever shown their homosocial desire on the streets of Chicago. The restaurant was filled with adults from the parade. The conversation revolved around the warm feeling from the day and the lingering sense of being a member of a large crowd. The straight waitress got in on the fun.

After dinner the group went to Bowie's apartment. The *Sound of Music* was interrupted to watch the 10:00 P.M. news. The kids snickered as they evaluated the coverage. "Channel 7 won best news cast honors," Jeffrey said. "Channel 5 was most homophobic," the kids felt. The NBC affiliate didn't mention the parade until after a piece about a newborn giraffe at the Zoo. According to Bowie, some youth thought that this arrangement reflected a "subliminal plot to show the goodness of natural reproduction and then follow it with a show of the disgusting queer thugs that wore beards and dresses, and paraded through the streets of Chicago." Some of the more closeted youth were worried about being spotted on the news but they did not have to worry. "As usual people in outlandish drag got the camera's attention," Jerry said. The next day it was discovered that Cable Network News had filmed the youth group marching and televised it nationally.[55] Luckily, only people that didn't mind coming out "nationwide" were shown. As Bowie concluded, "The Pride Parade brought a sense of togetherness and warmth stronger than ever. Youth group members are already looking forward to next June."

The kids feel vulnerable being so visible for the first time. "I felt as though I was on display," Karyn said. "I've only been out for a year, not very long. It wasn't a good feeling ... but towards the end we were 'RAH! RAH!' It was great. At first it was like, 'Who is looking at me?' But once you hit that bend, WHAM! ALL THESE PEOPLE!"

For many youth the parade is an introduction to gay life and institutions, such as P-FLAG, beyond Horizons. The diverse roles and cultural norms of gay and lesbian life, both sexual and social, involve the local economy (bartenders, shops), gay and lesbian organizations, such as athletic groups, churches, newspapers, and the entertainment industry, such as performers, not to mention the political system of power and its brokers, the lawyers and politicians. They get to see the impressive number of professionals involved; gay doctors, lawyers, architects, and many others, some with their own contingents, such as the Business Association, and others who act in concert with different groups. "You could see the different cross-sections of the community—a cross-section that you would not normally see any where else if you just went out in the community." As Tiffany said, "I think it opened people's eyes that we're out there. It's not like when you turn twenty-one you think, 'Gay, straight, gay straight—flip a coin.' That's not how it happens."

The teenagers felt ratified by the enthusiastic response of the crowds. As Ken said, "The thing that sticks out is that when you were walking along, there were a lot of people cheering instead of yelling and screaming and calling you names. That was a different feeling to have. There were so many people happy to see us walking along. It was like a *homecoming* parade." What should the parade be for? Ken continued: "I'd like to see it as a big community morale booster. Not to make people aware of us. . . . We do that the whole year round. The parade is the time for the community to get together, and to be aware of the community. To get to know each other. In a high school homecoming parade, you're not doing it for the other schools, you are doing it for your own people."

Some adults in the gay and lesbian community felt that the impact of AIDS made it hard to celebrate in 1987. They wanted to cancel the parade and hold only a rally instead. The youth all disagreed with the proposal. Bowie was firm: "No! For people with AIDS, it might have been a real big boost, the parade. Starting any comment with "Because of AIDS" doesn't help the situation at all. The only thing that helps is saying, 'practice safe sex.' Trying to stop other things because of that is just an excuse! Having the health clinic and Chicago House in the parade—passing out their literature—raising awareness—that couldn't be bad!"

The parade is for "us" the kids say; "that's why it must be in the gay territory." Karyn was adamant: "It went through the community where the highest concentration of [gay] people involved in it actually live. . . . That's right. A Polish parade doesn't go through an Italian neighborhood. Go where you are going to get the biggest response. If you go downtown, you'll get people booing and hissing and throwing things . . ." The inclusion of themselves in the parade and in Newtown's confines thus stakes a new claim for their place in the culture, a subtle but profound shift in their perspectives.

The youth recall the parade in largely glowing and sometimes nationalistic terms. Jerry recalled: "What do I remember most? ALL THE PEOPLE! It was a major step for me! If you are walking in that parade, *you're gay—everyone knows it*." And this is what makes gay culture visible to them: "I didn't even know the community existed until I found the youth group. Where were they all hiding? Up to that point, I thought that the community was two or three thousand. And here were these 100,000 people. That was amazing to me!"

Death and Rebirth in Coming Out

We see from this chapter the scale of socially organized experiences that lead the youth from secrecy to coming out in the parade. As they enter the parade, the teenagers are at a turning point in their lives. Some of them are near the age of twenty-one, when they must exit the group and move on, out into American society. This latter stage of coming out, and the parade in particular, mark what anthropologists would call a rite of "intensification": that is, having passed through the early stages of transformation, from hiding to the youth group, and out into contexts of the community, including the assumption of social relations and possibly romantic and sexual intimacy with another, the youth moves on to demonstrate and celebrate with the community the claims to a new status. Appearing in the prom is a commencement of public ritual.

But what does the concept of ritual add to our understanding of the changes in the lives of the youth? Throughout this chapter we have used "ritual" to refer to a congeries of events and experiences loosely related to "coming out." Ritual, as a metaphor, signifies the sequence of prescribed social steps in status change which the gay and lesbian community increasingly recognizes as necessary for youth to come out.

The liminal period of the kids, betwixt and between passing as straight in the mainstream heterosexual society and being open in gay and lesbian culture, is a highly energized and morally charged resocialization. Remember that coming out refers both to self-transformation and a new claim to social rights. For the self, the rights of coming out are a commitment to establishing a new state of being in society, with new rights and duties woven around the cultural theme of expressing same-sex desires. But ritual often suggests an involuntary conscription into a group, and this aspect is seemingly missing from the youths' transition. One might think, at first, that no one forces the youth to come out; it seems self-selected, socially voluntary: they may or may not express their desires. Yet that is a heterosexualist interpretation. On the side of the self, one might just as well see the opposite: the youth have no "choice" but to come out, if they are to be "true to themselves," as so many of them say. They come in dire need—the desire to end secrecy and torment—to find a new social life. Anthropologists know that certain rites of passage express achievements of the person, such as marriage or promotion to a new social role, that are less "driven" by biology and more guided by social impetus. We also know, from some cultures around the world, that initiation is not coerced but rather a voluntary association, entered into for reasons of status elevation and social advancement.[56]

Coming out is one of these socially expressive rites of passage created out of the intense desire to live a social life in accordance with inner desires that can only be achieved by entering the new culture.

Let us review the cultural themes of this chapter as they point to the developing accord between same-sex desires and social values. The youth are being socialized into a community of new values. Their central rites emphasize again and again the accumulative effect of instilling a dislike of secrecy in favor of social solidarity with their group peers. The unlearning of the "naturalness and normality" of heterosexuality in favor of the values of "diversity" and "normal" same-sex desire are critical to their move into the youth group. Through the resocialization they discover first in themselves and later in society how much homophobia has marred human life. They also learn of new gender roles and identities in the gay and lesbian community, especially through the advisors, that do not require them to reverse or invert their sense of being masculine or feminine as they once believed was required. Rather, the many forms of androgynous "gender blending" prove to them the entirely conventionalized nature of male and female, which they ridicule or subvert. They learn the meaning of "responsibility" through safe-sex standards with partners and in their conduct with other kids at Horizons. This participation teaches also the value of "commitment" to their gay reference group, which supports them through the coming-out process. Thus they come to value equality in all relations, including their romantic and sexual interactions; and in the latter, they find a healing effect of being loved and desired by those they shunned in the past. Their final entry into the Gay and Lesbian Prom and Gay Pride Day Parade intensify an acceptance into the social community that claims its footing in gay and lesbian culture.

Of all these features of ritual that are compelling in the interpretation of coming out, there is one that stands out in understanding why ritual is so necessary. Death is all around and a constant guest at these events, from beginning to end. Before they can go on, the youth must deal with one of the most difficult of all human experiences: suffering the death of what they were, with the promise that a new person and self will take its place. As the young woman in the newcomer's group commented, a feeling of heaviness clings to the initial group so that it is like a "funeral." Another youth says, "I feel so bad from all of this, I feel like dying." Imagery of grief is so close to consciousness in process, but it defies it, until something happens; violence or rejection by someone, or an AIDS death.

Coming out is not only a claim for something new, it is a grief for the lost self. From their first fears of giving up the secrecy to their torment in passing through the threshold of Horizons, death is all around. It guards the fear of coming out, threatens violence on the street, is implicit in harassment and violence in the schools. The group is "really" about coming out, a black youth said, and yet he spoke mainly of loss. "I feel that I have to reckon with the child in me, when the child in me comes out. I feel, 'Yes, I am a faggot. It's my fault.' That sinking feeling comes to me, and I feel, 'Oh, my God.'" This same youth said that he was called a "whore" by an Hispanic man at his workplace. He was supported by his friend in the group. We might amend his comments to say that the group is really about death and rebirth of a new self.

People who undergo ritual transformations the world over experience a process of merging of individual identity with the group that we might refer to as the formation of a "group self." It is characterized by the loss of old identity markers and the strong association of age mates that erases the boundaries between bodies, minds, and souls. We have seen the intense emotion in the group, the intense physical contact of touching, holding, kissing, and among some youth, sex and lovemaking. They cry and laugh together. In this liminal state the timelessness of old moral norms can be changed and new ones introduced. The youth group, in this sense, becomes an object of and for the self, a living being that serves as a mirror that reflects the inner feelings and aspirations of individual members. To be defined in one's being by the cultural setting, not by one's individual body or self, is to feel the overflow of the sentiments and aspirations of the other as if they were the self. Past images of self and social relations are instantly shattered and must be rebuilt in a new selfhood—and rather urgently at that—with the energy and blessings of admired and loved authorities, the elders of the community and the ritual leaders of the group, that affirm the ritual emergence from seclusion to be the "right and natural" order of things. In this sense, participation in the Gay Pride Day Parade is the supreme act of coming out: a ritual of intensification that affirms the desired identity with the gay and lesbian culture. Rituals of coming out thus *embody* what is intensely personal in the social light of day.

How deeply the feeling of loss extends can be observed from the many stories of parents' reactions to coming out. A nineteen-year-old Caucasian youth from the suburbs said: "My parents couldn't deal with it. My mother said, 'You are dead to me. How can you be queer?'" She kicked him out of their home a year ago and refuses to acknowledge his existence today.

Both parents and children have to contend in the coming-out process. A story from the Pride Day Parade weekend helps to illustrate. Horizons hosted a social function for parents of the youth the day before the parade. It was Saturday afternoon. Soft drinks and snacks were served; balloons and banners were displayed. Someone put the rainbow flag up. A large punch bowl, in the good old fashioned midwestern style, was filled with dry ice to keep it cool in an overly hot room. About thirty youth showed up, some twelve advisors, and about twenty parents, some of them P-FLAG organizers. Among these were George and Selma Golden.

David, a new member in the group, had brought his mother along. He was twenty, a good-looking, black-haired young man, who attended a local college. He had only recently come out to his parents. David's mother was accepting to a degree, but his father had responded with anger and hurt. His father refused to join them. Several speeches, short in length, opened the social, followed by mixing in the crowd. David passed through the kids and adults, his mother in tow, proudly showing her off—in that special way children have of being flattered by their parents' presence at one of the great events in their lives. He introduced her to us as well. She was well groomed and in her late thirties, but she looked somewhat bowed and was visibly anxious. As the two of them moved through the center of the room, David's introductions seemed to make her socially embarrassed, and she grew even more distraught. She began to cry openly. She was the only one to interrupt the happy occasion, but there was so much noise that her crying was muffled. David was stunned, not knowing what to do. Then his mother broke away from him and passed through the crowd, apparently headed for the door.

As David's mother passed by Selma Golden, a large woman of immense presence and good nature, Selma actually grabbed her by the shoulder and pulled her over to her. "Honey, come over here," she said, firm but concerned, "I want to talk with you." The woman could only sob and looked away, visibly shaken. Mrs. Golden held onto her tightly, as if the mother might escape. Selma's voice was calm and reassuring, the study of a woman in her sixties who had been through this ritual many times before. In a minute, David's mother stopped crying. Then Mrs. Golden confided to her, "I know how you feel. I know it's hard to accept. When my son came out, I couldn't deal with it." She paused, and we wondered if she would cry too. "I had to cry. I cried for SEVEN years. But he didn't—couldn't—change. And then I realized, 'This is Raymond. He is one of our sons. I love him and I'm not going to give him up.'" She straightened her blouse and let loose of her hold on the mother. Selma looked straight into the other woman's eyes confidently: "If you love your son, you have to start dealing with the fact that he is gay; the other part of him is gone."

To come out is to deal with emotionally wrenching experiences of this kind all the time. The emotional loss is too much for the individual to cope with alone. It requires social support, the love and care of others in society, not only to undo the alienation and stigma of the past, but to create new social perceptions and images of these people for future relations. The ritual traditions evolving through Horizons and similar institutions around the country help kids to make the transition from straight to gay- or lesbian-identified people. Through the sequence of transitions the youth begin to accept that their old self has died. They begin to grieve for it; perhaps they will do so with their parents and friends. If successful, they eventually come to feel a kind of rebirth as a new self and social person, with a new status. Such is the process of giving up; the loss of the heterosexual self in the fantasies and dreams of both the children and, of course, of their parents—from whom some of these fantasies emanate. This is the protecting intent of gay cultural rites; they allow the youth to grieve forsaken heterosexual images and norms and to celebrate a new status.

But this is very hard to achieve overnight. The youth are struggling to articulate future goals, especially longer-term goals beyond their coming out, as we have seen. They cannot fully come out to everyone in their social lives. Some youth "drop out" of the group along the way, but before they reach their twenty-first birthday they may return at any time. One woman, discovered to be twenty-two, was asked to leave the group, though she was not yet ready. She cried and fretted openly and asked for support from the group, but the advisors, although sympathetic, were unyielding. They sense that the group must acknowledge the boundaries of ritual. An age boundary—in this case legal age—serves as a rough marker of independence and agency in our wider society.

We have seen how the stage is set at Horizons, from which the youth will now pass into other spheres of social life to demonstrate, that is, to perform and operate within, the new identity "gay and lesbian." As they do so, the "real life" facts of their individual lives intervene. First among these are their own sexual desires and wishes, which we will discuss in chapter 5. Second are the differences among them related to social status and standing: gender, class, family relations, ethnicity, and school. These differences provoke conflicts in their search for new identities in various social arenas and cultural domains of their lives forever after, as we shall see in chapter 6.

Ritual cannot do all of this for them. It can only open the way if they take the lead. In opening the way it provides the most powerful means known toward a new end: the achievement of full personhood and social acceptance in the gay and lesbian culture.

◆ ◆ ◆

CHAPTER FIVE

Milestones of
Sexual Identity Development

*My first sexual experience [at age 12] was with my best friend at the time. We were
really good friends in school. During the summer we had free time and would spend
the night at each other's houses. I was experimenting, I thought, but I was in love
with him. He was sleeping over at my house—he wanted to take all our clothes off
together. I was really excited—thought I would die—my heart was pounding so
fast. For Jim the excitement wore off. I wanted to continue being with him.
He would tell me, 'I wonder what it's like with girls?' He was straight and
just experimenting. I knew I was gay.*
—Mark, a seventeen-year-old African American

Mark's story is one of many such sexual awakenings that Horizons'
youth shared with us.[1] In talking about his life, Mark recounted viv-
idly how he first became aware of same-sex desires around age ten.
When he was twelve, as he says above, he had his first sexual experience with a friend of the same age. Today he is in the last semester of
the twelfth grade at a large multicultural public high school in Chicago. He lives at home with his mother and father, who are in their
early fifties; both parents are employed in blue-collar jobs. Mark is the
youngest of six siblings, and the three oldest children are out of the
house. He described relationships with both of his parents as having
been positive in the past. However, things had changed abruptly a few
days before we interviewed him in 1987. His mother was searching in
his bedroom and found a letter that Mark had received from a gay
male friend. She wrote him an angry note that was critical and rejecting, stating that she had "lost all respect for him." Although jolted
by the experience, Mark said somewhat nonchalantly that he was going to "give her a week or so to calm down" before discussing it with
her at length. Mark said that he generally feels accepted by peers at

school but is out to only a select few, the ones who are supportive of his gay identity; he hides being gay from those peers he perceives as homophobic. Mark told his interviewer he had two main worries in his life: "settling into a love relationship" and "discussing his sexual orientation with his parents."

The information from our interviews with Horizons youth indicates that they rate themselves within the parameters of same-sex attraction and that they self-identify as gay or lesbian. Their sexual identity is defined by how they identify with the cultural categories "gay/lesbian," "bisexual," or "homosexual"; their sexual orientation, the extent to which they are attracted to same- and opposite-sex partners; the extent to which their sexual fantasies take same- or opposite-sex partners, or both; and the stability or exclusivity of all of these elements. From this body of material we have created a theory that attempts to explain some of their developmental changes into gay and lesbian culture.

Desire for the same sex emerges early in development. We have found that the youth of Horizons begin experiencing desires for the same sex before puberty. The early objects of homoerotic desire need not be persons in the immediate environment of the child. Some youth describe attractions to media figures or celebrities, movie stars, singers, or people in books and films. Kevin, a twenty-one year old black, described his first awareness of homoerotic attraction in his response to a singer on television: "I was watching television and I saw Rick Springfield and I was sitting down and said, 'I wish I looked like that.' And then he did a love scene with someone and I said to myself, 'I want to be there too.' I still like Rick Springfield a lot." But somewhere along the development path real people will become involved. A fifteen-year-old Caucasian girl described her earlier attraction to a same-aged peer in these terms: "We were friends. We had very strong emotions. One night we kissed and felt so much passion. We were both holding back. It wasn't planned. Then it lasted eleven months. It became very romantic."

Homoerotic attractions to the same sex are viewed as "adolescent" in a doubly negative sense. American teenagers have long been regarded in cultural terms as potentially rebellious and amoral. Margaret Mead's well-known journey to Samoa in the 1920s was undertaken to find out whether American adolescent turmoil and sexuality were shaped more by the universals of biology or by local culture.[2] Seventy years later adult American attitudes continue to reflect the long-standing feeling that youth are usually "confused" and "risky" at sexual awakening. The youth's same-sex experiences are interpreted by others (if they are known at all), especially parents and older siblings, as a *passing* phase of development. They should lead to something else, our cultural reasoning and folk science has taught us. But these experiences are also considered to be "adolescent" because they are attributed to conflict and turmoil, and above all to immaturity—thus is sustained that great myth of our culture that same-sex desires are less than adult. They are believed to be a product of adolescent distress and irresponsibility, of surging hormones and the antisocial or rebellious behavior discussed by early psychologists, including Freud.[3] The youth may be admonished with statements such as "you'll outgrow this," or "it's just a stage—we all go through it." One nineteen-year-old girl in the youth group spoke up during a discussion of parents' reactions of this kind. She advised a younger boy in the group who was having family problems, "You have to please yourself. My parents said I was just going through a phase . . . they sent me to a psychiatrist. But after two years, and after I had a female lover, they stopped saying that. I don't see the shrink anymore. I have to please myself."

On the way to the presumed heterosexual bliss of adulthood, such a "derailment" is still viewed by many parents as a cause for anguish and the suspicion of developmental regression or fixation. Given the cultural bias, the reason is understandable. As the late Robert Stoller has written, many psychiatrists and psychoanalysts continue to regard "the homosexual" as a bogeyman, bizarre and unnatural, based upon a fictitious construction of "the heterosexual" which is equally flimsy and false when it comes to support of the empirical evidence. Richard Isay has also taken them to task for their homophobic theory on the subject.[4] But still, these stereotypes continue to prevail.

That heterosexualness among teenagers in the United States is largely taken for granted is apparent from our major institutions.[5] Particularly within the organizations that have the strongest and most long-lasting impact on youth—families and schools—adults assume that all youth are "naturally" heterosexual. The social organization of schools and the socializing influences of families prepare youth for heterosexual roles and life goals, from childhood through old age. As we noted in chapter 4, these institutions impose the most difficult of all developmental hurdles for gay and lesbian youth: unlearning the assumptive heterosexual identity and forging a gay or lesbian one. In this chapter we will explore the individual emergence of this new identity.

Rethinking Gay Youth Sexual Development

Perhaps the most profound, and yet the most common error, that adults in all kinds of roles—as parents, teachers, mental health professionals—make in understanding the development of same-sex desire is to lump together the two identities "homosexual" and "gay/lesbian." This error is compounded when they confuse the stigma of homosexual adults from their own past—the people whom they knew in growing up, in going to school, or from newspaper stories that usually portrayed the sad fate of the "homosexual"—with the feelings and expressions of today's self-identified gay and lesbian youth. They may think that same-sex experiences in youth are merely signs of confusion, or Oedipal conflict, or fear of the opposite sex—all are key folk notions of the past. To understand the effects of a new cultural world on the formation of individual youth requires us to sort out these confusions in thinking about sexual identity development.

Adolescence has long been understood as a time of identity development. Largely through the work of G. Stanley Hall and Anna Freud, the teenage years have been thought to initiate an upsurge of "libidinal drives."[6] According to these theorists, the adolescent phase of the cultural life course is linked to the tribulations of coping with "surging hormones," leading to many kinds of "problem behavior" for teens. Emotional turmoil is the most common but least serious of the so-called "problems." In the past, prominent psychologists identified the more severe problems as rebellion against family authority, antisocial activities, including juvenile delinquency, promiscuous sexual conduct, participation in street gangs, and homosexual experimentation.[7] Learning how to be a "mature and competent heterosexual"—as the old textbooks of psychoanalytic theory prescribed—in the face of these "conflicts," was critical to "successful" entry into adulthood.[8] Alfred Kinsey's empirical evidence from the 1930s and 1940s identified some adolescent same-sex erotic behavior as a normative, but only as it was limited and transitional into opposite-sex behavior, notably among boys.[9] In the domain of sexual identity, experimentation through masturbation and other sexual actions was thought a routine accompaniment to the supposed psychological "moratorium" of youth, described by Erik Erikson in the Cold War period.[10] As it turns out, this moratorium was more historical than psychological, as the sexual revolution bore witness to many changes in sexual experimentation among teenagers and young adults in the 1960s, including the birth of the gay and lesbian movement.[11]

Among developmental scientists it is still widely assumed that the normal and natural condition of sexual development is heterosexual. The evolution, functions, and outcomes of sexual development are still largely perceived as taking shape from the "natural fact" that desire for the opposite sex and reproduction guide all human affairs. Thus the occurrence of same-sex desire and action has been seen in negative terms. Homosexuality during adolescence has been explained by attributions to a variety of negative causes: to sexual abuse and seduction (typically imposed by an older perpetrator on a younger "victim"); to social learning through the associative pairing of sexual gratification within a same-sex dyad, often in situations of antisocial behavior, delinquency, and other forms of psychopathology; and to the lack of opportunities or restricted options for heterosexual outlets.[12] As Evelyn Hooker argued long ago, such biased research on the "problem of homosexuality" creates preoccupations with the "abnormal" causes of same-sex attraction rather than leading to study of the effects of same-sex attraction on development, including positive outcomes.[13] The extent of this bias is demonstrated dramatically by the facts that research publications on gay and lesbian youth are very recent, and discussions of development still routinely omit gay youth from their outlines of a supposedly universal human development and nature.[14]

Beginning in the early 1970s a small number of studies that were positive toward gays and lesbians began to emerge, including studies of the coming-out process.[15] This body of work helped to shift perspectives, leading to new questions and findings. Striving to have their research accepted as "normal science," the authors of these works largely ignored cultural context and routinized the schemas for explaining people's desires.[16] This had the unfortunate effect of slanting models of development toward adults and ignoring the kind of historical cohort and cultural change we have discussed in preceding chapters. Researchers began to talk about stages of coming out and identity formation and phases of the development of same-sex coupled relationships.[17] There was a tendency here, as in our Eurocentric Caucasian middle-class culture and science more broadly, to forget that identities and their contexts of human action continue to change, just as history and culture introduce new notions of being and doing gay and lesbian, or of being in a same-sex coupled relationship. Rather than thinking of gay and lesbian identity development in ineluctable "stages or phases," we now conceptualize their experiences as different processes of distinctive developmental subjectivities, each with its own pathways to adulthood.

The concept of sexual identity as a state of being—an ontology—stipulates an ideal self as well as a practicing, adaptive self, in an imperfect world. The course and fate of desires are in certain respects shaped by what happens to the person in the subjective and time/space worlds. An idealized self for gay youth is perhaps even more necessary than in other aspects of human development, as we have glimpsed in prior chapters, because of the great barriers and taboos of society with which the youth who desires the same sex must cope while developing.[18] Nowhere in human development are the person's desires and relationships subject as much to what Freud called the "accidental series" of our life histories as in sexuality. Whatever our desires might be, our being in a particular world shapes the possibilities we have for expressing our being, across the boundaries of culture, race and ethnicity, gender, class, religion, and the personalities of our parents and ourselves. For instance, Peter, a seventeen-year-old Caucasian boy, related an experience he had when he was six years old: "I used to live by the beach and I'd see these guys playing baseball. They really attracted me. I didn't know why. They had most of their clothes off." Peter's experience is shaped by growing up near the beach, seeing the men and boys in their swimsuits. He might have had a different set of experiences had he been reared in the ghetto of New York or the backwoods of Wisconsin. Furthermore, his culture is organized to regard these beach men as healthy and virile, figures of sexual action and as mythic movie stars. His culture offers female objects of desire as well, but he did not select the girls or women lying on the beach as objects of fantasy; something inside trained his interest and desire on the men.

In this chapter, by developmental subjectivities we mean the experience of adaptation across the course of life, the conventions and taboos of social roles that inform the experiences, the mental health conflicts and resilience linked to them, the cultural meanings they infuse in the stories people tell about their lives, and the interpretations of them made by significant others. Sexual identity is represented as including two modes of organization: *"sexual being,"* which includes such matters as sexual desire, sexual orientation, sexual pleasure and objects; and *"sexual relations,"* that concern erotic tastes and practices, developmental sequences of behavior, and sexual lifestyles. Where the former mode draws more upon the inner world of desires, the latter evokes much of what is important in the social expression of sexuality. We use the concept of sexual identity as a link between individual development, history, and culture. Unlike sexual orientation, which is focussed upon the "sex object" of the person, sexual identity is more fundamentally concerned with the definition of social and psychological reality. Identity is the culturally informed process of expressing desires in a social role and with socially shared cultural practices within a social context. Sexual identity formation remains one of the great keys to understanding the nature of the person in the process of cultural adaptation.

We view sexual identity development as an interlocking and overlapping set of processes embedded in historical cultural context. These processes begin, we think, with a given, perhaps a biologically grounded, form of "desire." The term desire is used advisedly, rather than other concepts, such as Freud's "drives," because of our concern with the development of *subjective* experience, not with the mechanisms of sexual function.[19] Desires, we believe, originate from within the nature of the person, as a state of being and adaptation. We think of these elements as "internal" in the sense of the potentials of being a person; however, desires interact with cultural experiences and social learning to achieve particular set goals or end points.[20] Desire is not a timeless universal either; both form and content are historically, culturally, and psychologically negotiated throughout life. Yet the earliest desires, we believe, are ontologically prior to and directive of all later cultural learning and teaching, especially after the entry of the child into school and diverse peer groups; subsequent socially learned desires build upon them. It is fruitless venture to search for "nature/ nurture" dichotomies here.[21]

Homoerotic development has its own impetus, desires and fantasies, particular contexts of expression, life tasks and goals, as shaped by the individual and his or her significant others in the social surround. The first experiences are concerned with early development from birth to puberty. Desire is here based in aesthetic feelings and responses that are neither purely of the body nor of the culture. They are not discreetly "erotic." Yet these early experiences are more strongly influenced by intrinsic desires and feelings than later ones.

Prior to puberty, Horizons youth refer to this process by feelings of being "different," with a faint suspicion that their desires diverge from the norm.[22] The individual's fuller awareness of attractions for gendered individuals brings a flood of attempts to interpret them through the lens of parents' actions and cultural tradition. The later experiences following puberty focus upon the erotic arousal and events of orgasm. These may be influenced by feelings from before; exploratory sexual play and arousal for the same and opposite sex before puberty. The final process of development, which is mainly concerned with social adaptation, usually begins to occur after puberty and finds its compression in the strong pressures exerted on the individual to conform to familiar and peer expectations of what constitutes "natural" human conduct. These social desires are channeled into first sexual and romantic experiences. Confusion may result from the conflict between earliest erotic desires and these later social attempts to desire conformity to custom and roles.

Many youth in our study recall reckoning with such assumptions and social norms. A sixteen-year-old boy recalled of his transition around puberty: "I just started having a feeling . . . I was more interested in men. It scared the hell out of me! I kind of forced myself to be interested in girls at the time. It felt very bad. I guess at the time it freaked me out. I thought, 'I can't be like that—no, I can't be.'" Thus the self may experience its own desires as alienating because the self has been hitherto defined socially as heterosexual.

First Desires

When does the earliest remembered same-sex desire occur? The individual interviews with each of the girls and boys in our study, revealed that the youth were able to recount their developmental experiences to us. They could usually report the ages at which they first became aware of their homoerotic attractions and fantasies and their first homoerotic sexual experience. The qualities and detail of these stories varied, but few of the youth were unable to locate themselves in a concrete social reality of the past, where they could recall many of the feelings and meanings of their desires at the time. In examining the emergence of the youth's same sex desires, we found that most youth reported a sequence of developmental desire. It began with an awareness of their same sex desires, followed by sexual fantasies about others, and this typically led to some type of same-

Table 5.1 Mean Ages (in years) and Standard Deviations (SD) of
Developmental Markers Reported by Gay and Lesbian Youth

Development Marker	Males (N=147)			Females (N=55)			Total (N=202)		
	M	SD	n	M	SD	n	M	SD	n
1st same-sex attraction	9.6	3.6	(146)	10.1	3.7	(55)	9.7	3.6	(201)
1st same-sex fantasy	11.2	3.5	(144)	11.9	2.9	(54)	11.4	3.3	(198)
1st same-sex activity	13.1[a]	4.3	(136)	15.2[a]	3.1	(49)	13.6	4.1	(185)
1st opposite sex activity	13.7	3.6	(87)	13.6	3.6	(44)	13.6	3.6	(131)
Age at 1st self-disclosure	16.0	2.4	(104)	16.0	1.8	(36)	16.0	2.3	(140)

[a]$t = -3.64, p < 0.001.$

sex experience. Table 5.1 shows the average ages at which youth reported the occurrence of five specific markers of their sexual development.

The average ages of first same-sex experience reported by the youth in our study are somewhat earlier than what has been reported by other researchers studying adult samples of gay men and lesbians.[23] While the age of sexual initiation is decreasing for all teens,[24] among gay and lesbian youth we find a time lag between the average age of first same-sex experiences, boys having their first same-sex experience significantly earlier than girls.[25] Statistical analyses of our interviews have confirmed this finding of earlier first same-sex experience for the Horizons boys.[26] The girls were more likely to report later ages for their first same-sex encounters. We wondered if the apparent gender difference was actually produced by some other variable. Thus we also controlled for other influences that might affect the age of same-sex desire for sexual contact, such as the minority status, employment status, residential status, and current age of the teens.[27] We found that the gender difference still held.

However, despite the fact that the genders act on their homoerotic desires at different ages, there was no gender difference in the average ages of first same-sex attractions and fantasies as reported by boys and girls. For boys the first attraction to someone of the same-sex occurred on average at nine and one-half years, quite similar to that reported by girls as occurring at ten years. Most youth were aware of these attractions before the onset of puberty, indicating that sexual development does not begin with the onset of puberty.

Horizons youth had many types of early desires to the same sex that defy stereotyping. The nature and object of these attractions also differed for the genders. Some youth tell how they were first attracted to peers of the same age, often innocently, and without an understanding of the early erotic aspect. For example, Troy, a sixteen-year-old black boy, described his first desire at age thirteen: "I was at school. I liked girls until eighth grade; then I started noticing boys. I guess that's how I changed. That's when I started looking at guys at school. . . . I didn't understand what happened. Why would I start to notice boys?" Sandy, an eighteen-year-old girl of mixed ethnic background (black and Caucasian), described her first desire during early adolescence in terms more general than the erotic: "It was a girlfriend I knew from school. The sex part has always come second to wanting to be with the person. I'd always want to be around her. I'd always find some way to touch her." Sexual interaction may not have been a part of these experiences, which may contribute to the remembered sense that the desire was "normal." Jerry, an eighteen-year-old Caucasian boy, described an attraction at age six: "[I was to] my cousin Alan. Same age. He moved in with us with his mother. We had, like . . . an attraction. We never did anything, sexually, we were very protective of each other. I knew what I was feeling. I was normal." Jerry's feelings grew in later years to become the desire for a same-sex lover.

Others became aware of their attractions through media images of older adults whom they idealized. Jose, a twenty-year-old Mexican-American, described his first awareness of homoerotic attraction at age four looking at a photonovela: "The only clear thing I can recall—my mom had these paperback Spanish novels with pictures in them. Some were of guys. I liked seeing them. I would look at them and kiss them sometimes." Gene, an eighteen-year-old black, described his first attraction at age ten to a man in a sexually explicit movie: "I saw an X-rated film. I liked when there were two guys and one woman. That's when I knew I was gay. I always liked to see the male body." Such desires contribute to the development of stable mental representations of real or fictitious persons, the source of homoerotic daydreams in later years, that further shape the individual's sexual identity.

Since school is such a large part of children's lives, it is not surprising that teachers are often reported as the first person to whom a student feels an attraction. Marta, a eighteen-year-old Puerto Rican girl, described her first attraction at age six: "It was my teacher. I used to like to hang around her . . . help her clean up the tadpole dish. It felt good just to be around her." Similarly, Jean, a seventeen-year-old girl of mixed ethnic background (black/Caucasian) recalled her first attraction: "My sixth-grade teacher—she was really nice to me. It was just a crush. She helped me out a lot. She was pretty. It was a good feeling, really nice."

Horizons youth experienced various types of sexual fantasies in the process of growing up. Their same-sex fantasies were reported to have occurred on average by age eleven among the boys, and by nearly age twelve among the girls. While the ages are similar, the content of these fantasies are gender-divergent. This is not surprising in itself; but the intensity and explicitness of the fantasies reveals important clues for understanding the genders. Boys reported fantasies that were often more explicitly erotic than did the girls. Here is a characteristic scenario from Tina, a sixteen-year-old black girl, who remembered this fantasy from age ten: "I always thought it would be nice to have a house with a woman. There would be no kids—just us. We'd each have a car—go to our different workplaces. Maybe have some cats, a real family structure. Two women together, cats, work, a home, no kids—I felt it was a fantasy I needed to fulfill in order to be happy. Sex was involved in this fantasy, but it was not the main focus." On the other hand, Terry, an eighteen-year-old black boy, described his first sexual fantasy also at age ten: "I fantasized about me and another guy, or two guys. . . . I felt guilty after climax, but it felt good. I couldn't see myself with a girl doing that."

The boys who reported their first sexual awakening before puberty seemed to regard these experiences as troubling for several reasons. Primary among these is perhaps the internalized guilt for breaking the taboo in our society against sexual experience between children. When it occurs with a same-sex partner it is compounded by homophobia. Later, the guilt may be fueled by the cultural myth that "homosexuality" is caused by childhood seduction (in which myth says an older male is the initiator). The long suggested link between prepubertal sexual "precocity" and homosexuality may be another factor.[28] On the other hand, as they move into adolescence, individuals may remember what they felt in childhood through the lens of gay and lesbian ideology: a cultural value suggests that homosexual/gay men have a "sex drive" eroticism more powerful than that found among heterosexuals.

Why are there differences between the fantasies of boys and girls? Teenage girls may be more reluctant to express explicitly sexual fantasies because of their family and school experiences, which discourage expressions of female erotic desire. On the other hand, boys may be more likely to respond with explicit sexual fantasies because it is a defining feature of masculine ideals. Whatever the source of the gender difference, most youth have great difficulty in accepting their own fantasies as "normal" at the time. Tina describes her feelings at eleven: "I had a cousin I was attracted to. . . . And [there would be fantasies from] seeing things on TV. I entertained the thought of me and her kissing. It would come and go . . . I felt like an oddball—that I was out of place, that I shouldn't feel that way. I grew up trying not be close to other females. I knew it wasn't normal. I didn't want people to say, 'she likes girls.'" Mack, a twenty-year-old black youth, described how his first sexual fantasies felt "unnatural" but were nonetheless highly arousing. "I thought they were unnatural desires. It was kind of degrading. Bad. A kid at school, a Greek kid. I haven't seen him in years and I really want do." It is not until subsequent social relations bring opportunities for the desire to become a reality that the next milestone must be hurdled.

The First Homoerotic Experience

We were about five. He was a friend of mine. A school friend. We didn't do much really. We laid on top of each other, felt around. We were really just playing."
—*Michael, an eighteen-year-old Caucasian*

Children are not typically ambivalent about their needs and wants. By age three they begin to receive messages and communications—more indirectly than directly, and more tacitly than explicitly—which begin to define for them the parameters of love and sex, of what is socially approved or disapproved—which in the Judeo-Christian context translates into the well-known states of being "good" and being "evil." Through socialization both overt and covert, adults teach children what is okay and what is not; soon these notions are translated into what is "dirty" and "clean." The erotic desires of childhood are likely to be the discoveries of curiosity. This curiosity, Freud believed, begins with a child's questioning of his/her origins as a body and a gendered being.[29] Children's curiosity and detective work (at least in fantasy) extends into the bed of mother and father, making them into "quasi-scientific" excursions: the child as a scientist/explorer (similar to the metaphor Piaget early adopted of the child as a moral philosopher[30]). Children are, perhaps intrinsically, curious about many things, including the human body—about its functions and purposes, and all of these curiosities carry the seeds of desire. The explorations of childhood sexual play, Kinsey tells us, are actually a common occurrence, with many sexual interactions between same- and opposite-sex playmates, and between same-sex playmates, particularly among boys.

Most of the boys and girls of Horizons—88 percent to be exact—reported engaging in their first same-sex experience when they were ten years old or older. However, a smaller group of boys (12 percent) and girls (3 percent) reported an age of nine years or younger (two female respondents did also). Those from the smaller group reported, in at least half of these cases, same-sex activity with a same-aged peer, which often was described as "playful." From their descriptions, these desires appear to be different from the first desires described by other boys and girls at a later age (around age eleven, on average).

Let us begin with the youth who have the earlier experience. Around age seven on average, a small number of Horizons boys and two girls told us that they began to feel an attraction, a drawing near, to other children of the same sex. The number may be larger than we think.[31] Many want to imitate their mothers and fathers heterosexuality, wanting to do what they have seen and thought older people were doing. By age seven they felt what they recall to be an erotic interaction with someone of the same sex. A few youth described these as volitional childhood experiences: they had a self-consciousness of the meaning of the sexual interaction at the time. Thus, a twenty-year-old Hispanic youth described his feelings at age five: "I never really imagined being straight, so my homosexual thoughts were normal for me—I wasn't torn between heterosexual and homosexual . . . it just felt normal. [First sexual attraction] was to some kid, fourteen or fifteen, in the neighborhood. I hardly remember him other than being attracted to him. I used to go to his house. I'd go alone. I was sexually attracted. He made me feel excited to be around him."

While these experiences are uncommon for the group, they point toward a trend: earlier childhood experiences felt as pleasingly erotic in the more diffuse rather than in the genital sense. The relatively unique nature of the Horizons population prevents generalizing to other groups of teenagers regarding the typicality of this pattern for boys. The younger and older groups may represent different paths of initiation into male sexual identity and lifestyles, as reported by the youth themselves. (This set of boys who engaged in early same-sex relations may also account for the gender difference in average age at first same-sex experience.)

The largest group of youth who have a prepubertal experience remembered a more explicit erotic feeling at the time. Randy, a nineteen-year-old Caucasian boy from the suburbs, describes his sexual emergence as a blend of awareness and naivete. "In third grade, I was most curious. I didn't know what to do with penises. But there was a boy— I felt good about my feelings about him. I just told mom that he was cute. I just thought it was admiration for another person. I didn't tell him, because it was third grade. I didn't know anything. Around age ten, I asked mom what homosexuality was. I could only imagine anal sex as what homosexuals did." Soon, Randy had come out to his mother, and shortly thereafter he self-identified as gay. He has never come out to his father, who he said, is "macho" and "hates gays."

Youth without Same-Sex Experience

There are also youth, however, who self-identify as gay or lesbian in the absence of any overt sexual experience in their life history. Seventeen of the Horizons kids reported having never had a homoerotic relationship, and yet they self-identified as gay or lesbian. While this is a small number (8 percent), its significance is great in the light of the long debate on whether same-sex desires are "learned" though early sexual experience.[32] These kids did not "learn" their desires from anyone else in the simple sense; they report them as being a part of their existence for as long as they can remember. These teens, for one or another reason, have also decided to postpone homoerotic relations. A few of these youth discussed their desire to delay sex with someone of the same sex until they had found the "right" person. As one boy said, "I'm not just going to fuck anyone. I want to wait for someone I feel good about."

A couple of boys have also expressed fears of contracting AIDS as a factor in their delay of same-sex relations, consistent with the themes of chapter 4. A sixteen-year-old black youth linked his not having sex to his concern about AIDS. "You just don't know who has it [AIDS] and you have to be real careful. People just want to sleep with you just to sleep with you. I'll be careful whenever I start. . . . I feel you don't have to have sex to keep a relationship. If someone likes you, they like you. They just don't want to have sex with you." For others, AIDS has made homoerotic relations something about which they were very cautious and fearful. One eighteen-year-old black male told us he had never had either heterosexual or homosexual sex. He went on: "There's no such thing as safe sex. I call it 'responsible sex.' I want to get to know the person . . . that is important, also wear a condom and all that."

As they get older, youth are closer to the consciousness of positive gay and lesbian cultural images, through various sources, such as media. Here is Randy, an eighteen-year-old black who was open (but still uncomfortable) talking about sex.

> My first attraction [was] at age nine—[it was] mostly sexual thoughts. . . . At age thirteen, [I had sex for the first time] with a friend. It was great. But the only thing I regret is that his parents didn't know he was gay. We had to keep it hush hush. He did. I didn't. It was mutual . . . we're still friends. It started out to study [homework]. We went upstairs, sat on the bed. He said, "What do you think of gay people?" I said, "There's nothing wrong with them," and he said, "Give me a kiss," and it started. He was gay but not out. But he is now.

Today Randy is out, dates other boys, and is actively involved in a sexual life.

Contexts of Sexual Initiation

Unlike the society of the past, many new contexts are available for youth to gain sexual experience. The gay and lesbian youth in our study reported a variety of interpersonal contexts in which they initiated a first same-sex experience. Whether with the same or the opposite sex, these experiences hold implications for sexual identity development in the coming months and years. While our study of gay youth is not concerned with the causes of homosexuality, our data on gay and lesbian youth peripherally address this issue by examining the context in which youth become aware of and first express their same-sex desires.

Table 5.2 displays the average ages of youth according to the context of their first same-sex experience. (Responses to questions regarding first homoerotic activity were coded for the context in which these sexual relations began.) The three key contexts of first same-sex experience can be identified as "sexual," "dating," and "friendship," as discussed below.[33] Statistical analyses of our data revealed a signifi-

Table 5.2 Relational Context of First Same-Sex Experience

	Males		Females		Total	
	n	%	*n*	%	*n*	%
Sexual	35	24	3	5	38	19
Dating/Romance	21	15	12	22	33	17
Friendship	33	23	25	45	58	29
Childhood Play	18	12	2	3	20	10
Abuse	26	18	7	13	33	16
No Sex	11	8	6	11	17	8
Total	144	100	55	100	199	200
Uncodeable/missing	3	...	...	...	...	...

cant relationship between the gender of the youth and the context of the first sexual experience. The boys were more likely than the girls to initiate a first homoerotic experience in a sexual context. The experiences of girls were typically described as evolving in the context of friendships. Thus, the motivations for first expressing homoerotic desires may be quite different among the male and female youth. In general, boys attached more emphasis to sexual pleasure, while the girls viewed emotional closeness as more important. But the boys also clearly express needs for emotional closeness, and lesbian youth certainly did not disregard sexual pleasure. However, the valuations of sexual expression are different for the boys and girls.[34]

Sexual Contexts. The transformative impact of puberty in the lives of gay and lesbian youth is a critical aspect of sexual identity development that has been ignored. For the majority of the gay and lesbian youth in our study, sexual interaction with the same sex begins after biological puberty.[35] Puberty involves a rather dramatic set of changes in which a child's body gradually comes to approximate that of an adult. Homosexual and heterosexual teenagers may be similar in many respects, including their experiences of puberty. A nineteen-year-old Caucasian boy from the suburbs described his first orgasm: "I was masturbating. It scared me. I thought I'd hurt myself. But it felt fun. I was home, in the shower." His report is quite like that of other heterosexual boys.[36]

However, the eroticizing impact of puberty in transforming desires and attractions opens the door to alternative developmental pathways for lesbian and gay youth. For example, one of the outcomes of puberty is the attainment of mature reproductive potential. With the possibility to reproduce comes greater social and moral pressures to conform to "normal and natural" roles. The new physical status of the postpubertal adolescent, physical size, body shape, and appearance is accompanied by a variety of social and psychological expectations. Important people such as friends, teachers, and family members may begin to react differently to a young adolescent, effecting a shift in the ways in which a teenager is viewed by others.[37] This potential affects the adolescent's self-image, as well as his or her assumptions and expectations regarding sexual behavior and social relations.

Nearly a quarter (24 percent) of the boys but only 5 percent of the girls initiated their first homoerotic relationships in a sexual context, at an average age of 15.5 years for boys. That the desire for erotic contact formed the basis for beginning these relationships is clear: the youth had neither been friends with nor had prior knowledge of, their sexual partners, at the time the homoerotic activities began. One boy described his first experience at age fifteen. "I was with this group of people, and we went to a house party. I met this guy Jeff. We went into somebody's bedroom. We started touching each other. It became more intense."

Dating Contexts. The girls were much more likely than the boys to report first homoerotic experiences in the context of a dating or romantic relationship or in a friendship context. A seventeen-year-old Caucasian girl described meeting an age-peer at the group. "We met last summer at Horizons. We talked about how we felt. She was waiting for me to initiate. Sex was very minor; it wasn't planned and it happened a long time after we first met." (Sexual contexts were relevant among only 5 percent of the girls at an average age of 16.3.) Seventeen percent of the youth (15 percent boys and 22 percent girls) reported initiating sexual activity in the context of dating and romance. Interestingly, the average age of boys in this context was nearly eighteen (17.9), while for girls it was a younger age of 16.4. An eighteen-year-old boy described such a first sexual experience with an age-peer. "It was beautiful. The sex wasn't planned. It was already a relationship. We'd just kissed and hugged before. I'm romantic. The relationship lasted two years. It was very romantic. I'd go to his house. We'd go out to dinner."

Friendship contexts were the most common relational setting for the first same-sex relationship following puberty. More than two-thirds of the youth's first homoerotic experiences occurred with peers or friends of similar ages. The expression of homoerotic desires were, excluding the group who reported coercive or abusive experiences (16 percent) described below, initiated by choice with an age-peer partner. For girls (45 percent) this occurred on average at age 13.8 years of age. For over one-fifth of the boys (23 percent) it occurred at a markedly later age (15.7 years). Friendships that evolved into sexual relationships were qualitatively different for boys and girls. Not only does gender shape first sexual experiences, but their timing may also affect the forms of these relationships. Mary described her first sexual relationship arising out of a friendship: "Brenda and I were friends in school. I spent the night at her house and as we were lying in bed together, we started going at it. This first time was not planned. But afterward we began planning the relationship. . . . We'd go to the movies, biking, dinner. We spent quality time together. We lasted for two years."

But not all of the responses to first homoerotic relations with friends are positive. Some youth remain frightened and closeted. Sixteen-year-old Tammy describes her feelings for another girl of the same age: "I was drunk, afraid. She told me she had liked me for two years. I was scared. I didn't want to be friends then, but we stayed friends and one night we got drunk and it happened. I didn't really like her sexually—afterward I just wanted to go hide somewhere. I didn't see her as often as I did before. 'Cause she wanted to get serious—I told her I was drunk and let's leave it alone.'" A year later, Tammy had still not come out and had not had a positive same-sex experience. Another fear concerns sexual disease risk. One boy in this group described his first homoerotic experience at age eighteen with a twenty-year-old. "I met him at the group. Then he asked me if I wanted to come over to his place. He was the one that led, in everything. He started touching me. One thing I worry about, which I regret—I didn't use protection and he didn't. Now I'm worried about myself."

With whom do the youth engage in their first same-sex experience? Table 5.3 presents the distribution of first sexual partners of the youth (excluding cases of abuse). Three-quarters of the youth reported a first sexual partner who was a friend or peer (defined as not more than three years older or younger than the respondent). A slightly larger percentage of girls (81 percent) reported a first sexual partner in this category than did the boys (73 percent). Nine percent of the youth reported an older first sexual partner, and 15 percent reported an adult (defined as over twenty-one years). These older partners were largely those of the oldest youth in our study (age twenty-one).

Table 5.3   Gender of Respondent by Sequencing of First Sexual Experiences[a]

Sequencing of First Experiences	Males		Females		Total	
	n	%	n	%	n	%
Same-sex, then opposite-sex	46	36	16	34	62	35
Opposite-sex, then same-sex	28	22	21	45	49	28
Same-sex exclusively	54	42	10	21	64	37
Total	128	100	47	100	175	100

[a]$X^2 (2, N = 175) = 10.53, p < 0.0052.$

Heteroerotic Experience

A significant number (55 percent) of our gay and lesbian interviewees (thirty-seven girls and seventy-four boys) reported having had some type of heteroerotic experience (see table 5.3.) For gay and lesbian youth, such heterosexual experimentation may be parallel to the same-sex encounters described by heterosexual youth.[38] Heteroerotic experiences occurred among a higher percent of girls than boys. For the boys this occurred at 13.7 years on average, very close to the average age of 13.6 years for girls. Both boys and girls reported mixed reactions to opposite-sex sexual activity. Kevin, a Caucasian (twenty-year-old) youth, described his first heteroerotic experience at age thirteen this way:

> It was just kissing—she felt me out, I didn't put my hands in her pants or any of that. I was a little turned on by it, but it wasn't great for me really. We went out together a few times. A little later, when I was seventeen, I met a girl who was fifteen. I saw her for a couple of months. It was my last-ditch effort. I felt good about it. I was glad to be this involved, but there was still something missing. I had her, but my feelings about guys just didn't change or go away.

The gender difference we have discovered in the sexual development of youth helps us to understand the social pressures they experience in growing up. The divergence of average ages for first homoerotic and heteroerotic experiences of boys and girls suggests the first clue: that they have divergent sexual developmental pathways, particularly for the first same-sex experience. To understand the development of the genders' sexual subjectivity of these experiences, we classified youth according to which of a series of three sequences occurred in their initial sexual encounters (that is, those who had heteroerotic or homoerotic experiences first). We found that the first homoerotic sexual experience of boys was typically preceded by a first hetero-erotic experience. For girls, the average age of same-sex experiences was later than the average age at first sex with a male. These differences are very significant in knowing how the heterosexual/homosexual dichotomy influenced the development of the individual. Do boys or girls experience the same heterosexualist pressures? Our evidence suggest the pressures shift and change, with girls experiencing pressures to conform to normative heterosexual roles in such a way that they "delay" the expression of their same-sex desires longer than the boys. We also find that because the boys have somewhat more "freedom" to "test" their same-sex and opposite-sex feelings, they may have a tendency to feel an earlier and stronger uncertainty about how and where to express their homoerotic desires.

Thirty-five percent of the youth were categorized in the same-sex/opposite-sex pathway; 28 percent were in the opposite-sex/same-sex sequence; and 37 percent in the same-sex only category.[39] Larger proportions of boys were found in the same-sex/opposite-sex and same-sex only groups. The percentage of girls was higher in the opposite-sex/same-sex group. Thus, girls were significantly more likely to have had an opposite-sex erotic experience before their first same-sex erotic experience. Statistical analyses of these data have confirmed that the sex of the youth allowed us to predict the sequencing of first same-sex and opposite-sex experiences, regardless the influence of other factors such as the youths' ethnicity, employment status, or age at the time of interview.[40]

The youth's descriptions of their experiences suggest that they used the meanings that they felt to clarify their desires. One of the girls in the same-sex/opposite-sex pathway group reported comparing her own feelings with the demands of societal norms. She said she felt: ". . . confused as to whether I should be with a guy because society said so, or if I should be with Brigit [her female lover]." Other recollections suggested that by comparing them, the youth began to regard the same-sex experience as more desirable. As one boy (in the opposite-sex/same-sex pathway group) told of his first homoerotic experience: "I liked it, it felt natural to me. I'd had sex with a woman before, and this felt better to me, more natural." One's basis for comparison may effect how positively or negatively one judges an intimate experience.[41]

Even youth who were ambivalent about their first homoerotic experiences found that comparing these experiences to heteroerotic ones helped them to admit or accept feelings otherwise difficult to comprehend. For example, a boy in the same-sex/opposite-sex group described his first homoerotic experience as one in which "we enjoyed the act but didn't enjoy thinking about it." Yet he subsequently found that when he tried out sexual intercourse with a woman, the experience was not gratifying to him: "I was very romantic with her, only I was fantasizing about guys [when I was] with her. . . . It felt worse than I did with my first relationship with a guy! . . . I felt like I was leading her on."

How the youth felt about these initial sexual encounters may also have served as a context for the way in which they constructed their gay and lesbian identities. A theme running through the accounts of youth describing their first heteroerotic experience was that it was "sex without feelings," which they "kept trying" but did not particularly find rewarding or fulfilling. Regardless of whether it was preceded by a homoerotic experience or not, a feeling of "unnaturalness" and a lack of affective intensity in their first heteroerotic sex was mentioned repeatedly. This theme was present in the accounts of both boys and girls, although girls tended to describe heteroerotic experiences as something that they simply *expected* to happen, while boys indicated that they often *sought* out the experiences. One girl put it this way: "I went to his house, we had sex. Initially it hurt. I'd go to his house about twice a week. Finally it didn't hurt, but there was no feeling for me. I didn't enjoy the experience." Barry, another boy, recounted his first sexual experience with a girl, "Her parents were away for the weekend, we went back to her house. It felt weird, I thought it was because it was the first time. But we went out for a year and it never did feel right." In contrast first homoerotic activity was often described as quite "natural" by the boy. Thus, the effect seemed magnified if the experience had been preceded by a heteroerotic one with which to compare it.

The youth's descriptions of their feelings about first same-sex experiences were classified on a five-point scale from very negative to very positive. Good to excellent reactions were reported by over half the youth (56 percent), with ambivalent or mixed reactions reported by another 29 percent. Some youth did not regard their first homoerotic sexual activity as "real" sex and stated that they were not disturbed or upset by these first same-sex experiences. Somewhat less than a third reacted negatively to their first same-sex experience (even though they admitted that they had enjoyed its erotic component) and followed this experience with an opposite-sex experience. Girls responded more positively to their first same-sex activity than boys.

The relationship between the youth's reaction to first same-sex experience and gender revealed a significant but weak statistical relationship.[42] Boys felt significantly more positively than girls about their first opposite sexual experience. Despite these differences, the more positive ratings by boys were not a motivation for continuing heteroerotic experiences. In fact, whether they experienced same-sex relations before or subsequent to sexual relations with the opposite sex, the youth tended, on average, to feel better about their homoerotic experiences than their heteroerotic experiences. These ratings were similar to those who had only engaged in homoerotic sexual behavior. It is possible that those youth who have only engaged in a first homoerotic experience initiated their sexual activity later, and therefore had not yet had an opportunity to have a heteroerotic experience at the time of the interview. Table 5.4 presents the relationship between the sequencing of sexual behavior and the average ages at which the behavior first occurred, as well as the average ratings of the youths' reported feelings about their first sexual experiences. The data in the first and second rows of table 5.4 indicate that this possibility is not the case, since the average age at first same-sex for the exclusively same-sex group (14.1 years) was later than that for the same-sex/opposite-sex group (11.5 years). Otherwise, these ages were as expected, given the sequencing that each category represents (i.e., for the opposite-sex/same-sex group the average age at first opposite-sex was younger than that for first homoerotic sex, while the reverse was true for the same-sex/opposite-sex group).

The third and fourth rows of table 5.4 compare the youths' ratings of feelings about first homoerotic and heteroerotic experiences for youth in each of the three pathways. These self-ratings ranged from 1 through 5 (1=very bad, 2=bad/not good, 3=average/OK [mixed positive and negative], 4=good, and 5=very good). The teenagers in all three groups rated their initial homoerotic experiences fairly positively (between OK and good). They are also similar in the uniformly lower ratings they give to their first heteroerotic activity. There is nearly a one point drop in the average rating from same- to opposite-

Table 5.4 Youths' Sequence Group by Ages at First Sexual Experience and Responses to First Same-Sex and Opposite-Sex Sexual Experience

Mean Ages and Ratings of First Sexual Experiences	Opposite-Sex, then Same-Sex (*n*=49)	Same-Sex, then Opposite-Sex (*n*=62)	Same-Sex Exclusively (*n*=64)
M age of 1st same-sex	15.4 years	11.5 years	14.1 years
M age of 1st opposite sex	11.9 years	14.9 years	...
M response[a] to 1st same-sex experience	3.6	3.7	3.5
M response[a] to 1st opposite-sex experience	2.8	2.8	...

[a]Response scores range from 1 through 5; 1 = very bad, 2 = bad/not good, 3 = average/ok, 4 = good, 5 = very good.

sex activity for both same-sex/opposite-sex and opposite-sex/same-sex groups (from 3.6 to 2.8 among the opposite-sex/same-sex youth and from 3.7 to 2.8 among the same-sex/opposite-sex youth).

The developmental sequencing of the youth's first sexual experiences does not appear related to the ages at which same-sex and opposite-sex activity first occurred, nor to the youth's feelings regarding these events. Instead, gender appears to play a major role in the sequencing of first homoerotic and heteroerotic sexual activity, independent of these factors. Just as same-sex contact between heterosexually identified adolescent boys is typically not defined as "homosexuality" and does no necessarily lead to the sexual identity "gay" or "homosexual,"[43] likewise the participation of these gay and lesbian youth in heteroerotic experiences does not identify them with "heterosexuality." The youth's descriptions of their participation in sexual relations with the opposite sex highlights how the normative socialization of teenagers includes strong pressure to conform to mainstream norms.[44]

The accounts of the boys revealed that they often sought heteroerotic experiences, while female youth typically described heteroerotic sex as something that had previously happened to them at an earlier age. It is possible that the greater likelihood of sexual pressure and coercion experienced by girls from heterosexual boys predisposes them to the sequence of heteroerotic then homoerotic experiences, as a consequence of growing up in a society where girls encounter such experiences much more commonly than boys. Sexual socialization of young girls, in public schools for example, typically prepares them to experience their sexuality in passive ways.[45]

The girl's initial (and relatively less pleasurable) heteroerotic activity may serve as a basis of comparison that facilitates their transition to lesbian identities. For the first time, it may also permit them to feel like they are the agents of their own sexual desires—both in body and in social relations.[46] While both boys and girls are the object of heterosexualist assumptions (from family, peers, and significant others), boys may at first experience greater cultural and familial expectations for heterosexual behavior, in part because they commence sexual experience at an earlier age than the girls. This heterosexualist pressure might impel them to experiment with girls, regardless of their primary erotic desires. And of course, similar to findings reported on gay and lesbian adults,[47] some of the youth have told us of their magical wish—that by engaging in heteroerotic behavior, their same-sex desires would go away. Girls may experiment in a similar manner as time unfolds; however, as they physically mature, the pressure to engage in heterosexual dating and intercourse may exceed that experienced by the boys. At least one major recent study reports that Danish girls underestimate the age of their first male sexual partner, suggesting heightened pressure on girls at younger ages to begin their sexual careers.[48]

Sixteen percent of the sample described first sexual experiences that were of a coercive or abusive nature (18 percent boys and 13 percent girls). They involved partners who were of either the same or opposite sex to that of the youth. These experiences spanned a range, from direct assault to subtle forms of coercion. For example, a female described a first sexual relationship she had at age eleven: "She was my teacher in martial arts. . . . I never really realized or thought of it as sexual experiences. Sex made me feel secure in a frightening place. Our world was dark and lonely and didn't have a lot of room for emotion. To be free to love someone was the best part of my life then." It should be noted that girls in our sample were more likely to report sexual abuse and coercion in first heterosexual relationships than did boys.[49] A twenty-one-year-old male described an abusive first experience at age seven with an eleven-year-old male. "My older cousin molested me. He rubbed his body against mine. He wanted to have anal sex, but I said no." In general, the youth seem to have weathered these experiences with the resilience shown in other areas of their adaptation. Still, the presence of coercive experience in their past is a reminder of the harsh and sometimes violent events surrounding sexuality in a society that remains preoccupied with sexual ignorance in children and sexual sophistication in adults.[50]

Bisexuality

Many youth reported engaging in behavior that society would more broadly define as "bisexual." Yet their opposite-sex contacts were transient and irregular. Transient sexual contact with the same sex, Kinsey told us, was most frequent before age fifteen and more likely to be experienced by boys than by girls.[51] Today, these experiences are usually felt to be discrepant with the erotic desires and feelings of Horizons youth, as we have seen. Participation in opposite-sex experiences suggests that these youth were "testing" their own homoerotic desires. They were simultaneously engaging in socially expected heterosexual relations, while also internally comparing these to their same-sex experiences, making these events a benchmark of comparison. The youth's accounts of their feelings about their same-sex and opposite-sex experiences highlighted the comparisons.

We have seen that in the Horizons youth group, as in American society in general, bisexuality is a contentious and often confusing issue. The bisexual is "betwixt and between" sexualities; and at Horizons its follows that for many youth, though by no means all, bisexuality is a social phase, a certain developmental step, into coming out. Youth depend upon a process of emergence to awaken in them new and perhaps hidden and threatening feelings. For example, sixteen-year-old Jesse, an ambiguously identified youth at Horizons, was bisexual in his self-presentations. He was from South Side Chicago's black community, and there, he said, it was a lot harder to be openly gay. In fact, it was impossible. His history reflected this need for secrecy. "My identity has been mostly straight. I could be mostly gay in self-identity." But in life-style, "I have felt and still feel mostly straight."

But consider, by contrast, the problem that "Straight Sam" presented to the youth group. Sam was a youth who preferred homosocial settings. The Horizons group invented his nickname in part to poke fun at him, and in part to mock his frequent assertion, "I'm straight." Sam was a gangly nineteen-year-old Caucasian youth, skinny and clumsy, who had a bad case of acne. He was the original "nerd," complete with horned-rimmed classes and a big mop of brown hair, uncombed and flying in every direction. His appearance was striking against the usually carefully coiffured other youth.[52] In both a formal interview and two additional informal interviews, Sam consistently maintained that he was "heterosexual."[53] According to his assessment of himself in interviews, he rated higher opposite-sex interest in almost all dimensions of identity, though he felt attraction to the same-sex emotionally, and in his social life he liked to interact with gays more than straights. Upon questioning, Sam said that he had never been involved with the opposite or same sex intimately. He came to the group, he said, to "get rid" of his homophobia, which he said he "inherited from his lower middle-class parents in the suburbs." He felt that he was "breaking down his prejudice" by coming to the group. He attended for about six weeks. The other youth never believed that he was straight but they accepted his presence. He claimed that he wanted to be a "better person" and this required being around gay and lesbian teens. He suggested at one point that he liked his "gay friends better than his straight friends." Sam told how he was actually the target of "queer" slurs in his high school, and these had bothered him a lot. Sam, it turns out, was the "school fag." He was the target of harassment, which he didn't talk about much in the group. Sometimes the youth tried to discover if there were other feelings. One of the boys suggested that Sam might "like to come to a party," insinuating something sexual, but Sam turned him down. Sam is a paradox: a boy who consolidated among gay youth his "straightness." Perhaps Sam enjoyed and needed a gay "symbolic space" but not an identity, a refugee from suburban life who was tenuously accepted. It was ironic for us to discover that in terms of his sexual sex identity scores, Sam was among the most confused youth we knew.

In listening to the stories of the Horizons youth it is apparent that the process of comparing their heteroerotic and homoerotic experiences is an important part of the development of eventual gay and lesbian identities. Many Horizon's youth express their identities with "bisexual feelings" at first. Seventeen-year-old John's experience tells this story: "She was interested in me and I wanted to make it work. I didn't have any drive for her, I felt removed, like looking through a window. . . . I thought, 'maybe it was the girl.' So, I thought I'd give myself three strikes, then I'm out. They [the next two girls] were basically similar. After the last one, there was no point in it." John found that his desires for the same sex were both more exciting and fulfilling for him, and he went on to become gay-identified in sexual and social relationships. Our dualistic culture, so strongly woven around the opposition between the old categories "heterosexual and homosexual," compels Horizons youth to commit themselves to a category of identity before they are comfortable in knowing their desires. For this reason, some of the youth at Horizons have made use of the category "bisexual" on the path to gay and lesbian identity development.

For the vast majority of the Horizons group, bisexuality is a purchase on time, both social and developmental time. The youth can decide who to tell and how to define the expression of their desires and tastes, sexual and social. The biding of time is problematic for friends, who may question their own sexual identity in the interim, or be threatened by the "inbetweenness" of this liminal period. The bisexual, in sum, is a chameleon, an embryonic being akin to the trickster of American Indian folklore, full of possibilities to be all and everything, but elusive to others and perplexing for the self that would fix a steady gaze on its own life.

Sexual Experience and Gay and Lesbian Identities

The lessening of cultural taboos in conjunction with the presence of a gay cultural community has enabled Horizons youth to give expression to their homoerotic desires in ways that are both personally meaningful and culturally expressive. This is striking in contrast to many lesbian and gay adults of today who attempted in their earlier development, often for significant periods of time, to live as, or as if, they were heterosexuals.

While many of the youth in our study have experimented with some heterosexual experience, they appear to have chosen a different life course trajectory during a critical phase of the life cycle, circumventing a protracted period of passing as "heterosexual." The stories of Horizons youth suggest the simple but profound point that they knew early on that their desires for the same sex would not go away. In fact, these desires were the signs of a new identity—budding but still secret—that awaited a new cultural context to be self-consciously expressed.

By middle adolescence, the majority of the Horizons youth are well into their second phase of sexual identity development. Their sexual histories include, for many, experiences with both boys and girls. They have different pathways of reaching the same point: sexual relationships with the same sex on a more or less regular basis. We have shown that the pressures to conform to heterosexual roles vary for the genders. Boys and girls experience a variety of social and psychological pressures to "try out" sexual relations with the opposite sex, and in most spheres of their lives, they have had to struggle with passing as "heterosexual." Though we cannot absolutely demonstrate the point, it is our impression that girls experience longer and greater pressures to conform and pass as "straight." Our study of suicidal experience in the Horizons group supports the impression: girls have a greater risk of taking their life before they come to the youth group.

Here, the mainstream society and gay and lesbian culture are in competition, a moral tug-of-war regarding the eventual outcomes of development for these youth in adulthood. What kind of community are the youth of Horizons adapting to? As a young adult nearly forty years ago, historian Martin Duberman described finding a group of homosexual friends in the 1950s. "I entered a subculture that blessedly brought me from individual isolation to collective secrecy—a considerable advance if one can understand, in this day where all furtiveness is decried, the quantum leap in happiness from private to shared anguish."[54] Today, as we have seen, the old pathway of youth who do not come out may still lead in the same direction as Duberman's "collective secrecy." The other direction leads youth to learn new ways of expressing and confirming their gay and lesbian identities at Horizons.

In spite of the pressures to conform and the difficulties they experience in their relationships, the Horizons youth are not confused about their sexual desires, as our sexual identity measurements demonstrate. Their desires are firm; the confusion they experience usually rests in how to express their desires in meaningful and valued ways in society. The experiences of the youth tell us that they have neither been seduced into same-sex relations by an adult,[55] nor have these youth ventured into same-sex relations because of a lack of heterosexual opportunities. Like coming to Horizons itself, this new level of experience in the development of their sexual identities represents an emerging tradition of milestones for understanding these adolescents. It is similar to aspects of the coming-out process as described by other studies of adult lesbians and gay men; but it differs in the young age of onset of the milestones, and the early age at which new identities are expressed. For the vast majority of the Horizons youth, we predict that by the time they reach young adulthood (age twenty-one), they will be in largely exclusive same-sex relations.

As we have seen from the historical and cultural chapters, the emergence of the gay and lesbian culture has provided a context in which these youth can integrate their sexual being with the sexual doing. They are in varying degrees of accepting the desires and necessities of their individual lives, and the differences in self-acceptance and coming out are a function of social stratification. The dilemmas of minority youth, whose experiences are complicated by racism, differ from those of Caucasians. The genders differ by virtue of conformist pressures and a biased opportunity structure in the mainstream society. Here, the cultural influences on coming out suggest that boys' and girls' first sexual experiences evolve out of contrasting social situations. Conflict with religious beliefs also poses a problem for some youth. Unlike the closet homosexual, however, it is more probable than ever before that youth will eventually "come out" across the range of contexts in which they situate themselves: school, home, work, and friendships. When they are threatened they may defend themselves with denial or deceit, as do their heterosexual peers. When supported and encouraged, they are at their best: full of energy, curiosity, and resilience. They respond favorably to positive support and adversely to negative reactions and devaluations of their being. The life course markers of the Horizons youth thus reveal the very opposite of the stereotypes that have traditionally informed the secret homosexual mythology of the past. These youth generally regard themselves as the pioneers of a new generation.

Sexual identity development is but one part of a larger story of moral thinking and the cultural management of identity implicit in our theory of coming out. Early and emergent desires are woven into a life story—a personal narrative—that includes a "choice" regarding the form and expression of one's cultural identity. One may not choose one's subjectively experienced desires; but the histories of Horizons youth suggest that they are actively choosing identities—ones which place a more positive stamp on their desires than ever before. The emergence and expression of desire through such milestones suggest a new tradition of subjectification that gay and lesbian culture is providing. The internal images, fantasies, perceptions, and goals of the youthful life course are being supported by the culture; and this has the effect of "objectifying" the cultural realities of longer and more positive futures for these teenagers. The youth are seeing the possibilities of living with their desires, not in hiding and alienation, but out in the public, in the light of social day—leading to adaptation and greater creative fulfillment than they could have imagined at the beginning of the process. They are launched on their new moral careers as persons, the subject of our next chapter.

CHAPTER SIX

◆ ◆ ◆

Being Out

Coming to the youth group was just so incredibly enormous for me. Before, I always thought that the reason I wasn't popular, why I didn't have friends, was because I was gay. . . . I never knew how to go about making friends. But then I would think, well, if I could be with people who would accept that I was gay, then we could go from there . . . we could deal with me, the way I really am. But what finally happened—I was in the group and people didn't care that I was gay, and it suddenly frightened me, because I didn't know what to do. . . . There I was, with people that I could form friendships with, and I didn't know how to go about doing it. At the same time I didn't know anything about being gay. I didn't even know about gay bars!

—*Robbie, a young African-American man and a member of the first Horizons youth group*

Adults of the prior generation never grew up knowing that they could live as gay men or lesbians. By comparison, the youth of the Horizons group attend a Gay and Lesbian Prom and walk in the Gay Pride Day Parade—rites of intensification of their budding status in the new culture. Clearly, the prior generation was not socialized for gay and lesbian social roles, for the simple reason that they did not exist. What gay and lesbian youth learn today is thus not sexual desire for the same sex, but how, when, and where to express these desires. Their discovery of how to be out and how to cope with the problems of expressing their desires in the cultural contexts of the mainstream society for the first time is the subject of this chapter.

From their first awareness of their desires to their first "declarations" of gay identity, as John Alan Lee described this phase of development, and on to a stage of identity "integration," "being and doing gay" are portrayed as a "final" stage of development for adults.[1] Whatever the importance of these hypothetical stages of development for the older cohorts of men and women, the youth of Horizons have not yet arrived at the final stage of development.[2] Youth begin, whether cautiously or boldly, to enter the everyday settings of their lives and announce that they are gay or lesbian. But what else do these declarations "say" to significant others and audiences in the cultural contexts of American society? To say, "gay" or "lesbian" is not to suggest that there is any single prototype of gay or lesbian youth. Indeed, one of the aims of this chapter is to demonstrate the range of diversity by gender and ethnicity that we have found at Horizons.[3] What was once considered a very public political act and declaration has changed in meaning, and the reason is that many kinds of people are coming out, people with differing experiences and intentions. Coming out, in our theory, is about transformation. It is a process of becoming and a developmental outcome that represents a deep individual change in unlearning one identity and learning a new moral career in the life course. Stories about coming out are not the end of this process, but only the beginning of a lifelong pathway, a means to another end: becoming worthy and excellent human beings.

By the action of coming out, the youth are not choosing a sexual desire, but they are choosing a certain identity. They are also, through Horizons, selecting (implicitly or explicitly) a certain pathway to adaptation: moving from the assumptive identities "heterosexual" to "homosexual" to "gay/lesbian." Their love and sexual needs are closer to them, more "experience near."[4] But near to what? In everyday life, lesbian and gay youth today, as Michele Fine has commented in a high school study in New York,[5] are more willing to discuss their desires than are other segments of the adolescent world. Perhaps their openness arises out of having to work so hard to know and feel, and then to express their desires. However, the experience of their peers who remain hidden, and who cannot or will not come to agencies such as Horizons, suggests a different perspective. The hidden youth are not only "experience distant" from gay and lesbian contexts; they are distant from their own developmental subjectivities simply because they are not free to explore themselves. They are seeking a divergent developmental pathway from the Horizons youth.[6] On the other hand, the moral voices of the youth we have explored offer clues, by the language and roles they take, that these youth are "experience nearer" to themselves because they have found the protective umbrella of gay and lesbian culture.

An Emerging Gay Life Course

In the individual developmental transition from secret and private to the most public of lives, the gay and lesbian teenager must create new norms, rules, and social roles where none have existed before. Advisors to the Horizons youth group and adults in the lesbian and gay community are their most important role models. But they are adults. They can advise youth, and, most importantly, affirm their social status. As the youth begin to accept their erotic desires for the same sex, they recognize that they will not have the same course of life as their parents and heterosexual peers. They will not have a heterosexual marriage; they may not have children or grandchildren. In short, they do not aspire to heterosexual life-course markers. Since for these youth sexual desires for the opposite sex are not a driving force of motivation, their awareness of homoerotic desires during adolescence is likely to initiate a sense of being developmentally "off-course." In a society such as ours, where much store is placed in competing and keeping up with one's friends and neighbors, such an identity crisis can unhinge not only sexuality but belief in all future life success.

Developmental *discontinuities* have been a common experience for the majority of adult gay men and lesbians. They skipped from imposed heterosexual life goals to claiming new gay and lesbian life goals—but without much attention to how one learns or expresses these desires and roles in society. For instance, it is one thing to come out to one's friends and quite another to come out at work. How does one tell a supervisor or colleague that being gay and lesbian are meaningful life goals in the workplace, and not merely at home, as is often assumed by heterosexuals? An important difference between the coming-out process among youth and among adults is related to the timing of developmental events. An adult who has previously suppressed/repressed his/her same-sex desires and subsequently chooses to come out, experiences being both "off-course" and "off-time." Not having had the opportunities for exploration and romance typically experienced by adolescents, being off-time may result in a major delay in sexual identity development.

The interviews with the youth of Horizons suggest that there are a set of critical developmental tasks which they have the unique opportunity to resolve during the new adolescent phase of the gay and lesbian life course. Simultaneous to overcoming the cultural stereotypes of homosexuality, the coming-out process entails giving up of previously internalized heterosocial life goals. This may involve some "grief work" and mourning for the formerly identified heterosocial self, as we saw in chapter 4. Youth begin to replace these heterosexual expectations with new ideals and ambitions. It is the formation of these emerging desires to take on gay and lesbian social roles in which we see the major developmental work of gay youth. Because they have been a hidden minority, however, adult gay and lesbian role models and "success stories" have been hidden from the youth. They wonder and question the adults they encounter: Is a certain teacher or a friend of the family gay? Is a woman employer or teacher a lesbian? Could a same-sex pair they see in a restaurant or shopping mall be a lesbian or gay couple? By restructuring the "average expectable life cycle" of heterosocial development, gay- and lesbian-identified youth have the opportunity to resolve their feelings of being "off-course" with regard to expected heterosexual life events. Thus, for these teenagers, life cycle expectations must often be created anew. Horizons and the gay community become the critical nexus of their resocialization.

What is different for gay and lesbian teens is that the opportunities for "doing" gay and for "being" gay occur simultaneously, during the adolescent phase of the life course, when they "put together" their social experience with their future plans and social relationships. The magnitude and nature of discontinuity is changing for younger generations. For example, large urban centers such as Chicago, with visible communities like Newtown, provide new contexts for learning how to come out among gay and lesbian youth, lessening the disruptive impact of cultural discontinuity and facilitating continuity into new forms of socialization and interpersonal relationships. The rituals of coming out as described in chapter 4 provide the clearest signs that an emerging cultural tradition in gay and lesbian culture is providing new life course goals and roles. Increasingly, these rituals suggest gay and lesbian lifeways for thinking about expressing how to be "on-course" in development and "on-time" with other gay and lesbian peers who are coming out. In short, norms of a specifically gay and lesbian social order have arrived; they define and normalize entry into stable social roles and status positions in the new culture.

Mental Health and the Risk of Suicide

Many Americans have expressed concern about the well-being and mental health of gay and lesbian youth, and for all of the factors of homophobia and alienation we have reported, their concerns are justified. Perhaps no issue is of greater importance than that ultimate risk—the taking of one's own life. We begin the description of learning to be out with a study of this issue for two reasons. First, we feel that its importance defines the mental health context of same-sex desire prior to the positive social support the youth receive at Horizons. Second, there is a high level of suicide risk among gay and lesbian youth, and a profound question of survival is suggested by our findings. At stake in removing the social oppression that continues to burden these youth are their lives.

We compared the youth in our study with groups of putatively heterosexual youth on a set of standard measures of mental health.[7] Overall Horizons youth compare favorably with adolescents at large in their psychological resilience and distress. While gay and lesbian youth do not reveal major differences in anxiety, confusion, or insecurity compared to adolescents in general, some tend to be more depressed, vigilant, and vulnerable compared to heterosexual peers. This is not surprising in view of the social pressures exerted on them to pass as straight and the problems of homophobia examined in this book. During the process of coming out, especially before they receive social support, a small number of youth may experience feelings of sadness and shame in giving up aspects of their normatively prescribed role and self-image as heterosexual. Another small number may also respond by becoming suspicious and hostile compared with their straight peers.

We asked the youth in our study whether they had ever attempted or thought about suicide. Twenty-nine percent of the total sample reported at least one suicide attempt prior to entering the Horizons' youth group.[8] Among those who attempted suicide, the lesbian teenagers are disproportionately represented: over half of the sample reported at least one attempt. By comparison, 20 percent of the gay males reported one attempt. There are no comparable reports from the research literature on young lesbians; however, on gay boys, these findings are comparable to studies of suicide among gay and bisexual males in other cities.[9] Although our information is not longitudinal, it suggests that lesbian youth may experience greater social pressures than gay youth to conform to heterosexuality. Our information in chapter 5 showed that girls typically have their first sexual experience with someone of the opposite sex. Barriers to the development of lesbian identity may therefore result in lowered self-esteem and aggression directed against the self. Further support for this idea comes from the larger adolescent literature, which shows gender differences in mental health among younger adolescents. Adolescent girls, in general, show increases in depressive feelings across adolescence, and while specific causes have not been identified, many cultural constraints on adolescent girls, such as pressures to conform to ideal standards of beauty and sexual attractiveness, probably result in more difficulties for all adolescent girls.[10]

Once they have crossed the threshold into Horizons, the majority of these youth have demonstrated little impairment in their ability for achieving close relationships with others. This fact is critical because of the strong assumption in the mental health literature on homosexuality and adolescence that such youth are impaired in forming intimate and warm relations. Through Horizons, the youth have friends with whom they can discuss their fears, hopes, and dreams. In general, they relate well to adults, family members, and peers. The problems they have experienced prior to coming to Horizons seem to be primarily the result of stigma and the kind of alienation we have described, rather than because of an incapacity for closeness or personality disorders. Their resilience in the face of these problems suggests that the youth do better with social support and understanding. When stereotypes and homophobic reactions are leveled against them, whether from parents, peers, or teachers, their well-being is endangered. This suggests a cultural perspective: when suicide is a recognized means of ultimate coping, and youth lack social support in a society, the risk of suicide is greater—precisely the conditions of gay and lesbian youth development in the United States.[11]

We believe that suicide risk among youth in the general population who desire the same sex is probably higher than the few studies and our information suggest. Further study is needed to discover if our guess is correct. However, research reports more than a decade old indicate a growing split may be occurring within the country—between youth who continue to hide and those who come out within the context of institutions such as Horizons. Certainly some youth express "confusion" regarding the expression of their desires and the influence of hiding, alienation, and such "confusion" upon personality development. "Confusion" is, however, a very loaded concept to use in this context, for the simple reason that present studies do not permit us to untangle the "chicken and egg" problem of whether the confusion leads to distress, or distress leads to confusion. Some of these young people may experience pervasive difficulties in making friends, in chronic conflict within the family, and in recurrent substance abuse—much as is found in our mainstream society. However, these risk factors must not be confused with same-sex desire and the barriers that inhibit its expression, particularly homophobia.[12] Our hunch is that the mental conflicts of these youth, especially prior to coming to Horizons, are less associated with their sexual orientation and more related to problems of not feeling close with others, which leads to a diminished sense of well-being. What we have shown is that the topic of suicide is not present in the group; that fears of it may lurk on the margins—too scary to express openly—and that when most youth locate support through the youth group, their closeness to others increases along with enhanced feelings of well-being.

Such is the positive context that leads to a willingness to reveal the self.

Revealing the Self

We asked each of the youth in their interviews to tell us what "coming out" meant to them, and whether they had come out according to their own definition. Eighty percent of the group told us that they had. There was no difference between boys and girls in this regard. On the average, the youth of Horizons come out as they define it at the age of 16.75 years, a bit shy of their seventeenth birthday.

The definitions of coming out offered by this group focus on communication with the self, rather than upon telling others. Most of the youth discuss their concepts of coming out in terms of a self-dialogue, involving self-recognition and acceptance of same-sex desire. A few others add the proviso that coming out also specifically means telling others—but here, the others are usually personal friends or family. A nineteen-year-old Italian-American boy said: "I have two definitions: One is coming out to yourself, realizing yourself—your own personal preferences—emotional, sexual, social.... Coming out to other people is letting other people know, not standing on rooftops waving cardboard signs, but telling your family, your closer friends."

Nearly all of our informants describe the experience in ways that highlight the search for freedom from fear. An eighteen-year-old black girl said: "No longer feeling the burden of homosexuality—accepting yourself finally." Another eighteen-year-old Hispanic girl described it this way: "I know it's a very frightening experience. It's like you're afraid of your sexuality or of what people will think of you."

The youth often expressed torment over knowing what is a moral possibility for the self and continuing not to express it. Not all of the youth of Horizons are out. Some remain hidden; a few deeply closeted. A sixteen-year-old Caucasian boy, who had not yet come out, said that being out meant: "Openly admitting it and freely showing it by my lifestyle and the things in my home." However, he added: "I am not out. I like living in the closet, especially in the suburbs, for social reasons." These young men and women thus feel the need to suppress the expression of their sexual identity when they interact with the family, at school, and in the workplace. Their hiding and passing poses problems of identity "management" simultaneous to those of identity development; that is, they must learn how to suppress their desires and perform and imitate heterosocial goals and roles pretty well, in order to succeed in passing. Of course, the older they get, the greater the social demands that are placed upon them to conform to heterosocial norms, especially marriage.

Despite these counteracting pressures, the largest majority of the youth are able to function reasonably well in school, at work, and in their families. In individual interviews each youth was asked about the ways in which coming out had affected seven areas of their life: grades, friends, self-esteem, work, daily hassles, future plans, and family relationships. At the end of the interview, they were then asked to assess comparatively, on a four-point scale ("positive," "neutral," "mixed," and "negative" assessments), their feeling about how coming out had effected each of these life domains. (See table 6.1.)

There was a variety of responses from the youth, but we observed some key patterns. A majority of boys and half of the girls feel that coming out has had a positive impact on their self-esteem. Boys report the most frequent positive effects on their self-esteem, followed by a positive effect experienced in their friendships. For a quarter of the boys, coming out had the most negative effects in the area of family relationships. For girls, family relations was also the domain most negatively affected by coming out, reported by 47 percent of the girls.

Table 6.1 Gay and Lesbian Youth's Perceptions of How Coming Out Affected Their Lives

	Negative		Mixed		Positive	
	M	F	M	F	M	F
Grades	12%	28%	71%	55%	17%	17%
Friends	11%	17%	44%	45%	45%	39%
Self-esteem	5%	13%	31%	37%	64%	50%
Work	8%	17%	82%	69%	10%	14%
Hassles	9%	23%	54%	37%	37%	40%
Future plans	13%	27%	56%	40%	30%	33%
Family relationships	24%	47%	56%	47%	20%	7%
Other Things	29%	...	46%	25%	25%	...

Less than one-fifth of the boys report negative effects for grades, friends, and making future life plans. A larger number of girls indicated "mixed" feelings about their success in grades, friends, and the future, suggesting again the gendered trend of greater heterosocial pressures on females. For the majority of boys and a large percentage of girls, "mixed" effects—both positive and negative developments—occur across all domains.

The positive effects of self-esteem building are not surprising, given that many youth reported feeling better about themselves through the self-disclosure process. Many describe this process as being first an admission to the self, prior to a discussion with others (if such occurs), in the "confessional manner" of recognizing a secret for the first time: an effect we have already noted in the period of coming to Horizons. The self-declaration is usually associated with the youth's early visits to the Horizons youth group, where for many, entering the building and then the group for the first time provoke anxiety and panic.

Who did the youth first tell of their sexual identity? Two-thirds of the boys and over half of the girls (63 percent of males; 55 percent of females) first made the revelation to a same-aged peer or friend. The majority of both the boys and girls told a same-sexed friend, although a quarter of each of these groups told an opposite-sex friend. The sexual orientation of these peers, as reported by our respondents, were both same-sex and opposite-sex attracted. This information suggests a trend in developmental subjectivity: youth feel most comfortable with their friends, and their comfort level is highest with a person of the same sex, regardless of the sexual identity of that person. The average age at which this first disclosure occurred was seventeen (16.75) for boys and sixteen for girls.

These youth are even more uncomfortable than their heterosexual peers in discussing their sexual desires with the parents. Only 5 percent of the males and females (6 percent of the males, 3 percent of the females) told their mother first, and none discussed this first with their fathers. And yet, virtually all Horizons youth aspire to tell their parents of their desires. The reason for this difference between desire and expression has undoubtedly to do with the strong pressure to conform to heterosexual roles their parents represent and push them toward. As we shall see later, this is a strong source of continuing anguish for many youth in coming out beyond the Horizons group.

Telling for the first time is perhaps one of the most frightening experiences that these youngsters face. For the first time they are contemplating challenging a basic assumption of their being—and by extension—their parents' role in discussing the child's being with them. We asked the youth how difficult or easy it was to disclose this information. We found a significant association[13] between the degree of difficulty experienced in this first disclosure and the sex of the youth. Boys found it more difficult to disclose their sexual orientation the first time than did the girls. This gender difference is not surprising in view of the sequence of sexual experiences the youth reveal, with boys having earlier sexual activity and girls having a trend toward opposite sex relations before same sex relations.

The decision about whom to first reveal their desires to is taken with great care and usually after much thought. Three-quarters of both the boys and girls perceived the response of the other person to this first disclosure as having been supportive. It seems that those who chose to disclose their sexual desires picked someone whom they perceived would generally support them. One of the boys remarked: "It was a while before I told anyone. I guess it helped a little. I told my friend. I knew she wouldn't react bad, but it just took so long to tell her." However, choosing a potentially supportive confident did not always obviate the difficulties involved in the disclosure. A Hispanic boy described first telling his sister: "It was sort of difficult . . . not too much. I was crying when I told her. I didn't know if she'd accept me. She did, even though I knew she thought it was wrong. She asked if somebody raped me. I said no. She asked how long I had these feelings. I said since I was young. She said, 'maybe you're confused.' I told her I tried to change and prayed, but I just can't." Another boy described his experience as positive but difficult: "[I told] a friend at school. It was difficult. I didn't know how. I handed her my journal. The first pages were about how I am, the later pages about how I'd like to be. But it's hard to be myself—cause I'm gay. We ordered pizza and talked. I had a feeling she'd understand and she did."

The youth's narratives of their first disclosures suggests that how and when they tell, and the responses they receive, influence their later disclosures to others. Telling parents usually comes after telling a peer and is problematic in different ways; for instance, the youth may desire to tell only one parent, often their mothers, and not the other. Thus the transmission of desires within the family or circles of friends may involve a period of partial outness, with family "secrets" and complicity with friends vis-à-vis others.

These first experiences serve as a kind of "testing of the waters" and often take great courage on the part of the teens; they never know when they might be rejected or even ejected from the family household. A positive reaction to the first disclosure thus consolidates in many youth their commitment to developing their gay and lesbian identities. Here is where the full impact of mainstream society comes into play.

Contexts of Coming Out

Youth opting to come out during the adolescent phase aspire to succeed, to be competent, to find happiness. These aspirations, governed by their sense of an ideal self, a highly condensed image of erotic and social desires, are not easily achieved. The roles they seek, and the tasks they must perform, are influenced by the context. We have found that social space and time intersect in a significant way; we shall call this the social geography of the emerging moral careers of gay and lesbian youth.[14]

If the mainstream society of parents, school, and peers was generally positive and supportive, the youth might experience an easier transition in giving up the norms and goals of "straight life" for the lifeways of gay men and lesbians. But then, of course, there would be less of a need for "coming out" in the first place, and the coming-out rites might never have come into being. We find that to be successful in their transition from a heterosexual to a gay-identified and lesbian-identified person, the youth must come out in a sequence of events and variety of contexts. We shall thus trace the experience of coming out in the most distinctive domains of the lives of Horizons teenagers—family, friends, school, and work.

Coming Out to Family

As we suggested earlier, perhaps the most difficult stumbling block to coming out and being out is the youth's relationship with their parents. The current generation of youth expect to come out to their parents, although they fear it. A young black girl told us: "I haven't come out yet to my parents. I'm sure it'll be a problem when I do."

A small body of recent literature on gay and lesbian youth suggests that disclosure of sexual orientation to family results in conflict and distress in family relations during an adolescent's transition to a "gay" or "lesbian" identity.[15] One recent report, based on a sample of New York City youth attending a shelter for gay youth, found many individuals whose self-disclosure to parents resulted in a serious disruption of parent-child ties, at least at the time of interview.[16] A recent survey by Richard Savin-Williams of more than three hundred gay and lesbian youth (ages fourteen to twenty-three) found that adolescent well-being was related to perceptions of parental acceptance of their "homosexuality."[17] Subsequent study revealed that positive parental relationships predicted which lesbians felt comfortable with their sexuality and were out to their parents, although positive parental relations did not predict the females' self-esteem.[18] The same relationships did not obtain for the males.[19] For the males in Savin-Williams' study, being out to mothers (but not fathers) predicted high self-esteem. Although the findings from such studies do not establish whether parental self-disclosure leads to higher self-esteem, or whether higher self-esteem may be associated with self-disclosure, they underscore that coming out is a process, not just an outcome. Coming out within a family context interfaces with the interior of the family as a whole, and with the life-course trajectories of individual family members.

Coming out to one's parents is a difficult step for adolescents to take. Even those with the most positive parental relationships reported difficulty in disclosing to them. However, in consequence of an earlier identity transition to gay or lesbian, some youth who have begun this process are "coming out" to parents during their adolescent years, posing problems for their families and themselves to negotiate during that phase of the life course. Recent changes in family size and spacing of children, combined with increased life expectancy, have given a long life to the parent-child relationship, typically lasting four to six decades. And for the greater part of its duration, these persons will interact as adults.[20] Coming out to parents in adolescence presages the contours of the future course of a long relationship between children and parents. To continue meaningful interaction, new styles of family interaction must evolve, with a pattern of social relations between youth and their parents unknown to previous cohorts of adult gay men and lesbians. How does one introduce one's same-sex partner to the parents or bring them around to Thanksgiving dinner with the grandparents?[21] Do the parents refer to their child's partner as "daughter" or "son" or by their personal name? Horizons youth who come out to parents do so with the hope of acceptance. One nineteen-year-old Caucasian male told us: "I don't think my mom is very accepting of gay people at all. It is not so much gay people as it is anyone who's different. I don't feel that she would reject me, but she would have a hard time accepting it if I told her. I will tell her when I move out because I think that when I tell her—we will need space for a while to think things out."

The intense reactions of a few parents are so negative that they lead to a complete break in all ties. We note that seven youth have reported being kicked out of their homes after their parents' discovery of their gay and lesbian identities. These estranged youth were living in shelters at the time of their interviews. Obviously, this is not the usual response of the parents, but it poses a difficult and wrenching break for this small number of youth.[22] More importantly, it serves as a symbol of what may happen in the lives of the other youth at Horizons, as we have seen, becoming a prospect of their worst fear.

Some parents, while reacting negatively to the disclosure by their children, do not let their feelings disrupt relationships with their children. A high schooler told us that his mother found out indirectly that he was gay. "She told me she was aware that I was leading an alternative lifestyle and she was concerned about me getting AIDS. I just about died. I felt like I was a big disappointment to my parents. But the joke's on me. Nothing changed between us. I thought there would be a lot of those long dragged out conversations about being gay, but everything remained the same." A nineteen-year-old male told us:

"My mother doesn't treat me as an issue. She regards me as her son who is gay and not her gay son."

Out of all family members, parents were those whom the youth most frequently named as being aware. Not surprisingly, a larger number of girls reported that their parents were aware of their sexual desires (63 percent of mothers and 37 percent of fathers) than did the boys (54 percent of mothers and 28 percent of fathers). Mothers are more frequently perceived to be aware of the youth's desires than are fathers, regardless of the gender of the youth. Perhaps this finding reflects a more general trend in American families for children to turn to their mothers with questions about sexuality.[23]

We found two types of parental awareness of same-sex desires in youth. Some youth reported that their parents knew about their sexual desires, although the teenager had not discussed it with that parent. For example, a fifteen-year-old female told us that her mother had read her diary in which she revealed her love for a female classmate; her feelings about being a lesbian were obvious. When asked if she had ever talked with her mother about this, or if her mother had ever brought it up, she responded: "No, it's never been mentioned. It would be too scary to tell your mom. I think I can tell her when I move out to go to college. . . . I overheard my Mom tell my Dad that she thought I was a lesbian because of what she read in the diary."

Other youth in our study directly discussed and disclosed their sexual desires with their mothers or fathers. This was the more common mode of parents learning about their children's sexual orientation. For example, an eighteen-year-old girl said: "Yes, I told her. I was so frustrated from hiding—that I just told her, so it wasn't that hard. But at that point I didn't care anymore. She thinks it's totally wrong and that I'm making a big mistake."

The analysis of these two types of awareness of parents again showed the greater prominence of the mother in receiving disclosures. We divided all youth who directly disclosed their same-sex desires in one category from those who had not. Both sexes disclosed more to mothers than fathers. However, a larger proportion of girls than boys directly disclosed to both mothers and fathers. Forty-seven percent of the total sample of girls directly disclosed to their mothers, and 24 percent did so with their fathers; 38 percent of the boys did so with mothers and 14 percent with fathers. It is likely that youth who disclosed their identities to parents were those with more positive preexisting relationships. Statistical analyses (controlling for the influences of a number of independent factors such as minority status, age, living situation, and employment status) were used to examine the associations between self-disclosure (both direct and indirect disclosure) of sexual identity to parents and measures of parent-child relations.[24]

Ethnic tradition and color influence the response of parents to coming out. One study of mulicultural gay and lesbian youth in Toronto found that when minority youth had come out to parents, the youth's relationships to their entire ethnic communities changed. Out of concern and care for their families, some of these Canadian youth experienced alienation from their communities, excluding themselves from cultural activities to avoid shaming their families.[25]

Religion is also a factor that influences coming out to families. Especially in religious families, as we found for some black and Hispanic youth, coming out is inextricably linked with religious attitudes about "homosexuality." A nineteen-year-old black youth told a detailed story about how his family has been unable to cope with his being gay. He had been very concerned with having to "give up" his religion and he wondered whether he should change religions. He had wondered whether God would accept him and whether he would go to hell as a result of being gay. For his family, the problem of "being gay and being damned in hell" are very closely intertwined. The problem of contracting AIDS is related to this, and he was very scared that he might someday die from the dreaded disease. This seemed to suggest that in his world, the problem of being open and out is so different from the larger Horizons youth group.

The issue of same-sex desire often becomes a silent discourse. Many youth in our study reported that their parents—both those who had some awareness and those who had been told directly—preferred to "sit on" the information or deny it, at least initially. In the descriptions of disclosure, adolescents told us that parents responded with such comments as, "you'll outgrow this"; a large number of youth themselves referred to their parents' responses as "denial." In support of this denial, these families' shared realities became a "demilitarized zone" surrounding features of the child's intentions regarding marriage, parenthood, and heterosocial relations. Some of the youth continue to bring up their desires with parents, while others agree to a conspiracy of silence.

While this identity transition begins with the youth, the self-disclosure to parents is likely to initiate a type of "family coming-out" process in the parents themselves. Parents are given the opportunity to restructure expectations and goals for the future life course of their children by revealing to others that they have a gay or lesbian child. From interviews with the youth it is clear that coming out communicates different meanings for mothers and fathers. Regardless of the gender of the adolescent, the process does not appear to be an easy one for many families. Nevertheless, for mothers—whatever their initial responses to the direct or indirect news of their children's gay and lesbian identity—the overall quality of their relationships is not affected. For fathers, meanings and responses are different and partially determined by the gender of the child.[26] In our study, fathers' awareness of their children's sexual identity (either through direct or indirect disclosure) was associated with more positive relationships. Direct disclosure to fathers was associated with changes in relationships, although the direction of these changes was not predictable. For some fathers it may be a relief to understand their children in a new way; to be aware of an aspect of their lives previously hidden or even confusing to them. For others it may result in anger, rage, or some type of rejection.

Our study suggests that fathers and daughters experience some difficulties unique from those of the other parent-child dyads in the family. Changes in father-child relations were found to be predicted by the gender of the child; the girls reported more negative changes in relationships than did boys, regardless of whether their fathers were aware of their lesbian identities. Margaret Schneider has discussed some differences between the experience of lesbian youth and those of gay boys.[27] The teenage girls in her study were less influenced by prevailing stereotypes than the boys; perhaps this was related to the advantages of their access to the feminist movement, including lesbian and feminist music, art, humor, and political thought, in addition to the resources of the lesbian community.[28]

The final outcome of the process of coming out to parents remains unclear. But it is certain that some of the same patterns of interaction we have identified among these families occur in American society more broadly.[29] Since our data are correlational, we cannot, of course, assume causal relationships between self-disclosure and parental relationships.[30] We must conclude that little is known of the events that characterize coming out between parents and their children.[31]

Coming out is among the most difficult processes that a parent will ever have to face in the relationships with their children. If the youth must battle with all the myths of their culture regarding the "sin, disease, and disgrace of homosexuality," all the more do the parents dread the confrontation, for they grew up in a time of much greater social intolerance than the youth of today, baby-boomers included.[32] If the birth of gay culture represents a utopian movement that celebrates sexual and cultural differences, there is no necessary reason why parents should want to join in the celebration. They have already made their own cultural way of life. (We use the verb "made" advisedly here, for we would no more suggest that parents chose to be heterosexual than that their offspring chose to be gay.) Nevertheless, what youth do not realize fully is that the stigma of homosexuality blights not only themselves but their parents too. As Anne Muller suggests for a Chicago study, there is a perception of status demotion that occurs when parents tell others they have a gay or lesbian child.[33] Part of the reason may be the tendency we have in our culture to blame parents for the lifestyles of their children. We see, however, the results in the actions of parents who reject their children. These parents cannot accept either the gayness or the wound to their own identity. This is an injury to parent and child that may heal only slowly, and sometimes never at all. Our study provides hope, however, that as social change in society proceeds, these parents may eventually find the wherewithal to build new futures with their children.

Coming Out to Friends

Friendship is the source of immense comfort and fulfillment in adolescence, and friendship circles provide that first measure of defining self and significant goals away from home on the road to autonomy. So often youth think of a "real" or "true" friend as someone who knows everything about them. To hide their deepest desires from their best friend is thus an intolerable burden. As we have noted, two-thirds of the boys and more than half of the girls of the Horizons group first come out to a friend, usually a same-aged and same-sex peer. A significant number of these close friends are other youth at the Horizons group.

One of the great options afforded by entry into the Horizons group is that they gain friends and comrades, and sometimes lovers, with whom they share experience of coming into being. Many of their new friends who know of their "true" identities hale from the group. Some of their initial "experiments" with opposite sex are partners from the group too. They are, in the parlance of anthropology, age-mates; members of a batch of like-aged, same-status youth—equally vulnerable and virginal in social experience. Of all the things they come to share over months and years, what matters most is that, unlike the lone child model of coming out in the late sixties or even the seventies—and most contrary to the received wisdom of the stage model psychologists who focus on individual norms and differences—these youth have a ready-made cohort for *coming out together.* We asked youth to tell us about their "best" friends and often they named one or two teenagers from the group.

Outside of the Horizons group, however, relations with friends are difficult and often mirror those with the family because they share the same community values. A black youth who attends the Wednesday evening group has come through the struggle. He was reared in a Catholic suburban school. "I couldn't come out in high school." He had to invent a girlfriend in high school to get his male friends "off his back." Her name was "Cassandra," he said; he felt bad about lying to his friends, but he felt that he had no other choice. "It's better with gays," he says. "It's more real." He has a niece, a lesbian, who came out to him. She is supportive. His parents aren't "handling his gayness well." Now he works in a pizza parlor. He still lives at home, and his parents do not allow any broach of sex as a subject. They don't allow any visitors. They won't take telephone messages for him. They hassle him, especially his mother. But he is finding new friends at Horizons who are easing the burden.

Ethnicity is a critical factor in how and when youth disclose their desires to friends as well as parents. We can find no statistical correlations from our study, but we have plenty of anecdotal evidence. We saw, in our description of "Joey Has AIDS," how youth of color face the conflict of giving up their ethnic identity and tradition in order to come out. Here is a nineteen-year-old black who talks about his difficulties with the issue: "Unfortunately I am not out, no; I still have a great fear of trying to explain it to my parents. To some of my friends I've given them hints. I don't usually reveal what I'm doing. They have their own suspicions but are afraid of asking. Eventually, yes, I do feel I will come out. I'm tempted to tell my parents. When I think of telling I get a great fear. They have been through enough traumas so I hold back, being the first born."

This youth reveals a semi-openness that admits of being lesbian or gay, but only if asked, or only if pressured into making a confession. It is not only common among minority youth, but many youth who are comparably conflicted about their old identities and their new ones. Here is sixteen-year-old Regina, talking about her sense of being "out" right now: "If people ever asked me, 'Are you gay?' I would say 'yes,' but they never ask me. So I don't say 'yes.' If they say about a guy, 'Do you think that he's cute?', I say 'no', but I don't say that I'm gay. No, I don't feel I have to hide it from people. . . . There's [just] certain people that I put off telling them, but I don't hide it from them."

Eventually, as they gain more friends who are gay and lesbian, a new concern enters awareness; the fear of losing their place in the mainstream society. One of the problems that worries youth—their parents would be surprised by this, they believe—is that they fear they will lose all of their contacts with the straight world. How many gay and straight friends do I have, some youth ask? One teenage Caucasian boy says: "I worry because all of my friends seem to be gay now; only my parents, my family, and my old girlfriend! are straight. . . . I could become too isolated." But of course this is the product of their liminal state at Horizons, and their transition into the new culture. Their greater concerns lie beyond—in coming out in the most significant institution beyond the family—their school.

Coming Out in School

Since school is the context in which youth spend the majority of their time, it is a critical context for understanding the coming out of gay and lesbian youth. One Saturday morning at the Horizons youth group, one of the kids brought a Xerox of a poem by Ian Paterson.[34] Its creases and tears suggested it had passed through many hands. He showed it to the group to poetically express the homophobia and pain that he had been feeling. It reads:

High School Faggot

A usual—
cold,
unfriendly—
school never changes,
nor the people.
Jocks,
Heads,
Rockers,
Always verbally,
sometimes physically
abusive.

Homo,
Faggot,
Queer,—
that's what they call me
everyday,
all day.
No one cares for my feelings,
they're blinded
by hate,
by homophobia.
Why can't they accept me
for who—
and what I am—
a person
with thoughts
with feelings
with emotions.
But I'll survive.
I'll read my books,
Give my views and opinions,
Wear my pink triangle
and be proud of who,
and what I am—
a male homosexual;
but most important
I am
a Person.

Many of the kids in the group that day remarked, "Yeah, that's it," and "Right on," and "That's how I really feel!" How and why they feel this way explains the problem of coming out in the public schools of the United States today.

School, many gay educators tell us, is a model of society.[35] High schools have a central role in the perpetuation of homophobia in American society—homophobia is condoned or at least tolerated by many school authorities. Though we shall focus on the youth, gay and lesbian teachers and counselors, who remain even more hidden, know the problems of homophobia only too well.[36] It is all too easy for the adult person today to forget the enormous social pressure exerted upon youth to conform to peer circles. Gay and lesbian culture is in intense competition with the youth culture of high schools—which emphasizes the heterosexual norms of dating, sports, and conformity to fashion. The high school is of such enormous influence in the lives of the youth; it provides the context for their problems and prospects; indeed, much of everyday life is comprised of its classes and encounters with friends and foes. Youth group discourse at Horizons reflected the high school experience. The effects of being identified as "queer" or "fag" or "dyke" or with "the pollution of homosexuality" in high school is immense; official school policies espousing equality have a nice ring, but little meaning to high schoolers struggling to survive the trials of daily harassment.

The youth in our study are represented in all manner of educational settings. The majority of these youth attend secondary school or college; they report positive feelings about school. Approximately equal numbers of boys (27 percent) report that coming out had either negative or positive effects on their grades; a third of the girls report improved grades; and one-fifth report poorer grades in school. However, these settings, as described by the youth, typically do not provide guidance, and youth typically withstand a variety of pressures to conform and must negotiate alone their school environments—which negate their sexual identities.

In individual interviews with the youth, we asked whether they felt they had to hide their sexual identity, to what extent they felt required to do so, and in particular, from whom. (See table 6.2.) Two-thirds of the youth told us that they felt they had to hide partially or totally. Less than a quarter of the group felt that there was no one from whom they had to hide being gay or lesbian. Frequently, both boys and girls stated that they had to selectively hide their identity from both teachers and peers. However, not unique to gay adolescents, their predominant concerns were focussed on peers.

The Chicago public schools are novel for several reasons. One is the size of the system. As of 1990, 408,714 students were enrolled. Over 85 percent of all students are members of racial or ethnic minorities. A second unique feature is a new program of education targeting counselors and teachers: the goal is to make school environments both more secure and more positive for lesbian and gay youth. The most significant impetus for this change was the increased visibility of the gay and lesbian movement, and the emerging voices of gays and lesbians who are asserting their identities and needs as young gay men and lesbians.[37] A third unique aspect and key source of response to these voices is the "Family Life Education Program" (FLE) in the Chicago public schools. Established in 1960s, the FLE is part of the central administration's Bureau of Science and is responsible for maintaining

Table 6.2 Degree to Which Youth Feel They Must Hide Being Gay or
Lesbian at School and Work

School	Males	Females
Very much hidden	33%	29%
Mostly hidden	20%	29%
Open to some, not others	13%	8%
Open to most people	13%	13%
Very open to everyone	22%	19%

Work	Males	Females
Very much hidden	37%	38%
Mostly hidden	11%	14%
Open to some, not others	16%	33%
Open to most people	7%	...
Very open to everyone	29%	14%

and implementing curricula on health, sexuality, and HIV/STD education.[38]

Attitudes and policy regarding "homosexuality" in the Chicago public schools have changed over the last twenty-five years.[39] Roughly between 1965 and 1975, homosexuality was not at all mentioned in resource material and was thus highly stigmatized as a "taboo" topic. Beginning around 1975 and continuing on—the "awareness decade"—several changes began to trickle into textbooks and resource material on sexuality. This included materials from the "Sex Information and Education Council" and Planned Parenthood, as well as gay and lesbian positive research (in the wake of the declassification of homosexuality as a mental illness by the American Psychiatric and American Psychological Associations). Four "taboo topics" previously excluded came into the Chicago Public Schools' "Family Life Resource Handbook:" contraception, abortion, masturbation, and homosexuality.

Chicago's Board of Education teacher-training programs began to reflect these changing perspectives. Observations of teachers reactions varied. Many were silent. Other teachers and counselors wanted to know what they could do to change students or "make kids be heterosexual." However, with the emergence of the AIDS epidemic, a small but growing number of openly gay teachers began to attend these teaching-training services and made their voices heard. The main accomplishment during this second period was that the silent treatment on the topic of homosexuality ended; positive images began to be represented. Teachers started talking openly about the topic and about biases.[40]

A new era of sensitization began in 1985. This was due in large part to the emergence and growing presence of gay and lesbian social service and advocacy groups, including the Horizons agency. The Board of Education and some schools began to utilize these groups for in-service education. Homophobia was also added as a topic of discussion for family life educators. With the development and implementation of AIDS education curricula and in-services, the topic of gay youth began to be covered in more positive ways. Many citywide in-services have covered these topics with openly gay and lesbian speakers, including gay youth. Additional resources are being made available to school libraries, including such books as *One Teenager in Ten*, and *Gay and Lesbian Youth*.[41] These books sometimes have "hot line" referral cards stuffed in flaps for the taking by youth who explore them.

Despite the fact that this generation of youth experiences their education in a city that has new structures to encourage positive gay and lesbian expression, may youth still describe school as a place where they were the target of constant assumptions regarding heterosexual roles and life-style choices. These include jokes and jabs about opposite-sex boyfriends or girlfriends, and insinuations about dating or the expression of other heterosocial markers. Such experiences result in almost all of the youth feeling, at some time, the need to suppress or hide their same-sex desires, particularly with some of their peers and teachers.

The youth of Horizons were asked about the degree of perceived acceptance they felt by same-sex and opposite-sex peers in school, including their personal peer group or clique. The girls report feeling more accepted by same-sex peers, while more boys report acceptance by opposite-sex peers. A large majority of both the males and females reported feeling accepted by their small group of friends or personal peer group.

Horizons youth employ diverse strategies to conceal their sexual feelings and identities at school. Probably the most common strategy is to "pass" as heterosexual, but there are diverse forms of passing in school. The issues of what Vivienne Cass has called "active" and "passive" coming out are relevant here.[42] Most of the time, as we have seen in many other contexts, youth simply allow their school friends to assume that they are straight. A high school youth remarks: "I'm totally hidden [at school]. The environment is not conducive to come out as people take an idea that already existed as negative without questioning. High school is small intellectually. I'm looking forward to college to be more open." Another high school girl, Sarah, permits her girlfriends to tell her that she should go out with "Freddie" because they share an interest in horses, and "Freddie is so cute." Sarah smiles and says that she will "think about it." She never returns to the topic because she has no desire for Freddie, and, in fact, her friend who suggests Freddie is the person whom Sarah is "in love" with. A boy at another high school described changing the pronouns of his sentences with friends—the "he" becoming "she" in reference to desires and feelings, when actually he referred to his boyfriend. Here he combines "actively" distorting his experience to hide, with passively allowing his friends to assume that he could only be interested romantically in girls. But the more active approach to hiding is used in situations where a youth is in a state of panic about the denial of desires or his friends are pushing him strongly to conform. A stronger form of passing is complete avoidance of peers and withdrawal from school activities as a way to hide what the youth describe as their "true" selves.

Unfortunately, teachers were not typically viewed as a source of assistance or protection. A seventeen-year-old girl said that she is: "Very much hidden [at school]. I was attracted to a few of my friends and tried very hard not to let it show. Mostly I'm afraid about classmates. I think most of my teachers were open-minded; one told me about the Gay Pride Parade." On the other hand, another eighteen-year-old girl said about her teachers: "I think once you get older, you become more and more closed minded, you get set in your ways. People your own age are still growing with you, so they're more open minded."

Many of the youth in our Chicago study described a kind of "double bind" regarding their sexual identity. This was organized around the fact that parents and teachers stress the virtues of truth and honesty; however, remaining true to themselves often results in traumatic experiences, including discrimination and harassment. Many changes will have to occur if schools are to become truly supportive and accessible to gay and lesbian youth. Eric Rofes has summarized these as a need to focus further on the needs of young people, rather than be exclusively concerned with community response.[43]

In this era of AIDS, education on safer-sex must also be a key part of curricula development for these and all students. Teachers, counselors, and students obviously need to feel comfortable with gay and lesbian issues. School curricula, of course, need to include the historical contributions of gay men and lesbians, as well as literature that reflects the experiences and culture of lesbian and gay writers. The presence of gay and lesbian youth in our schools may make the largest difference.

Coming Out at Work

A fourteen-year-old girl, active in the Horizons group, felt torn about appearing in the Pride Day Parade for fear of its repercussions on her finding a job. "I'm afraid to march. I need a job this summer, and an employer may see me on television. I can't risk losing out on a job like that."

Little is known of the problems faced by gay and lesbian youth as they embark on their moral career in the workplace. A generation ago, virtually everyone in our society assumed that their peers and colleagues at work were heterosexual; social life in the shops, office, and factories were notoriously heterosocial. The standards are changing, of course, but in the work contexts of teens, there is good reason to believe that the old standards still prevail. Some youth seek employment in professions or occupations perceived as "gay-sensitive," since they feel they will find less harassment and alienation there. Perhaps the strongest possibility of acceptance is to find work in a gay- or lesbian-owned business, though such opportunities may not be readily available. Some youth may seek work that has traditionally been marked as stereotypically gay, such as waitering, florist, fashion and design jobs. The youth group advisors at Horizons, however, demonstrate the range of professional possibilities toward which youth may strive: physicians, police, psychologists, air traffic controller, insurance and bank employees. The diversity suggests that the horizons of employment are broadening for the youth.[44]

Sixty percent of the youth in our project reported being employed, typically in part-time employment. A few had full-time work. A majority of the youth also feel they must hide their sexual identities from employers and fellow workers. Thirty-seven percent of the boys and 14 percent of the girls report that they can be open to people in the workplace. Unfortunately, most do not consider the workplace a "safe environment" in which to be gay.

Here the monetary incentive to pass as heterosexual reigns supreme. The anecdotes and stories told by the Horizons youth indicate that they face difficult prospects of obtaining satisfying and rewarding employment if they come out at work. We have the impression that in middle-class workplaces, an open-minded heterosexual supervisor can make a huge difference in the future of a gay or lesbian youth; conversely, a prejudiced boss can make the youth's life miserable. For instance, the teenager may be forced to invent a fictitious "steady" partner of the opposite sex, or construct fabricated stories of sexual conquests to fit into all-male office banter. Jean, a sixteen-year-old girl, reported that the only context in which she had ever been harassed for her sexual identity was at work. "At work—in my present job. This guy I'm friends with hassled me. . . . I told him that I was gay. We were discussing it. He was saying some stuff that was really pissing me off and I just hate that." After this incident Jean felt that she had to become more "closed" and circumspect at work. In general, most youth feel that they cannot come out to their employer, unless there is a definite indication of tolerance in the older adult, and that is unusual. This aspect of their moral careers deserves extensive study by future researchers, because it suggests that the workplace remains the critical context for hiding and passing in adulthood.

It is clear from these interviews that these young men and women differentially suppress their sexual identity in the family, with friends, at school, and in the workplace. How does one manage a stigmatized identity?[45] Their identities become articulated with courage and ingenuity through their own emerging moral voices. Horizons youth must develop creative strategies for expressing the self, in spite of counteracting pressures. In the process, the largest majority of the youth begin to develop cultural competence as a gay or lesbian person. But where does this lead?

Well Being and New Futures

The coming-out rituals bring Horizons youth to the edge of knowing what is possible, and they begin to design probable futures—up to a point. In imagining and constructing plans for their futures they have more difficulty than their heterosexual peers. Specifically, they have a hard time imagining life beyond their mid-thirties, unlike heterosexual peers who can predict events into their fifties. Why is this?

We asked youth about their expectations and images of their future life course. Future narratives are the beliefs which individuals hold about the timing and content of anticipated life events on the horizon. Such narratives are thought to assume particular salience during periods of developmental transition, because they shape goal-setting and planning activities, as well as much of later outcomes. The youth were asked to describe all of the events and experiences which they thought would occur in the future, in addition to the age at which each event would most likely to occur.

The gay and lesbian youth anticipated significantly fewer events compared to a sample of heterosexual youth.[46] Heterosexual youth anticipated a more even distribution of events across the projected life course and extended themselves to more distant points in the future than did the gay and lesbian youth. Differences were also found in the type of future events described by the gay and lesbian youth. Gay and lesbian youth described a higher percentage of achievement events (e.g., buying a house, starting a career, going to school). By contrast, heterosexual adolescents described a higher percentage of events concerning relationships and life-style. No differences emerged in the percentage of existential events, such as greater knowledge or spirituality. These findings are best understood as the combined effect of two cultural influences: negative sanctions regarding the expression of gay and lesbian identity by the culture, and the absence of explicit positive norms of gay and lesbian adulthood for the youth.

One of the great developmental tasks of gay and lesbian youth we can see, is the construction of a new set of future expectations of the gay and lesbian life course in the absence of clear plans and purposes from gay culture, and the presence of negative stereotypes from the mainstream. Here, as we found in chapter 4, is the benefit of positive role models—the youth group advisors at Horizons—whom the youth tell us are so central to their developing images of a future life. The facticity of possibilities in being gay or lesbian in the world is a guiding light. Indeed, discovering the existence of a gay and lesbian cultural community through the youth group provides the teens with a cultural context for their identities. Many, for example, described the experience of their first Gay Pride Day Parade as one of the most exhilarating events of their lives.

The future horizon for these gay and lesbian youth is expanding with more optimistic possibilities than ever before. We find that 30 percent of the boys and 33 percent of the girls think that their futures are bright and have been positively affected by coming out. While this is still a minority of the group, we believe that without the support of Horizons and the gay and lesbian culture, we would have found a far lower percentage of positive futures. We also expect that as the younger teens at Horizons are socialized into positive role and work models, they will raise their expectations, and the numbers who see positive futures will grow substantially over the coming years. With a new cultural context and social support, we can predict that these youth will as adults experience more positive and rewarding future events than were ever experienced by openly gay and lesbian adults in the past.

Solidarity and Diversity: Dual Themes of Gay Culture

Every culture represents an ideal design for life and a pragmatic lived reality, and often these are neither harmonious nor conflict free. Gay and lesbian culture as it has emerged in the past twenty years is no different. It struggles to create meaning systems that are compelling designs for living, as well as being morally "just," for its people. As youth enter the culture through the rites of passage, they must face the fundamental problem of living by the ideal of commitment to a common culture, in spite of many differences that might lead them away. A poetic expression of this problem comes from gay novelist David Leavitt's *Family Dancing*, which some of the Horizons youth had read and discussed. The novel's two lead characters, Andrew and Nathan, discuss the Gay Pride Day Parade and what it means for the individual:

> Andrew: "In any battle for freedom of identity there can be no distinction between the private and political."
> Nathan: "Oh, great, quote to me from the manual. . . . That helps. You know what's wrong with your party-line political correctness. Exactly what's wrong with your march. It homogenizes gay people. It doesn't allow for personal difference. It doesn't recognize that maybe for some people what's politically correct is personally impossible, emotionally impossible. And for a politics which is supposed to be in favor of difference, it certainly doesn't allow for much difference among the different."[47]

As soon as these youth begin to sense the happy "normality" and stability of these norms and roles, they are faced with a new problem—and one that will occupy them for many years to come: how do they express their own unique desires and goals as an individual in the culture they seek to enter? Central to the problem of adaptation to gay and lesbian culture is thus the struggle to find a meaningful niche, with a distinctive voice, amid the patterns of conformity, commitment, and diversity which they find awaiting them in the community. Gay men are not the same as lesbians. Blacks and Caucasians differ from Hispanics and Asian-Americans. The youth who desire to go on to college differ from those who seek full-time employment immediately following high school. How is one to be a professional gay or lesbian in a profession that continues to be homophobic? Where to fit in and how to fit into these blossoming gay and lesbian social status positions in the community are all questions which come to occupy them increasingly. Such issues form the basis, at least in part, for the appeal of Queer Nation as an alternative image and moral voice for some youth today.[48] Can an individual youth be true to his or her distinctive selfhood and social origins and still live up to the new cultural ideals of the gay and lesbian culture? These are very old cultural themes in American society; the tradition of expressive individualism that appeals to our deepest sense of how the person will create a social contract with society. This latter process of integrating the social desire to adapt to the new gay and lesbian traditions generates a discourse of new concern for Horizons youth.

Horizons creates a social institution of unique and large proportions in its effort to support and promote the moral justice of coming out among all people. It does so by its values of social justice and participatory democracy in the leadership and organization, as we shall see below. It does so directly in the symbolic and psychological nature of the youth group itself, which defines itself as a democracy that deplores discrimination of any kind, whether by race, gender, sexual identity, whatever. Of course not all of its members live up to this utopian ideal, any more than the members of our Congress are all scrupulous. But the cultural standard that is set by these utopian moral values, of being just and true to oneself, and of making a commitment to promote social justice as a way of being a real and full person, poses a common challenge to youth from diverse walks of life.

The issue of conflicting cultural meanings is critical to understanding how youth come out, because the social world of Horizons is like a small, face-to-face society—unlike the mass anonymity of society in general. What emerged from our description of Horizons was its "small town" flavor, the sense in which life is lived with people who are known and who know you; people one can fight with and still love; people who share commitments to values that color every aspect of the organization. In spite of the politics and controversies that divide any city, and notwithstanding the large and cosmopolitan nature of Chicago, this is a community in which face-to-face social relations matter greatly. As a long-time mental health researcher shrewdly observed some years ago, "People tend to have more detailed knowledge or each other's lives in gay and lesbian communities."[49] Horizons is a magnet in the culture, a place to see and be seen, a place to put your feet up; a place to call your own. Some of the central values that emerge from the agency include its focus upon gay and lesbian rights and liberation, commitment to community and solidarity building, its "equal access" and "equal opportunity" policies, its regard for providing service to the community, and its commitment to cultural and ethnic diversity. These values govern the social interactions between adults and teenagers, and the messages the youth receive in the process of socialization into lesbian and gay culture.

The social life of Horizons is a maze of competing political interests, which is itself a microcosm of gay and lesbian culture. Many of the key actors in the agency, volunteers mostly, are leading citizens in the community. They are active in gay and lesbian political and social organizations that have separate agendas; some of them sit on the boards of these organizations and raise funds for them; they are quoted in the newspapers, especially the local gay and lesbian papers; they may own businesses and serve as consultants to other organizations; they are professionals who have a stake in the community by virtue of their standing and reputations with gay and lesbian clients, associations, and businesses; and some of them have access to inner circles of power, such as advisory offices of the city and municipal or charitable organizations. As in the rest of American society, gender politics and hierarchy play their roles within the Chicago lesbian and gay community too, as reflected in the narratives of chapter 2. The oft-cited cliche that "gay men stick together" and "lesbians are for each other" is prominent as a cultural theme. The social conflict may take an egocentric form, in which a particular individual, strong-willed and outspoken, clashes with others on such issues as support for city or state ordinances or the emphasis upon AIDS fund-raising. However, what is more important are the cultural and political divides within the community.

How do these conflicting cultural ideas influence the socialization of the gay and lesbian youth in the community? For instance, after many years, there is still widespread disagreement regarding the representation of "diverse" gay and lesbian groups who march in the Gay Pride Day Parade. The conflict between solidarity and diversity is directly apparent in the reactions of the youth to the parade. Many youth disliked having "leather men" in the parade. Gay men who dress in full leather "drag" arouse debate. Some people feel that they present a "bad" image to mainstream society, and they should not be allowed to march in the parade. Transvestites also bothered some youth. They provoke the most heated discussion and disagreement among the kids when they talk about these persons who are photographed and put on television—an annual spectacle before the entire American society. But when some youth argued that they should not be allowed to march, a young lesbian argued back: "I don't agree with this. I think they are part of the community and they should present themselves and the way that they want to. Why should a community that is discriminated against then discriminate against its own people! If that's how the people are, if some people are more flamboyant than others, why should we say "Let's hide him because he is a stereotype. Where do you decide to hide the things that fit or don't fit the stereotype?" The majority, however, continue to feel that marching is everyone's right because the community "belongs" to everyone.

Who represents a "positive" role model and image for the society in general and the youth in particular? Implicitly, people in the debate are asking: Is this how we want our children to dress and act? The mainstream rhetoric and subordination of gay and lesbian values is of course a key battleground for acceptance of the culture into American society. Many community leaders voice their opposition to having their standards "dictated" by heterosexuals. The tradition of expressive individualism, popularized by the 1960s hippie adage "do your own thing," continues to privilege the rights of individuals to "be themselves." Yet the form of the rhetoric masks an underlying institutional change that is apparent within the city more broadly. As we pointed out in chapter 2, in the 1970s and early 1980s, many of the bars featured "men in leather," and virtually all of the gay bars in Chicago had drag shows, with transvestites a common fixture. Today, only a few bars have regulars who wear full leather drag, and no bar in the area (eighteen male bars, two female bars) has drag shows. The gender roles and identities of gay men and lesbians seem to be feeding into the mainstream today.

A cultural perspective allows us to see that the change in gender roles is but one example of a larger process of change that represents a paradox of belonging to the culture for gay and lesbian youth. We have pointed out that in the mainstream, youth experience a "double bind" in the messages they receive from parents and teachers. On the one hand they are taught to be honest and "true to themselves," while on the other they learn that it is unacceptable and even forbidden to express same-sex desires. We have seen numerous illustrations of how the resulting secrecy and alienation breeds contempt for the moral standards of the heterosexual adults in question. An analogous process is at play in the gay and lesbian community.

There are pressures in the youth group toward making a commitment to the community. Youth first learn how to be gay or lesbian, without being told so in so many words—but by observing the role models of the advisors. The advisors are teaching the youth to accept people "as they are." Let us call this a principle of "unconditional love," as one of the advisors put it. Related to this is another principle that one must "love oneself" and learn how to be "responsible for your own desires and needs." On the other hand, there are pressures to conform to the youth group's standards, as we have seen: to share in an ideology of unlearning heterosexist values and learning politically and morally proper rules and norms; to adopt "safe sex" practice; to shun secrecy; and of course, to accept the great value of coming out. There is a paradox here, a clash between some of the central values of gay culture regarding respect for diversity, and the pressures to conform. The explicit message the youth receive is to be themselves, as they come to the group for acceptance; but they also experience pressures to accept the standards and cultural images of what it means to be a gay or lesbian person in the center of the community.

All youth experience pressures to conform, but what differentiates this pressure from that of their families and communities is the fact that these youth are diverse and multicultural, and their socialization into norms at Horizons brings them into direct conflict with some of their earlier life experiences, and their current family and ethnic backgrounds. The signs of this conflict are all around the edges of the youth group, though they are seldom highlighted for discussion, as we saw from the example of the parade discussion. This is because the value of "solidarity" tends to bind people's energy to a common purpose in the face of outside opposition ("the mainstream"). When an outside threat is absent from group discussion, the discourse turns upon individual differences within the group, making these a potential source of hierarchy in direct opposition to the democratic values of the group. For instance, hiding from one's parents and not coming out to peers are matters of general discord, with large differences in the reactions of individual members, as we have seen.

A review of the key cultural themes that characterize the ritual coming-out process in the group, from beginning to end, will help to clarify how the conflict between individual expression and group adaptation emerges.

1. Hiding one's "true nature" in childhood before coming to the Horizons group signifies the existence of different kinds of family relationships, with differential opportunities to share awareness of same-sex desires with parents and friends.

2. The degree to which the youth have unlearned basic assumptions about stereotypes—heterosexual "normalcy," homosexual "abnormality," "gender inversion," and homophobia shapes the nature of their current secrecy, and also represents diversity in the group. As we have seen, awareness of desires emerges at an average of age of nine and a half, and yet boys and girls do not express their desires at the same age, suggesting that gender is a major factor of individual differentiation in transcending secrecy. Ethnic and class differences that create different pressures to continue to pass as heterosexual are highly significant here.

3. The experience of crossing the threshold at Horizons suggests significant individual differences in anxiety, fearfulness, and mental health, with a significant number of youth feeling alienated enough to try to take their own lives before they come to the group. The youth who do not come to Horizons are of course even more vulnerable in this regard; they follow a different pathway of development altogether.

4. The experience of the newcomers group is disheartening to some and positive to others, with the result that some youth leave and never return, while the ones who go on become regulars, building a network of new social relations. Yet, even within this network, there is a contrast between how well the youth do at being open and coming out: some cannot tolerate separation from the larger group; others opt for rapid activism that leads them into community activities.

5. The main group brings the youth into the socialization process: learning new values—commitment, solidarity, responsibility, belongingness, gender equality. These values are pivotal in the transition from the youth group into the culture, with the acceptance of the values as a necessity for acceptance into the community. Yet, as we have seen in differential responses of the genders and people of color, the youth's acceptance of these values is not uniform but rather spotty, and individualized.

6. The process of coming out in the community is presaged by venturing with friends from the group to local hangouts, such as the hamburger stand and the apartment. Many youth loathe the bars, but the others who go to them suggest a different emphasis upon socializing and sexual contact, akin to the previous generation. Youth who decline to socialize with their peers at this juncture implicitly signify a different pathway of development, with subgroupings of friends by gender or color. Adaptation to gay and lesbian roles in the culture requires a step in this direction of being out in public, and of coming out at school, but many youth postpone such outing until they leave home or go to college; the pressures are too great, and the desires are different. Their solidarity with their families, neighborhoods, and heterosexual peers remains strong—strong enough to hold them back from making a greater commitment to the gay culture at this point.

7. As romantic and sexual relations develop, the trajectory of change may widen: some youth may become so involved with a partner that their interest in the group wanes. The roles that they take in these relationships again vary by factors beyond the group, ethnicity, and gender, being significant. Because of the sequence of sexual experiences we have found, with boys having sexual experience earlier than girls, and girls having more heteroerotic experience than boys, gender obviously influences the pattern of sexual coming out. Many youth find some erotic experience within the group. Going to the Gay and Lesbian Prom is a major source of coming-out impetus, and a ritual that tends to confirm their growing commitment to the community's norms and roles. Since most youth who are regulars participate in the prom, it becomes apparent that they are making a stronger effort at instilling the values of the group and possibly will continue them into their adult futures.

8. Dealing with the challenge of AIDS and sexually transmitted disease by learning and practicing safe sex is a key to seeing how effective this aspect of the socialization at Horizons is for the youth. Deal-

ing with death and loss from AIDS, as we saw in reactions of the Horizons youth to Joey's death, suggests significant variation within the group—not just in attitudes about sex, but about dealing with the larger "loss" of their former heterosexual lives and identifications. Many youth avoided and denied the effect of Joey's death and stayed away from the pilgrimage to the Quilt. This suggested that they were not ready to make further commitments to the community in confronting the epidemic. It also suggests that as individuals, they continue to feel more conflict over the real-life fact of sexual risk and same-sex expression in their personal lives.

9. The Gay Pride Parade is an entry point of distinction in the group and the most visible means the youth have of intensifying their identities within the culture. Some youth hold back and do not march; they are not ready to make a commitment and express their solidarity to the community. They may fear the reactions of parents, high school friends, and employers. By excluding themselves they postpone a celebration of solidarity; but they may have good reason, in terms of their individual realities, to do so; and the effect of their decisions will not be known until later. To their fellow initiates, they may appear hesitant or confused; they may be treated as "different" by the youth who feel that their commitment to march has expressed what is "real" and morally just. The advisors generally praise the marchers' participation in the parade and related activities, signaling an emerging distinction between "full" and "partial" membership in the culture. To be a full person in gay and lesbian culture is to have passed through each of these successive ritual passages that culminates in marching in the parade. That is their jumping-off point into society, following which the youth apply what the youth group experience has taught them.

At each of these transition points, gay and lesbian youth may diverge from emerging group norms. How is the "difference" handled by the youth? We have found the ability of most youth to accept others' diversity amazing at times. But their capacity is not unlimited. The point is best illustrated by the case of Steve, the only chronically mentally ill youth who attended the group during the time of our study.[50] Steve had been going to the group for longer than anyone could remember (we calculated that he must have been attending for at least five years). In fact, he was probably over age, but no one took notice of this. Not much is known about Steve. The group did not know where he lived or how he got by. The most striking thing about Steve was his physical appearance: he was rather emaciated and gaunt. He dressed shabbily; some group members said they had never seen him in more than one change of clothes. He talked to himself sometimes. He always arrived on time. He carried reading material in a plastic bag, which he proceeded to take out and pour over. He seemingly paid no attention to conversations in the group, but when he was questioned it was clear that he had been listening. He made several unsuccessful attempts to become more involved, for instance, in the improvisation theater group, where his contributions were intelligent and witty. He was invited to the picnic; he didn't get actively involved except to complain about the smoke. The group was not sympathetic to him; he was a "spoiler." He was also invited to a party that a group member held. People at the party said that he only complained about the music. At other times, however, the group was very supportive of him and tried to be encouraging.

The group's reaction to Steve was ambiguous; they were never overtly hostile. Many tried to engage him in conversation, but he lacked social skills. Steve had a particularly negative effect on the new people. He frightened them. They were already uncomfortable and his presence threatened them with the possibility that they were "losing their minds"—a metaphor for their profound alienation from society and status change made possible by the rituals. In the main group, the youth were not as disturbed by Steve's presence and accepted him as a fact of life. Here the youth were vibrant and healthy, normative in most features of their lives, and typically mentally normal (as we have found from our psychological assessments). Unlike Steve and Joey, they were also living largely within the center of the sexual norms and practices of the gay and lesbian community, as represented by the role model of the advisors as well.

We cannot understand individual differences within the group without an accurate description of the norms and the "normal" individual of the society in which they take place. How red is a rose? How sweet is its smell? Such questions call for judgments, aesthetic assessments of relative comparison, based upon other sorts of roses and the fragrances of many flowers. Thus a developmental theory of gay and lesbian is explicitly comparative and implicitly evaluative. Many of us are uncomfortable with such value judgments; they challenge our received American ideology of equality. What does a "norm" and a "normal individual" mean in the emergence of a new culture? The fact is, no one knows: as a cultural pattern emerges, individuals respond to its roles and norms by a central tendency to conform to competing and, sometimes conflicting, cultural standards. The ideology of "solidarity" to gay and lesbian culture is clear enough, but it competes with another ideological value, "cultural diversity." By attending a gay and lesbian social event or political cause, people implicitly commit themselves to the value of "solidarity." Actors from an ethnic minority are more visible, which affirms another value, "diversity." This explains why marching in the parade poses such a conflict for gay men and lesbians of color. Gay and lesbian persons are from all walks of life in the United States; their erotic desires may or may not link them as consociates; but their social desire to participate in common causes makes them a culture.

By arriving at this conclusion we finally see the problem that the experience of coming out presents to youth of diverse backgrounds who enter Horizons with the desire to come out. Their disparate backgrounds lead them to a pathway of adolescent development that is fraught with all of the ambivalence of stage fright and collective culture-building simultaneously. The youth do not have to surrender their individuality to join Horizons or enter into the rituals of coming out. Indeed, they may celebrate their gendered, ethnic, class, and religious heritages. However, there is a continuous "push" into the gay culture and "pull" back into their diverse lifestyles that poses a continuing challenge for the individual. As they proceed to more positive futures, they begin to integrate their new identities into the mainstream social roles and relationships from the past. But this integration often requires all the creative energy and resourcefulness they can muster within themselves to achieve the double adaptation of being gay or lesbian in the mainstream and in the gay and lesbian culture.

Like other Americans, we are also troubled and disagree with the social structure of homophobia that has suppressed the cause of gay men and lesbians, preventing them from sharing in equal justice and social rights. Our society is changing in this regard, in some areas faster, while in others, such as the high schools and the armed services, the change is fiercely resisted and barely noticeable. As a cultural process, coming out and its creation of same-sex identities and social relations belongs not only to a particular historical society, but to a moral ideology of norms that shapes these events.

What is good and just in our society today, the youth of Horizons ask? Our society has inherited much homophobic prejudice that does harm to the developing person. The teenager—especially during the traumas of coming out—is challenged by gay and lesbian culture to revise some of his or her most fundamental social perceptions and beliefs about society, including their particular ethnic and community values. They discover that homophobia exists in everyone, including their parents and themselves. They learn that harassment of gays and lesbians is common in American society; that discrimination in the armed forces and churches, government, and business is an acceptable practice; and that crimes against gays, both violent and nonviolent, are reported in the newspapers everyday. To affirm the reality of these challenges to cherished myths is to undo some of their basic commitments to their natal homes and communities and transform them in the context of gay and lesbian culture.

Is the purpose of Horizons to confirm a desired sexual identity as gay or lesbian for the aspiring person? For the younger person who comes to the organization, the answer is yes: without the existence of this new cultural entity, they might not come out. From the perspective of the collective, however, the answer differs. It requires another look at the process of symbolic death we have found so striking in the rituals of coming out.

As we have shown, coming out amounts to a kind of death of the self, the former heterosexual self and personhood. Because rites of passage around the world so often employ the symbolism of death of the old role and rebirth of a new self and role, the anthropologist is not surprised to find in the lives and stories and rituals of coming out themes of loss, grief, and death. However, for a long time—at least since the early 1970s—this negation of the past, the loss of mainstream goals and norms through coming out, has generally been avoided and suppressed by the political rhetoric of the gay and lesbian movement. Adults who had come out wanted to make visible and celebrate only the positive and life-cherishing functions of gay and lesbian roles in the face of rampant homophobia. They had suffered enough; they had known the bad press for too long; they did not want to be reminded of the old rhetoric of sin and disease which said that they were "bad," or "flawed in their bodies or natures," or "juveniles who refused to grow up." The last thing gay and lesbian people wanted to be reminded of was what they were losing symbolically in the declaration of their same-sex desire by joining gay culture.

The reason why the adults of the prior generation could not accept the idea of having lost something was because there was no gay culture for them to turn to as haven and home. They lacked a safe refuge.

They could not go back to passing as straight—that compromise of integrity to which they had been subjected their whole lives. They may have sometimes felt great pressure from parents, friends, and employers—the great temptation—to do so. Had they a positive and supporting environment, they could have gained the comfort of a supporting cultural attitude: "Well, I've lost straight life, but I have gained gay culture." It is with the symbolic loss of this kind—or rather, its denial—that adults and youth have had to contend in the ritual process of coming out for so very long. The generations of the past could not rely upon ready-made cultural attitudes of this kind simply because they did not exist. They were not socialized into gay and lesbian culture. How could they put to rest their stage fright and temptations to pass when they did not have the support of the ritual process we have examined in this book? It is in the light of such immense developmental and cultural loss, which might include not only the withdrawal of one's parents' love, the loss of one's job, one's friends, and even banishment from one's church, that we must interpret the larger meaning of individual differences in coming out.

Individuals vary in their capacity to cope with loss and be resilient in adapting to uncertain futures. Of the various aspects of their adjustment that we have examined, one of these deserves a final look: their native culture, the pre–coming-out values, beliefs, and norms of their families and friends, nationalities, and ethnic neighborhoods.

In the minds of some youth, giving up heterosexual roles and institutions is more than a "sexual" matter; it is a loss of cultural identity, a break with historical tradition. The Asian who finds that he will not be able to carry on the family and clan tradition, the black who may no longer attend the neighborhood church, the Italian-American who is rejected by his parents and can no longer attend extended family functions—these are soul-wrenching losses of such an immense magnitude that they signify the loss of a *whole way of life*. To lose all of this in order to gain the public expression of sexual desires may seem like a bad trade-off. Some adults can handle the anxiety created by this declaration, but for many youth it is too much to bear. Youth who struggle with the idea of giving up a normative heterosexual life course, including marriage and having children, feel that this is too much to surrender in exchange for habits of the heart. The old American tradition of expressive individualism, the supreme ideal that tells them to follow their particular dreams and feelings of the self, should lead them on to gay and lesbian culture. However, another kind of cultural identity—their native heritage—is in direct competition with it. The older closet homosexual knew these demands only too well. Assimilation to the mainstream heterosexual norms may have been painful, with its isolating preclusion on intimacy in most social relations, but closet homosexuals did not have to reckon with the loss of the cultural traditions of their childhood and adult family and friends, on which their public success as competent individuals in the workplace and community was based. The ones from the earlier generation who were able to overcome these losses were indeed resilient and exceptional; most, however, could not. Some youth of today suffer from a similar paralysis, except that they have a stronger and more powerful possibility of adaptation: gay and lesbian culture will fight for them.

The youth who face choosing a cultural change in their identities or continuing to pass as heterosexual are thus at a historic crossroads. Their ability to successfully achieve the transitions afforded by the rites of coming out augers a willingness, as individuals, to undergo a long process of grieving for what was before, in order to find a future of uncertain success. The road to successful adaptation, to a new "normal" life in the future, is bumpy and requires a courageous effort—a kind of heroic expressive individualism that American society in general and gay and lesbian culture celebrates. It is a paradox of cross-cultural study that the same value that leads to being out—heroic individualism—is celebrated by both mainstream and the gay culture as a unique contribution of the American tradition to the moral understanding of individual development, even though they disagree mightily on the means to the end—declarations of being out in diverse contexts—and to the end itself: being gay- and lesbian-identified in society. The cultural history of the gay and lesbian movement in the United States in general, and in Chicago in particular, suggests that rituals of coming out stand for the creation and transmission of a new cultural tradition that makes this moral understanding an inevitability of life in the twenty-first century.

CHAPTER SEVEN

◆ ◆ ◆

Conclusion:
Gay Culture and the
Moral Career of Youth

Many adolescents experience emotional upheaval and "identity cri-ses" in American culture at large,[1] and perhaps it is true that most adolescents yearn to remake society. "The adolescent mind becomes a more explicitly ideological one, by which we mean one's search for some inspiring unification of tradition or anticipated techniques, ideas, and ideals."[2] Like many adolescents the Horizons youth are idealistic. Unlike other youth, however, the children of Horizons share their idealism with a growing nation of adult gay men and lesbians who strive for freedom in American life. Horizons youth would settle for acceptance, but love is what they hope to find.

Our defense of gay and lesbian teenagers moral right to follow their hearts and minds in search of a culture best suited for them is more than a matter of our politics or a reverse prejudice on our part. It is also based upon a reading of the history and cultural changes wrought by gay men and lesbians. The Horizons kids are correct in thinking that coming out is an unprecedented cultural phenomenon, yet they are largely oblivious to its historical foundations. Ironically, the relationship between ritual pedagogy and same sex expression in the creation of the social body is an ancient theme in our cultural ancestry; moreover, coming out is a century-old device of personal change and development in the American tradition.[3]

Nearly three centuries ago the desire for the same sex was punished by death in many western nations. For example, in Holland between the seventeenth century and the early nineteenth centuries, the "sodomite" was tried and condemned to death, initially in secret, and then in public, execution.[4] Many people were put to death during this period of approximately 150 years. The evidence from their love letters and confessions suggests that some of these sodomites had a clear sense of desiring the same sex. Why were the early executions secret? Because sodomy was loathsome: such a crime against God and nature that it should not be discussed in public; it was a truly silent discourse.[5] By 1811 the worst abuses were over, and eventually the Netherlands was to become not only the most enlightened of countries, but with increasing secularization, the most progressive in the area of same-sex rights. Execution for same-sex desire is gone; yet in countries like the United States we continue to see its signs in an absolute taboo on same-sex desire enduring in social consciousness. It is a "cultural survival" in our society; indeed, in each of us. Gay and lesbian culture challenges this moral ideology in its formulation of a new cultural consciousness.

The gay and lesbian rhetoric for building a new culture is threatening to the old heterosexual/homosexual dualism. As a new form of sexual and gendered life, "gay and lesbian" challenges basic and cherished folk assumptions, such as the "need" for each individual to form a nuclear family and rear children as a heterosexually married couple. The idea of a "same sex couple" which lives openly and adopts or creates biological children is breaking down these accepted norms of social life; that is, the historical social contract between individual and society known since the founding of the Republic. By introducing new cultural ideas of sexual desire and identity, pleasure and love, with associated social relationships in public, gay men and lesbians suggest the basis for a new theory of "human nature" and a conception of being human, that is, the foundation of a new thinking.

As the coming-out rites have thus increasingly challenged moral norms in the United States, members of the gay and lesbian youth groups of Chicago, Minneapolis, Los Angeles, or New York, and many other cities have opened up new ways of thinking, talking, and doing sexuality through self-help and self-awareness friendship networks. They seek to transform what they thought was all "bad" into something to be cherished, even loved, when they tell their own stories of struggling to come out.

Individuals are always placed in situations of making decisions about what is ethically "right" and "wrong" in society. From childhood until old age, we face a continuous series of decisions—how to express our thoughts, and what choices to make between alternative paths of acting to further our interests and goals. Gay and lesbian teenagers are placed in situations that create moral conflicts between what is expected of them and what they feel is "true" of their desires. In simple terms, the youth experience their decisions as representing what is "good" or "bad," according to the cultural logic of being heterosexual or homosexual. From the perspective of daily life—however painful this process might be—it contains the potential for promoting their development. It does this by causing the youth to question their moral thinking; to understand why they should think of their desires as "bad" and why they should not regard gay and lesbian culture as a "good thing in its own right." These moral conflicts lead the youth to question their moral precepts of what is right and wrong. Eventually, they begin to feel that it is not their self that is "bad," it is society that is "bad" for harboring such prejudice. This questioning leads them ultimately to challenge their assumptions of heterosexual "naturalness" and "normalcy," as we so frequently encountered in the youth's stories. Being resocialized through the youth group, teens redefine what they felt was "bad" about themselves, learning of "homophobia" as a cultural idea that displaces the older content of shame and self-hatred. In this way, their identities emerge as morally positive and ethically "good" by virtue of their support and acceptance in the new gay and lesbian culture.

We have referred to this process as a "compromise of integrity." Many adolescents have to make compromises all the time, in adjusting to familial and peer demands and to societal expectations at school or at work, prior to leaving home and becoming economically or socially independent. However, the moral conflicts of gay and lesbian-identified youth are of another order—the basic compromise between their erotic desires and social roles that violates their very sense of being. In the development of same-sex desire, as we showed, the moment of hiding is also the moment of denial of the self's desires, which constitutes self-alienation. This violation, we suspect, is at the root of the high rate of suicide risk among gay and lesbian youth. The teens are exposed to a "double bind" from parents and teachers; on the one hand, they are expected to be "honest" and "truthful," while on the other they learn that their desires are "bad" and should be hidden, an intolerable torment to their mental health. From knowing people who hide and pass as heterosexual, including teachers or friends of the family, to reading in the newspapers about the double-standards of the government when it comes to matters of equal and fair protection under the law, the youth become increasingly aware of ethical compromises throughout their society. "What am I going to do?" the youth wonders. "Am I just going to sit back when the teacher tells me to get a date for the high school prom?" And, "Why should my boss at work need to know what I do in bed—it's none of their business!" Their moral thinking compels them to act in one way, to defend and adapt themselves, while on the other hand they feel a moral responsibility to tell others how they truly feel. "The teacher should not assume that I am straight," and "I don't ask my boss what he does in bed—everyone should have the right to their own desires."

Moral dilemmas come from the double-standards of society, it is true; but the judgments of the youth are not just about other people, they are about themselves. Their idealism leads them to an extreme sensitivity regarding what is right and wrong in themselves. Adults become attenuated to these issues; many have long adapted pragmatically to stable social roles and jobs that cause them to suppress moral sensibility. Teenagers, however, are acutely sensitive to moral principles. They look so closely at what people do and say because they are watching for signs of compromise that would lead into more double binds for themselves. The compromise of integrity thus leads many of these youth into a new way of moral thinking which actually promotes development by redefining their precepts and feelings, adjusting them to their positive identities and futures as adult gay and lesbians.

If the youth succeed in wrestling with these moral compromises and questioning the moral precepts of their existence, a symbolic rebirth as gay and lesbian waits in the wings. This is the protecting intent of gay cultural rites; it allows, in its wiser seclusion, the youth to grieve for what has been "lost": heterosexual images and norms. Only this symbolic mourning may pave the way for the celebration of the new moral thinking. This mourning process was not available to earlier generations; they did not have the benefit of the rites of passage afforded by institutions like Horizons. But such a process is crucial to handling the revolutionary identity changes required of coming out, soothing the individual's passage through society as well as the redefinition of the self as positively gay or lesbian. The coming-out rites have the symbolic function of both restoring the self and healing. They make whole what has remained incomplete and sore in the body, mind, and the soul of the gay and lesbian as well: that is, the ineffable sense of coming into being as a real person with dignity, who is loved in, and belongs to, this social world.

The social rituals of heterosexual, homosexual, and gay are divergent and competing cultural ideals. The key confirmatory rites of each include church-ordained marriage, for the heterosexual; passing as heterosexual, for the closet homosexual; and coming out, for the lesbian and gay. Each embodies distinctive symbolic traditions: their social roles and practices diverge, and their mythical images spring from different sources, as we have repeatedly seen. The rituals of coming out not only critique the moral compromises of the closet homosexual, they are also a critique of heterosexuality as a moral ideology and a lifeway as well. Gays and lesbians are refashioning what "reproduction" means in the creation of a social community; they are negotiating new ways of adopting and bearing children. But not everyone is in agreement about the values of coming out and its cultural practices; for instance, in the area of creating a committed, life-long same-sex couple relationship; in having children; and in being openly gay in all walks of life.

The responses of adults to these idealistic youth vary immensely, by virtue of the fact that gay men and lesbians now span the widest possible range of the life course that has ever existed before in history. There is a plethora of age cohorts, as we discussed in chapter one; adults in their twenties and thirties, largely gay and lesbian-identified; people in their forties and fifties, less distinctively identified demographically; others up to their eighties who remain totally closeted. From a global perspective it is only their erotic desire that links them; they do not form a single fabric of culture. Their social attitudes and tastes, their own particular desires for social life, compromise, and adaptation are enormously different. Each group has different perspectives on the teenagers. The advisors at Horizons are closest in chronological age and worldview to the youth; they are motivated to do for the youth what they would have liked others to have done for them in assisting their own development. Some of the oldest people living, the ones in their seventies and eighties, may ironically be more positive than others, in their fifties, who are still living under heterosexual pressures to which they compromised themselves. They sometimes reflect quite negative attitudes toward the youth; the attitude that the kids are simply "jailbait." Some suffer the oppression of homophobia that binds the old homosexual to the fear of being accused of seducing, of promoting "homosexuality," in youth. Here is a large stumbling block to the creation of a positive social foundation for adult support of youthful gays and lesbians today. More importantly, these generational differences pose a fundamental problem for the transmission of the culture to the young.

The purpose of the rites of coming out is not to perpetuate the gay and lesbian culture, but to promote individual freedom. But, without sufficient power and collective solidarity, the rights which the individual seeks are open to violation for all. They may be cancelled, undone. The renewed controversy over the *Roe v. Wade* decision of the United States Supreme Court, which allowed women the freedom to elect an abortion and which is now being challenged in the legislatures and courts, suggests that social rights, once assumed to be irrevocable, can be eaten away, even abolished.[6] To suggest that rights of sexual identity are immutable because they are based in "biology" is no ultimate protection either. Magnus Hirschfield, the champion of homosexual liberation in the earlier twentieth-century Germany, was to learn this bitter lesson after the rise of the Nazis in Germany. His idealistic formula, "Knowledge Equals Justice," did not protect homosexuals: the Nazis' simply proceeded to remove the "disease" they felt could not be changed or cured by exterminating thousands of people who desired the same sex, including many for whom this was a false accusation.[7] What begins as a medley of moral critiques expressing individual rights and social justice may end in a symphony of conformism and even oppression.

The right to come out, we believe, should be viewed as a cultural right offered the individual who seeks freedom. Yet as soon as traditions become visible and institutionalized, such as the rituals of coming out, they begin to create pressures toward conformity. When the impetus changes, and the tradition is placed first for political or moral reasons, then this spells trouble in the matter of individual moral thinking. For then, as Edward Sapir once wrote, we are no longer dealing with a genuine culture, aimed at creating a harmonious and graceful way of living in accord with a desired social life. We are instead confronted with a spurious culture that seeks to justify itself by whatever means available, including the negation of the values of individual freedom. The debate touches upon the ultimate value of coming out itself.

Throughout this book we have referred to *rituals* of coming out, using a concept of ritual that implied something that was valuable and meaningful as a category of collective social action. For many Americans, indeed, for many Westerners, such an assumption is questionable. That ritual is less prevalent or popular today in American society proves that we are in a period of long-standing social change, even secularization of purpose, interest, and being. The long decline in ritual practices in the Western tradition, first in the religious sense, and then in forms of secular social living, was abruptly halted by social formations of the late 1960s and 1970s, of which the historical construction of coming out as a ritual entry into gay culture is among the most prominent.

When the right to seek individual freedom is made secondary to the political import of the process of coming out, then, and then only, will these rituals become an "empty" form. For some people, especially those who are not "religious," ritual is a vapid or authoritarian category. It is meaningless, devoid of personal intent, and goals. What anthropology has taught us, however, is that this quality of ritual is produced by the change to a "spurious" culture. When a ritual lacks meaningfulness for individual actors, one of two processes emerges. Either there is a loss and decline of individual signification by identification with the tradition, in which case, the cultural reality of the rites no longer reflect collective action.[8] Or else, the individual actor has new options which satisfy the same goal, and he or she may no longer make the rational choice of "investing" their symbolic capital in a rite that lacks personal intent or collective reason. When the rites of coming out fail to meet the needs either of the emerging gay and lesbian culture or, when they come into conflict with the struggle for individual freedom, then will they become "empty rituals." Until that time they remain the safeguard of the process, just as the advisors at Horizons serve as the guardians of the youth.

Whatever the origins of this new culture, it is clear that many of those gay- and lesbian-identified adults who claim membership as its citizens, share a utopian vision of what their society can and must be into the twenty-first century. In our study we have discovered that having children remains one of the key unresolved issues of the generations of both youth and adults. They are creating new social roles and institutions, such as Horizons, to deal with the issues. Like the hermaphroditic *hijras* of old India,[9] whose divine nature is blessed by the Mother Goddess, the lesbian and gay adults of American society today feel a special sympathy for any youth who would brave the icy waters of homophobia to come out. The Indian *hijras* lay a ceremonial claim of kinship to any child who desires to belong among them; likewise, with adults and teenagers, the gay and lesbian culture of Horizons claims for its own all children similarly born who reveal the mark of a different nature: their desire for the same sex and gay selfhood.

All of us are aware of the legacy of the disease and pathology stereotypes of homosexuality. We grew up with them; they stigmatized us and our friends; they caused generations to feel the sense that they had sinned or had committed a crime by loving the same sex. A hundred years of this tradition created the conditions for negative symptoms of all kinds, including poor self-esteem, depression, maladaptive coping mechanisms such as alcoholism, and of course the dreadful closet of passing as straight—the slow and symbolic self-negation inherited from the past. We mention these issues to declare our interest in seeking positive models of development and mental health for the youth of tomorrow. Adults must become intensely aware of the absence of positive role models that haunt the field of lesbian and gay mental health care.

The liberal democracies of the West have had to live with the notion of cultural variation for centuries, and gay and lesbian culture is but a further expansion of freedom based upon this old principle. The gay and lesbian movement stands for reform of many kinds, but we notice that it's moral commentary on our society is a way of suggesting back to the critics of gay and lesbian culture that it represents a stronger desire to live fuller, happier, less compromised lives. Its "good" is that it inspires the coming generation to love life and to join society, rather than to shun or hate it, because of the imposition of false standards that deny the existence of those who desire the same sex. Laws are expensive; morality is cheap. What we look forward to is an inevitable evolution of social reform, based upon the new moral thinking of coming out, translated into more expensive laws and social entitlements.

Think about this: in 1908, the social reformer, Edward Carpenter, opened his significant essay on the "intermediate sex" with a moral voice and vision that is so contemporary it still defines the needs of gay and lesbian youth:

> But we may point out how hard it is, especially for the young among them, that a veil of complete silence should be drawn over the subject, leading to the most painful misunderstandings, and perversions and confusions of mind; and that there should be no hint of guidance; nor

any recognition of the solitary and really serious inner struggles they may have to face! If the problem is a difficult one . . . the fate of those people is already hard who have to meet it in their own persons, without their suffering in addition from the refusal of society to give them any help.[10]

Carpenter's plea from more than eighty years ago has gone unheeded for long. All of us who are concerned with positive development in society, whether heterosexual, homosexual, or gay, have the opportunity to support the understanding of the parallel path of growth and development of gay and lesbian youth, with optimal mental health outcomes in all the walks of life. Likewise, we must resist any effort to deny the sexual development of children, or to reduce the full person to his or her sexual life. Above all, we must challenge the notion that confusion in identity is the primary reason that someone is gay or lesbian. These reductionisms dehumanize the full and dignified person, and they have no place in a larger conception of human nature.

We would like to address a different plea to the parents of gays and lesbians. Too many parents in the past have blamed themselves for having a "homosexual" child. This is nonsense. Whatever the causes of same-sex desire—there are a hundred ways to get to heaven—gay and lesbian children are not in any simple way the product of what parents do or don't do. Yet parents *are* responsible for dealing with the problems of homophobia and stigma that are present in all of us, the parent and child included. When a parent acknowledges that a child is growing up, or getting married, such a parent is coping with reality; more importantly, the parent can influence the developments by being loving, understanding, and supportive.

We have found from our study of parents and their gay and lesbian children that the perspectives of loss and gain differ dramatically. Parents focus on what they are losing, while children emphasize their gain in coming out. Where the parents are grieving for lost dreams and goals, such as having grandchildren, their children are looking forward to a new freedom by being out. As in these other areas of growing up, the parents' responses may be equal in magnitude to the youth's responses to coming out. If the child is gay or lesbian, this may activate a subjective process within the parent, regarding their own identities, which can be positive or negative. On the positive side, if the child is telling the parents about feelings, it is one of the most wonderful gifts the parent could receive. The youth is sharing who they feel themselves to be. If parents find out accidentally, they need to be told why they were not informed directly. On the negative side, if the parents simply react, it may set off a "chain reaction" in their relationship with the child that will lead to more hiding, alienation, and destructiveness than ever. We are learning that the preexisting relations within the family are significant in predicting whether the responses will be more positive or negative. The more involved both parents are, the more positive their relationships with the child will be as a factor of the child's coming out, including the effects upon the marital relationship between the parents. Here again a new moral thinking may emerge. If the parents are open to "coming out" and revealing to their relatives and friends that they have a gay or lesbian child, this is a positive sign of dealing with the homophobic attitudes regarding their social status change. And if the parents are open to the child, the teenager will begin to teach them about their own heterosexual assumptions and expectations. This will not only introduce them to the ideas of gay and lesbian culture; it will create a new and better social bond with the child. Parents can make a decisive difference in all of these areas of future development of the child.

All of us have the opportunity in social programs, teaching, research, and counseling to define a new moral vision of human development. We cannot ignore the anguish and pleas of those who seek help, nor can we remove ourselves from the dilemmas of activists, whether in the arena of AIDS or of gay nationalism or lesbian alternative health care networks, who seek to restore the dignity of the person. Our responsibility is to find new and creative ways to define the positive mental health of this new cohort of adults and young people, which includes the emergence of same-sex desire and gay lesbian social roles. Some twenty years ago a survey study of openly gay men suggested that the more engaged in gay culture they were, the more well-being they felt in most areas of their lives.[11] This was an early indication of the positive effects of gay and lesbian culture we have discovered in our own work. We hope that this book adds to the growing perspective in mental health research that it is unhelpful to appeal to nineteenth-century images of the nuclear family and heterosexual models of childhood for optimal mental functioning, or to urge conformity to heterosexual norms and mental health guidelines, for this will mean that injury will be done to the gay and lesbian child in development.

If our optimistic view is correct, then we would predict that in twenty years or so—one more historical generation—that the coming-out process will no longer be necessary, at least in urban centers. In the twenty-first century, around the time of puberty, youth who feel desire and enjoy relations with the same sex will simply begin to express these feelings publicly—much as heterosexual youth begin to moon over their boyfriend or girlfriend, initiating dating and the courtships that lead to later life partnerships. Expressing such desires, like opposite sex desires today at puberty, will be celebrated: not as a matter of individual coming out, but as a recognition of the nature and being of the individual. There will no longer be the delay for years, with the negative effects on social development in many other areas, such as friendship, that was inflicted upon prior generations. Homophobia will not disappear entirely, of course; but like the nastier forms of racism condoned in the old plantation and slavery system, it too will diminish, becoming gradually invisible, until it fades into a happy death. Such a steady hand of social process takes many years; and it is beset with all of the problems that await the gay and lesbian child in growing up in this extraordinarily turbulent and burgeoning society.

By the time the process is completed, the children of Horizons and thousands more like them in major cities across the United States will have achieved not only expression of their sexual identity and desires; they will have also joined in the larger and more ambitious task of adaptation to life, part of the project of becoming a new citizen of the growing polity—gay and lesbian culture. What we can do to help prepare ourselves for this coming generation is to create social arrangements that promote positive development for these youth. All things human built on respect and dignity for the individual, and equal rights for individuals as members of cultures in our society, will, in turn, create life-cherishing social relations. So says our own optimistic Americanism.

EPILOGUE:
GROWING UP GAY AND LESBIAN
IN THE AGE OF AIDS
♦ ♦ ♦

The AIDS epidemic in the United States has had the paradoxical effect of mobilizing the gay and lesbian community into a more cohesive and effective political and social organization, while simultaneously killing thousands of its most dynamic, creative, and influential members. The plague continues to exact such a terrible toll on those who support and remember—lovers and friends, family and buddies— that its social and psychological toll on lesbians and gays will take many generations to calculate. That such a disease both produced a new level of cultural consciousness and sapped the vitality of the very same population is remarkable and may be without parallel in history. One thing is sure—the burden of grief has made rituals of remembering those who have died of AIDS a necessary but painful part of gay and lesbian communal life, prematurely "aging" what was hitherto a rather "young" culture.

Enter now the perilous problem of lesbian, gay, and bisexual adolescence in the AIDS epidemic. As we have shown, the emergence of gay-identified youth who come out in early adolescence is in many ways the crowning point of the progress of lesbian and gay culture over the past twenty-five years. Moreover, AIDS was rightly perceived to be a direct threat to gay youth years ago by activists and leaders of the lesbian and gay community, and the steps taken long ago to protect those youth were bold and far-reaching. At the time of our original study at Horizons in the late 1980s, the AIDS epidemic had generally not stricken gay youth in Chicago. Of course, AIDS had touched their lives, especially through Horizon's constant HIV education campaigns, but the threat remained an abstraction to many. It was not until the death of Joey from HIV that the youth group began to experience (firsthand) the sting of mortality, which showed just how close to home the deadly virus could strike.

Today, the epidemic affects all aspects of the coming out process. Against increasing evidence that a rising tide of HIV infection among gay teens and young men poses a new and greater threat, it is important that we update our study of the emergence of gay culture by examining this threat and the empowerment of lesbian and gay youth that is necessary to combat it.

American teenagers coming into sexual maturity today enter a world saturated with the presence of AIDS and other sexually transmitted diseases. Youth are being infected with HIV at an increasingly younger age, and all adolescents—straight and gay—are more at risk of infection than at any prior time in the epidemic. New studies estimate that 25 percent of individuals infected with HIV between 1987 and 1991 were under twenty-one years of age. Sexual contact accounts for approximately 35 percent of AIDS cases among youth who are thirteen to nineteen years old; the figure rises to 70 percent among young adult men aged twenty to twenty-four.[1] With the heightened risk for HIV infection to heterosexuals, the risk to women—particularly those who are economically underprivileged and often of color—is of great concern. This increasing rate of infection for AIDS seems to be caused by people taking more sexual risk and ignoring information about safe sex. This is true in spite of the fact that society in general and gay and lesbian institutions in particular are more diligent in promoting prevention and teaching safe-sex education.

When we conducted our study in Chicago, the Horizons agency was already providing a vigorous program of "safer" sex education for HIV and STDs. The program, which was highly visible and explicit, was far ahead of its time and beyond anything that had been previously implemented in the schools. Teens who attended the Horizons youth group regularly participated in discussions involving speakers, in films and plays about HIV/AIDS, and in a variety of social and political fund-raising, care-taking, and related events. The education for safe sex that youth received was aggressive; "in your face," as they liked to say of it.

On a less visible level, gay and lesbian adult role models provided positive images to emulate, counseling, and sex socialization information seldom available for straight youth whose parents and teachers were and still are afraid to broach the subject of sex. Looking back, we can see the courage it required for gay adults to help educate youth at a time when their community was under attack and straight parents were not doing the teaching. Indeed, Horizons' youth participated in AIDS prevention programs to the point that they grew weary of the constant reminders of the "Big A" as they referred to AIDS. But this changed drastically when the youth group lost a member. From the death of their peer Joey in the late 1980s, many youth realized the lethal importance of practicing safe-sex; since AIDS had struck so close to home, it was no longer an abstraction, and many youth told us of their renewed efforts to protect themselves, and even more, to remind and hasten their peers to protect their own bodies. Socialization into the gay and lesbian community through institutions such as Horizons—which in 1995 remains strong and vital—has had a positive effect on teaching and implementing safe-sex practices in society at large.

By the time we had completed our field study in 1989, fear about sexual risk for HIV was already high among gay male youth. That was, however, six years ago—short by the standards of history but a very long time by the clock of an epidemic. AIDS is around more; the same kinds of risk are present, but there is more infection than before. We can only speculate that unlike the youth we studied at Horizons, younger teens are not protecting themselves as much. Of course, there were and are strong cultural ideals about practicing safe sex, and these may have biased the reporting in our study and may be a factor in the statistics today. Practicing safer sex became a powerful group expectation—so powerful that it might have biased some youth to hide their real behaviors and pretend they were being "safe" even when they were not. This cannot be ruled out, as we noted before, but we have a hunch that the frequency of infection has actually gone up.

Many of Horizons' youth experienced a time when they saw themselves as "bisexual," although they did not typically communicate these dual desires as part of their "cultural identity." We found that many engaged in sexual relations with both genders, with a higher number of girls having their first sexual experience with the opposite sex, and a higher number of boys having an exclusive history of same-sex relations. Their risk-taking was found to be a function of their experience or ignorance of sexual intercourse with the same or opposite sex. Lesbian youth during the time of our study felt that AIDS education was insufficiently addressed to them, since it was not personalized to their particular sexual risk for HIV. But it was the HIV risk-taking by boys in anal sexual practice that was of most concern. Allow us to summarize AIDS findings from our study that were not available when this book originally appeared.[2]

As mentioned earlier, the youth group provided the cultural environment of an active and ongoing safer-sex program. The teens were socialized into awareness of "riskier" and "safer" sexual practices. Both males and females demonstrated a high degree of positive knowledge of HIV and safe sex. An assessment of attitudes about safer sex obtained through our study demonstrated that teens expressed strong attitudes of approval of safer sex. Both sexes appeared sophisticated regarding sexual risk behaviors and generally were in agreement about what constituted safer-sex practice. Youth were more suspicious and wary of getting HIV-infected from their older partners than from those of their same age; boys more than girls believed that they had to take greater precautions with partners older than themselves, and especially with those over the age of twenty-one.

In Chapter Five we showed that many girls reported having engaged in sexual behavior with a man one or more times. This experience often occurred before the girls had expressed their same-sex desires and before they were aware of the risk of HIV. A few girls engaged in sex with males who were gay or bisexual, some of whom they met in the group. Young women typically reported that HIV among women having sex with women was a topic confined to "sex education" and often wrongly assumed that they were at little risk of infection. An eighteen-year-old girl of mixed ethnic background typified the attitudes of her female peers in this way:

> AIDS hasn't affected me. I will not involve myself with a bisexual female—I figure that way I am safe. It hasn't changed how I think about myself. I wasn't aware of AIDS when I first came out. Not really. I guess I found out at Horizons . . . and the media. Safe sex means to me—leave girls who have sex with guys alone! [But] No, I don't practice safe sex.

In the study of Horizons' boys, we discovered a strong relationship between accurate knowledge of AIDS and their sexual behavior. As a general rule, the boys reported that they practiced safer sex in anal intercourse by using condoms. The boys engaged in a high degree of anal sex, but they protected themselves as well. We found that 47 of our 87 boys (or 54 percent) experienced anal intercourse at least once in the last twelve months. About two-thirds of these boys had been anally-receptive at least once, and of those boys, 96 percent reported having protected themselves by using a condom during anal sex. In terms of oral sex 83 percent had experienced oral intercourse at least once, with about 95 percent having fellated another male at least once. Only about 58 percent of these boys, however, reported that their partners used a condom. The sexually active males in the groups tended to engage in "higher" (54 percent) and "lower" (83 percent) risk behavior; the greater the perceived HIV risk, the more likely they were to protect themselves.

Here is what Joseph, an eighteen-year-old African American male, said about his sexual experience.

> It's scary, cause now that I'm old [sic!], I want to have strong relations with somebody. I got scared, because after my first, I had a rash. I went to see the doctor. (He's the third person I came out to!) He gave me the HIV antibody test and it came out "no." Since then I've been really lucky. I still feel something against the same-sex . . . scared about making sure he doesn't have it. Since AIDS started coming out in the news, I said to myself, "Life ain't fair." I waited to get old enough to fool around, and now that I am, it's a blockage.

From narratives such as this, it seems clear that all efforts to increase risk awareness and prevention must begin with examining individuals situated in a particular time and place. In the cultural community of gays and lesbians, actions and motivations for change and stability often come from shared beliefs, ideals, and values. In short, to analyze sexual risk-taking and HIV, we must not take the isolated person as the unit of study, but, instead, the individual who occupies specific social environments which thereby enhance or reduce risk. To facilitate such analysis, we suggest the concept of a "cultural risk milieu." In an earlier time, epidemiological risk vectors referred to broad populations and to the significance of "context variables" in models of HIV-disease prevention that are insensitive to cultural environments.[3]

By cultural risk milieu, we are referring to two kinds of social and behavioral settings in which the perceptions, decisions, and actions of persons affect their risk-taking or vulnerability to AIDS. First there are risk-enhancing milieus that promote the taking of risk and diminish the individual's capacities to sustain or repel risk-taking. The conditions of being homeless, using drugs, or living on the street, and the recklessness of young street gangs, daring each other to acts of bravado or demonstrations of loyalty to the group, all enhance the possibilities of HIV infection. Second, there are risk-reducing milieus, in which the cultural settings or institutions and support groups teach safer sex practices, thereby supporting these persons' abilities to make reasoned and empowering decisions. As suggested above, the norms of the group make it less likely that people will engage in unsafe sex. However, exceptions may also be harder to detect, since people may be reluctant to talk about the transgression of norms. The promotional actions of the culture do facilitate self-protection nevertheless, bringing a new kind of empowerment to the youth. The gay and lesbian agency of Horizons is such a risk-reducing milieu, as the lower incidence of reported sexual risk-taking among its lesbian and gay youth members demonstrates.

The individual's risk-taking is contingent upon his or her cultural competence in negotiating different cultures and risk milieus. Here is where the risk reducing milieu may teach youth to be better able to protect themselves across different situations. Individuals migrating from one culture to another, moving from one community to another, changing high schools or entering into new friendship or sexual networks—all of these entail new vulnerabilities of not knowing "the rules of the game." Here we must make a distinction between knowledge and behavior that comes as a lesson from the failure of the so-called "health belief model" of predicting behavior change. Simply knowing the correct rule or practice to protect oneself from risk is insufficient when it comes to HIV risk. Several things are required: one is a sense of identity, another is efficacy, others include resistance skills that empower the person against the pressure from peers or authorities in different milieus.

There are at least three factors that enhance the risk of HIV infection to youth. First is the basic issue of whether the individual is gay or lesbian, bisexual, or transgendered in their identity. Helping teens means learning never to assume that one knows about their sexuality; instead, it is necessary to learn about an individual's sexual orientation in order to help him or her cope better with the risk of HIV. Second, there is the economic need and disenfranchisement of youth, especially acute among underprivileged teens highly at risk to HIV— through poverty, physical violence or abuse, selling sex, or pressure from gangs and peer groups. It was discovered by Michele Fine in her path-breaking study of adolescent development and sexual education that heterosexual teens who are economically underprivileged and socially vulnerable can better promote their own self-interests by forming discussion groups in high school.[4] Learning to articulate desires and stresses is a means to self-help and protection. Third are conditions involving the presence or absence of emotional support from partners, family and friends, and, more broadly, the gay and lesbian community who support self-protection. We might call all of them "consistent caretakers" if these people are typically present and can be relied upon to socially and psychologically protect the youth. Such qualities characterize the adult lesbian and gay advisors at Horizons, thus making them valuable role models as well.

Another factor that influences HIV infection is the relapse into unsafe sex that occurs in sexual behavior later on. It is reported that gay men in San Francisco, more than ever before, are now engaging in greater HIV risk-laden practices and are not protecting themselves properly.[5] The trend seems related to the accumulating losses of friends and lovers due to AIDS, which may result in depression and a fatalistic attitude toward life.

Homophobia and the general persistence of hatred and violence against gays and lesbians must surely be counted among the deep cultural roots of the AIDS statistics.[6] The great effort of the gay and lesbian movement has been for reform of basic civil rights and acceptance of same-sex desire in a heterosexist tradition, one that initially responded to the AIDS epidemic by wrongly labelling it the "gay disease." The opposition of politicians and the governmental medical bureaucracies of the 1980s, as dramatized in Randy Shilts' *And The Band Played On*, changed only when the wider threat to the population drew a clamor for action and enhanced AIDS funding.[7] The obstructionism from politicians has continued in a variety of ways. That Surgeon General Jocelyn Elders could be fired in 1994 for advocating teaching youth about masturbation in the promotion of safer-sex behavior demonstrates how politics repeatedly undermines the rational effort to educate and prevent the spread of the epidemic in the United States. In general then, risk for HIV is a function of the socioeconomic context. It is with this idea in mind that we realize how the risk for HIV must be seen as a basic indication of the force of society: the perpetuation of political, social, and economic barriers or demands that facilitate the spread of the disease throughout the population.

We have found that a more fully developed gay identity tends to reduce the risk of HIV infection, both at the levels of subjective perception of risk and of objective behavior. Virtually all of the narratives of the teens reflected how AIDS had permeated their coming out process. Furthermore, AIDS education significantly affected the sexual practice of more than half of the youth we interviewed—in the direction of reduced HIV risk-taking. There was again a gender difference, since many girls felt less threatened than boys. In general, however, the teens had a high level of HIV/AIDS knowledge and a consistent and accurate understanding of what makes a sexual encounter "safer." (The favorite motto of the time regarding sexual practice was, "on me not in me!") Of course, as these findings show, not all youth at the time practiced safer sex, and those who did so were not always consistent. The greater degree of involvement and identification with the gay and lesbian culture, the less risk and greater self-protection occurred in the development of the youth. Such a finding should not totally surprise us, since a cross-country study done twenty years ago demonstrated that positive mental health among gays and lesbians was associated with involvement with the gay community.[8] A new study from Holland shows that when a gay man is comfortable with his sexual being (such as enjoying anal sex), he will then be more capable of taking the necessary steps to protect himself.[9]

The issue of bisexuality is relevant to understanding sexual risk and is probably more complicated than it was at the time of our original study. Many youth of today report that being bisexual is more acceptable and even approved of than before. The emergence of Queer Nation and Queer theory in activist and educated circles has certainly contributed to the impression that bisexuality is "cool." However, keeping in mind that education for AIDS sexual risk is enhanced through social institutions such as Horizons, and the absence of such leads to less prevention, we must think about the effect of "bisexuality" as a sexual identity in the current coming-of-age population. This is because there are far fewer "bisexual groups" that would step in to offer the sort of positive safer-sex education provided by gay and lesbian organizations and, in some instances, public schools and clinics. The recent example of a bisexual center in San Francisco studied by Weinberg and colleagues is instructive, since AIDS education seemed less present in the bisexual cultural atmosphere. (The center closed soon after their study was completed.)[10]

The issue here is not merely one of protecting youth, but of their social and psychological empowerment as well. Empowerment is, among other things, being able to express and articulate desires; it is the process of allowing teens to understand how they may become agents of their own desires. For gay and lesbian youth, their psychological and cultural "outness" is a decisive factor in their ability to protect themselves because it helps empower them to confront the homophobia, street violence, everyday harassment that can occur in the classroom, and risk involved with sexual encounters. Blocking this empowerment is a danger and a constant liability to the psychological and social development of the youth. We noted the importance of distinguishing between youth who are more open and those who are more closeted in understanding their exposure to and risk for a variety of problems, from violence and harassment to AIDS. Youth who are more secure in their identities are less willing to take risks and do reckless acts that lead to infection.

What we are saying is this: when youth are able to feel comfortable with who they are and with their sexuality, and when they receive positive and consistent support from the people around them, they do much better. They can handle the challenges and risks in their environment. They can even reach out to help their friends and peers in school. But youth who lack this empowerment face greater difficulties and even danger due to their inability to protect themselves better.

Much of the impetus of safer-sex campaigns and AIDS awareness efforts on the part of the lesbian and gay community arose from the chilling realization of the urgency to undertake initiatives to protect youth, "the symbolic children" of gay culture, from the disease's epidemic of death. Year after year of involvement in this effort saps the strength of the group. New volunteers come forward to help out. They may be less aware of the losses of the past. They may also be lulled into the false security of thinking that everyone already "knows" about the risk of AIDS. But cohorts come and go, of course, and with each new group of faces there is the need to impress upon them in a fresh way the imperative of protecting against infection.

Today, as children of Horizons mature and move into the community to assume their positions as the next generation of young adults, younger cohorts of teens of course take their place. The great advantage enjoyed by the current generation of lesbian and gay youth who are coming into sexual maturity is the vigorous support and assistance they receive from institutions such as Horizons. The range of benefits and resources that enable their coming out is impressive, even from the perspective of world cultures. Increasingly, American gays and lesbians stand out as a progressive force for teaching and learning in a society intimidated by change. Education and prevention for AIDS and other sexually transmitted diseases is but one of these areas of support. As these youth grow and change we shall see them inherit the traditions of their culture—and the symbolic and protective role of their lesbian and gay elders. We hope that they will be as equally courageous in their support of the young who have yet to appear. Only time will tell how the process works, but there is every reason to believe that this generation will create a strong and dynamic cultural milieu of its own for future children of Horizons.

NOTES

◆ ◆ ◆

Preface

1. The concept of "normal life" is used by many youth themselves, by which they mean to describe the experience of not feeling bad, odd, or alone, but instead feeling connected, understood, and confirmed in a community of others who share common perspectives on life, including the development of a social consciousness of solidarity with other gay men and lesbians.

2. Throughout this book we use the terms "homosexual"/"homosexuality" and "heterosexual"/"heterosexuality" in the marked sense of their signs as historical and social categories of being and of identity, separate from individual experiences of them. By problematizing the concept, we join with those researchers who no longer accept the privileged status of the concepts, but rather see a wider spectrum of cultural identities and meanings that apply to them. Whether they are placed in quotation marks or not, we usually mean this interpretation to apply to the words, unless otherwise stated.

3. Gilbert Herdt is identified primarily with work on New Guinea, sexuality and homosexuality, and gender roles and development: *Guardians of the Flutes: Idioms of Masculinity* (New York: McGraw-Hill, 1981); *Rituals of Manhood: Male Initiation in Papua New Guinea*, ed. (Berkeley: University of California Press, 1982); *Ritualized Homosexuality in Melanesia*, ed. (Berkeley: University of California Press, 1984); *The Sambia: Ritual and Gender in New Guinea* (New York: Holt, Rinehart and Winston, 1987); Gilbert Herdt and Robert J. Stoller, *Intimate Communications: Culture and the Study of Erotics* (New York: Columbia University Press, 1990); and lately, on gay and lesbian youth and culture, *Gay and Lesbian Youth*, ed. (New York: Haworth Press, 1989) and, on gay men, *Gay Culture in America*, ed. (Boston: Beacon Press, 1992). Andrew Boxer is known for work on adolescent development and sexuality, the family and parent/child relations, and AIDS prevention: A. M. Boxer et al., "Historical Time and Social Change in Adolescent Experience," in D. Offer et al., *Patterns of Adolescent Self Image* (San Francisco: Jossey-Bass, 1990); "Parents' Perceptions of Young Adolescents," in R. S. Cohen et al., *Parenthood: A Psychodynamic Perspective* (New York: Guilford, 1984); A. M. Boxer and Bertram

265

Cohler, "The Life Course of Gay and Lesbian Youth: An Immodest Proposal for the Study of Lives," in G. Herdt, ed., *Gay and Lesbian Youth* (New York: Haworth Press, 1989).

4. Our study of parents and gays and lesbians was conducted to understand how the coming-out process effects the parents' lives and may change their familial relations. That study will be published elsewhere.

5. John Gonsiorek, "Organization and Staff Problems in Gay/Lesbian Mental Health Agencies," *Journal of Homosexuality* 13 (1982): pp. 203–204.

6. Take note, however, that by the canons of modern biological science no aspect of the investigator or the cultural context of study is allowed to inform the research narrative. Even the recent controversy surrounding the biologic basis of sexual identity differences, as for instance in the work of Simon Levay, has not challenged this canon; while the public may be very interested in the motives and identity of the investigator, it is not published as part of the study.

7. Herdt and Stoller, *Intimate Communications.*

8. On the issues in anthropology, see, for instance, Kenneth E. Read, *Other Voices* (Novato, Calif.: Shandler and Sharpe, 1980), appendix 1; Walter Williams, *The Spirit and the Flesh* (Boston: Beacon Press, 1986); and Gilbert Herdt, "Ten Years after Ritualized Homosexuality in Melanesia: Introduction to the New Edition," in G. Herdt, *Ritualized Homosexuality in Melanesia* (Berkeley: University of California Press, 1992). More generally see Herdt and Stoller, *Intimate Communications;* Joseph Carrier, "Homosexual Behavior in Cross-Cultural Perspective," in J. Marmor, ed., *Homosexual Behavior: A Modern Reappraisal* (New York: Basic Books, 1980); and the reviews of gay men's development and culture in Herdt, ed., *Gay Culture in America.*

9. Bruno Bettelheim, *Children of the Dream* (New York: MacMillan, 1969).

I. Birth of a Culture

1. By "true nature" the youth refer to their inner feelings as if these were the sole product of their personal experience and not of the social milieu; and while social constructionist theorists are right to point out the folk theory of essentialist sexual orientation which the youths' views imply, teenagers nevertheless express the matter as located in themselves, especially at first. We discuss this issue in subsequent chapters.

2. Our concept of desire thus diverges from the "wish" construct of Freudian theory by seeing the fulfilment of satisfaction as primarily outside of mental life; it differs from Freud's theory of "drives and libido" by making the striving both a part of the physical body and a part of cultural reality, but not restricted to purely intrinsic motivations (see Sigmund Freud, *Three Essays on the Theory of Sexuality,* London: Hogarth Press, 1962 (1905). It differs from Kinsey's concept of "sexual drive" in much the same way, though we locate the meanings of sexual desire more fully in historical and social context than he did (see Alfred Kinsey et al., *Sexual Behavior in the Human Male,*

Philadelphia: W. B. Saunders, 1948); it differs from Foucault's concept of desire primarily by making desire more of an affective, and less of an abstract, striving, with the intentionality of satisfaction-seeking located in individual actors, regardless of the social or historical sources of desires at any moment of social action. Like Foucault, however, we assume that desires can be collectively represented and exploited for a variety of purposes, such as the social control of action through the cultural framing of discourse about sexuality and society. We also differ from Foucault's framework somewhat by seeing the emphasis upon desires less in terms of the search for objects, and more in the recognition of the subject as the signifier of feelings (see Michel Foucault, *The History of Sexuality*, vol. 1, trans. W. Hurley, New York: Random House, 1980). Hence, we emphasize the subject more than the object, though we see them as part of an expanding system of interpretation which must ultimately transcend the subject/object dualism, as for instance Eve Sedgewick has argued (*Epistemology of the Closet*, Berkeley: University of California Press, 1990). Finally we reject the naive realist claim that desire is a single, monolithic entity, innate in human development (see, for example, James D. Weinrich, "Is Homosexuality Biologically Normal?" in William Paul, ed., *Homosexuality: Social, Psychological and Biological Issues*, Beverly Hills: Sage, 1982, pp. 197–208); we see it more as a heuristic for interpretation.

3. Freud, *Three Essays*; Kinsey et al., *Sexual Behavior in the Human Male*; reviewed by Gilbert Herdt, "Developmental Continuity as a Dimension of Sexual Orientation Across Cultures," in David McWhirter, J. Reinisch, and S. Sanders, eds., *Homosexuality and Heterosexuality: The Kinsey Scale and Current Research* (New York: Oxford University Press, 1990), pp. 208–238.

4. Foucault, *History of Sexuality*; and Michel Foucault, *The Use of Pleasure*, trans. R. Hurley (New York: Random House, 1986).

5. John Gagnon, "Sexuality Across the Lifespan in the United States," in C. F. Turner et al., eds., *AIDS: Sexual Behavior and Intravenous Drug Use* (Washington, D.C.: National Academy Press, 1989); John Gagnon and William Simon, *Sexual Conduct: The Social Sources of Human Sexuality* (Chicago: Aldine, 1973).

6. Where sexual desire is ontologically given, however, identity is largely culturally formed; that is, through both internal and external processes of experience and symbolic formation, the person comes to associate the self and body with social categories of identity. All persons growing up in our Western cultural tradition experience a powerful tendency—actually a strong inference—to presume that the self and other are "heterosexual," by which we mean here: desires for the opposite sex are preferred over desires for the same sex, with respect to sexual intercourse, partnership, and adaptation across the lifecourse.

7. See, for example, Carole S. Vance, "Social Construction Theory: Problems in the History of Sexuality," in D. Altman et al., eds., *Homosexuality, Which Homosexuality?* (London: GMP Publishers, 1989), pp. 13–34; John D'Emilio and Estelle Freedman, *Intimate Matters* (New York: Harper and Row,

1988); Thomas Laqueur, *Making Sex* (Cambridge, Mass.: Harvard University Press, 1990); Cf. Foucault, *History of Sexuality, Use of Pleasure;* Gagnon, "Sexuality Across the Lifespan;" and Sedgwick, *Epistemology of the Closet.*

8. See, especially, our reviews of the literature in Gilbert Herdt and Andrew Boxer, "Introduction: Gay Youth, Emergent Identities, and Cultural Scenes at Home and Abroad," in G. Herdt, ed., *Gay and Lesbian Youth* (New York: Haworth Press, 1989), pp. 1–42; Gilbert Herdt and Andrew Boxer, "Introduction: Culture, History, and Life Course of Gay Men," in G. Herdt, ed., *Gay Culture in America* (Boston: Beacon Press, 1992), pp. 1–28.

9. By "mainstream" we index "heterosexual rules, beliefs, and social roles," and while such a construction is mythic and ideological in lumping together many disparate entities, a widely shared consensus rhetoric in science and popular culture defines its boundaries; see for instance the historical views of Paul Robinson, *The Modernization of Sex* (New York: Harper and Row, 1976); and for postmodern critiques, see Sedgewick *Epistemology of the Closet;* Diana Fuss, ed., *Inside/Out: Lesbian Theories, Gay Theories* (New York: Routledge, 1991).

10. See the older comparison made by Martin S. Weinberg and Coline J. Williams, *Male Homosexuals* (New York: Oxford, 1974), which finds a positive evaluation of homosexuality by the Dutch and Danish, compared to American responses. For a comparative study including Sweden, see Michael Ross, "Gay Youth in Four Cultures," in Herdt, ed., *Gay and Lesbian Youth,* pp. 219–314.

11. See the discussions of Steven Epstein, "Gay Politics, Ethnic Identity: The Limits of Social Constructionionism," in *Forms of Desire,* ed. Edward Stein (New York: Garland Publishing, 1990), pp. 273–293; Richard Mohr, *Gays/Justice: A Study of Ethics, Society, and the Law* (New York: Columbia University Press, 1988).

12. Reviewed in Roy Cain, "Disclosure and Secrecy among Gay Men in the United States and Canada," *Journal of the History of Sexuality* 2 (1991): 25–45.

13. See Barry Adam, *The Rise of a Gay and Lesbian Movement* (Boston: Twayne, 1987); John D'Emilio, *Sexual Politics, Sexual Communities* (Chicago: University of Chicago Press, 1983); D'Emilio and Freedman, *Intimate Matters.* Cf. George Mosse, *Nationalism and Sexuality* (New York: Howard Fertig, 1985).

14. D'Emilio, *Sexual Politics;* Adam, *Rise of a Gay and Lesbian Movement;* and for comparative views, see Christopher Plummer, "Lesbian and Gay Youth in England," in Gilbert Herdt, ed., *Gay and Lesbian Youth* (New York: Haworth Press, 1989), pp. 195–224.

15. See chapter 2; and for comparisons, see D'Emilio, *Sexual Politics;* Jeffrey Weeks, *Sexuality and Its Discontents* (New York: Routledge and Kegan Paul, 1985).

16. Little wonder that the sociologist John Gagnon has referred to it as the birth of a new "cult of manliness" among the formerly disparaged "effeminate" closet homosexuals. Eventually, the same process has led to gender

changes in lesbians' social relations too. See J. Gagnon, "Disease and Desire," *Daedalus* 118 (1989): 47–77.

17. Herdt, ed., *Gay and Lesbian Youth;* and see chapter 5.

18. This argument is developed in Herdt and Boxer, "Introduction: Culture, History, and the Life Course of Gay Men;" cf. Gilbert Herdt, "Representations of Homosexuality in Traditional Societies: An Essay on Cultural Ontology and Historical Comparison, Part II," *Journal of the History of Sexuality,* 2 (1991): 602–632.

19. G. Herdt, "'Coming out' as a Rite of Passage: A Chicago Study," in Herdt, ed., *Gay Culture in America,* pp. 29–67.

20. Vance, "Social Construction Theory;" Sedgewick, *Epistemology of the Closet;* George Chauncey, Jr., "From Sexual Inversion to Homosexuality: Medicine and the Changing Conceptualization of Female Deviance," *Salamagundi* 58–59 (1982): 114–146. Cf. Carol Smith Rosenberg, "The Female World of Love and Ritual: Relations between Women in Nineteenth Century America," *Signs* 1 (1975): 1–29; Randolph Trumbach, "London's Saphists: From Three Sexes to Four Genders in the Making of Modern Culture," in Julia Epstein and Kristina Straub, eds., *Body Guards* (New York: Routlege, 1991).

21. See Epstein, "Gay Politics, Ethnic Identity"; cf. Carol Warren, "The Stigma of Homosexuality," in J. Marmor, ed., *Homosexuality: A Modern Reappraisal* (New York: Basic Books, 1980).

22. Reviewed in Andrew M. Boxer and Bertram Cohler, "The Life Course of Gay and Lesbian Youth: An Immodest Proposal for the Study of Lives," in Herdt, ed., *Gay and Lesbian Youth;* A. M. Boxer, J. Cook, and G. Herdt, "To Tell or Not to Tell: Patterns of Self-Disclosure to Mothers and Fathers Reported by Gay and Lesbian Youth," in K. Pillemer and K. McCartney, eds., *Parent-Child Relations across the Lifespan* (New York: Oxford University Press, 1991), pp. 59–93. On the problem more generally see Bertram Cohler, "Personal Narrative and Life Course," in P. Baltes and O. G. Brim, Jr., eds., *Life-Span Development and Behavior,* vol. 4 (New York: Academic Press, 1982); B. Cohler, "Adult Developmental Psychology and Reconstruction in Psychoanalysis," in S. I. Greenspan and G. H. Pollock, eds., *The Course of Life,* vol. 3 (Washington D.C.: GPO, 1981).

23. See, for example, Joseph Harry, *Gay Children Grown Up* (New York: Praeger, 1982); Alan Bell and Martin Weinberg, *Homosexualities* (New York: Simon and Shuster, 1978); and Alan Bell, et al., *Sexual Preference: Its Development in Men and Women* (Bloomington: University of Indiana Press, 1981).

24. These writers have emphasized *stage* models of identity development, devoid of context and bereft of social and historical processes; this has had the effect of creating false or outdated norms and goals. See, especially, Boxer and Cohler, "The Life Course of Gay and Lesbian Youth."

25. For example: "Childhood cross-gender behavior, as we have seen, is a universal and inevitable aspect of homosexual orientation, emerging wherever homosexuals are to be found." Frederick L. Whitam and Robin M. Mathy,

Male Homosexuality in Four Societies (New York: Praeger, 1986), p. 68. Scholars across a range of fields—including history!—seem to rely upon the time-warp view. For instance, the historian John Boswell (*Christianity, Social Tolerance, and Homosexuality,* Chicago: University of Chicago Press, 1980), the psychologist Joseph Harry (*Gay Children Grow Up*), the earlier work of anthropologist Walter Williams (*The Spirit and the Flesh,* Boston: Beacon Press, 1986), and the psychiatrist Richard Green (*The "Sissy Boy" Syndrome,* New Haven: Yale University Press, 1987) all stress *continuity* between the present and the social roles, identities, and categories of the past. In *Gay and Lesbian Identity: A Sociological Analysis* (New York: General Hall, 1988), Richard Troiden states (p. 106): "Homosexual identity development involves increasing acceptance of the label homosexual as applied to the self," in spite of the fact that the title of the book refers to gays and lesbians. The point is that these writers have failed to see the difference between homosexual and gay and to put their distinctive social and psychological identities in historical context.

26. Glen Elder, *Children of the Great Depression* (Chicago: University of Chicago Press, 1974); Glen Elder, "Adolescence in Historical Perspective," in J. Adelson, ed., *Handbook of Adolescent Psychology* (New York: John Wiley and Sons, 1980), pp. 3–46.

27. Elder, *Children of the Great Depression,* p. xv.

28. See Herdt, "Coming Out as a Rite of Passage," and below in this chapter, with a review in chapter 2.

29. But see Chauncey, "From Sexual Inversion to Homosexuality," who finds that in New York during an earlier period, the concept of "gay" was used. In *Coming Out Under Fire: The History of Gay Men and Women in World War II* (New York: Free Press, 1990), Allan Berube describes the actors as "gays," but this is surely a misnomer; neither their stories nor their concepts of themselves suggest a consistent meaning of "gay" or "lesbian" as these terms have been used in the past twenty years.

30. See D'Emilio, *Sexual Politics.*

31. See Robert J. Kus, ed., *Gay Men of Alcoholics Anonymous: First-hand Accounts* (North Liberty, Iowa: Winter Star Press, 1990).

32. See Randy Shilts, *And the Band Played On* (New York: St. Martin's 1987).

33. Evelyn Hooker tells us that in her work on the National Institute of Mental Health panel to declassify homosexuality as a disease in 1969, many felt that she was being overly optimistic in seeking so much change so fast; she specifically names Judd Marmor, who was supportive, but felt that these changes were too much (personal communication to G. Herdt, 7 March 1992). These changes are reviewed in Ronald Bayer, *Homosexuality and American Psychiatry* (Princeton: Princeton University Press, 1987), pp. 60–64, and passim. For a new look, see Stephen F. Morin and Esther D. Rothblum, "Removing the Stigma: Fifteen Years of Progress," *American Psychologist* 46 (1991): 947–949; Gregory M. Herek, et al., "Avoiding Heterosexist Bias in Psychological Research," *American Psychologist* 46 (1991): 947–963.

34. See, for example, Dorothy C. Holland and Margaret A. Eisenhart, *Educated in Romance: Women, Achievement, and College Culture* (Chicago: University of Chicago Press, 1990); and Judith Butler, *Gender Trouble: Feminism and the Subversion of Identity* (New York: Routledge, 1990); Sarah Lucia Hoagland, *Lesbian Ethics* (Palo Alto, Calif.: Institute of Lesbian Studies, 1988).

35. Gayle Rubin, "Thinking Sex," in Carole S. Vance, ed., *Pleasure and Danger: Exploring Female Sexuality* (London: Routlege and Keagan Paul, 1984), pp. 267–319; Saskia Wieringa, "An Anthropological Critique of Constructionism: Berdaches and Butches," in D. Altman, et al., *Homosexuality, Which Homosexuality?* (London: GMP Publishers, 1989), pp. 215–238; Hoagland, *Lesbian Ethics*; on heterosexual concepts, see Robert J. Stoller, *Pain and Passion* (New York: Plenum, 1991).

36. See for instance, Barry Adams, *The Survival of Domination* (New York: Elsevier, 1978); Michael Warner, ed., "Fear of a Queer Planet" (Special Issue) 29, *Social Text* (1991).

37. See Margaret Mead, *New Lives for Old* (New York: Dell Publishing, 1956); and also Herdt, ed., *Gay and Lesbian Youth*.

38. See G. Herdt, *The Sambia: Ritual and Gender in New Guinea* (New York: Holt, Rinehart and Winston, 1987); cf. Vance "Social Construction Theory," and Marvin Harris, "Why The Gays Came Out of the Closets," in M. Harris, *America Now* (New York: Simon and Schuster, 1982).

39. G. Herdt, "Introduction," in *Ritualized Homosexuality in Melanesia*, (paperback ed., Berkeley: University of California Press, 1993), pp. vii–liv. See also David Greenberg, *The Construction of Homosexuality* (Chicago: University of Chicago Press, 1988).

40. Herdt, ed., *Gay and Lesbian Youth*; Herdt, ed., *Gay Culture in America*.

41. For the classical statement see Arnold van Gennep, *The Rites of Passage*, trans. M. K. Vizedom and G. L. Caffee (Chicago: University of Chicago Press, 1960); G. Herdt, ed., *Rituals of Manhood Male Initiation in Papua New Guinea* (Berkeley: University of California Press, 1982).

42. Victor Turner, "Betwixt and Between: The Liminal Period in Rites de Passage," in *The Forest of Symbols* (Ithaca: Cornell University Press, 1967); V. Turner, *The Ritual Process* (Chicago: Aldine, 1971); Gilbert Herdt, *Guardians of the Flutes: Idioms of Masculinity* (New York: McGraw-Hill, 1981).

43. Quoted from Clifford Geertz, *Local Knowledge* (New York: Basic Books, 1984), p. 85, in the context of intersexuality and cultural categories.

44. See Evelyn Hooker, "Male Homosexuals and Their Worlds," in J. Marmor, ed., *Sexual Inversion: The Multiple Roots of Homosexuality* (New York: Basic Books, 1965); Adrienne Rich, "Compulsory Heterosexuality and Lesbian Existence," *Signs* 5 (1980): 631–660.

45. Alexis de Tocqueville, *Democracy in America*, edited and abridged by Richard D. Heffner (New York: New American Library, 1956).

46. See especially the critiques by feminist and lesbian theorists, Butler, Vance, and Hoagland, and Jonathan Ned Katz, "The Invention of Heterosexuality," *Socialist Review* 20 (1990):7–34.

47. See A. Kinsey et al, *Human Sexual Behavior;* John H. Gagnon, "The Creation of the Sexual in Early Adolescence," in J. Kagan and R. Coles, eds., *Twelve to Sixteen: Early Adolescence* (New York: Norton, 1971).

48. Herdt, ed., *Gay and Lesbian Youth;* Barbara Ponse, "Secrecy in the Lesbian World," *Urban Life* 5 (1976): 313–338; C. Warren and B. Laslett, "Privacy and Secrecy: A Conceptual Comparison," in S. K. Teft, ed., *Secrecy: A Cross-Cultural Perspective* (New York: Human Sciences Press, 1980), pp. 24–34.

49. See Allan Berube and Jeffrey Escoffier, "Queer /Nation" *Outlook* 11 (1991): 13–14; Alexander Chee, "A Queer Nationalism," *Outlook* 11 (1991): 15–19; Douglas Crimp and Adam Rolston, "Mourning and Militancy," in Russell Ferguson, et al., eds., *Out There: Marginalization and Contemporary Culture* (Cambridge, Mass: MIT Press, 1990), pp. 233–246; Catherine Saalfied and Ray Navarro, "Shocking Pink Praxis: Race and Gender in the ACT UP Frontlines," in Fuss, ed., *Inside/Out*, pp. 341–372; and on the critique of "outing," see Richard D. Mohr, *Gay Ideas: Outing and Other Conroversies* (Boston: Beacon Press, 1992).

50. See *The Celluloid Closet;* Richard Meyer, "Rock Hudson's Body," in Fuss, ed., *Inside/Out*, 1991, pp. 259–290.

51. Max Gluckman, ed., *Essays in The Ritual of Social Relations* (Manchester: Manchester University Press, 1962).

52. See the review in Mary Douglas, "The Healing Rite," *Man* 5.2 (1970): 302–308.

53. Robert Bellah, et al., *Habits of the Heart* (Berkeley: University of California Press, 1985), p. 137.

54. These youth would agree with the value-laden search of Edward Sapir, the American anthropologist, who sought to distinguish patterns of culture that were "genuine" from those that were "spurious"; see "Culture Genuine and Spurious," in E. Sapir, *Selected Writings in Language, Culture, and Personality,* ed. D. G. Mandelbaum (Berkeley: University of California Press, 1949), pp. 308–331.

55. Erik Erikson, *Childhood and Society* (New York: Norton, 1963); E. Erikson *The Life Cycle Completed: A Review* (New York: Norton, 1982). We critique these views in Herdt and Boxer, "Introduction: Culture, History, and Life Course of Gay Men." See also the critique of Erikson in Klaus F. Riegel, "Adult Life Crises: A Dialectic Interpretation of Development," in N. Datan and L. Ginsberg, eds., *Life-Span Developmental Psychology: Normative Life Crises* (New York Academic Press, 1975), pp. 99–128.

56. Erik Erickson, *Identity, Youth, and Crisis* (New York: W. W. Norton, 1968).

57. Freud, *Three Essays;* Freud, "The psychogenesis of a case of homosexuality in a Woman," *Standard Edition* (London: Hogarth Press, 1955 [1920]), vol. 18, pp. 145–172. For his change of views, see Freud, "Letter to an American Mother [1935]," reprinted in Ronald Bayer, *Homosexuality and American Psychi-*

atry (Princeton: Princeton University Press, 1986); see also R. Isay, *Homosexual Development* (New York: Farrar, Straus, and Giroux, 1988).

58. Kinsey et al., *Human Sexual Behavior.*

59. See Robert J. Stoller, "Psychoanalytic 'Research' on Homosexuality: The Rules of the Game," in Stoller, *Observing the Erotic Imagination* (New Haven: Yale University Press, 1985), pp. 167–183.

60. Martin P. Levine and Richard R. Troiden, "The Myth of Sexual Compulsivity," *Journal of Sex Research* 23 (1988): 347–363; see especially pp. 353–355, on changes in conceptions which emerged during the sexual revolution of the 1960s and 1970s.

61. Carol Gilligan, *In A Different Voice* (Cambridge: Harvard University Press, 1982).

62. See Richard Mohr, "Gay Studies as Moral Vision," *Educational Theory* 39 (1989): 121–132.

63. The Reverend Pat Robertson in his address to the Republican National Convention in August 1992, for instance, asserted on national prime time television that women who would believe in feminism and independence must be like witches and lesbians. One must read Richard Plants's *The Pink Triangle: The Nazi War Against Homosexuals* (New York: Henry Holt, 1989) with a cold heart not to hear the echos of today in the nationalistic attacks on women's sexuality, the right to elect abortion, and homosexuality that were launched by the Nazis during the 1930s and 1940s; Himmler's fanaticism is uncannily reminiscent of "new right" attacks of this kind.

64. Meyer, "Rock Hudson's Body.

65. Oscar Wilde, *The Picture of Dorian Grey and Other Writings of Oscar Wilde,* edited by R. Ellman (Toronto: Bantam Books, 1982).

66. Mark Booth, *Camp* (London: Quartet Books, 1983); Susan Sontag, "Notes on Camp," in *Against Interpretation and Other Essays* (New York: Farrar, Straus and Giroux, 1964); and see our commentary on Vitto Russo and Susan Sontag in Herdt and Boxer, "Introduction: Culture, History, and the Life Course of Gay Men."

67. The first part of the joke, on kitch, we owe to the late Robert J. Stoller, *Observing the Erotic Imagination* (New Haven: Yale University Press, 1985.

68. The term comes from Michael Warner, "Introduction: Fear of A Queer Planet," *Social Context* (1991): 3–17; see his discussion of "the folk theory of breeder-identity," p. 9.

69. See Erving Goffman's classic and still useful discussion in *Stigma* (Englewood Cliffs, N.J.: Prentice-Hall, 1963), pp. 79 and passim; Richard Plant, *The Pink Triangle: The Nazi War Against Homosexuals* (New York: Henry Holt and Co.: 1986).

70. Editors, Harvard Law Review, *Sexual Orientation and the Law* (Cambridge, Mass.: Harvard University Press, 1990), p. 9.

71. Fuss, ed., *Inside/Out;* Hoagland, *Lesbian Ethics.*

72. For a remarkable, nutty, and reactionary attack on the scientific founda-

tions of social science research on sexuality in this matter, see Judith A. Reisman, et al., *Kinsey, Sex and Fraud: The Indoctrination of a People* (Lafayette, La.: Lochinvar-Hunting House Publications, 1990). The book is recommended by Patrick Buchanan on the cover as "social dynamite." The old debates on "essentialism" and constructionism," still current in some quarters, are relevant here (see Vance, "Social Construction Theory") as are the older theological and ethical essays on sex and morality (see the reviews in Mohr, *Gay Ideas*).

73. Even this philosophical nihilism is not entirely correct. To distinguish between the desires and what to do with them is an academic matter; in fact, actors in ordinary life seldom make the distinction because, to them, having a desire suggests that something must be done with it, and this entails, at the stage of anticipatory social action—fantasy—already the opening or foreclosing of the desire. And the social facts of gender and ethnicity suggest that all actors are not equal in their room to maneuver. But this is a point best deferred until chapters 5 and 6.

74. See the reviews in Gilbert Herdt and Shirley Lindenbaum, *The Time of AIDS* (Newbury Park, Calif.: Sage Publications, 1992).

75. Magnus Hirschfield's favorite motto, "Justice Through Knowledge," was ultimately a defeated axiom after the Nazi's came to power following the collapse of the Weimar Republic: See Plant, *Pink Triangle*, pp. 29 ff. In addition to Plant's study, reviews of Hirchfield's influence include Charlotte Wolff, *Magnus Hirschfield: A Portrait of a Pioneer in Sexology* (London: Quartet Books, 1986).

2. From Homosexual to Gay in Chicago

1. Richard Herrell's primary analysis is contained in R. Herrell, "The Symbolic Strategies of Chicago's Gay and Lesbian Pride Day Parade," in Gilbert Herdt, ed., *Gay Culture in America* (Boston: Beacon Press, 1992), pp. 225–252.

2. The Vice Commission of Chicago, *The Social Evil in Chicago* (Chicago: The Vice Commission, 1911), p. 3.

3. Reported by Vice Commission member William Healey, M.D., interviewed by John Burnham in 1960. John Burnham Papers, Chicago Historical Society, pp. 293, 295.

4. James Kiernan, "Classification of Homosexuality," *Urologic and Cutaneous Review* 20 (1916): 350, cited in George Chauncey, Jr., "From Sexual Inversion to Homosexuality: Medicine and the Changing Conception of Female Deviance," *Salamagundi* 58–59 (1982): p. 142. Chauncey's article on New York City provides a valuable comparison for the Chicago material of this period.

5. Vice Commission, *Social Evil in Chicago*, p. 297.

6. Constance Weinberger and Saul Alinsky, "Diamond Lil's," MS. Ernest W. Burgess Papers (126:10), University of Chicago Library, Special Collections, 3 pp.

7. Ibid.

8. Allan Berube, *Coming Out Under Fire* (New York: Free Press, 1990).

9. Ibid., p. 107.

10. See John D'Emilio, *Sexual Politics, Sexual Communities* (Chicago: University of Chicago Press, 1983).

11. Berube, *Coming Out Under Fire*, p. 113.

12. Ibid., pp. 320, 116–117.

13. See, for example, Edmund White, *A Boy's Own Story* (New York: E. P. Dutton, 1982) and *The Beautiful Room Is Empty* (New York: Random House, 1988).

14. Subsequent notes identify this interviewer by initials (DS: David Sonnenschein; AB: Alan Bell; AK: Albert Klassen) and provide the date of the interview if available.

15. Bell and Weinberg, *Homosexualities*, p. 10.

16. DS interview, October 19, 1967.

17. Ibid.

18. DS interview, October 30, 1967.

19. DS interview, October 6, 1967.

20. AB group interview 1, August 7, 1967.

21. AB group interview two, August 8, 1967.

22. Ibid.

23. DS interview, September 30, 1967.

24. DS interview, November 2, 1967.

25. DS interview, October 10, 1967.

26. DS interview, October 3, 1967.

27. AB group interview 1, August 7, 1967.

28. AB group interview 2, August 8, 1967.

29. See John D'Emilio, *Sexual Politics, Sexual Communities* (Chicago: University of Chicago Press, 1983), pp. 58–60 and passim.

30. AB group interview 2, August 8, 1967.

31. AK fieldnotes, May 28, 1967.

32. DS interview, October 5, 1967.

33. DS interview, September 7, 1967.

34. DS interview September 7, 1967.

35. For comparison, see Manuel Castells, "Cultural Identity, Sexual Liberation, and Urban Structure: The Gay Community in San Francisco," in M. Castells, *The City and the Grass Roots* (London: Edward Arnold Ltd., 1983), the best all-around community study published to date. See also Stephen O. Murray, "Components of Gay Community in San Francisco," in Herdt, ed., *Gay Culture in America*, pp. 107–146; and Martin P. Levine, "The Life and Death of Gay Clones," in Herdt, ed., *Gay Culture in America*, pp. 68–86.

36. This analysis is based upon community statistics in Louis Wirth and Margaret Furez, eds., *Chicago Local Community Fact Books* (Chicago: Chicago Recreation Commission, 1938); Louis Wirth and Eleanor H. Bernert, eds., *Chicago Local Community Fact Books* (Chicago: University of Chicago Press, 1949); Philip M. Hauser and Evelyn M. Kitagaw, eds., *Chicago Local Community Fact Books* (Chicago: Chicago Community Inventory, University of Chicago, 1963); Chicago Association of Commerce and Industry, *Chicago Local Community Fact*

Books (Chicago: Chicago Association of Commerce and Industry, Research and Statistics Division and OSLA Financial Services Corporation, 1974); and the *Chicago Fact Book Consortium* (Chicago: Chicago Fact Book Consortium, University of Illinois, 1984).

37. The community and institutions described in this chapter are depicted as they were during the time of our study. Newtown is rapidly changing and not every aspect of it described here has remained the same. For example, the Rodde Center and Horizons have subsequently moved to other locations on the margin of the Newtown neighborhood.

38. These establishments include Paris Dance, a popular dance club to the north, Women and Children First (a bookstore specializing in books and recordings for women) to the south, *Outlines* (one of the three gay and lesbian periodicals in Chicago) to the west, and the Women's Gym. Women informants generally placed all of these businesses beyond Newtown.

39. Gerald D. Suttles, *The Social Construction of Communities* (Chicago: University of Chicago Press, 1974).

40. Alexis de Tocqueville, *Democracy in America* (New York: Knopf, 1945, first published in 1835). Robert N. Bellah, et al., *Habits of the Heart* (Berkeley: University of California Press, 1985).

41. W. Lloyd Warner, *Yankee City* (New Haven: Yale University Press, 1963).

42. See for instance, Levine, "Life and Death of Gay Clones"; Barry Adam, *The Survival of Domination* (New York: Elsevier, 1978).

43. Herrell, "Symbolic Strategies."

44. See the controversy surrounding this lack of involvement in Daryl Yates Rist, "AIDS as Apolcalypse," *Christopher Street* 132/11 (1989): 11–14, and the responses that follow it. Cf. Levine, "Life and Death of Gay Clones"; Catherine Saalfield and Ray Navarro, "Shocking Pink Praxis: Race and Gender in the ACT UP Frontlines," in Diane Fuss, ed., *Inside/Out: Lesbian Theories, Gay Theories* (New York: Routledge, 1991).

45. This section, "The Living and the Dead," borrows its title from Warner, *The Family of God: A Symbolic Study of Christian Life in America* (New Haven: Yale University Press, 1961).

46. See, for example, Harlon Dalton, "AIDS in Blackface," *Daedalus* 118 (1989): 205–227; John L. Peterson, "Black Men and Their Same-Sex Desires and Behaviors," in Herdt, ed., *Gay Culture in America,* pp. 147–164; and cf. John Gagnon, "Disease and Desire," *Daedalus* 118 (1989): 47–77.

47. On the issue more broadly, see E. Michael Gorman, "The Pursuit of the Wish: An Anthropological Perspective on Gay Male Subculture in Los Angeles," in Herdt, ed., *Gay Culture in America,* pp. 87–106; Levine, "Life and Death of Gay Clones"; Stephen Murray and Kenneth Payne, "Medical Policy without Scientific Evidence: The Promiscuity Paradigm and AIDS," *California Sociologist* 11 (1988):13–54; and Paula Treichler, "AIDS, Homophobia, and Biomedical Discourse: An Epidemic of Signification," *Cultural Studies* 1 (1987): 32–70.

48. See for example, Roy Cain, "Disclosure and Secrecy among Gay Men

in the United States and Canada." Peter M. Nardi, "AIDS and Obituaries," in D. Feldman, ed., *Culture and AIDS* (New York: Praeger), pp. 159–168.

49. See Randy Shilt's story of the events in *And the Band Played On*.

50. See the discussions in Shilts *And the Band Played On*, 187, and Gagnon, "Disease and Desire."

51. See Murray and Payne, "Medical Policy Without Scientific Evidence" and Darrell Y. Rist, AIDS as Apocalypse," *Christopher Street* 11.11 (1989): 11–14.

52. See Gagnon, "Disease and Desire;" Ralph Bolton, "Mapping Terra Incognita: Sex Research for AIDS Prevention—An Urgent Agenda for the 1990s," in G. Herdt and S. Lindenbaum, eds., *The Time of AIDS* (Newbury Park, Calif.: Sage Publications), pp. 124–158.

53. Michael Gorman, "Anthropological Reflections on the HIV Virus among Gay Men," *Journal of Sex Research* 28 (1991): 269.

54. F. Tönnies, *Gemeinschaft und Gesellschaft* (Leipzig, 1887), trans. C. P. Loomis, *Community and Society* (New York: Harper Torchbooks, 1963).

55. Clifford Geertz, *The Interpretation of Cultures* (New York: Basic Books, 1973), p. 131.

3. "Horizons" and the Youth

1. George S. Buse, "Gay Youth Speaks Out," *Gay Life*, May 18, 1979, p. 9.

2. Ibid.

3. See Robert Bellah, et al., *Habits of the Heart* (Berkeley: University of California Press, 1985). The idea is developed in Gilbert Herdt, " 'Coming Out' as a Rite of Passage: A Chicago Study," in G. Herdt, ed., *Gay Culture in America* (Boston: Beacon Press, 1992).

4. The neighborhood clinic is controversial for many reasons, including the politics of AIDS that surround its services and funding. It attracts the most laudatory and negative comments from locals. As the anthropologist well knows, such sentiments denote the very heart of intense cultural sociality, of being and belonging to a community.

5. Horizons Community Services, Inc., "Agency Fact Sheet." This document is associated with the agency's 1987 Annual Report, Chicago, Illinois.

6. In fact, all of these programs overlap; anyone who has ever worked with a grass-roots organization knows that the titles refer to shifting, often amorphous programs and entities, that change with the needs of the community. To the ethnographer, however, these code words, such as "information and referral," also indicate areas of social organization and the influence of particular personalities on the agency.

7. The agency board was unhappy to find itself under-represented for women and minorities in 1987. In the subsequent two years, the situation changed dramatically, as the percentage of women on the board enlarged to more than half of its members. Several minority members also joined. In 1990 a new director of the agency was hired, a woman who served for some time in the post.

8. The man who did not use his real and full name is a local doyen and a

large financial contributor to the agency. Because he is not out to his family, he used only his last initial. In fact, he did not use his true name inside the agency, although this fact was little known.

9. George S. Buse, in the same 1979 *Gay Life* article, reports: "Frequently overlooked by the gay community these are gay kids who are not runaways, who are not in trouble with the law, and who remain in school preparing themselves for the future as carefully as their straight contemporaries. While some fast and loose types might even call them square, they could never call them straight" ("Gay Youth Speaks Out").

10. This may be the first time in which a gay youth–oriented program made it onto national television.

11. A discussion in the youth group regarding this Oprah Winfrey Show revealed that two young women members and a woman advisor were highly offended by its contents. They didn't like Oprah's attitudes about lesbians, which were "poor" they said. They wondered aloud if Oprah may be accepting of gay men but disapproving of lesbians.

12. That was in 1988. In 1990 an additional group, a coming-out group for persons over twenty-one years of age, was also added to the Horizons program.

13. Gary David Comstock, *Violence Against Lesbians and Gay Men* (New York: Columbia University Press, 1991); see especially chapter 2. From a variety of sociological surveys and interview studies, Comstock shows that the incidence of hate crimes has risen historically, including general violence as well as murders.

14. Ibid., p. 2.

15. See, for instance, the review of Peter M. Nardi and Ralph Bolton, "Gay Bashing: Violence and Aggression Against Gay Men and Lesbians," in R. Baenninger, ed., *Targets of Violence and Aggression* (North-Holland: Elsevier Science Publishers B.V., 1991), pp. 349–400.

16. The event was written up as an AIDS-related "backlash" event of the kind thought to be occurring in many parts of the United States at the time. See, Dirk Johnson, "Fear of AIDS Stirs New Attacks on Homosexuals," *New York Times*, April 17, 1987. A photo of Jeffrey McCourt, editor of the *Windy City Times*, is featured.

17. See Linda Gorov, "Gay Bashers Have Gone Batty—and Violent," *Chicago Sun Times*, March 24, 1987.

18. The reasons for identifying suspects vary, but anyone suspected of having a sexual interest in youth is firmly declined. Anyone who seems uneasy or uncomfortable with their own gay or lesbian sexual identity is channeled into another area of service—an issue that we shall address below.

19. This function was initiated and sponsored by our University of Chicago research team, and was undertaken first to inform the youth group of our interim progress in research, and second to allow the youth to bring in their parents for an open group discussion. It allowed us an opportunity to enlist parent-volunteers in our study of parents of gays and lesbians, which

was done simultaneously to this project, but not reported here. (See A. M. Boxer, J. Cook, and G. Herdt, "To Tell or Not to Tell: Patterns of Self-Disclosure to Mothers and Fathers Reported by Gay and Lesbian Youth," in K. Pillemer and K. McCartney, eds., *Parent-Child Relations Across the Lifespan* (New York: Oxford University Press, 1991.)

20. E. Goffman, *Asylums* (Garden City, N.Y.: Anchor Doubleday, 1961), p. 60.

21. Of course there are adults, heterosexual and homosexual by cultural label, who are attracted to children and adolescents, and some of them live and act out these tendencies. Among closet homosexuals, the gay cultural stereotype is known as either the "chicken hawk" (who preys upon young males, who are the "chicken") or the "sugar daddy," which has the meaning of an adult who supports a younger person in return for sexual favors (current in heterosexual and closet homosexual discourse). These symbolic types are distinct from the more dreaded monster and vampire images described above. Here again a critique of moral development must begin with an understanding of historical social oppression that inhibited same-sex desire and move to an understanding of how sexual identity is constructed in and through the mores of the older homosexual system that today competes with the newer gay and lesbian cultural system. See, in this regard, the discussions in Herdt, ed., *Gay Culture in America*, and Gilbert Herdt and Andrew Boxer, "Introduction: Culture, History, and the Life Course of Gay Men," in ibid.

22. Reviewed in Comstock, *Violence Against Lesbians and Gay Men*, chap. 5.

23. One of these youth, a lesbian, was very "difficult" to handle, according to the advisor who assisted at the time. She was a real "live wire." Among other things, she was rumored to have been sexually involved with an advisor.

4. The Rituals of Coming Out

1. Gilbert Herdt, ed., *Gay and Lesbian Youth* (New York: Haworth Press, 1989); Andrew M. Boxer and Betram Cohler, "The Life Course of Gay and Lesbian Youth: An Immodest Proposal for the Study of Lives," in Herdt, ed., *Gay and Lesbian Youth*.

2. For theoretical study of this process, see Gilbert Herdt, "Fetish and Fantasy in Sambia Initiation," in G. Herdt, ed., *Rituals of Manhood: Male, Initiation in Papua New Guinea* (Berkeley: University of California Press, 1982), pp. 44–98; and Gananath Obeyeseke's work, especially his *The Work of Culture* (Chicago: University of Chicago Press, 1990).

3. Gilbert Herdt and Andrew Boxer, "Introduction: Culture, History and the Life Course of Gay Men," in G. Herdt, ed., *Gay Culture in America* (Boston: Beacon Press, 1992).

4. Carol A. B. Warren, *Identity and Community in the Gay World* (New York: John Wiley and Sons, 1974), p. 4.

5. Arnold van Gennep, *The Rites of Passage,* trans. M. K. Vizedom and G. L. Caffee (Chicago: University of Chicago Press, 1960), p. 86.

6. Ibid., pp. 114–115.

7. Ibid., pp. 81, 115.

8. See, for instance, Gilbert Herdt, *Guardians of the Flutes: Idioms of Masculinity* (New York: McGraw-Hill, 1981).

9. See Max Gluckman, ed., *Essays in the Ritual of Social Relations* (Manchester: Manchester University Press, 1962).

10. E. Goffman, *Asylums* (Garden City, N.Y.: Anchor Doubleday, 1991), p. 32.

11. See John Gagnon, "The Creation of the Sexual in Early Adolescence," in J. Kagan and R. Coles, eds., *Twelve to Sixteen: Early Adolescence* (New York: W. W. Norton, 1971); we know that these fantasies may involve either the same or opposite sex, though the same-sex desires may or may not be expressed, and they do not necessarily indicate a gay or lesbian identity; see also Herdt, ed., *Gay and Lesbian Youth*.

12. At the University of Chicago, for example, this is a low-visibility group, with minimal social and political activity.

13. Carol A. Warren, "Fieldwork in the Gay World: Issues in Phenomenological Research," *Journal of Social Issues* 33 (1977): 93–107.

14. See Richard Shweder, *Thinking Through Cultures* (Cambridge: Harvard University Press, 1991).

15. On the historical representation of "inversion" see Michel Foucault, *The History of Sexuality* vol. 1, trans. W. Hurley (New York: Random House, 1980); Gilbert Herdt, "Representations of Homosexuality in Traditional Societies: An Essay on Cultural Ontology and Historical Comparison," part 1, *Journal of the History of Sexuality* 2 (1990): 602–632; Randolph Trumbach, "London's Sapphists": From Three Sexes to Four Genders in the Making of Modern Culture, in Julia Epstein and Kristina Straub, eds., *Body Guards* (New York: Routledge, 1991).

16. See Kurt Wolff, ed., *The Sociology of Georg Simmel* (Glencoe: Free Press, 1950), pp. 355–356.

17. In fact, during the time of our study, at least one of the advisors, Kyle, had gone through the youth group himself; he was twenty-three years old and had quit the group at twenty-one, as prescribed. Some of the older advisors were a bit skeptical of his maturity, but he was a steady helper in the group.

18. Wolff, *Sociology of Georg Simmel*.

19. Tiresias, the famous soothsayer of Ancient Greece, was renowned in the ancient world for having been born a female, changed into a male, and changed back again into a female.

20. One of our graduate student interviewers was critical of the advisors on this point: "Why don't they make it easier on these kids? Some of these advisors seem so immature themselves!" As the later process revealed in this chapter makes clear, the advisor's own responses in this way are a significant part of the ritual passage and hurdle that the youth must pass through.

21. For a report on "Project 10," see Virginia Uribe and Karen M. Harbeck, "Addressing the Needs of Lesbian, Gay, and Bisexual Youth: The Origins of PROJECT 10 and School Based Intervention," *Journal of Homosexuality* 22 (1991): 9–29.

22. Their major criticism of Horizons was that it was too "social." Some of the complaints centered on the wish for a smaller, more intimate, group. Yet the initiates who spoke felt that their lives were better now, because they were entering the community, and finding a niche in the Newtown.

23. Horizons has implemented an outreach program to the schools that has been highly successful in spreading the word.

24. In the coming year these goals were largely achieved.

25. See G. Herdt, "Fetish and Fantasy in Sambia Initiation."

26. See especially Gilbert Herdt and Robert J. Stoller, *Intimate Communications: Culture and the Study of Erotics* (New York: Columbia University Press, 1990) and on the topic of homosexuality see Herdt, "Representations of Homosexuality."

27. Van Gennep, *Rites of Passage*, p. 67.

28. On the historical issues see, for instance, Jeffrey Weeks, *Sexuality and Its Discontents* (New York: Routledge and Kegan Paul, 1985), chap. 3; Judith Butler, *Gender Trouble: Feminism and the Subversion of Identity* (New York: Routledge, 1990), chap. 1, especially pp. 57–59; Gilbert Herdt, "Cross-Cultural Issues in the Development of Bisexuality and Homosexuality," *Handbook of Sexology*, vol. 7 (Berlin: Verlag-Springer, 1990), pp. 111–128.

29. On the measurement and counting issues, see, by comparison, Richard Green, *The "Sissy Boy" Syndrome* (New Haven: Yale University Press, 1987), who is more confident than are we in this regard.

30. See John Money, *Gay, Straight and In-Between: The Sexology of Erotic Orientation* (New York: Oxford University Press, 1988).

31. Are the advisors projecting here? Is their own coming-out process still ·bound up with old ideas about bisexuality? We think that the social values and commitments of the advisors lend itself to this interpretation. Yet they also struggle with holding the group together at times when anxiety-producing events intrude, and in this they may register feelings at a deeper (unconscious) level that the youth are unable to articulate yet.

32. *Gentleman's Quarterly*, a traditional high-fashion magazine, captures a style of chic, fancy self, and attire, which goes by that name, but more in the older cohort of gay men then in the younger.

33. Maurice Leznoff and William A. Westley, "The Homosexual Community," *Social Problems* 3(1955): 256–263; John D'Emilio, *Sexual Politics, Sexual Communities* (Chicago: University of Chicago Press, 1983); K. Vacha, *Quiet Fire* (Trumansburg, N.Y.: Crossing, 1985).

34. In Barry Dank's 1971 classic study "Coming Out in the Gay World," *Psychiatry* 34 (1971): 180–197, such cruising places are given prominence as the places informants said that they "came out." See, in the recent period, the

detailed memory culture of cruising scenes provided by Martin Duberman's important biography, *Cures: A Gay Man's Odyssey* (New York: Dutton, 1991).

35. Kenneth E. Read, *Other Voices* (Novato, Calif.: Shandler and Sharpe, 1980).

36. See, for instance, this theme throughout the work of Dennis Altman, especially his *Homosexual: Liberation and Oppression* (New York: Avon Books, 1973) and *Coming out in the Seventies* (Boston: Alyson, 1981); compare John A. Lee, "Going Public: A Study in the Sociology of Homosexual Liberation," *Journal of Homosexuality* 3 (1977): 49–78; Ken Plummer, ed., *The Makings of the Modern Homosexual* (London: Hutchinson, 1981).

37. John Gagnon, "Disease and Desire," *Daedalus* 118 (1989): p. 53.

38. Robert J. Kus, ed., *Gay Men of Alcoholics Anonymous: First-hand Accounts* (North Liberty, Iowa: Winter Star Press, 1990).

39. An ad in the paper for "Mountain Moving Coffee House" read as follows: "For Womyn and Children—Back by popular demand ... Hunter Davvis rings with her hits from latest albums "Harmony, etc. "No wommyn is ever turned away. NO male children over the age of ten."

40. In the period of our project, the oldest well-established hustler bar closed down. It had been a well-known landmark in the homosexual history of Chicago. This is the kind of place we have in mind. During our study, only two or three youth ever mentioned having visited the place, and most of them did not, in fact, know of its existence (it was far south, in a seedy part of the downtown).

41. For reviews, Herdt and Boxer, "Introduction: Culture History, and the Life Course in Gay Men"; Douglas A. Feldman, "Gay Youth and AIDS," in Herdt, ed., *Gay and Lesbian Youth*, pp. 185–194.

42. See, for instance, Martin P. Levine, "The Life and Death of Gay Clones," in Gilbert Herdt, ed., *Gay Culture in America* (Boston: Beacon Press, 1992).

43. Gilbert Herdt and Andrew Boxer, "Sexual Identity Development and AIDS Sexual Risk," in T. Dyson, ed., *Anthropological Demography and AIDS* (Liege, Belgium: International Union for the Scientific Study of Demography, 1992).

44. Herdt attended this prom and those of 1988 and 1990 with his long-time partner. See Gilbert Herdt, " 'Coming Out' as a Rite of Passage: A Chicago Study," in Herdt, ed., *Gay Culture in America*, pp. 52–54.

45. In 1987 there were two black youth who dressed in women's clothes; one of them, who was tall and gorgeous, and wore the full make-up of a fashion model, made a real sensation.

46. Max Gluckman, "The License in Ritual," in *Custom and Conflict in Africa* (New York: Barnes and Noble, 1969), pp. 109–136; V. Turner, *The Ritual Process* (Chicago: Aldine, 1971).

47. On the concept of minstrelization see Troiden, "The Formation of Homosexual Identities," *Journal of Homosexuality* 17 (1989): 43–73.

48. They have lived together in their own apartment for some time and remain lovers today. One twist is that Bowie eventually split up with his lover,

moved to another state for a time, but then returned to Chicago. He had no place to turn and moved in as a roommate with Herb and Jeffrey. Through such contacts some members of the group remain steadfast friends today.

49. Herdt and Boxer, "Sexual Identity Development and AIDS Sexual Risk."

50. On subjectification and objectification as symbolic processes, see Obeyesekere, *Medusa's Hair* (Chicago: University of Chicago Press, 1981).

51. The reactions of the youth to the notion of "master/slave" were disconcerting not only because this confounded their ideal of equality between partners, but because Joey insinuated not only that he enjoyed the sexual practice, but welcomed the role of playing the "slave." And this was very puzzling to some.

52. The meeting was suggested by Herdt and Boxer and represents our only significant intervention in the youth group during the two years of our study. From private interviews with youth and adults, we came to the conclusion that the issue of Joey's unprecedented death in the group had touched a nerve that was being avoided, and was ultimately injurious in that way. Hitherto there were no guidelines for how the youth group would handle infection or death due to AIDS. We recommended to the advisors that they have a meeting to discuss the youth's reactions to Joey's death, in a climate that included an empathic film and supporting conversations with professionals, including the psychologists on our research team. Such an intervention must be approached very, very cautiously, but it cannot be sidestepped long; when an apparent conflict threatens the emotional life of a group, one must act out of deference to professional and ethical responsibility.

53. One evening in 1991 we were surprised to be haled by a passing patrol car operated by a policewoman who was openly lesbian—a woman who had served on our Horizons project and was, once upon a time, a member of the youth group a few years ago. In the 1992 Pride Day Parade a contingent of gay- and lesbian-identified police marched for the first time.

54. In the 1992 Chicago Pride Day Parade, the contingent of gay and lesbian police officers appeared for the first time, smiling and proud, not far back from the new Police Commissioner of Chicago, whose appearance was the first of its kind. This police group received huge applause and was highlighted in newspaper articles about the parade as the greatest breakthrough of the year.

55. The widening cultural consciousness that begins to emerge in the youth group finds its highest expression in the parade. An acute awareness of the role that the media play in televising the parade is apparent. In the regular group the media is frequently mentioned, including favored movies that show gay themes and talk shows such as the "Oprah Winfrey Show." *Time* and *Newsweek* clips are mentioned, and there is constant discussion of newspaper stories. The gay and lesbian community papers are most often discussed. Negative stories are mentioned. The media are brought into the cultural environment more and more as a social consciousness emerges: "we

are not isolated individuals; we are a group." The aspect that soon emerges in all discussions is a focus on how the individual story tells of a pattern, of prejudice, of notoriety, etc. The youth begin to create a link between their new attention to the culture and their own personal feelings and perceptions. In this way the youth reveal an emerging enculturation into the gay and lesbian local culture.

56. Reviewed in Y. A. Cohen, *The Transition from Childhood to Adolescence* (Chicago: Aldine, 1964); J. La Fontaine, *Initiation* (New York: Penguin, 1985).

5. Milestones of Sexual Identity Development

1. Mark was interviewed by Floyd Irvin, Ph.D. All of the material contained in the following chapter, unless otherwise indicated, came from the individual interview study conducted on the premises of Horizons with 202 youth. These interviews usually took between two and a half to four hours to complete, depending upon the length of the individual's narrative. The project study was the combined effort of Gilbert Herdt, Andrew Boxer, and Floyd Irvin. The interview data were subsequently coded, entered, verified, and analyzed at the University of Chicago, primarily under the direction of Andrew Boxer.

2. Margaret Mead, *Coming of Age in Samoa* (New York: Dutton, 1927).

3. Sigmund Freud, *Three Essays on the Theory of Sexuality* (London: Hogarth Press, 1962 [1905]), pt. 3.

4. Robert J. Stoller, "Psychoanalytic 'Research' on Homosexuality: The Rules of the Game," in Stoller, *Observing the Erotic Imagination* (New Haven: Yale University Press, 1985), pp. 167–183; Richard A. Isay, *Being Homosexual: Gay Men and Their Development* (New York: Farrar, Straus, and Giroux, 1989). The issues are reviewed in Andrew M. Boxer and Bertram Cohler, "The Life Course of Gay and Lesbian Youth: An Immodest Proposal for the Study of Lives," in Gilbert Herdt, ed., *Gay and Lesbian Youth* (New York: Haworth Press, 1989).

5. Reviewed in Herdt, ed., *Gay and Lesbian Youth;* and Andrew M. Boxer, Bertram J. Cohler, Gilbert Herdt, and Floyd Irvin, "Gay and Lesbian Youth," in P. H. Tolan and B. Cohler, eds., *Handbook of Clinical Research and Practice with Adolescents* (New York: Wiley, 1993).

6. Anna Freud, *The Ego and the Mechanism of Defense* (New York: International Universities Press, 1946). G. S. Hall, *Adolescence: Its Psychology . . .* (New York: Appleton, 1904).

7. See, for example, Erik Erikson, *Identity, Youth, and Crisis* (New York: W. W. Norton, 1968). Even the liberal minded L. M. Terman clung to the view that homosexuals were overly motivated by sexual needs, a condition which leads them into many troubles. We discuss Terman's views elsewhere (Gilbert Herdt and Andrew Boxer, "Introduction: Culture, History, and the Life Course of Gay Men," in G. Herdt, ed., *Gay Culture in America* (Boston: Beacon Press, 1992).

8. See the critiques of Isay, *Being Homosexual;* Stoller, "Psychoanalytic 'Research' on Homosexuality."

9. Alfred Kinsey, et al., *Sexual Behavior in the Human Male* (Philadelphia: W. B. Saunders, 1948).

10. Erik Erikson, *Identity and the Life Cycle.* (New York: W. W. Norton, 1959). Compare Erikson, *Identity, Youth, and Crisis.*

11. Reviewed in John D'Emilio and Estelle Freedman, *Intimate Matters* (New York: Harper and Row, 1988).

12. Kinsey, et al., *Sexual Behavior in the Human Male;* Robert J. Stoller and Gilbert Herdt, "Theories of Origins of Homosexuality," *Archives of General Psychiatry,* vol. 42, pp. 399–404.

13. Evelyn Hooker, "Male Homosexuals and Their Worlds," in Judd Marmor, ed., *Sexual Inversion: The Multiple Roots of Homosexuality* (New York: Basic Books,) pp. 83–107.

14. See Boxer and Cohler, "The Life Course of Gay and Lesbian Youth."

15. These are reviewed in chap. 1; and see Herdt, ed., *Gay and Lesbian Youth;* Boxer and Cohler, "The Life Course of Gay and Lesbian Youth."

16. A common focus was the objectification of phases of coming out, making use of stage models of development.

17. David P. McWhirter and Andrew Mattison, *The Male Couple* (Englewood Cliffs, N.J.: Prentice-Hall, 1984).

18. Self psychology, as developed by Heinz Kohut and others, conceptualizes processes of idealization as a central aspect of development. See Heinz H. Kohut, *The Analysis of the Self* (New York: International Universities Press, 1971).

19. The distinction is most clearly articulated in the work of Robert J. Stoller, *Sexual Excitement* (New York: Random House, 1979).

20. We do not know the cause of such desires in an ultimate sense; we presume, along with such scholars as Stoller that they are the result of a biological force through such precipitants as hormones, genes, gonads, and brain states. See Robert J. Stoller, *Sex and Gender,* vol. 2, *The Transsexual Experiment* (New York: Jason Aronson,), especially chap. 2.

21. Boxer and Cohler, "The Life Course of Gay and Lesbian Youth"; cf. Richard Green, *The 'Sissy' Boy Syndrome* (New Haven: Yale University Press, 1987).

22. See Thomas Weinberg, *Gay Men, Gay Selves* (New York: Irvington Publishers, 1983); and see also Vivienne Cass, "Homosexual Identity: A Concept in Need of Definition," *Journal of Homosexuality* 9 (1983/84): 105–126.

23. See Alan Bell and Martin S. Weinberg, *Homosexualities A Study of Diversity Among Men and Women* (New York: Simon and Schuster, 1978).

24. Over the last three decades, first sexual experiences of all teenagers have been occurring at increasingly earlier ages. Andrew Boxer, R. Levenson, and A. C. Peterson, "Adolescent Sexuality," in J. Worrell and F. Danner, eds., *The Adolescent as Decision-Maker* (New York: Academic Press, 1990); R. R. Troiden, "The Formation of Homosexual Identities," in G. Herdt, ed., *Gay*

and Lesbian Youth, pp. 43–74; Gary Remafedi et al., "Demography of Sexual Orientation in Adolescents," *Pediatrics* 89 (1992): 714–721.

25. This time lag between age of sexual initiation among boys and girls has also been reported in other studies of adult gay men and lesbians and continues to persist.

26. Based on whether the teenager was male or female, we were able to predict the average age of a first same-sex experience. This suggests a stable cultural and psychological pattern of desire that differentiates the genders.

27. Andrew M. Boxer, "Life Course Transitions of Gay and Lesbian Youth: Sexual Identity Development and Parent-Child Relationships." Unpublished Ph.D. dissertation, Committee on Human Development, The University of Chicago, Chicago, Ill., 1990.

28. See Bell and Weinberg, *Homosexualities.*

29. Freud, *Three Essays.*

30. Jean Piaget, *The Moral Judgment of the Child* (New York: Free Press, 1965).

31. We did not ask all of the youth in our study whether or not they had ever had a sexual experience during childhood. In retrospect, this missing information might have helped to clarify aspects of early development. It is likely that some additional youth would have reported homoerotic experience in childhood had we asked them about the matter.

32. R. R. Troiden and E. Goode, "Variables Related to the Acquisition of a Gay Identity," *Journal of Homosexuality* 5 (1980): 383–392.

33. Narrative responses to questions regarding first same-sex activity were coded for the relationship context in which they were initiated (Leslie Pratch, Interpersonal Contexts of First Sexual Experiences: A Coding Manual. Unpublished manuscript, Committee on Human Development, The University of Chicago, Illinois, 1989). First homosexual sexual experiences were coded as *abuse,* based on standardized criteria developed by Gail Elizabeth Wyatt ("The Sexual Abuse of Afro-American and White-American Women in Childhood," *Child Abuse and Neglect* 9 (1985): 507–519), if the participation in sexual activity was described as involuntary or achieved through (physical or psychological) coercion; or, if the respondent was twelve years or younger at the age of initiation and the age difference between respondent and partner was greater than five years. First sexual experiences were coded as *childhood sex play* when described as occurring prior to age ten and with a partner who was no greater than four years older. *Friendship* was coded as the relational context if the respondent described his/her sexual partner as a friend prior to the initiation of same-sex sexual activity. *Sexual relationship context* was coded when the respondent described the first sexual relationship as initiated only by a desire for sexual activity and/or with no prior knowledge of or relationship with the partner. *Dating/romance* was coded when respondents described a romantic, dating, or intimate relationship prior to initiating sexual activity. Interrater agreement on these categories was 0.83.

34. B. C. Leigh recently found, among a probability sample of men and women of differing sexual orientations, that men's and women's stated reasons for having sex were different regardless of their sexual orientation (Leigh, "Reasons for Having and Avoiding Sex: Gender, Sexual Orientation, and Relationship to Sexual Behavior," *Journal of Sex Research* 26 [1989]: 199–209). In other words, sex differences in motivations for sexual behavior were greater than differences by sexual orientation.

35. However, because our standardized interview did not specifically ask youth about sexual experiences which occurred prior to puberty, it is possible that many youth who reported sexual experiences after puberty also may also have experienced some type of childhood sexual play, which they did not consider a true first "sexual" experience.

36. See John Gagnon, "The Creation of the Sexual in Early Adolescence," in J. Kagan and R. Coles, eds., *Twelve to Sixteen: Early Adolescence* (New York: W. W. Norton, 1971).

37. M. Tobin-Richards, A. Boxer, and A. C. Petersen, "Psychological Significance of Puberty Change," in J. Brooks-Gunn and A. C. Petersen, eds., *Girls at Puberty* (New York: Plenum Press, 1983), pp. 127–154.

38. Kinsey et al., *Sexual Behavior in the Human Male*.

39. In the total group of 202, only 27 (13 percent) of the youth did not fit into any of these developmental pathways. The reasons varied, from having had no sexual experiences (neither with the same or opposite sex) at the time of the interview (N = 6), to having had only opposite-sex experiences exclusively (N = 11), to having had their first same-sex and opposite-sex experiences at the same age (N = 9), and because of missing information regarding sexual sequencing (N = 1).

40. Preliminary analyses of the sexual sequence were presented by J. Cook, A. Boxer, and G. Herdt in "First Homosexual and Heterosexual Experiences Reported by Gay and Lesbian Youth in an Urban Community. Paper presented in the session, "Homosexuality," at the Annual Meeting of the American Sociological Association, San Francisco, Calif., August 10, 1989.

41. We can make a distinction between having a sexual desire and being socialized about how to express it. Clearly, the prior generation was not socialized into gay and lesbian roles, for the simple reason that they did not exist. "Nobody who now identifies himself or herself as a part of that world was deliberately socialized to become a homosexual," sociologist Carrol Warren wrote in *Identity and Community in the Gay World* (New York: Wiley, 1974). Doubtless she did not mean to suggest what we infer. But the implication is that homosexuals were not socialized. What gay and lesbian youth today learn is not the desire itself, but how, when, and where to express it.

42. The statistical relationship was ($r = 0.18$, $p = <0.02$).

43. John Gagnon and William Simon, *Sexual Conduct: The Social Sources of Human Sexuality* (Chicago: Aldine, 1973).

44. M. Fine, "Sexuality, Schooling, and Adolescent Females: The Missing Discourse on Desire," *Harvard Educational Review* 58 (1988): 29–53; D. E. H.

Russell, "The Incidence and Prevalence of Intrafamilial and Extrafamial Abuse of Female Children," *Child Abuse and Neglect* 7 (1983): 133–146; G. E. Wyatt et al., "Kinsey Revisited. Part 1: Comparisons of the Sexual Socialization and Sexual Behavior of White Women over 33 Years," *Archives of Sexual Behavior* 17 (1988): 201–239.

45. Fine, "Sexuality, Schooling, and Adolescent Females."

46. Again, see Michele Fine's "Sexuality, Schooling, and Adolescent Females." Young lesbians, as the literature suggests, are faced with a dilemma different from gay boys: their bodies can bear children. Though the boys may continue to pass as heterosexual, making up stories and inventing fictitious girlfriends and heterosexual exploits for the amusement of their male peers, they are not asked to prove their biology through the ultimate fact of reproductivity like the girls are. Some girls may experience a pressure from outside in peer circles and inside themselves, regarding the need to have a baby for the completion of an idea of being a full adult person. Thus, the resistance to heterosexual relations at this point is a liberation of two kinds: from the heterosexual body and from heterosexualist social relations. And the girl may experience this as a deeper than hitherto recognized order of agency.

47. Martin S. Weinberg and Coline J. Williams, *Male Homosexuals* (New York: Oxford, 1974); Alan Bell et al., *Sexual Preference: Its Development in Men and Women* (Bloomington: University of Indiana Press, 1981).

48. See Hanna Wielandt, et al., "Age of Partners at First Intercourse Among Danish Males and Females," *Archives of Sexual Behavior* 18 (1989): 449–454.

49. Carol Warshaw, Coercive and Abusive Homosexual and Heterosexual Experiences of Gay and Lesbian Youth. Unpublished manuscript, Evelyn Hooker Center, University of Chicago.

50. As Ruth Benedict "Continuities and Discontinuities in Cultural Conditioning," *Psychiatry* 1 (1938): 161–167. might have suggested, abuse in such a society is an almost inevitable result of an extreme discontinuity between the two sides of naivete and sophistication. When people are not trained regarding their sexuality in positive ways to prepare them for adulthood, we can expect such abuses.

51. Kinsey, et al., *Sexual Behavior in the Human Male.*

52. Carefully coifured does not mean hairsprayed and prissy; for some youth it meant punk chic, with every hair out of place in just the perfect way. "Straight Sam" did not care about his hair or comb it in any way, suggesting that his physical appearance played a different role in how he conveyed himself as someone to be desired.

53. Herdt interviewed Sam in part because our graduate student interviewers were reluctant to take him on. They felt that he was a fake, and they could not understand his self-image; another manifestation of the issues related to transference and counter-transference in a project of this kind. In fact, Herdt found him benign and confused.

54. Martin Duberman, *Cures: A Gay Man's Odyssey* (New York: Dutton: 1991), p. 22.

55. There are a few exceptions to this generalization. However, they are complex cases that do not conform to the stereotype, and we shall elsewhere publish our findings on them.

6. Being Out

1. John A. Lee, "Going Public: A Study in the Sociology of Homosexual Liberation," *Journal of Homosexuality* 3 (1977): 49–78.

2. Much confusion continues to reign in understanding the differences between adult and youthful gay men and lesbians in this regard, and we would highlight the gender differences between lesbians and gays that continue to be ignored. See A. M. Boxer, J. Cook, and G. Herdt, "To Tell or Not to Tell: Patterns of Self-Disclosure to Mothers and Fathers Reported by Gay and Lesbian Youth," in K. Pillemer and K. McCartney, eds., *Parent-Child Relations across the Lifespan* (New York: Oxford University Press, 1991).

3. Studies on coming out have often been defined either by the overcoming of particular internal psychological traits or states, such as denial or "suppression," or by the sociologist's attention to the process of self-labeling. This includes the acquisition of a particular constellation of role features which define a "gay" person and the symbolic construction of their shared meanings, as in the subgroup that Martin P. Levine called "gay clones," ("The Life and Death of Gay Clones," in G. Herdt, ed., *Gay Culture in America*, Boston: Beacon Press, 1992, pp. 68–86). Compare the following findings with those reported in A. D. Martin "Learning to Hide: The Socialization of the Gay Adolescent," *Adolescent Psychiatry* 10 [1982]: 52–65), and in the reports published in Gilbert Herdt, ed., *Gay and Lesbian Youth* (New York: Haworth Press, 1989).

4. The contrast "experience near" and "experience distant" comes from Heinz Kohut but has been popularized by Clifford Geertz. See his "From the Native's Point of View: On The Nature of Anthropological Understanding," in K. Basso and H. Selby, eds., *Meaning in Anthropology* (Albuquerque: School for American Research, 1976), pp. 221–237.

5. Michelle Fine, "Sexuality, Schooling, and Adolescent Females: The Missing Discourse on Desire," *Harvard Educational Review* 58 (1988): 36: "The absence of safe spaces for exploring sexuality affects all adolescents; it was paradoxical to realize that perhaps the only students who had an in-school opportunity for crucial sexual discussion in the company of peers were the few students who had organized the gay and lesbian organization at the High School."

6. As we have suggested repeatedly in this book, we recognize that many youth who desire the same sex do not come to openly visible gay and lesbian support groups. We think that there are many reasons for their decision to stay away, but of course, on a general level, homophobia is a primary cause.

7. These measures included a symptom checklist as well as specially designed measures of gay and lesbian self-esteem. Floyd Irvin conducted pre-

liminary analyses of these data. F. S. Irvin, "Resilience and Vulnerability among Gay and Lesbian Youth." Paper presented at the Annual Meeting of the American Psychological Association, 1988.

8. One of our students, Shiela Healy, has undertaken a more detailed analysis of these data. S. Healy, "Suicidal Behavior among Gay and Lesbian Youth." Unpublished Master's Thesis, Committee on Human Development, The University of Chicago, 1992.

9. See, for example, R. F. Kourany, "Suicide Among Homosexual Adolescents," *Journal of Homosexuality* 13 (1987): 11–117; G. Remafedy, et al. "Risk Factors for Attempted Suicide in Gay and Bisexual Youth," *Pediatrics* 87 (1991): 869–875. See also Paul Gibson, "Gay Male and Lesbian Youth Suicide," in Marcia R. Feinleib, ed., *Report of the Secretary's Task Force on Youth Suicide*, vol. 3, *Prevention and Interventions in Youth Suicide* (Rockville, Md.,: NIMH), pp. 110–137. No data on lesbian suicide are presented.

10. For example, see Anne Petersen, "Adolescent Development," *Annual Review of Psychology* 39 (1988): 583–607; Michael Rutter, "The Developmental Psychopathology of Depression: Issues and Perspectives," in M. Rutter, ed., *Depression in Young People* (New York: Guilford, 1986); Daniel Offer and Andrew Boxer, "Normal Adolescent Development," in M. Lewis, ed., *Child and Adolescent Psychiatry: A Comprehensive Textbook* (Baltimore: Williams and Wilkins, 1991), pp. 266–278. On heterosexual pressures on girls, see especially Dorothy C. Holland and Margaret A. Eisenhart, *Educated in Romance: Women, Achievement, and College Culture* (Chicago: University of Chicago Press, 1989).

11. The cross-cultural point is made in more general terms by Louise Jilek-Aall, "Suicidal Behavior Among Youth: A Cross-Cultural Comparison," *Transcultural Psychiatric Research Review* 25 (1988): 87–105.

12. Debra Boyer, "Male Prostitution and Homosexual Identity," *Journal of Homosexuality* 17 (1989): 151–184) has shown that some young men engaging in homosexual prostitution seek affirmation of their gay identity by using the only means they have at their disposal. For such youth, prostitution provided an identity and mode of conduct that corresponded to their cultural image of the "homosexual." With increased acceptance of the gay and lesbian teen, the use of homosexual prostitution as a pathway into gay identity should decline.

13. The relationship is (chi square = 11.378, $df = 4$, $p < 0.02$).

14. We thus follow in the tradition of George Herbert Mead, and those sociologists, such as Erving Goffman (*Stigma: Notes on the Management of Spoiled Identity*, Englewood Cliffs, N.J.: Prentice-Hall, 1963), who locate the presentation of the self and social action in real life contexts.

15. M. F. Myers, "Counseling the Parents of Young Homosexual Male Patients," *Journal of Homosexuality* 7 (1982): 131–143. R. Robertson, "Young Gays," in J. Hart and D. Richardson, *The Theory and Practice of Homosexuality* (London: Routledge and Kegan Paul, 1981), pp. 170–176; R. R. Troiden, *Gay and Lesbian Identity* (New York: General Hall, 1988).

16. A. D. Martin and E. S. Hetrick, "The Stigmatization of the Gay and Lesbian Adolescents," *Journal of Homosexuality* 16 (1988): 163–183.

17. R. L. Savin-Williams, "Parental Influences on the Self-Esteem of Gay and Lesbian Youths: A Reflected Appraisals Model," *Journal of Homosexuality* 17 (1989): 93–109.

18. R. L. Savin-Williams, "Coming Out to Parents and Self-Esteem of Gay and Lesbian Youths," *Journal of Homosexuality* 18 (1989): 1–35.

19. Although in families where males rated parents as an important part of their self-worth, perceived parental acceptance was related to their comfort with being gay (which in turn predicted self-esteem); Savin-Williams, "Coming Out to Parents."

20. G. Hagestad, "Problems and Promises in the Social Psychology of Intergenerational Relations," in R. W. Fogel et al., eds., *Stability and Change in the Family* (New York: Academic Press, 1981).

21. Kath Weston, *Families We Choose: Lesbians, Gays, Kinship* New York: Columbia University Press, 1991).

22. Much further research is needed to examine the characteristics and processes in families of gay and lesbian teens who are forced to leave home; see also Martin and Hetrick, "The Stigmatization of the Gay and Lesbian Adolescent."

23. See, for example, Andrew M. Boxer, Judith A. Cook, and Gilbert Herdt, "To Tell or Not to Tell: Patterns of Self-Disclosure to Mothers and Fathers Reported by Gay and Lesbian Youth," in K. Pillemer and K. McCartney, eds., *Parent-Child Relations Across the Life Span* (New York: Oxford University Press, 1991), pp. 59–93.

24. Ibid.

25. Bob Tremble, Margaret Schneider, and Carol Appathurai, "Growing Up Gay or Lesbian in a Multi-Cultural Context," in Gilbert Herdt, ed., *Gay and Lesbian Youth* (New York: Haworth Press, 1989), pp. 253–268.

26. Andrew Boxer et al., "Parents' Perceptions of Young Adolescents," in R. S. Cohen et al., *Parenthood: A Psychodynamic Perspective* (New York: Guilford, 1984); Boxer, Cook, and Cohler 1986.

27. M. Schneder et al., 1989.

28. A process of relationship "cooling" may have already begun between the fathers and their daughters prior to any actual disclosure to fathers.

29. While we have been emphasizing the relationships between self-disclosure and parent-child relations, these data also highlight many similarities between the parental relationships of these youth and those found in other studies drawn from presumed heterosexual samples. Males and females in this study reported more positive relationships with mothers than with fathers; and older youth reported better relationships than did younger youth. In addition, more females reported changes in parental relationships than did males.

30. Antecedent relationships of these youth with their parents may shape many aspects of the self-disclosure process for which there are no available

data. See, A. Caspi, D. J. H. Bem, and G. H. Elder, Jr., who suggest that disruptive life transitions highlight dimensions of personality continuity: "Continuities and Consequences of Interactional Styles Across the Life Course," *Journal of Personality* 57 [1989]: 375–406). It is possible that those youth in our sample whose parents reacted particularly badly to their disclosures also had difficult parental relationships earlier in their lives. Additionally, many youth had not yet directly disclosed their identity status to their parents. Further analyses of causal relationships can only be adequately assessed through longitudinal follow-up.

31. Understanding the full impact of the self-disclosure process within the family will require prospective studies. Such research must also take account of ethnic and social class differences in cultural norms and responses to homosexuality (see, for example, S. Jue, "Identifying and Meeting the Needs of Minority Clients with AIDS," in C. G. Leukefeld and M. Fimbres, eds., *Responding to AIDS* (Silver Spring, Md.: National Association of Social Workers, Inc., 1987). Based on data presented in this chapter, it is difficult to determine now the full effects of coming out on parent-child relations. Follow-up of this sample's transition to adulthood provides the opportunity for further examining this process during a subsequent phase of the life course.

32. Anne Muller, *Parents Matter* (New York: Naiad Press, 1987). Boxer, Cook, and Herdt, "To Tell or Not to Tell."

33. Muller, *Parents Matter.*

34. Reprinted with permission of the author, Ian Paterson (P.O. Box 93504, Nelson Park Post Office, Vancouver, BC, Canada, V6E-4L9).

35. See, for example, the important work of James T. Sears, "Educators, Homosexuality, and Homo Sexual Feelings," *Journal of Homosexuality* 22 (3/4) (1991): 29–79; and Anthony R. D'Augelli, "Teaching Lesbian/Gay Development: From Oppression to Exceptionality," *Journal of Homosexuality* 22 (3/4) (1991): 213–227.

36. Karen M. Harbeck, ed., "Coming Out of the Classroom Closet" (special issue), *Journal of Homosexuality* 22 (3/4) (1991).

37. Eric Rofes, "Opening the Classroom Closet," *Harvard Educational Review* 59 (1989): 444–453.

38. The FLE is also responsible for in-service teacher training and provision of classroom resources, as well as monitoring and oversight of curriculum implementation. FLE is part of the regular curriculum typically taught in science, health, home economics, or special education classes. During the last two years, the governance of individual public schools in Chicago has been decentralized and now resides with elected Local School Councils (LSCs); while the structure and functioning of these LSCs are standardized, the magnitude of their involvement in educational processes varies from school to school. Thus, the extent to which schools will actively and programmatically provide more supportive environments for gay and lesbian youth will now reside, in part, with LCSs.

39. This model on attitudes and policy to follow was conceptualized by our colleague and friend, Beverly Johnson Biehr, Coordinator of Family LIFE/HIV Education in the central office of the Chicago Public Schools.

40. A survey of all public high schools in Illinois by the Illinois Gay and Lesbian Task Force further reinforced the need to provide more positive information and determined a high need for educational materials in order to effectively serve the needs of gay and lesbian youth.

41. A Heron, ed., *One Teenager in Ten: Testimony by Gay and Lesbian Youth* (New York: Warner Books,); Herdt, ed., *Gay and Lesbian Youth.*

42. Vivienne Cass, "Homosexual Identity: A Concept in Need of a Definition," *Journal of Homosexuality* 9 (1984) 105–126.

43. Rofes, "Opening the Classroom Closet."

44. The labor of adolescents in our society is typically viewed as a marginal experience. E. Greenberger and L. Steinberg have examined the impact of work on the development of youth (*When Teenagers Work: The Psychological and Social Costs of Adolescent Employment,* New York: Basic Books, 1986). They conclude that there are few positive effects, given the type of work which is typically available to them. Fast-food servers, busboys, waiters and waitresses, and basic secretarial work are some of the typical jobs available to teens in our society.

45. Goffman, *Stigma.*

46. Anita Greene et al., Future Narratives Among Gay and Lesbian Adolescents. Paper presented at Biennial Meeting, Society for Research on Adolescence, Washington, D.C., March 1992.

47. David Leavitt, *Family Dancing* (New York: Warner Books, 1983), p. 188.

48. See sources given in n. 49, chap. 1.

49. John C. Gonsierek, "Organizational and Staff Problems in Gay/Lesbian Mental Health Agencies," *Journal of Homosexuality* 7 (1982): 193–208.

50. According to Floyd Irvin, the psychologist who conducted the usual interview with him, Steve is schizophrenic. This diagnosis was made on the basis of a three-hour interview, and use of the psychological measures we implemented, including the Psychiatric Symptom Checklist.

7. Conclusion

1. The causes and consequences of this upheaval have been in dispute since before Margaret Mead's *Coming of Age in Samoa.* (New York: Dutton, 1927). And now compare: Derek Freeman, *Margaret Mead and Samoa* (Cambridge: Harvard University Press, 1984).

2. Eric Erickson, *Identity, Youth, and Crisis* (New York: W. W. Norton, 1968), p. 130.

3. One need only recall the commentary of Max Weber on Attic culture Greeks, in which he wisely suggested that the erotics of man/boy love were not merely the product of some "naive naturalism of sex," but rather was the center of their society and aesthetics, what he referred to as the "total being

of man" or a way of life. Likewise, there is the far-reaching sentiment of Sir Kenneth Dover in his classic study *Greek Homosexuality* (New York: Cambridge, 1978) that sees the Hellenistic form not merely as a perverse pederasty but rather as the base of educational philosophy and a mode of social life.

4. Theo Van der Meer, *De Wesentlijke Sonde van Sodomie en Andere Vuyligheeden: Sodomietenvervolgingen in Amsterdam 1730–1811* (Amsterdam: Tabula, 1984).

5. Compare Michel Foucault, *The History of Sexuality,* trans. W. Hurley (New York: Random House, 1980), on the public secret of the homosexual in the nineteenth century, with Van der Meer, *De Wesentlijke Sonde van Sodomie en Andere Vuyligheeden.*

6. Editors, Harvard Law Review, *Sexual Orientation and the Law* (Cambridge: Harvard University Press, 1990).

7. Richard Plant, *The Pink Triangle: The Nazi War Against Homosexuals* (New York: Henry Holt and Co., 1986), pp. 108–110.

8. See Gilbert Herdt, *Guardians of the Flutes: Idioms of Masculinity* (New York: McGraw-Hill, 1981); *The Sambia: Ritual and Gender in New Guinea* (New York: Holt, Rinehart and Winston, 1987); " 'Coming Out' as a Rite of Passage: A Chicago Study," in G. Herdt, ed., *Gay Culture in America* (Boston: Beacon Press, 1992).

9. Serena Nanda, *Neither Man Nor Woman: The Hijras of India* (Belmont, Calif.: Wadsworth Publ. Co., 1990).

10. Edward Carpenter, *Selected Writings,* vol. 1, *Sex* (London: GMP Publishers, 1984), p. 194.

11. Martin S. Weinberg and Colin J. Williams, *Male Homosexuals: The Problems and Adaptations* (New York: Oxford University Press, 1974), especially chap. 14.

Epilogue

1. Center for Disease Control, "Update: Mortality Attributable to HIV Infection/AIDS Among Persons Aged 25–44 Years—United States, 1990 and 1991," *Morbidity and Mortality Weekly Reports,* 2 July 1993: 481–486; R. M. Selik et al., "HIV Infection as Leading Cause of Death Among Young Adults in U.S. Cities and States," *Journal of the American Medical Association* 269 (1993): 299–194.

2. Gilbert Herdt and Andrew Boxer, "Sexual Identity and Risk for AIDS among Gay Youth in Chicago," in Tim Dyson (ed.), *Sexual Behavior and Networking: Anthropological and Socio-Cultural Studies on the Transmission of HIV,* pp. 153–174 (Liege, Belgium: Editions Derouax-Ordina, 1992).

3. Gilbert Herdt and Andrew Boxer, "The Ethnographic Study of AIDS," *Journal of Sex Research* 28 (1991): 171–189; Richard Parker, Gilbert Herdt, and Manuel Carballo, "Sexual Culture, HIV Transmission, and AIDS Research," *Journal of Sex Research* 28 (1991): 75–96.

4. Michele Fine, *Disruptive Voices: The Possibilities of Feminist Research* (Ann Arbor: University of Michigan Press, 1992).

5. Stall, R., et al., "Relapse from Safer Sex: The Next Challenge for AIDS Prevention Efforts," *Journal of Acquired Immune Deficiency Syndrome* 3 (1990): 1181–87.

6. See Bradford N. Bartholow and Linda Doll, et al., "Emotional, Behavioral, and HIV Risks Associated With Sexual Abuse Among Adult Homosexual and Bisexual Men," *Child Abuse and Neglect* 18 (9) (1994): 747–761.

7. See Cindy Patton, *Inventing AIDS* (New York: Routledge, 1990).

8. Martin S. Weinburg and Colin J. Williams, *Male Homosexuals: Their Problems and Adaptations* (New York: Oxford, 1974).

9. de Witt, John, et al., "Behavioral Risk Reaction Strategies to Prevent HIV Infection Among Homosexual Men: A Grounded Theory Approach," in J. de Witt (ed.), *Prevention of HIV Infection Among Homosexual Men: Behavior Change and Behavior Determinants,* pp. 98–115 (Amsterdam: These Publishers, 1994).

10. Martin S. Weinberg et al., *Dual Attraction: Understanding Bisexuality* (New York: Oxford University Press, 1993).

INDEX

♦ ♦ ♦

Abortion, 248

Advisors, Horizons Youth Group, 87–93; meeting of, 93–96; sex taboo between teens and, 96–99

AIDS, 6, 11, 22, 215, 217; awareness, 127, 140, 142, 143; bisexuality and, 131–132; and Cohort Four, 9, 12; education about, 95, 225; fear of catching, 110–111, 186–187; first diagnosis of, 118; fund-raisers for, 134, 232; and Gay and Lesbian Pride Parade, 166; and Horizons, 73, 74, 95, 98; and Howard Brown Clinic, 73; impact of, on Chicago's gays and lesbians, 56–60; impact of dealing with, 25, 141, 236–237; Joey's death from, as ritual of coming out, 154–158, 220; and "Names Project" Quilt, 60–63, 67, 159–162; and *Windy City Times*, 86

Alcoholism, 136, 250. *See also* Bars, homosexual

Alley (Chicago), 138

American Airlines, 32

American Psychiatric Association, 11, 224

American Psychological Association, 11, 224

Apartment, as setting for ritual of coming out, 152–154

Arlington National Cemetery, Tomb of Unknown Soldier in, 66

Asians and Friends (Chicago), 56

AUGIE C. K.'S (Chicago), 47, 163

Bars, homosexual, in Chicago, 34, 46–47, 49, 52; alternatives to, 41–42, 80, 137–138; closing of, 33; history of, 37, 38; seeking, as ritual of coming out, 136–140; World War II's creation of, 29–31

Bartlett, Roy Spencer ("Diamond Lil"), 28–29

Being out, 203–204; contexts of coming out, 213–228; emerging gay life course, 205–206; mental health and risk of suicide, 207–209; revealing the self, 209–213; solidarity and diversity, 230–242; well being and new futures, 228–230. *See also* Coming out; Rituals of coming out

Bell, Alan, *Homosexualities: A Study of Diversity among Women and Men* (with M. Weinberg), 32

Bellah, Robert, 18, 53

Berlin, The (Chicago), 130

Bisexuality, 197–199; as ritual of coming out, 129–132

Biways (Chicago), 93

Black and White Men Together, 62

Board of Education (Chicago), 224, 225

Boxer, Andrew, 85

"Breeders," 47

Burger Queen (Chicago), 133

Business Association, 165

Busse (Mayor of Chicago), 27

Byrne, Jane, 41

Cable Network News, 165

Carpenter, Edward, 250–251

Cass, Vivienne, 225
Castro District (San Francisco), 39, 41, 52
Chicago, University of, 28, 86
Chicago House, 59, 166
Chicago Reader, 48
Child molestation, 117
Circus Inn (Rock Island, IL), 30
Civil rights movement, 67, 162
Closet, The (Chicago), 47, 163
Cohn, Leonard, 61
Cohort(s), four historical age, of Chicago, 6–9; One, 9; Two, 9–10; Three, 10–12; Four, 12–13
Cold War, 10, 30, 176
Collective secrecy, 200
Coming out, 2–4, 9, 10, 69, 201; AIDS and, 57; contexts of, 213–228; definitions of, 209–210; to family, 214–219; to friends, 219–221; future outlook for, 253; lowering of age of, 6; parents' reactions to, 105, 170–171, 212, 213, 214–219, 251–252; in school, 221–227; two meanings of, 101; violence and context of, 84–87; at work, 227–228; among youth vs. adults, 205. *See also* Being out; Rituals of coming out
Committee of Black Gay Men (Chicago), 56
Compromise of integrity, 3, 245–246
Condoms, use of, 143
Consenting Adult (film), 81, 120
Cruising, sexual, 134, 139, 143
Culture, dual themes of gay, 230–242

Daley, Richard J., 31
Danger and safety, as ritual of coming out, 104–109
Death: desire for same sex punishable by, 243–244; Joey's, from AIDS, as ritual of coming out, 154–158; and rebirth in coming out, 166–172, 240
Declaration of Independence, 16
De-individuation, process of, 113–114, 115
Democratic Convention (1968, Chicago), 31
Denial, by parents of youth coming out, 217
Desire(s), 179–180; conception of, 1–2;

emergence of same sex, in sexual development, 174–176; first, 180–184. *See also* Sexual identity development, milestones of
Diamond Lil's (Chicago), 28–29
Dignity (Chicago), 41
Discontinuities, developmental, 205
Diversity, conflict between solidarity and, 230–242
Dolan, Terry, 61
Dominick's (Chicago), 42, 44
Double bind, 234, 245
Drag shows, 10, 233
Duberman, Martin, 200

Early Frost (film), 81
Elder, Glen, 8
Equality, social attitude of, 123
Erikson, Erik, 19, 176
Ervin, Floyd, 85–86
Escort service, 133

Fairfax High School (Los Angeles), 125
Family, coming out to, 214–219. *See also* Parents' reactions to coming out
"Family Life Education Program" (FLE), 223–224
"Family Life Resource Handbook," 224
Fine, Michele, 204
Finnie's Club (Chicago), 30
Foucault, Michel, 2
Freud, Anna, 176
Freud, Sigmund, 2, 19, 175, 178, 179, 184
Friends, coming out to, 219–221
Fung, Richard, "Asian Positive" (video), 58
Futures, well being and new, 228–230

Gacey, John Wayne, 117
Gagnon, John H., 2, 25, 26, 136; his study of homosexual life in Chicago, 31–32, 35
Gay Alcoholics Anonymous (Chicago), 41, 51
Gay and Lesbian Adolescent Social Services of West Holywood, 68
Gay and Lesbian Pride Day Parades, 23, 50, 56, 68, 88, 90; ambivalence about marching in, 54–55, 227, 237; conflict between solidarity and diversity in,

233; cultural analysis of, 27, 63–64; exhilaration from marching in, 229; and Horizons Youth Group, 26, 63, 69, 75; and March on Washington, 65, 66–67; meaning of, for individual, 230; and "Names Project" Quilt, 62; as ritual of coming out, 100, 162–166, 168, 169, 203; and Stonewall Tea Party, 5, 63–64

Gay and Lesbian Prom, 88, 95, 168, 236; as ritual of coming out, 148–152, 203

Gay and Lesbian Youth, 225

Gay-bashing, *see* Violence

Gay Chicago, 38, 44, 157

Gay Horizons, 42; founding of, 71–72. *See also* Horizons Community Services, Incorporated; Horizons Youth Group

Gay/lesbian, homosexual vs., 6–7, 18–24, 176

Gay/Lesbian Youth Prom, *see* Gay and Lesbian Prom

Gay Liberated Zone, 66

Gay Liberation Front, 36

Gay Liberation Movement, 76

Gay Life, 70

Geertz, Clifford, 69

Gender blending, 110, 135, 149–150, 168

Gender reversal, 110, 149–150, 152

Generation gap, 13, 71

Gerber-Hart Library (Chicago), 55

Germ theory, 110

Ghetto, gay and lesbian, 3, 11, 104; in Chicago, 36, 39, 48. *See also* Newtown

Girth and Mirth (Chicago), 56

Gluckman, Max, 17

Goals, discussion of, 127–128

Golden, George, 163, 164, 170

Golden, Selma, 163, 164, 170–171

Golden Nugget Pancake House (Chicago), 42

Gorman, Michael, 63

Gray Pride (Chicago), 56

Great Depression, 8

Greenwich Village (New York), 39

GRID (Gay Related Immune Deficiency syndrome), 118. *See also* AIDS

Group: main rap, as ritual of coming out, 121–125; meeting, listening in on

rap, as ritual of coming out, 125–128; meetings, youth, as ritual of coming out, 112–113; new people's, as ritual of coming out, 113–121. *See also* Organizational life

Hall, G. Stanley, 176

Hay, Henry, 35

Healing rite, coming out as, 17

Herdt, Gilbert, 25, 85

Herrell, Richard K., 25, 68

Heteroerotic experience, 191–197

Hijras, Indian, 249–250

Hirschfield, Magnus, 23, 248

His 'n' Hers (Chicago), 42

HIV, 58, 60, 62, 74, 155, 157; risk of, 12, 57. *See also* AIDS

Homoerotic experience, first, 184–186

Homophobia, 4, 87, 91, 103, 111, 168; and AIDS, 60; as cultural idea, 245; defined, 85; diminishing of, 253; family life educators and, 225; internalized, 13, 116, 139; and mental health and risk of suicide, 207–209; oppression of, 247–248; poetic expression of, 221–222; prevalence of, 240; social, 136; social structure of, 239; struggle dealing with, 161

Homosexual, gay/lesbian vs., 6–7, 18–24, 176

Hooker, Evelyn, 15, 177

Horizons Community Service, Incorporated, 7, 12–13, 27, 34, 39; aims of, 74; coffee house of, 42, 73, 80; demographic profile of youth sample at, 75–76; founding of, 11; and Gay and Lesbian Pride Day Parade, 63–64, 69, 75; Gay Parents Group at, 48, 50; history of, in Newtown, 71–75; impact of, 51; location of, 44, 51; membership of, 74–75; programs of, 74; volunteers at, 71, 90–92

Horizons Youth Group, 48, 56, 67, 70, 74; activities of, 81–82; advisors, 87–96; and Gay and Lesbian Pride Day Parade, 26, 63, 69, 75; history of early, 76–84; organizational structure of, 80–81; publicity for, 82–83; reforms at, 78; sex taboo at, 96–99; violence at,

Horizons Youth Group (*continued*)
    84–87; visibility of, 83. *See also* Rituals
    of coming out
Howard Brown Clinic (Chicago), 59, 73
Hudson, Rock, 20, 61
Human Rights Ordinance, 68

Identity crisis, 100, 205, 243
Illinois Gay and Lesbian Task Force
    (IGLTF), 25, 42, 51, 59
Institute for the Protection of Gay and
    Lesbian Youth in New York, 125
Institute for Sex Research, 31
Intensification, rites of, 167, 203
Internal Revenue Service, 66
Isay, Richard, 175

Jane Addams Center (Chicago), 42
Jewel (Chicago), 44
Johnnie Walker's (Chicago), 138–139

King, Martin Luther, Jr., 31, 66, 67
Kinsey, Alfred, 2, 19, 176, 185, 197
Klassen, Albert, 32
Koff, Bruce, 74–75, 86

Lady Bug (Chicago), 47
Leavitt, David, *Family Dancing*, 230
Lee, John Alan, 203
Lesbian and Gay Academic Union
    (LGAU, Chicago), 41, 55
Lesbian and Gay Youth Prom, *see* Gay
    and Lesbian Prom
Levy, Phyllis, 82, 142
Liberace, 58, 60, 61
Liberation, coming of, to Chicago, 36–39
Life course: emerging gay, 205–206; giv-
    ing up heterosexual, 241–242
Lionheart Theater Company (Chicago),
    56
Love and sex, new rituals of, in coming
    out, 141–147

McCourt, Jeffrey, 86, 87
Magical thought, as ritual of coming out,
    109–112
March on Washington for Lesbian and
    Gay Rights (October 1987), 61, 63,
    65–68, 155
Marigold Bowl (Chicago), 42
Marriages of compromise, 10

Masturbation, 176, 188
Matlovich, Leonard, 68
Mattachine Society, 10, 34–35, 36
Mead, Margaret, 13, 174
Medusa's (Chicago), 137–138
Melrose Cafe (Chicago), 44, 164
Mental health, and risk of suicide,
    207–209
Metropolitan Community Church (Chi-
    cago), 41, 42, 47, 51, 62, 71, 151
Milk, Harvey, 66, 68
Molly's Restaurant (Chicago), 50, 56, 62,
    93, 95, 120, 138; Gay and Lesbian
    Prom at, 148–152
Money, John, 130
Monroe, Marilyn, 61
Moral conflicts, 2, 245–246
Moral development, critique of, 18–24
Mountain Moving Coffee House (Chi-
    cago), 138
Muller, Anne, 219

"Names Project" Quilt, 5, 56, 67, 69, 155;
    discussion of, 60–63; pilgrimage to, as
    ritual of coming out, 159–162, 237
National Institute of Mental Health, 31
Navy Pier (Chicago), 67, 159–160
Nazis, treatment of homosexuals by,
    248
New places to come out, 133–136
Newtown (Chicago), 36, 37, 54, 56, 104,
    206; contemporary cultural voices in,
    43–53; gay and lesbian businesses in,
    44, 50–51; profile of, 39–43
New York Times, 85
"Night of 100 Parties," 95
Northeastern Illinois University, 48

Off-course, feelings of being, 205, 206
O'Hare Airport (Chicago), 32
One Teenager in Ten, 225
"Oprah Winfrey Show," 82–83
Organizational life, gay, in Chicago,
    53–56
Orgasm, 188
Outlines, 52

Palmer House (Chicago), 30
Parents' reaction to coming out, 105,
    170–171, 212, 213, 214–219, 251–252

Parks, Rosa, 162
Paterson, Ian, "High School Faggot," 221–222
P-Flag (Parents and Friends of Lesbians and Gays), 74, 163, 164, 165, 170
Piaget, Jean, 185
Planned Parenthood, 224
PLWAs, 92, 95, 154
Prostitution ring, male, 133–134
PWAs (Persons with AIDS), 59, 62, 67

Queer-bashing, see Violence
Queer Nation, 9, 16, 129, 135, 152, 231
Quilt, see "Names Project" Quilt

Racism, 123, 253; Chicago's, 52
Read, Kenneth, Other Voices, 136
Reductionism, moral rhetoric of, 22
Reich, Jon, 62
Rich, Adrienne, 15
Rites of passage, 102, 129, 132, 158, 167–168, 246
Rituals of coming out, 4, 13–18, 87, 100–103, 247; apartment as, 152–154; bisexuality as, 129–132; danger and safety as, 104–109; and death and rebirth, 166–172; ending of secrecy of sexuality as, 103–104; Gay and Lesbian Pride Parade as, 162–166; Gay and Lesbian Prom as, 148–152; Joey's death from AIDS at, 154–158; listening in on rap group meeting as, 125–128; magical thought as, 109–112; main rap group as, 121–125; new people's group as, 113–121; and new places to come out, 133–136; and new rituals of love and sex, 141–147; pilgrimage to Quilt as, 159–162; purpose of, 248–249; seeking bars as, 136–140; youth group meetings as, 112–113
Rocks (along Lake Michigan), 145–146, 150
Rocky Horror Picture Show (film), 136
"Rodde" Center (Chicago), 44, 48, 51
Roe v. Wade decision, 248
Rofes, Eric, 226
"Rosie the Riveter," 30

Sadomasochism, 12, 143
Safe sex, 111, 127, 142–143, 144, 154, 155

St. Peter's Episcopalian Church (Chicago), 41
St. Sebastian's Catholic Church (Chicago), 41
Same-sex experience, youth without, 186–187
Sapir, Edward, 248
Savin-Williams, Richard, 214
Schneider, Margaret, 218
School, coming out in, 221–227
Schulte, Steve, 68
Second Unitarian Church (Chicago), 41, 42, 48
Secrecy of sexuality, ending of, as ritual of coming out, 103–104
Self, revealing, 209–213
Sex, new rituals of love and, in coming out, 141–147
Sex Information and Education Council, 224
Sex taboo, between teens and advisors, 96–99
"Sex Talk" show, 82, 142
Sexual being, defined, 178–179
Sexual fantasies, various types of, 183–184
Sexual identity development, milestones of, 173–176; bisexuality, 197–199; contexts of sexual initiation, 187–190; first desires, 180–184; first homoerotic experience, 184–186; heteroerotic experience, 191–197; rethinking gay youth, 176–80; sexual experience and gay and lesbian identities, 199–202; youth without same-sex experience, 186–187
Sexual initiation, contexts of, 187–190
Sexual relations, defined, 179
Shilts, Randy, 10
Simmel, Georg, 113–114
Simon, William, 25, 26; his study of homosexual life in Chicago, 31–32, 35
Sodomy, 244; statutes, 21
Solidarity, conflict between diversity and, 230–242
Sonnenschein, David, Some Homosexual Men: Interviews from 1967, 32
Stereotypes, homosexual, 96–97, 105–106, 107, 110, 175, 250
Stoller, Robert, 19, 175

Stonewall Tea Party, 10, 23, 26, 32, 36, 57; described, 4–6; and Gay and Lesbian Pride Day Parade, 5, 63–64; and Horizons, 72; impact of, 8, 13
Suicide, 120–121, 200, 245; attempts at, 111, 120; mental health and risk of, 207–209
Supreme Court, United States, 248

"Tales of the Closet" (gay comic book), 125
Terkel, Studs, 29
Tiresias, 119
Tocqueville, Alexis de, 16, 53, 55
Tönnies, F., 65
Town and Country bar (Chicago), 30
Transvestites, 110; disagreement over, 233
Treasure Island (Chicago), 44
Turner, Victor, 17
Tyler, Robin, 67

van Gennep, Arnold, 17
Vice Commission of Chicago, 27, 28

Violence: and context of coming out, 84–87; in Newtown, 52
Vulnerability syndrome, 87, 121, 144

Wabash Baths (Chicago), 30
Wardell, Al, 25
Warner, W. Lloyd, 54
Warren, Carol, 101, 108
Weinberg, Martin, *Homosexualities: A Study of Diversity among Women and Men* (with A. Bell), 32
Well being, and new futures, 228–230
Wellington Avenue Church (Chicago), 41, 62
White, Edmund, 30
Whitman, Walt, 71
Wilde, Oscar, *The Picture of Dorian Grey*, 21
Windy City Gay Chorus, 62
Windy City Times, 52, 82, 86–87, 134
Work, coming out at, 227–228
World War II, 8, 9–10, 12, 29, 57
Wrigley family, 40

Yidro Coffee House (Chicago), 138

BOOKS OF RELATED INTEREST
FROM BEACON PRESS

Gilbert Herdt
Gay Culture in America: Essays from the Field

"For all serious students of gay and lesbian issues, this book is a must."
—Evelyn Hooker

[0-8070-7915-4, PAPERBACK]

Warren J. Blumenfeld, editor
Homophobia: How We All Pay the Price

"This invaluable collection of essays makes forcefully clear that homophobia stunts the hater even as it oppresses the hated. In a country like ours, so intolerant of differentness, there can be no more important message."
—Martin Bauml Duberman

[0-8070-7919-7, PAPERBACK]

Warren J. Blumenfeld and Diane Raymond
Looking at Gay and Lesbian Life

"The single most complete source of information about homosexuality now available."
—*Bay Windows*

[0-8070-7923-5, PAPERBACK]

**Available at bookstores or directly from Beacon Press,
25 Beacon Street, Boston, Massachusetts 02108-2892**